Yearbook of Cultural Property Law
2009

YEARBOOK OF CULTURAL PROPERTY LAW

Series Editor: **Sherry Hutt**

Sponsored by the Lawyers' Committee for Cultural Heritage Preservation

The *Yearbook* provides those in the heritage-management world with summaries of notable court cases, settlements and other dispositions, legislation, government regulations, policies, and agency decisions that affect their work. Interviews with key figures, refereed research articles, think pieces, and a substantial resources section round out each volume. Thoughtful analyses and useful information from leading practitioners in the diverse field of cultural property law will assist government land managers; state, tribal, and museum officials; attorneys; anthropologists; archaeologists; public historians; and others to better preserve, protect, and manage cultural property in domestic and international venues. All royalties go directly to the Lawyers' Committee for Cultural Heritage Preservation.

Yearbook of Cultural Property Law

2009

Sherry Hutt
Editor

David Tarler
Assistant Editor

Routledge
Taylor & Francis Group
LONDON AND NEW YORK

First published 2009 by Left Coast Press, Inc.

Published 2016 by Routledge
2 Park Square, Milton Park, Abingdon, Oxon OX14 4RN
605 Third Avenue, New York, NY 10017

Routledge is an imprint of the Taylor & Francis Group, an informa business

ISSN 1931-5627
LCCN 2006213755
ISBN 978-1-59874-419-4 (hbk)

Contents

Articles

Resources

Tributes: Recognizing Career Achievements in Cultural Resource Protection

Preface

Welcome to a review of the year 2008 for the genre of law that is cultural property law. It has once again proven to be a substantive year as measured by the number of news articles, court actions, and journal articles that were generated and are noted in this volume. The *Yearbook* series seeks to bring together thoughtful pieces that explain these issues, inform and educate, and assemble source materials useful to those who will seek to represent clients and use the law as a means to protect cultural property.

As well as inform the reader and support cultural property practitioners, the *Yearbook* seeks to give identity to cultural property law, or cultural heritage law as some refer to it, as an identifiable area of legal practice. The *Yearbook of Cultural Property Law* series joins together federal, state, local, tribal, museum, historic preservation, marine resources, art market, international, and criminal law in one volume, where the common thread of cultural property law is identified, discussed, and analyzed. In this manner, the components of cultural property law can be seen and precedent can be addressed in a meaningful context. The reader will note that cases or discussions may appear in more than one section or article in the volume, allowing them to be viewed from different perspectives within cultural property law. It is hoped that genre identification will allow meaningful precedent to be developed in court cases. Cultural property law, although unique, is of the same standing as other well-recognized legal areas, which interrelate, such as: environmental law, Indian law, contracts, torts, administrative, international, and criminal law.

At the core of the *Yearbook* are the Practice Area sections, each with a section editor who is a practitioner and scholar in that particular area of cultural property law. If you the reader feel that something should be covered in the coming year, the editors would be pleased to receive your comments. In some instances, cases that saw litigation during the year are not reported, as the sentencing or culminating event had not occurred by year's end.

The articles in the *Yearbook* are peer reviewed and the topics are chosen to add further depth to the Practice Areas, to give the reader insight into major events, and to provide source data that are not published elsewhere. The *Yearbook* is intended as an ongoing aid to legal practice, ranging from scholarly analysis of emerging issues to practical aids for practitioners and educators. The *Yearbook* is similar to a law journal in the scholarly treatment of cutting edge topics, but it strives to blend cross-disciplinary styles of writing, combining legal and scientific forms. Contributors to the *Yearbook* are creative and forward thinking, seeking to identify the course of the law, but they are also mindful of their responsibility to fully inform the reader of the parameters of issues. The series strives for credibility upon which practitioners can rely. Thus, items accepted for the *Yearbook* are not advocacy pieces, except to the extent they generally promote cultural resource protection through use of the law.

Once again this year, the *Yearbook* has been produced as a project of the LCCHP, the nonprofit organization of lawyers, which is dedicated to scholarship, education, and cultural heritage preservation, and which receives the proceeds from the sale of this volume. The regular contributors to the *Yearbook* are members of LCCHP. For more information on the benefits of membership please visit www.culturalheritagelaw.org or email the LCCHP at LCCHP@yahoogroups.com. The editors, editorial board, the LCCHP and authors who contributed to this volume also offer their appreciation to Mitch Allen and the staff at Left Coast Press, our publisher, for their continued efforts to seek out and promote scholarship to benefit cultural resource preservation, protection, and education.

The *Yearbook* editors continue to seek information for the next edition, particularly actions that may not have been published or may have been resolved without a final judgment. Expression of interest to publish articles that meet the mission of the *Yearbook* are also welcome. Articles are desired that address topics of current interest in a scholarly and complete manner, that will be of assistance to practitioners, but that leave advocacy to those practitioners. Please send information or inquiries to: Hutt_Sherry@yahoo.com. Thank you.

The information in the Yearbook is drawn from public records. The views expressed in the Yearbook are those of the LCCHP members and the authors, and do not necessarily reflect the views or policies of the federal agencies or the public or private firms whose employees contributed to this volume.

Introduction

• • •

Introduction to Yearbook 2009

The *Yearbook* strives to provide substantive information on current topics of interest, in papers, interviews, articles, and Practice Area sections, authored by those who have sufficient expertise in the field to offer meaningful analysis and insight. Each volume presents cultural property law topics that have been featured in press articles and conferences and that will inform court cases. Sometimes, different perspectives on the same topic might appear in more than one Practice Area section in order to illuminate various facets or issues.

In 2008, one of the notable items was certainly the June 4, 2008, "New Report on Acquisition of Archaeological Materials and Ancient Art," issued by the Association of Art Museum Directors (AAMD). The AAMD has issued prior documents of this nature, as discussed by Jennifer Anglim Kreder in her essay "Cultural Property, Law and Ethics," but none of the prior pronouncements gave museums such clear guidance on setting acquisition policies. Professor Kreder teaches Cultural Property Law and other courses at Salmon P. Chase College of Law at Northern Kentucky University and is a graduate of the Georgetown University Law Center. To gain further insight on the AAMD Report, the *Yearbook* was honored to have been given an interview with Peabody and Essex Museum director and AAMD committee member Dan L. Monroe, who led the team that drafted the Report. In addition, Professor Marilyn Phelan, looks briefly at the AAMD Report in her article "International Mediation of Cultural Property Ownership Issues—It's the Right Thing to Do! " She places the Report in the context of international cultural property actions, which may be served by dispute resolution through mediation as proposed by the International Council of Museums (ICOM) formal mediation process, finalized in 2007 and to be effective in 2009, upon the training of mediators. Professor Phelan is uniquely qualified to discuss the new mediation process as she was reappointed for another three-year term on the Legal Affairs Committee of the International Council of Museums (ICOM). As a member of this committee, she prepared the mediation procedure for ICOM to recommend when individuals or countries make claims to stolen or illegally exported objects in museums' collections. The AAMD Report is also discussed in the Practice Area sections on Museum, by Lucille A. Roussin, art law practitioner in New York City; and International Cultural Property, by Patty Gerstenblith, professor of law at DePaul University College of Law, where she is Director of DePaul's program in art and cultural heritage law, and Washington, DC, cultural property lawyer, Laina Lopez, of Berliner, Corcoran & Rowe LLP..

Also returning this year to edit Practice Area sections for the *Yearbook* are, in Federal Land Management, James Van Ness, the acting Deputy General Counsel (Environment & Installations), Department of Defense, responsible for advising senior DoD officials on legal matters related to natural and cultural resources management, environmental planning, and consultation; in State and Local, Kelly Yasaitis Fanizzo, who works with federal agency compliance at the Advisory Council for Historic Preservation; in Tribes, Tribal Lands, and Indian Arts, Rob Roy Smith, who is of counsel with the Indian Law Group of the law firm Ater Wynne, LLP, in Seattle, Washington; in Art Market, Thomas R. Kline and L. Eden Burgess, practicing in the Washington, D.C., office of Andrews Kurth LLP, where they represent governments, museums, churches, foundations, and families, including Holocaust survivors and heirs, in recovering stolen art appearing in the United States; and in Enforcement, David Tarler, who is the enforcement and training coordinator in the Washington, D.C., office of the National Park Service, in the National NAGPRA Program. Joining the Board of Editors this year, for the Marine Environment Practice Area, is Nathaniel R. Orpen, a recent graduate of the William Mitchell Law School.

The *Yearbook* is also assisted by the following contributing editors: in Marine Environment, Caroline Blanco, the Assistant General Counsel for the Environment at the National Science Foundation, where she provides advice on the environmental and cultural resources laws implicated by the Foundation's mission in promoting cutting edge science; and in Enforcement, Elise

Foster, who is an attorney with the U.S. Department of Agriculture, Office of the General Counsel in Ogden, Utah, where, since 1997, she has been active in the development of ARPA civil penalty practice.

The *Yearbook* is also pleased to publish winning submissions of the 2008 Lawyers' Committee for Cultural Heritage Preservation (LCCHP) Law School Writing Competition, generously sponsored each year by the law firm of Andrews Kurth LLP. The entries this year presented in-depth analysis of several areas of interest to cultural property practitioners, making it beneficial to publish three of the top papers. The 2nd place article by Bryan Stockton, a student at Georgetown University Law Center, takes a thorough look at the Religious Land Use and Institutionalized Persons Act (RLUIPA), in the context of the current case of the Third Church of Christ Scientist. He examines this ongoing case, and concludes that Free Exercise of Religion protections need not hamper historic preservation. Finalist Jillianne M. Arguello, in her article on risk as a relevant factor in determining the fair market value of antiquities donated and taken as deductions from taxable income, makes a compelling case for amendments to IRS valuation policies. She urges the IRS to consider items with a broken chain of title differently from those with an unbroken chain of title in order to ensure that the purpose of the donation is ultimately achieved. Finalist Jessica Kennedy has contributed an article on the Visual Artists Rights Act (VARA), which will put in context a law that is not well understood. The article will be of interest to those involved with public art.

The *Yearbook* editors are pleased to recognize those cultural property practitioners who inspire us and who have made a positive impact on the field. This year we focus on two individuals of substantial note. Professor Colin Renfrew, an archaeologist, teacher, and highly acclaimed and prolific author, has devoted most of his life to being a strong and steady voice of conscience on the loss of culture and scientific knowledge due to looting and illicit trade in artifacts. He was honored this year by SAFE (Saving Antiquities for Everyone) for his lifetime achievement, which is also noted here. FBI Agent Robert Wittman retired this year from the FBI, although not from the field of cultural property protection investigations. He was a member of the first FBI Art Crime team, helping to establish the stature of the team in international art theft cases while offering his time to train law enforcement agents in many agencies. In coming years, the *Yearbook* will focus on the accomplishments of others who make a notable contribution to enhance care and protection of cultural property. Nominations are welcome.

In a continuing effort to meet the needs of practitioners and law professors, the *Yearbook* includes a section on published resources, websites, and blogs. Gary Nurkin has once again compiled a comprehensive list of items and electronic resources published and created in the last year. It is notable that each year the list of newly published items is long, reflecting the attention by scholars to the importance of cultural property law as an identified area of practice.

It is our hope that you, the reader, will find the information in the *Yearbook* to inspire your practice.

Note: The most recent citation to the cases discussed in the text is to be found in the table of cases.

Sherry Hutt
David Tarler

2009

Cultural Property, Law and Ethics

• • •

by Jennifer Anglim Kreder

We witnessed in 2008 the dramatic culmination of various scandals in the cultural property and heritage community. To name just a few of the high-profile events: (1) armed robbery of four paintings by Van Gogh, Cezanne, Degas, and Monet from the Emil Bührle Foundation in Zurich, Switzerland; (2) restitutions of spectacular Etruscan objects from some of the most prestigious U.S. museums and elite collectors to Italy; (3) FBI raids on four California museums whose employees allegedly engaged in antiquities trafficking and the exchange of inflated appraisals for donations to perpetuate tax fraud; and (4) the death of archaeologist Roxanna Brown in FBI custody. These scandals did not arise in a vacuum. The law and ethics of the cultural property market is changing—dramatically. Those interested in cultural property will appreciate the value of some history to understand the current environment.

In 1969, Clemency Coggins laid bare the unauthorized destruction of pre-Columbian sites to obtain objects to sell on the international market. She traced specific objects from looted find-spots to specific display cases in prestigious U.S. museums. Ever since, a raw, polarizing philosophical and ethical debate has raged between archaeologists, on the one hand, and collectors and museums, on the other, as to the extent of the trickle-down impact that the antiquities market has on archaeological sites worldwide.

A main purpose of the UNESCO Convention on the Means of Prohibiting and Preventing the Illicit Import, Export and Transfer of Ownership of Cultural Property of 1970 (UNESCO Convention) is to curb widespread pillaging of archaeological sites. The UNESCO Convention initially did little directly to change the legal landscape in the United States, except in regard to a relatively few categories of objects, the importation of which the United States agreed to prohibit pursuant to various statutes and bilateral agreements. The Convention rejected the "blank check" approach, which would have required art importing nations, of which the United States is the largest, to try to block importation of any object exported in violation of any source nation's export regulations. The Convention thus seemingly left undisturbed the international law mantra that nations do not enforce other nations' customs regulations or criminal provisions. The *Hollinshead*, *McClain*, and *Schultz* cases, however, have established (at least in the Second, Fifth, and Ninth Circuits) that one may be prosecuted under the National Stolen Property Act for removing an object from a source nation in violation of a clear national ownership law. The widespread adoption of the Convention, the entrenchment of the McClain doctrine, and the continued dialogue between archaeologists, collectors, and museums have significantly impacted the antiquities market and museum acquisition practices.

Generally, museums, collectors, and archaeologists, of course, are bound to follow applicable law. The debate continues, however, as to whether one in the United States should acquire an object without detailed documentation showing it was exported from a source nation in compliance with that nation's export laws when no U.S. law has been broken. The most common framework for the debate has been that of *cultural nationalism* versus *cultural internationalism*, as was first articulated by Professor John H. Merryman of Stanford Law School. Regardless of the philosophical debate, if the source nation lacks a clear national ownership law applying to objects excavated after its enactment, then the risk of criminal prosecution in the United States is minimal under the McClain doctrine. The same is true of civil liability.

On the other hand, assuming compliance with all applicable U.S. customs regulations and assuming the source nation has a clear national ownership law in place, then the necessary inquiry to evaluate legal risk in the United States becomes an evidentiary matter concerning whether it can be shown that the object was removed from a find-spot within the modern source nation after enactment of a clear national ownership law. A criminal prosecution also would require a showing that the acquirer possessed the requisite level of intent to deprive the owner of the benefit of ownership and a prosecutor willing to bring the case. That case might be brought in the form of a civil forfeiture action, which would shift the burden of establishing right to possession onto the purchaser claiming title.

Perhaps the most important impetus for the dramatic change in law and ethics pertaining to the antiquities market is the recent high-profile revelation of the extent of criminal activity providing a steady stream of illicit objects to the high-end antiquities market. In particular, developments in Italy have shown that the market in Etruscan artifacts has been infected with illicit excavation and organized international crime for quite some time. Illicit objects were laundered for years by sophisticated dealers into the international market and wound their way into respected collections and esteemed museums in the United States. We have seen the prosecution of previously esteemed collectors, a museum curator, and tombaroli, which is an Italian word meaning "tomb raiders."

Italian Criminal Investigations and Prosecutions

The popular press attributes Italy's recent success reclaiming its cultural patrimony to the book *The Medici Conspiracy* by Peter Watson and Cecilia Todeschini.[1] Although the book is interesting and revealing, the truth is that Italy's recent successes have resulted from events dating back to 1902, when it passed its first "in-the-ground" statute, which vests ownership of unearthed ancient artifacts in the state. Italy ratified the UNESCO Convention in 1978, and Italy signed a Memorandum of Understanding (MOU) with the United States in 2001. Pursuant to the MOU, which was renewed in 2006, the United States agreed to protect pre-Classical, Classical, and Imperial Roman architectural material. Thus, U.S. customs and enforcement agents have been committed to the goal of recovering covered artifacts. Italy, however, has not sat back and waited for the United States to do the heavy lifting.

In the mid-1990s, Italy began to firmly press U.S. museums to return objects Italy believed had been illegally exported. It has long been understood that artifacts illegally excavated in Italy are transported through Switzerland before reaching the international market to evade Italian protection laws. Accordingly, Italian police sought assistance from Swiss police in 1995 to conduct a raid on the Geneva warehouses of Italian art dealer Giacomo Medici. As relayed in *The Medici Conspiracy*, the raid uncovered a vast treasure trove of smuggled antiquities, many fresh from the ground, and others in various stages of the market preparation process. A parallel investigation in

Italy uncovered a piece of paper referred to as "the organigram" which seems to reflect an organization/flow chart of a vast smuggling ring implicating key players in the international antiquities market, including a number of U.S. museums, former J. Paul Getty Museum (the Getty) curator Marion True, and prominent art dealer Robert Hecht. The author of the organigram, however, was dead by the time it was found. The chart alone cannot tell us whether these key players knew they were trading in looted antiquities. Nonetheless, the Italian government viewed the organigram in conjunction with other evidence, particularly photographs found at the Medici warehouses, and brought criminal charges against key and lesser players. The photographs have been described as "a smoking gun" in the prosecution and negotiations.

Medici was arrested in 1997 and convicted in 2004, after a lengthy trial in Rome with testimony by Italian tombaroli. Medici was sentenced to ten years in jail and fined $10 million. He remains free pending his appeal. Hecht and True were indicted in Rome in 2002 for conspiracy to traffic in antiquities. Hecht was (in)famous for having sold the Euphronios krater to the Metropolitan Museum of Art in New York (the Met) for a controversial $1 million in 1972, the first million-dollar sale of a piece of antiquity. A raid of Hecht's residence uncovered his personal journal, which has been pivotal in his prosecution. True, who had tightened the Getty's questionable acquisition policies during her tenure as curator there, was the first U.S. museum employee ever to be indicted for alleged illegal antiquities trading. Under True's stewardship, the Getty implemented a policy requiring objects to be acquired from "established, well-documented collections" and to have been in published catalogues before 1995.[2]

Negotiations between the Italians and the Getty were difficult—it took several years before the parties could agree on exactly which antiquities the Getty would return to Italy. On October 25, 2007, the Getty formally agreed to return 40 of the 51 artifacts demanded, including the prized Cult Goddess limestone and marble statue. In the agreement, the Italian Culture Ministry agreed that the Cult Goddess could remain on display at the Getty until 2010, but the other artifacts were to be returned immediately. Pursuant to the agreement, Italy has loaned other artifacts and will continue to engage in "cultural cooperation," including research projects and joint exhibitions. For example, on February 1, 2008, Italy lent the Getty "a bounty of Berninis."[3] Pursuant to the agreement, such loans will be of a four-year duration, which many criticize as too short to accommodate serious academic study.

In the midst of the negotiations in August 2007, Italy dropped the civil charges against True and reduced the criminal charges, but the criminal trial of True and Hecht continues. It is likely that the Italian statute of limitations, which continues to run until the conclusion of a prosecution, will expire before the end of True's trial, and possibly also Hecht's, which would preclude their conviction. In late November 2007, an Italian judge ruled that a local cultural group's claim to the bronze "A Victorious Youth" was barred by the statute of limitations. The Italian government and the Getty are continuing negotiations concerning the statue, with the Getty claiming it had been found in international waters and thus is not subject to restitution.

Additionally, the Greek government charged True with antiquities smuggling, and the Getty returned four objects to Greece, including the prized gold funeral wreath, a photo of which used to grace the cover of the Getty's brochure. A Greek judge dismissed the criminal charges against True, which pertained solely to the gold funeral wreath, in late November 2007 on statute of limitations grounds.

True vigorously maintains her innocence, claiming that she never knew any of the antiquities in question were looted. In late December 2006, in the midst of the negotiations, in a two-page letter she wrote to her former colleagues at the Getty, she railed against their "calculated silence" and "lack of courage and integrity." She wrote specifically in regard to the return of the gold funerary wreath and other objects to Greece:

> Once again you have chosen to announce the return of objects that are directly related to criminal charges filed against me by a foreign government . . . without a word of support for me, without any explanation of my role in the institution, and without any reference to my innocence.[4]

Many curators of U.S. museums have publicly supported True, while others have distanced themselves.

Meanwhile, the Italian government on February 21, 2006, finalized negotiations with the Met for the return of the prized Euphronios krater, other vases, and Hellenistic silver. The museum continues to dispute Italy's claim that the silver's find-spot is located in Morgantina, Italy. The Boston Museum of Fine Arts, in September 2006, agreed to return thirteen objects, including a statue of Sabina. On October 26, 2007, the Princeton University Art Museum agreed to return four objects immediately and four more in four years. In January 2008, the University of Virginia agreed to return two ancient Greek sculptures. The Cleveland Museum of Art reached an agreement with Italy on November 19, 2008 to return fourteen objects.

Italy has proudly displayed many of the returned objects in the Presidential Palace, the Quirinal, in Rome, in an exhibition entitled "Nostoi," which means "homecoming" in Greek. No museum acknowledged any wrongdoing; all received promises for future loans of Italian antiquities or other "cultural cooperation." Not all objects initially demanded by Italy were returned.

The Italians reportedly have since turned their sights on other museums, dealers, and collections implicated in the photo chain linking tombaroli looting to the market. New York art dealer Jerome Eisenberg of Royal Athena Galleries agreed to return eight Etruscan and Roman artifacts on November 6, 2007. Collector Shelby White returned nine spectacular objects in January 2008, and will return another currently on loan with the Museum of Modern Art in New York in 2011. It also should be noted that White reportedly reached an agreement with Greece to return two objects in July 2008.

Archaeologists David Gill and Christopher Chippendale had called the Shelby White–Leon Levy collection into question many years ago. The Gill and Chippendale study revealed that 93 percent of the objects comprising the 1990 Glories of the Past show at the Met, which displayed more than 200 objects from the Shelby White–Leon Levy collection, had no known ownership history, and hence no archaeological provenience. Most archaeologists would draw the inference that the objects likely were looted from clandestine digs at archaeological sites. Many collectors would not be so quick to reach that conclusion, because the antiquities market norm in the 1990s was that few purchases were supported by completed provenance documentation. A reported sticking point in White's negotiations with the Italians was whether the Italians would pledge never to pursue another piece in her collection if she returned those sought. Reportedly, "Italy agreed that it would not lay claim to any additional objects that were catalogued [for the 1990 show]. . . . But if evidence were to surface that any other artifacts she owns were looted in Italy, the accord would allow Italian prosecutors to pursue their return."[5]

Other major players in the international antiquities market reportedly targeted by Italy, but not yet having reached any public agreement, include the New Carlsberg Glyptotek (Copenhagen, Denmark), the Miho Museum (Shiga, Japan), the Barbara and Lawrence Fleishman collection, the Maurice Tempelsman collection, dealer Fritz Bürki (Switzerland), Galerie Nefer (Switzerland, owned by Frida Tchacos, wife of Werner Nussberger who donated two items to the Getty), Atlantis Antiquities, and dealer Robin Symes (UK), who in 2005 served 7 months of a 2-year sentence for misrepresentations about his antiquities holdings in the course of his bankruptcy filing. Symes was a prominent dealer who had sold some extremely high-profile artifacts, including the prized Cult Goddess that the Getty will return to Italy in 2010. Symes was implicated in *The Medici Conspiracy* as having been part of the Medici cordata, which was depicted in the organigram as the smuggling ring that laundered looted objects onto the international market, including to the Getty.[6] An October 2008 auction at Bonhams, to pay Symes' creditors, was halted at the last minute at the request of the Italian embassy in London.

Earlier reports mentioned the Toledo Museum of Art and Minneapolis Institute of Arts, but more recent statements by Francesco Rutelli, Culture Minister of Italy, have not mentioned these two institutions. Additionally, the Bunker Hunt collection, which constitutes part of the Shelby White–Leon Levy collection, was mentioned separate and apart from the Shelby White restitution.[7]

Finally, the Italian government busted an international ring of antiquities smugglers, which led in early January 2008 to the largest criminal case against antiquities smugglers to date. On January 17, 2008, General Giovanni Nistri, head of the art squad within the Italian Carabinieri, reported statistics which in his view "show how, at the moment, international trafficking is surely declining."[8] Certainly, if that is the case, Italy's active pursuit of restitutions from high-profile entities and individuals and criminal prosecutions are part of the reason, as well as the 2006 bilateral agreement signed by Italy and Switzerland requiring Swiss customs agents to verify proof of origin and legal export of antiquities arriving in Switzerland from Italy. This is a dramatic legal change to the Geneva Freeport procedures described in *The Medici Conspiracy*.

The U.S. Museum Community's Reactions

Naturally, the American museum community reacted to these events. Again, some history is in order to understand the significance of most recent events. The Association of Art Museum Directors (AAMD), the institution most influential upon art museums' individual missions and guidelines, in October 2001 issued a Position Paper that underscored that acquiring works is a "vital part of a museum's mission."[9] The report stated:

> While it is highly desirable to know the archaeological context in which an artifact was discovered because this can reveal information about the origin of the work

and the culture that produced it, this is not always possible. Nevertheless, much information may be gleaned from works of art even when the circumstances of their discovery are unknown. Indeed, most of what we know about early civilizations has been learned from artifacts whose archaeological context has been lost.[10]

Since 2001, the museum community has been steadfast in supporting the cultural internationalist position, which maintains that liberal international exchange of cultural objects is preferable to retention of objects within the boundaries of their countries of modern discovery. The Position Paper described the nature and extent in 2001 of museums' due diligence concerning title and legal importation of an object from another country. It noted: "Conclusive proof is not always possible, because documentation and physical evidence may be inaccessible or lost."[11] Finally, the Position Paper noted that in an effort to deter the illicit trade in artifacts and "to ensure that the importation of art and artifacts from other countries is conducted in a lawful and responsible manner," museum directors considered the following questions:

- Is the country's cultural patrimony in jeopardy from pillage of archaeological and ethnological materials and/or other illegal actions, and how will the acquisition affect such activity?
- Is the importation of the cultural artifacts consistent with the interests of the international community, especially for scientific, cultural, and/or educational purposes?
- Is the importation consistent with applicable law, including relevant international conventions?
- How did the work come into the possession of the seller?
- Is there information and documentation that can be reasonably obtained to shed further light on the origins of the work and the circumstances of its acquisition?
- Is there evidence that the work is being legally exported?[12]

The Position Paper did not give any firm direction to art museum directors as to how the individual questions should be weighed or balanced in the evaluation process. Particularly significant is the last question regarding legal exportation. During the debates concerning the drafting and U.S. implementation of the UNESCO Convention, U.S. collectors and the U.S. museum community adamantly opposed the "blank check" approach, which would have required the United States to give effect to all foreign nations' export restrictions. Thus, it is quite significant that in 2001, the AAMD decided to include the legality of the exportation of an object among the factors directors should consider.

In 2004, the AAMD revisited the issue of acquisition of archaeological materials and ancient art in its June 4, 2004, Task Force Report. It reaffirmed within the Report's Statement of Principles that incomplete documentation of ownership history should be excused, at least in some cases, because of an object's "rarity, importance, and aesthetic merit," "in the absence of any breach of law" or the Principles.[13] Such objects "may be acquired and made accessible not only to the public and to scholars, but to potential claimants as well."[14] Thus, the Report takes the position that in some cases acquisition of an incompletely documented object might benefit a true owner whose chances of finding the object may be increased.

The 2004 Report noted that "it is increasingly important that [the museum] rigorously research the provenance of a work . . . ."[15] The 2004 Report, like the 2001 Position Paper, provided a laundry list of factors for a museum to consider before acquiring a work, but no precise direction as to how to weigh or balance the factors. The 2004 factors are:

- the ownership history of the work of art;
- the countries in which the work of art has been located and when;
- the exhibition history of the work of art, if any;
- the publication history of the work of art, if any;
- whether any claims to ownership of the work of art have been made;
- whether the work of art appears in relevant databases of stolen works; and
- the circumstances under which the work of art is being offered to the museum.[16]

These 2004 factors are directly relevant to legal defenses that may be raised to defeat a civil claim to the work of art, such as statute of limitations, laches, and waiver. Legal claims and litigation are costly for museums to evaluate and defend.

Additionally, Guideline II(A)(2) instructs that museums should "make a concerted effort to obtain accurate written documentation with respect to the history of the work of art including import and export documents." Guideline III states that museums "should require sellers, donors, and their representatives to provide all available information and documentation, as well as appropriate warranties regarding the origins and provenance of a work of art offered for acquisition."

Additionally, outside of the Guidelines, Part C is entitled "Legal Considerations." It requires that museums "must comply with all applicable local, state, and federal U.S. laws, most notably those governing ownership and title, import, and other issues critical to acquisition decisions." It continues to note the problematic complexity of the law applicable in antiquities cases:

> The law relevant to the acquisition of archaeological materials and ancient art has become increasingly complex and continues to evolve. Since the status of art under foreign law may bear on its legal status under U.S. law [pursuant to the McClain doctrine], member museums must be familiar with relevant U.S. and foreign laws before making an acquisition.[17]

Moreover, Part D deals exclusively with the UNESCO Convention. It provides that member museums should not acquire objects falling into any of these categories:

1. any archaeological material or work of ancient art known to have been stolen from a museum, or a religious, or secular public monument or similar institution (Article 7b of the Convention);
2. any archaeological material or work of art known to have been part of an official archaeological excavation and removed in contravention of the laws of the country of origin; or
3. any such works of art that were removed after November 1970 regardless of any applicable statute of limitation and notwithstanding the fact that the U.S. did not accede to the Convention until 1983.[18]

In comparison to the 2001 factors, the 2004 factors focus with precision on key legal standards. Although the 2001 factors mention "applicable law," which presumably meant criminal law and U.S. import regulations, and one factor implicating foreign export law, the 2001 factors' core theme reflects concern about the impact of museum acquisitions upon unauthorized excavation in foreign lands and destruction of the archaeological record. In contrast, the 2004 factors take on a more legalistic, and perhaps defensive, approach that primarily reflects fear of costly lawsuits. They inherently implicate legal evaluation of the ability to defeat claims that may be brought.

This is not to say that the Guidelines foreclosed acquiring an object with knowledge that there was a distinct chance it might later be restituted, but museum deaccessioning generally is strongly disfavored. Guideline F in the 2004 Report states that if a member receives a claim to an object, it should seek an "equitable resolution," "even though this claim may not be enforceable under U.S. law." "Possible options that should be considered include: transfer or sale of the work of art to the claimant; payment to the claimant; loan or exchange of the work of art; or retention of the work of art."[19]

Additionally, archaeological ethics remained a concern for the AAMD. Part E of the 2004 Report, entitled "Incomplete Provenance," provides that in cases where rigorous research could not provide "sufficient information on the recent history of a proposed acquisition," "museums must use their professional judgment . . . in accordance with the Statement of Principles" to determine whether to acquire an object. The exercise of judgment should "recognize that the work of art, the culture it represents, scholarship, and the public may be served best through the acquisition of the work of art by a public institution dedicated to the conservation, exhibition, study, and interpretation of works of art." Examples are provided:

1. "if the work of art is in danger of destruction or deterioration"; or
2. "the acquisition would make the work of art publicly accessible, providing a singular and material contribution to knowledge, as well as facilitating the reconstruction of its provenance thereby allowing possible claimants to come forward."[20]

Another notable factor that museums were instructed to take into account was:

> whether the work of art has been outside its probable country or countries of origin for a sufficiently long time that its acquisition would not provide a direct, material incentive to looting or illegal excavation; while each member museum should determine its own policy as to length of time and appropriate documentation, a period of ten years is recommended.[21]

In this very important respect, the 2004 Guidelines injected a factual assessment of the acquisition's likely impact upon looting. In 2004, the AAMD's view was that a ten-year separation between the likely date an object was improperly excavated and its acquisition date meant that the acquisition likely had no "direct, material incentive to looting or illegal excavation." Most archaeologists would dispute this assessment.

Regardless of who was right factually, by 2004, the AAMD approach to weighing the pros and cons of a possible acquisition became primarily, but not exclusively, a legalistic one. Although the AAMD recognized that acquisitions—even those that would not violate any applicable law—should not encourage destruction of the archaeological record, risk to the museum's budget became the primary guiding light.

On February 27, 2006, the AAMD Subcommittee on Incoming Loans of Archaeological Material and Ancient Art issued a Report largely extending the 2004 Principles and Guidelines to loans and particularly to long-term loans like those arranged between various U.S. museums and Italy. There are a few important distinctions in the 2006 Report. For example, in regard to determining ownership history, in addition to asking lenders for information and appropriate warranties, the Guidelines provide: "In some cases, the museum may decide that it is responsible and prudent to make further inquiries from other possible sources of information and/or databases." As to loans for visiting exhibitions, the Guidelines provide that principal responsibility for researching ownership history falls upon the AAMD member museum primarily responsible for organizing it. The Guidelines also caution that while the borrowing institution generally will accept the lending institution's assessment of the ownership history, legal issues may arise for the borrowing institution. Finally, it should be noted that the Statement of Principles in Section I(A) heavily reflects the December 2002 Declaration on the Importance and Value of Universal Museums, signed by some of the world's largest and most prestigious museums, including some of those that received restitution demands from Italy.

The AAMD's January 2007 Position Paper, "Art Museums, Private Collectors, and the Public Benefit," presents a long laundry list of factors by which to evaluate a potential loan or donation. None of the factors listed is unusual. Additionally, because the Position Paper applies to all art acquisitions and loans, the de-emphasis of issues related to archaeological ethics does not signify a departure from the Principles and Guidelines previously expressed.

It also is significant that whereas the prior reports, guidelines, and position papers did not in any way address how to weigh or balance the factors, this 2007 Position Paper states: "Each of the 176 institutions represented by the membership of the Association of Art Museum Directors (AAMD) answers these questions according to the unique mandate of its mission and the interests of its community."[22] Thus, AAMD member museums have now been given the directive to individually determine how the factors should be weighed or balanced.

On June 4, 2008, the AAMD issued its "New Report on Acquisition of Archaeological Materials and Ancient Art" (New Report). It announced the creation of a new AAMD website where museums will publish images and information about new acquisitions. The New Report represents a shift in focus from the prior approaches while allowing flexible, case-by-case assessment. Instead of leaving it to individual museums to assess the potential legal risk and the object's possible link to clandestine excavation within the last ten years on a full case-by-case basis, the New Report partially adopts the "blank check" approach in the UNESCO Convention previously rejected by the United States. It "recognizes the date of the [UNESCO] Convention, November 17, 1970," (1970) "as providing the most pertinent threshold for the application of more rigorous standards to the acquisition of archaeological materials and ancient art as well as for the development of a unified set of expectations for museums, sellers and donors."[23] Guideline E states, in relevant part, that AAMD member museums should not acquire a work unless its provenance research:

1. substantiates that the work was outside its country of probable modern discovery before 1970, or,
2. was legally exported from its probable country of modern discovery after 1970.

Thus, in the AAMD's view, amnesty is the rule for objects excavated prior to 1970. The blank check approach, which was so vigilantly fought by the museum and collector community during the UNESCO debates, now has been adopted by the AAMD.

Principle I(F) nonetheless still retains flexibility of judgment when complete ownership history is unavailable. It states:

> Recognizing that a complete recent ownership history may not be obtainable for all archaeological material and every work of ancient art, the AAMD believes that its member museums should have the right to exercise their institutional responsibility to make informed and defensible judgments about the appropriateness of acquiring such an object if, in their opinion, doing so would satisfy the requirements set forth in the Guidelines below and meet the highest standards of due diligence and transparency as articulated in this Statement of Principles.[24]

Guideline II(F) expands upon this flexibility, which can be fairly described as an intentional loophole:

> The AAMD recognizes that even after the most extensive research, many works will lack a complete documented ownership history. In some instances, an informed judgment can indicate that the work was outside its probable country of modern discovery before 1970 or legally exported from its probable country of modern discovery after 1970, and therefore can be acquired. In other instances, the cumulative facts and circumstances resulting from provenance research, including, but not limited to, the independent exhibition and publication of the work, the length of time it has been on public display and its recent ownership history, allow a museum to make an informed judgment to acquire the work, consistent with the Statement of Principles above.[25]

The overarching guiding light to operating within the loophole and deciding whether to acquire an object with incomplete ownership history back to 1970 is stated in Guideline II(F) (second paragraph): "In both instances, the museum must carefully balance the possible financial and reputational harm of taking such a step against the benefit of collecting, presenting, and preserving the work in trust for the educational benefit of present and future generations."[26] This emphasis is less legalistic than that of the 2004 Report. The guiding light is not that of preserving archaeological context, but that of the bottom line of the museum. This approach also underscores the importance of museum leaders' fiduciary obligations to manage museums and the objects within them for the public. As stated by Philip de Montebello, the esteemed former Director of the Met, who led the institution for thirty years, in regard to the "close correlation between public trust and a museum's reputation":

> A nick on either one constitutes a serious breach of both. In essence, a museum should have zero tolerance for even a single derisory comment from a credible source occasioned by even a single wayward step from its mission, and to that end, every effort should be made to assure the absolute integrity of all we do.[27]

The 2008 Report largely mirrors the remaining due diligence standards of the 2004 Report, but a few differences should be highlighted. Guideline II(A) seems to strengthen the due diligence standard: "Member museums should thoroughly research the ownership history of archaeological materials or works of ancient art . . . prior to their acquisition, including making a rigorous effort to obtain accurate written documentation with respect to their history, including import and export documents."[28] Moreover, Guideline II(C) states that member museums "should require sellers, donors, and their representatives to provide all information of which they have knowledge, and documentation that they possess, related to the work being offered. . . ."[29] Thus, the AAMD is recognizing that the old days—of almost unquestioned faith in representations by esteemed donors about an object's ownership history—are over. The market's previous standard of full anonymity and secrecy is changing.

The American Association of Museums (AAM) also weighed in on the debate in its new "Standards Regarding Archaeological Material and Ancient Art" (AAM Standards), approved by its Board of Directors on July 2008. The new AAM standards largely mirror the AAMD approach, but arguably put even more of an emphasis on the date UNESCO was opened for signature, November 17, 1970 (1970). The AAM Standards state that even if an acquisition would be legal, museums "should not acquire any object that, to the knowledge of the museum, has been illegally exported from its country of modern discovery or the country where it was last legally owned."[30] The standards "recommend" that "museums require documentation that the object was" (1) "out of its probable country of modern discovery" by 1970; or (2) legally exported out of its country of modern discovery. The AAM policy also contains a loophole "when there is substantial but not full documentation" of provenance, and states that if a museum utilizes the loophole, "it should be transparent about why this is an appropriate decision in alignment with the institution's collections policy and applicable ethics codes."[31]

Dr. Kwame Opoku, a frequent contributor to the debate concerning repatriation of African objects from Western museums, who wrote an essay in 2008 that attracted a rejoinder on Afrikanet.info from de Montebello, critiqued the AAM loophole:

> The solution of the AAM is what one often finds where there is division of opinion and both sides are almost equally strong: a bold general principle with an exception which almost negates totally the general principle. Both sides win. One step forward and one back.[32]

Certainly the expression of the U.S. museum community's new attitude toward the "blank check" approach represents a significant development. Also significant is the fact that the Getty and the Indianapolis Museum of Art had already adopted the 1970 "blank check" approach for new acquisitions—without a loophole—in 2006 and 2007, respectively.[33]

The AAM standards apply to new acquisitions, but the standards take a revolutionary position in regard to existing collections. They state in relevant part:

> In order to advance further research, public trust, and accountability museums should make available the known ownership history of archaeological materials and ancient art in their collections, and make serious efforts to allocate time and funding to conduct research on objects when provenance is incomplete or uncertain. Museums may continue to respect requests for anonymity by donors.[34]

This standard is revolutionary because there is no limit to the number of objects within a museum's collection to which the standard applies, and some of the most prestigious institutions' collections contain hundreds of thousands of objects. The task of full provenance research as to all archaeological and ancient art objects obtained after 1970 would be enormous. As stated by Lee Rosenbaum, who pens the influential CultureGrrl blog: "Did they realize what they were saying?"[35] It should be noted, however, that the new standards are aspirations, not requirements.

Finally, the new AAM Standard 4 seems to be a more reconciliatory approach toward handling claims to objects as well. It states:

> Museums should respectfully and diligently address ownership claims to antiquities and archaeological material. Each claim, whether based on ethical or legal considerations, should be considered on its own merits.
>
> When appropriate and reasonably practical, museums should seek to resolve claims through voluntary discussions directly with a claimant or facilitated by a third party.[36]

This new standard heavily reflects the cooperative approach to claims to Nazi-looted art previously advanced by the AAMD and the AAM, as well as what are referred to as the "Washington Principles," eleven principles acceded to by 44 governments, at a conference held in Washington, D.C. on December 3, 1998, which were reinforced in 2000, in Vilnius, Lithuania.[37] The AAMD, on June 4, 1998, issued guidelines that called on member museums to resolve legitimate claims to art in their collections "in an equitable, appropriate, and mutually agreeable manner." The Washington Principles drew heavily from the AAMD guidelines and call for nations to reach "just and fair" solutions to Nazi-looted art claims. The AAM November 1999 Guidelines, amended in April 2001, echo the AAMD standard. Similarly, the museum standards recommend the use of mediation over litigation, while Washington Principle 11 encourages nations "to develop national processes to implement these principles, particularly as they relate to alternative dispute resolution mechanisms for resolving ownership issues."[38] AAM Guideline 5 highlights that museums must review such claims while minding their fiduciary obligations to hold collections in the public trust. All of these standards and guidelines recognize that there is a tremendous variety in individual cases, and thus call for case-by-case evaluation. Although conciliatory in nature, it cannot be denied that the guidelines and principles are vague and lack instruction as to what is "equitable," "appropriate," or "just and fair" in difficult cases. Things have changed since this conciliatory tone was struck in 1998.

Ten years after the pivotal AAMD Report and Washington Principles in 1998, we are in an era where museums have begun to file declaratory judgment actions against claimants. They are throwing down the litigation gauntlet against fragile, perhaps weak, claims. It is telling that in May 2007, the AAMD issued a Position Paper stating that despite the large amount of Nazi-era provenance research that had been conducted in museums between 1998 and July 2006 (which one should note had not been uniformly progressive in all institutions), only "twenty-two works in American museum collections have been identified as having been stolen by the Nazis and not properly restituted after the war."[39] Although those who instructed the filing of declaratory judgment actions certainly felt such action was necessary to fulfill their fiduciary obligations to preserve museum collections for the public, it certainly seems a dramatic turn away from the spirit of 1998 and 1999. Is the same in store for antiquities? Will we transition out of this new phase of openness, to a period of preemptive litigation strikes to defeat claims?

Conclusion

As a consequence of these developments and others, objects with quality documentation of their ownership history are now highly prized by collectors and museums. Does that mean that one should presume, without more empirical research, that objects lacking impeccable documentation are looted?

Many archaeologists, consistent with policies of the Archaeological Institute of America, would say, "yes." Those policies reflect concern about the destruction of the archaeological record, as well as weaknesses a market filled with unprovenanced objects poses for science. For example, the market demand for undocumented Coptic sculptures allowed fakes to infiltrate museum and private collections for more than forty years, which has distorted our understanding of ancient Egypt and the importance of Christian iconography there.[40] At the Brooklyn Museum alone, approximately one third of its formerly prized collection of Coptic sculptures are believed to be fakes. At this point, it will be hard, for even experts, to tease out all of the fakes from collections throughout the United States and the world. To try to stop archaeologists from inadvertently enhancing the value of looted artifacts, the American Schools of Oriental Research (ASOR) and the Archaeological Institute of America (AIA) prohibit initial publication in their journals of unprovenanced objects, with the exception of an article highlighting the looting problem.

On the other hand, collectors and many within the museum community would respond, "no." The customary practice of the collecting market has never required such a high level proof of ownership—even if it should have done so. Additionally, chance finds are possible. Floods and earthquakes happen, people find objects on private property to which national ownership laws may not apply, and old collections do exist. If we ban such objects from museums and scholarly study, what consequences will we experience? What information will we lose in the overarching fight to preserve archaeological context?

Some scholars of antiquity are caught in the middle. In August 2007, the Biblical Archaeological Society issued a Statement of Concern in relation to the "movement that has received much publicity lately that condemns the use of unprovenanced antiquities from consideration in the reconstruction of ancient history."[41] Although they noted their uniform condemnation of looting, as has the AAM and the AAMD, they stated that a history of the ancient Near East and the Mediterranean basin "cannot be written without the evidence from unprovenanced antiquities." The Statement identifies many important unprovenanced and looted antiquities: "the Dead Sea Scrolls, the Nag Hammadi Codices, the recently reported Gospel of Judas, the Wadi Daliyeh papyri," coins, stone seals, and "hundreds of thousands of cuneiform tables, the basis of our understanding of Mesopotamian history." The Statement in particular criticizes the ASOR and AIA publication policies, claiming that it is "almost universally recognized" that the policies have "had little or no effect on looting." At an October 2008 conference in Chicago, at De-Paul University College of Law, some in the museum community were saying the same is true of museum acquisitions. The Biblical Archaeological Society Statement asserted: "Scholars cannot close their eyes to important information." It continued:

> 7. We do not encourage private collection of antiquities. But important artifacts and inscriptions must be rescued and made available even though unprov-

enanced. When such objects have been looted, the antiquities market is often the means by which they are rescued, either by a private party or a museum. To vilify such activity results only in the loss of important scholarly information.

8. We would encourage private collectors of important artifacts and inscriptions to make them available to scholars for study and publication. Too often collectors who do make their objects available to scholars are subject to public obloquy. As a result, collectors are disinclined to allow scholars to study their collections, and the public is the poorer.[42]

To conclude, it seems there has been a dramatic shift in significant segments of both the archaeologist and museum/collector camps concerning the best approach for museums and collectors who acquire objects. The initial cultural nationalism versus cultural internationalism framework was useful to start the discussion, but at a point the discussion seemed to become too polarized to lead to useful solutions. The revelation of the extent of infection of the market in certain objects with fraudulent or looted goods has caused the conversation to evolve in both the archaeologist and museum/collector camps. Regardless of one's view of cultural nationalism, the market in cultural objects, or politics,[43] present acquisitions invite a whole host of more complex legal issues to consider. Although hard empirical data would be useful to fully understand the ramifications of acquisition and publication policies, such data necessarily will be very difficult to obtain, because of the clandestine, and often criminal, nature of activities at an object's source, and the path of the object to the seemingly licit market. We cannot allow the lack of such data to become an excuse to close down open communication. Members of the cultural heritage community must continue to let informed logic and ethics guide their policies and practices as they act as stewards of objects for the public trust.

Notes

1. Peter Watson & Cecilia Todeschini, *The Medici Conspiracy: The Illicit Journey of Looted Antiquities* (2006).
2. This policy has since been tightened further, as discussed in Section II.
3. Elisabetta Povoledo, *Getty Is Lent a Bounty of Berninis*, N.Y.Times, Feb. 2, 2008. *See also* Elisabetta Povoledo, *Italy Makes Its Choice of Antiquities to Lend Met*, N.Y. Times, Mar. 15, 2006.

4. Associated Press, *Ex-Getty Curator Says She's Taking Fall*, Dec. 29, 2006.
5. Elisabetta Povoledo, *Collector Returns Art Italy Says Was Looted*, N.Y.TIMES (Jan. 18, 2008).
6. Watson & Todeschini, at 79.
7. A bronze krater seemingly of Trebenishte type is currently on loan to the Museum of Fine Arts in Houston from the Shelby White–Leon Levy collection, and there are calls for the museum to release its ownership history. The most probable find-spot for such a krater is within the Former Yugoslav Republic of Macedonia.
8. Associated Press, *Italy's Art Squad Says Archaeological Looting Declining*, Jan. 17, 2008.
9. Association of Art Museum Directors, Art Museums and the International Exchange of Cultural Artifacts, Oct. 2001.
10. *Id.* at 1-2.
11. *Id.* at 2.
12. *Id.*
13. Association of Art Museum Directors, Report of the AAMD Task Force on the Acquisition of Archaeological Materials and Ancient Art, June 4, 2004, at I(D).
14. *Id.* Other AAMD Reports, Position Papers and Guidelines discuss evaluating claims and deaccessioning objects.
15. *Id.*
16. *Id.* at II(A)(1).
17. *Id.* at Part C.
18. *Id.* at Part D.
19. It should be noted here that the AAMD in a November 2007 Position Paper stated that one consideration when determining whether to deaccession an object is whether "evidence has come to light that the work was stolen from another institution or that it was illegally exported or imported in violation of the laws of the jurisdiction in which the museum is located." Association of Art Museum Directors, Art Museums and the Practice of Deaccessioning, Nov. 2007, at 2. Note that the concept of the violation of a foreign nation's export regulation is not a listed consideration.
20. *Id.* at Part E.
21. *Id.*
22. Association of Art Museum Directors, Art Museums, Private Collectors, and the Public Benefit, Jan. 2007.
23. New Report at Statement of Principle I(E).
24. Association of Art Museum Directors, Art Museums, New Report on Acquisition of Archaeological Materials and Ancient Art, June 4, 2008, at Statement of Principle I(F).
25. *Id.* at Guidline II(F).
26. *Id.* at Statement of Principle II(F), ¶ 2 (emphasis added).

27. Philip de Montebello, *Art Museums, Inspiring Public Trust, in Whose Muse?*: Art Museums and the Public Trust 151-52 (James Cuno ed., 2004).
28. New Report at Guideline II(A) (emphasis added).
29. *Id.* at Guideline II(C).
30. American Association of Museums, Standards Regarding Archaeological Material and Ancient Art, July 2008, at Section 2, ¶ 3.
31. *Id.* at Standard 2, ¶ 6.
32. Kwame Opoku, *New AAM Standards for the Acquisition of Archaeological Material and Ancient Art: A Minor "American Revolution"?*, Museum Security Network Email, Sept. 7, 2008.
33. The Indianapolis Museum of Art policy was a stop-gap pending the adoption of new standards by the AAMD. According to a statement issued by its Director, Maxwell Anderson, and published in THE ART NEWSPAPER on April 30, 2007, the British Museum acknowledged 1970 as a bright line in March 2004. The British Museum is one of the signatories of the 2002 Declaration on the Importance and Value of Universal Museums.
34. AAM Standards at Standard 3.
35. Lee Rosenbaum, *AAM's New Antiquities Acquisition Standards: More Sweeping Than AAMD's*, Aug. 12, 2008, http://www.artsjournal.com/culturegrrl/2008/08
36. AAM Standards at Standard 4.
37. Nations met again in 2000, to build upon the Washington Principles in Vilnius, Lithuania, under the auspices of the Parliamentary Assembly of the Council of Europe. http://www.lootedartcommission.com/lootedart_councilofeurope.htm (last visited Nov. 1, 2008). The Vilnius Forum generated a declaration expressing continued support of the Washington Principles without significantly refining them or expanding upon them. http://www.lootedartcommission.com/vilniusforum (last visited Nov. 1, 2008).
38. Washington Principles at Principle 11.
39. Association of Art Museum Directors, Art Museums and the Identification and Restitution of Works Stolen By the Nazis, May 2007, at ¶ 3.
40. The fakes themselves seem to date back to the 20th century.
41. The Statement of Concern is reprinted in John H. Merryman, *Art Law Issues*, SM056-ALI-ABA 481 (2007) (available in Westlaw).
42. *Id.* at ¶¶7-8.
43. See generally James Cuno, *Who Owns Antiquity?* (2008) (railing against "nationalist retentionist cultural property laws").

Dan L. Monroe: Art Museums and Collections Policy

• • •

At the end of May 2008, the Association of Art Museum Directors (AAMD) released its "New Report on Acquisition of Archaeological Materials and Ancient Art." Dan L. Monroe, Executive Director of the Peabody and Essex Museum, in Salem, Massachusetts, chaired the committee of AAMD tasked with producing the report. In developing the report, the AAMD took on some of the most sensitive, high profile, divisive, and legally complex issues facing museums at the time. The acquisition of archaeological material and ancient art presents a long-standing conundrum for museums. The desire to own amazing items, to boost membership, financial support, and scholarly standing, is pitted against the ethical and legal issues of sustaining a trade in items, which may encourage an illicit market. Praise for the action of AAMD has come from all sectors of the cultural property arena, including those most concerned with protecting archaeological sites.

The inherent risk to museums of obtaining and holding items of questionable provenance was made clear earlier in the year in the wave of search warrants involving four museums in Southern California. The J. Paul Getty Museum, in Los Angeles, and the Metropolitan Museum of Art, in New York, have also faced contentious issues regarding claims of source nations to items in their collections. Both have embraced the AAMD recommendations as museum policy.

The guidelines recommend that AAMD member museums should not normally acquire items unless the museum's research substantiates that the object left its "probable country of modern discovery" prior to 1970, in acknowledgement of the UNESCO Convention. The onus is on the museum to conduct thorough provenance research, including information from donors. However, museums may acquire antiquities when there is no provenance information or when provenance information is incomplete, if they deem that the "benefit of collecting, presenting, and preserving the work in trust for the educational benefit of present and future generations" outweighs the harm of acquiring a possibly looted antiquity.

Certainly Dan Monroe did not act alone in drafting this report, and the entire committee, as well as AAMD, is due recognition for seizing the issue and acting responsibly. Still, his mark as a statesman, one who does not shy from sitting on the head of a pin, and doing so with panache, resounds through the report. As Executive Director and CEO of the Peabody and Essex Museum since 1993, he has increased the size and scope of the collection, visitor attendance, operating revenues, and the endowment several times over. PEM has become a world renowned institution under his leadership. Dan Monroe is not unaccustomed to dealing with controversy. As Vice-Chairman of the American Association of Museums, he guided national museum response to Mapplethorpe and other NEA controversies in Congress, and was the lead museum authority in the drafting and passage of the Native American Graves Protection and Repatriation Act, currently serving as a member of the Native American Graves Protection and Repatriation (NAGPRA) Review Committee. He then served as chairman of AAM and the International Council on Museums, America.

This fall, Dan Monroe granted an interview with the editors of the *Yearbook* regarding the AAMD and its efforts.

Yearbook: How would you describe the genesis of the AAMD and its role as a leader in guiding art museum policy?

Monroe: AAMD is an association of art museum directors. Unlike other museum professional organizations, individuals, not institutions, comprise AAMD's membership. Participation in AAMD is by invitation only based on professional qualifications and institutional size. Art museums often face special issues and challenges. AAMD has, for several decades, provided primary guidance to art museums on a broad spectrum of issues.

Yearbook: On June 4, 2008, the AAMD issued its "New Report on Acquisition of Archaeological Materials and Ancient Art," following reports and guidelines in 2000, 2004, and 2006. As a package, what do they give art museums?

Monroe: Acquisitions of archaeological material and ancient art have long been contentious and complex: witness the ongoing debate over the Elgin Marbles or the recent spate of illegally or improperly acquired works of art returned to Greece or Italy by several major American museums. Standards and practices regarding acquisition of archaeological material and ancient art inevitably change through time. Practices judged entirely acceptable today may be judged improper tomorrow. Likewise, the legal environment pertaining to cultural property is complex, sometimes contradictory, and constantly shifting as a result of the passage or amendment of national laws or as a result of interpretation of current laws through the courts.

Many of the nation's art museums collect, preserve, and interpret antiquities. AAMD's "New Report on Acquisition of Archaeological Material and Ancient Art" provides new guidelines to govern the complex processes involved in acquisition of archaeological material and ancient art. The new guidelines adopt more stringent research standards regarding provenance of objects, recognize for the first time the UNESCO 1970 Convention on Cultural Property as a pertinent threshold for consideration of possible acquisitions, provide an unprecedented level of public transparency for all acquisitions of objects that lack complete provenance through a new AAMD website, and lay out a process for acquisition decision making. The new guidelines have been widely recognized as progressive and responsible.

Yearbook: Do you see the efforts of AAMD as having had an effect on policies of art museums?

Monroe: AAMD's policies and guidelines have had a substantial effect on the policies of individual art museums in the areas of governance, ethics, deaccessioning, acquisitions, and a host of other issues.

Yearbook: Just recently it was reported that the Portland Art Museum placed a statue of Ganesha on the AAMD website. Is this an indication that the guidelines are working?

Monroe: AAMD's new website dedicated to presenting archaeological material or ancient art lacking complete provenance acquired by member museums is working effectively, as evidenced by the Portland Art Museum's recent posting of a Ganesha sculpture. Some critics have complained there are few objects on the website. This is ironic since the paucity of objects on the new AAMD website reflects the level of acquisitions activity among American art museums for archaeological material and ancient art lacking complete provenance.

Yearbook: What do you see as the current best practice model for art museum acquisitions in light of issues of provenance—that is, broken or unbroken chains of title?

Monroe: Art museum professionals and archaeologists have engaged in a long and generally bitter debate regarding acquisition of archaeological material and ancient art. The outlines of this debate are well documented. Archaeologists firmly believe UNESCO 1970 Convention provisions help stem looting and destruction of archaeological sites and resources by containing the black market for such materials. Many art museum professionals do not agree that art museums should never acquire works of art lacking complete provenance after the UNESCO 1970 bright line. Two things seem indisputable in this debate: (1) UNESCO provisions have not significantly stemmed the tide of looting and destruction of archaeological sites and resources; and (2) the art museum/archaeology debate on this topic has effectively prohibited any joint effort by these two key communities to launch new, cooperative efforts to preserve archaeological sites and resources. In effect, disagreement over means and methods, not goals, has prevented positive collaboration.

Art museums continue to believe it is in the best interest of the public they serve to, under certain circumstances, acquire works of art lacking complete provenance. The current best-practice model for making such acquisitions is laid out in the new AAMD guidelines referenced above. Art museums must, on a case-by-case basis, carefully balance the potential negative financial and other liabilities associated with acquisition of objects lacking complete provenance against the important and positive benefits associated with acquisition of certain objects for the benefit of the public, scholars, and researchers.

Yearbook: The AAMD 2008 Report sets 1970 as the date by which museums will henceforth be required to have documented provenance (source) for acquisitions, and prior thereto proof is only required that the items were essentially in the marketplace. Do you think this standard will be accepted by museums, will be workable, and will achieve the desired results? What are the desired results?

Monroe: The 2008 AAMD Report does not dictate that art museums uniformly and invariably adhere to UNESCO 1970 Convention provisions. The Report specifically recognizes that art museums may, in certain circumstances, wish to acquire objects that lack complete provenance after 1970, and it clearly endorses such decisions if all other elements of the Guidelines have been fulfilled in a museum's decision-making processes. Many archaeological and ancient objects lack complete provenance and no amount of expense, time, or effort will provide complete information. Though such works often lack contextual information, it is the firm view of many art museum directors that such works are aesthetically and culturally important and that they should reside in the public domain. A museum must carefully weigh potential damage to its reputation or pocketbook caused by an acquisition that turns out to be improper or illegal against the gain that will be realized in helping share a part of our collective artistic and cultural heritage.

The 2008 AAMD Report has been unanimously adopted by AAMD's members, and I fully expect complete compliance with the provision of the new Guidelines.

Yearbook: In lively interactions between archaeologists and museum directors the issues often come down to protection of provenance (the site) and the knowledge to be gained from putting the object in context, versus access, knowledge intrinsic to the item, and preservation in museum curation. Must these two perspectives always be in conflict? How would you resolve the two?

Monroe: The interactions between archaeologists and art museum directors have, indeed, often been lively but, I contend, largely unproductive. Neither side has advanced arguments persuasive to the other. The bitterness of the dispute has only assured that art museum professionals and archaeologists have been unable to transcend their differences to work together on shared values and goals. Both communities abhor destruction of archaeological sites and resources.

There are many dimensions to the arguments. Art museum professionals and archaeologists agree that contextual information acquired through properly conducted excavations is extremely valuable. Archaeologists generally believe objects lacking such information are useless. Art museum professionals strongly disagree.

These and other disputes—such as the impact of museum acquisitions on the black market—have produced well-worn rhetorical and intellectual arguments. Essentially, twenty-some years of debate have resulted in "armed" camps so divided it has become extremely difficult to engage in productive exchange of ideas, let alone cooperative joint efforts to help preserve archaeological sites and resources worldwide.

The solution? Recognize we do not agree on several issues and focus our efforts to work together positively, constructively, and collegially on issues and shared values we hold in common. If we had taken this approach two decades ago, more of the world's archaeological sites and resources might have been preserved and protected.

Yearbook: Will the AAMD reports and guidelines have an effect on review by museums of the ownership status of current collections?

Monroe: AAM's cultural property guidelines ask museums to review the ownership status of current collections. AAMD's guidelines do not make this demand. I doubt many museums, including natural history museums with major holdings of archaeological material or ancient art, will carry out comprehensive reviews of ownership status of current collections. The time, energy, and cost of such review is prohibitively expensive. It often takes many staff members many months to review the ownership history of a single object. Furthermore, since it is often impossible to construct a full ownership history even after intensive research, the value of such reviews is open to question. It is far more important for museums to assure their collections are readily accessible to the public, researchers, and scholars.

Yearbook: Over the last year the global economy has crumbled. The National Academy Museum in New York broke with AAM and AAMD prohibitions against selling accessions to pay operating costs, by deciding to sell two Hudson River School paintings, and the punitive action was immediate. What options do museums have to survive in the current economic environment absent deaccessioning objects to support operations?

Monroe: Deaccessioning objects to support operations fundamentally compromises the public trust requirements and integrity of a museum. Museum collections, not museum organizations, are held in public trust. An absolute firewall must exist between collections and operational support for museums. Donors who give works of art or other objects to a museum collection do so with the understanding that the work in question will be used to support education, interpretation, and research activities. If museums routinely sold objects to support operations, donors will inevitably decrease their gifts of art or other objects to museums. The public loses as a result. If museums routinely sold objects from their collections to support operations then donor motivation to provide support for operations will also be diminished. Collections are not fungible assets—a fact recognized by the Financial Accounting Standards Board.

Allowing any art museum to sell works of art to support operations undermines the integrity of the art museum community as a whole. Both AAM and AAMD have consequently adopted very stringent prohibitions against deaccessions to support operations. When an organization, like the National Academy of Arts, chooses to sell extremely valuable works of art from their collection to support operations AAMD and AAM have no choice but to censure and/or sanction their actions to protect the public's trust in museums.

Collections have priority over organizational existence. If a museum, for whatever reason, is unable to fulfill its mission in a financially sustainable manner, then it must reassess its governance, management, programs, mission, fund raising, and other activities. Many strategies may be pursued to achieve sustainability, but these strategies do not include using collections as liquid assets to support operations. If a museum cannot develop a viable operating strategy, then it should give its collections to other museums and cease to exist. Fortunately, the overwhelming majority of museums manage to uphold their mission and public trust responsibilities through good times and bad.

Yearbook: Over the last two decades you have had leadership roles in AAM and ICOM, served on the NAGPRA Review Committee, and now in AAMD. How would you reflect on your experiences, lessons learned, and guidance you would offer art museum professionals and the lawyers who serve them?

Monroe: I have had the great privilege to play a part in helping address a wide variety of national or international museum issues, among them issues surrounding the "Culture Wars," NAGPRA, Codes of Ethics, and national and international cultural property issues.

I do not believe leadership can be reduced to specific prescriptions or characteristics. Different situations and issues require different kinds of leadership strategies. So I am reluctant to do more than make some very general observations in answer to the above questions.

Most complex professional issues involve ethical, legal, and political factors. Leadership often involves the development of processes designed to draw out diverse views and potential solutions, methods to evaluate them, and agreed means to reach viable decisions. In opposition to this predominant approach to leadership, it is sometimes necessary to take a strong personal stand on issues even if doing so is not popular in certain quarters of one's constituency. Ultimately, most complex issues are resolved by integrating ideas and values in ways nearly all participants can accept and support.

Lawyers can and often do play a very important part in these processes. They bring not only knowledge of law but also training in technical and detailed analyses of issues and potential solutions.

Leadership in the cultural community requires an ability to listen to and appreciate diverse viewpoints, willingness to commit to finding the best solution, which often may not be one's own, and capability to respect divergent and antithetical perspectives. The cultural community is a collegial community. Finally, it is always essential to connect cultural issues to the world at large and to do one's best to understand long-term consequences to immediate actions.

Federal Land Management

• • •

Section Editor: James Van Ness

Indentifying Historic Properties: The "Reasonable and Good Faith Effort" Standard

It has been some time since a court of law last addressed the "reasonable and good faith effort" standard[1] for the identification of historic properties under section 106.[2] In *Quechan Indian Tribe of the Fort Yuma Indian Reservation v. U.S. Department of the Interior,*[3] the District Court of Arizona did just that, and in doing so provided us with another useful touchstone for judging the adequacy of agency efforts to identify historic properties within an area of potential effects.

The facts of the case are these: In 1951, the Wellton-Mohawk Irrigation and Drainage District (District) was created to provide domestic water, irrigation water, and other services to the Wellton and Mohawk Valleys in Arizona. In 1998, the District—having fully repaid the government loans related to the project—entered into a Memorandum of Agreement (MOA) with the Bureau of Reclamation (BOR) to effect transfer of title to the irrigation works, facilities, and associated lands to the District. In 2000, Congress enacted legislation authorizing the Secretary of the Interior to carry out the terms of the MOA, subject only to the BOR's compliance with certain federal laws, including the National Environmental Policy Act and the National Historic Preservation Act.

To satisfy the NHPA process, the BOR, in consultation with the Arizona State Historic Preservation Office (SHPO) and certain Indian tribes, designed and implemented a cultural resources program to determine the nature and extent of cultural resources on those lands proposed for title transfer. The first phase of the program, begun in 2003, involved a literature and archival search of archaeological investigations related to the 57,000 acres originally proposed for transfer, plus a 2.5 mile buffer around the perimeter of those lands. Thereafter, 2,124 acres of culturally sensitive lands were removed from the area proposed for title transfer, as were another 4,833 acres of undisturbed lands subjected to a pedestrian survey by an outside archaeological consulting firm. As ultimately configured, the proposed title transfer area included 47,538 acres containing 19 known Register-eligible historic properties. The Arizona SHPO and the Advisory Council on Historic Preservation (ACHP) both approved the BOR's cultural resources investigation.

During the four-plus years it took to complete the National Historic Preservation Act (NHPA) process, the BOR consulted frequently with various Indian tribes to obtain information on the location of traditional cultural properties. Beginning in July 2004, the BOR conducted monthly tribal consultation meetings, eventually conducting more than 30 informational and government-to-government meetings with various Indian tribes, including the Quechan Tribe. Throughout this period, the Quechan Tribe did not identify any specific TCPs or other eligible sites in the title transfer area that the BOR failed to investigate.

In December 2006, the BOR issued its Final Environmental Impact Statement, and on March 26, 2007, issued its Record of Decision. On that same date, the BOR transferred to the District approximately 39,000 acres of land. The BOR retained approximately 8,000 acres subject to the title transfer legislation; all 19 known Register-eligible sites are located on these retained lands.

In its Complaint for Injunctive Relief, the Quechan Tribe alleged the BOR violated the NHPA in several ways. First, the tribe alleged the BOR failed to make a reasonable and good faith effort to identify historic properties, including properties of traditional cultural significance, that could be affected by the federal undertaking. The court disagreed, finding that the BOR's cultural resources program—which included telephone calls, meetings, and on-site visits with members of local tribes, and cost more than two million dollars—constituted a reasonable and good faith effort to identify eligible sites in the title transfer area. Notably, the court pointed out that neither the NHPA nor the ACHP regulations require the BOR to conduct a complete survey of all

47,538 acres of the transfer lands, it being enough that every parcel of undisturbed land was subject to a pedestrian survey.

Second, the tribe alleged that the BOR violated the NHPA when it transferred the lands on which no eligible sites were found, while retaining those lands on which the 19 eligible sites were found until completion of the Section 106 process. The court was not persuaded that this alleged "segmentation" constituted a violation of the NHPA. Examining subsection 110(*l*),[4] the court found that the last sentence of the subsection requiring a Section 106 memorandum of agreement to cover the "undertaking and all of its parts" to be limited to only those parts of the undertaking that may adversely affect any property included in or eligible for inclusion in the National Register. Because the land transferred by the BOR did not include any known Register-eligible properties, it was not unlawful for the BOR to limit the scope of its MOA to just those retained lands upon which the 19 eligible sites are located.[5]

Lastly, the Quechan Tribe alleged the BOR failed to comply with the ACHP regulations requiring ongoing and continuous consultation with affected tribes during the Section 106 process. In this regard, the tribe made three separate but related arguments. First, the tribe complained that the BOR did not engage in government-to-government consultations with the tribe until after various surveys were completed and recommendations made. While true, the court found that this timing alone did not constitute a violation of the ACHP regulations, because the record indicated that the tribe made numerous requests during the subsequent consultations, all of which were acted upon by the BOR (including the conduct of additional pedestrian surveys requested by the tribe). Second, the tribe argued that the BOR failed to formally "invite" the tribe to be a consulting party in the effort to identify eligible properties. The court disagreed, finding that while the BOR may not have extended such an invitation to the tribe in so many words, the record as a whole showed that the BOR had invited the tribe to consult on the identification of eligible historic properties beginning as early as March 2002. Third, the tribe alleged that the BOR violated the ACHP regulations when the BOR failed to invite the tribe to sign the memorandum of agreement. Looking at 36 C.F.R. § 800.6(c)(2)(iii), the court concluded that only those parties that "assume a responsibility under the memorandum of agreement" must be invited to sign the agreement. Because the tribe had no responsibilities under the agreement, it was within the BOR's discretion whether or not to invite the tribe to sign.[6]

Postreview Discoveries and Consultation Under Section 106

Under what circumstances must an agency re-initiate consultation under Section 106 to address previously unanticipated effects? That was the question before the District Court for the Southern District of New York in *Concerned Citizens of Chappaqua v. U.S. Department of Transportation.*[7]

Inspections in 1994, 1996, 1999, and 2004 revealed that the National Register–eligible Route 120 bridge in the Hamlet of Chappaqua was structurally unsound and in need of repair or replacement. The New York State Department of Transportation (NYSDOT) evaluated three general options for the bridge: (1) take no action (and simply maintain the existing bridge); (2) repair and rehabilitate the bridge; or (3) replace the bridge. Given the necessity of making the structural repairs, and the desirability of adding a third lane to the bridge to ease congestion, NYSDOT elected to replace the bridge and add the additional lane. The addition of this third lane required NYSDOT to replace and extend the bridge's retaining wall. In 2005, the retaining wall was projected to extend 25 feet; NYSDOT expanded this projection to 144 feet in 2006, and eventually to 298 feet in 2007.

In December 2005, NYSDOT issued a report that identified three historic structures potentially affected by the bridge replacement: the bridge itself; the nearby Chappaqua train station; and the depot plaza. The report concluded, not surprisingly, that the bridge would be adversely affected by the proposed plan to replace it, but that neither the train station nor the depot would be affected by the construction. NYSDOT and the Federal Highway Administration (FHWA) concluded that replacement of the bridge was nonetheless required, and, in September 2006, executed a Memorandum of Agreement with the New York State Historic Preservation Officer that concluded that retaining the bridge was not a "reasonable alternative" and outlined appropriate mitigation measures to preserve the historic property to the extent feasible. Mitigation amounted to a full documentary and photographic preservation of the bridge. Thereafter, in July 2008, the FHWA submitted the MOA, along with evidence of the mitigation measures having been completed, to the Advisory Council on Historic Preservation; the Council responded that the submission "complete[d] the requirements of Section 106."

In October 2006, following the execution of the MOA, NYSDOT also issued a 148-page Final Design Report that concluded, among other things, that the measures articulated in the MOA were sufficient to mitigate adverse effects on historic properties and that the bridge project qualified for a "categorical exclusion"[8] under the National Environmental Policy Act. At the time of this report, the assumption was that the retaining wall would need to be extended 144 feet, to accommodate the new bridge. Subsequent to the report, the Town of New Castle, which contains the Hamlet of Chappaqua, asked NYSDOT to enlarge the bridge project to include the construction of a new intersection. This change necessitated a further extension of the retaining wall to 298 feet to support a new right-turn lane. In October 2007, NYSDOT determined that the bridge project redesign did not affect the eligibility of the project for a categorical exclusion; NYSDOT did not re-initiate consultation with the New York State SHPO.

The plaintiffs, Concerned Citizens of Chappaqua, are principally concerned with the loss of 61 large trees near the bridge that must be felled to accommodate the construction. Although the NYSDOT's October 2006 report concluded that any environmental and visual effects resulting from the tree removal would be mitigated by final landscaping, revegetation, and tree planting, the plaintiffs argued that NYSDOT and the FHWA erred by not re-initiating consultation with the New York State SHPO when the retaining wall was extended to 298 feet, threatening an additional four to fifteen trees.

National Historic Preservation Act

The court observed that NYSDOT's initial Section 106 review, which resulted in the 2006 MOA and concluded with the Council's 2008 concurrence in the conclusion that NYSDOT had satisfied Section 106, was adequate. The court, however, found the question of whether the revised project design for the retaining wall necessitated a fresh evaluation under Section 106 to be a close one. The plaintiffs claimed that the extended wall constituted an "unanticipated effect . . . , on historic properties" under 36 C.F.R. § 800.13(b), because of the wall's visual impact on the bridge, the train station, and the depot plaza. While the court agreed that "visual effects" can constitute an adverse effect on an historic property, the court observed that to do so the complained-of visual effect must "diminish the integrity of the property's significant historic features."[9] In this instance, the court concluded that the plaintiffs failed to show that the features qualifying the train station and depot plaza for National Register listing would be adversely affected by the extended retaining wall's visual impact. The court's conclusion was bolstered by an affidavit from the New York State SHPO that concluded that the 298-foot retaining wall, tree removal, and other work reflected in the October 2007 redesign would have no additional adverse impact not considered in the 2006 MOA.

National Environmental Policy Act & Section 4(f) of the Department of Transportation Act

The plaintiffs also alleged deficiencies in NYSDOT's compliance with the National Environmental Policy Act (NEPA) and Section 4(f) of the Department of Transportation Act. With respect to NEPA, the plaintiffs complained that the complete replacement of a National Register–eligible property could not conceivably qualify for a categorical exclusion. In a largely conclusory and thinly supported analysis, the court determined that the mere fact that the bridge is historic does not necessarily make the project ineligible for a categorical exclusion. Seemingly reading impacts to historic properties to be something other than conventional environmental impacts cognizable under NEPA,[10] the court held that in light of the "broad environmental assessment" performed by the NYSDOT (i.e., the 148-page Final Design Report that concluded that a categorical exclusion was justified) the court could not conclude that the categorical exclusion classification was clearly erroneous.

More transparent was the court's conclusion that NYSDOT did not violate section 4(f) of the Department of Transportation Act. The court rightly pointed out that, unlike the NHPA and NEPA, which are procedural statutes only, this section of the Department of Transportation Act imposes a substantive burden to avoid "land of an historic site" unless there is no "prudent and feasible alternative to using that land."[11] The court went on to conclude that the no action/maintenance alternative was properly rejected as *infeasible* because it would fail to correct the structural deficiencies plaguing the bridge, and that the repair and rehabilitate alternative was properly rejected as *imprudent* for failing to meet the transportation objectives of the project. Because the plaintiffs did not challenge the replacement alternative under section 4(f), the court held that NYSDOT adequately considered the relevant factors under Section 4(f), and that the agency's evaluation of "prudent and feasible alternatives" was reasonable.

Prudential Standing Under the NHPA

A plaintiff seeking to bring suit under the National Historic Preservation Act must satisfy twin requirements for standing: Article III standing, which enforces the Constitution's case or controversy requirement; and prudential standing, which embodies judicially self-imposed limits on the exercise of federal jurisdiction. In *Role Models America, Inc. v. Geren,*[12] the plaintiff failed to satisfy one of the elements of prudential standing and found its case dismissed.

Role Models is a nonprofit Maryland corporation that desires to use Fort Ritchie, a former Army base in western Maryland selected for closure in 1995, as an educational institution for at-risk and out-of-school youth. Role Models applied to the Department of Education for a no-cost public benefit conveyance of the Fort Ritchie property, but its application was denied. Disappointed by this decision, Role Models brought suit under the NHPA to block the Secretary of the Army from conveying Fort Ritchie to the PenMar Development Corporation, the redevelopment authority designated by the Maryland General Assembly to develop the Fort Ritchie property.

Located at the foot of Quirauk Mountain in the Catoctin Range of the Blue Ridge Mountains, Fort Ritchie is home to Camp Ritchie, a National Register–eligible historic district. Despite this fact, and while Role Models brought its suit alleging the defendants violated the NHPA by failing to consider the effects of the property transfer to PenMar on the Camp Ritchie Historic District, Role Models did not allege that it was concerned about preserving historic sites like Fort Ritchie. Rather, Role Models made it abundantly clear that its motivation in bringing the suit was to acquire the Fort Ritchie property to use it as an educational facility for at-risk youth.

The Supreme Court has defined prudential standing as encompassing three separate bars: (1) a general prohibition on raising another person's legal rights; (2) a prohibition on the resolution of "generalized grievances" that should be addressed to the political branches; and (3) a prohibition on hearing claims outside the "zone of interests" protected by federal law.[13] In this case, the Court of Appeals for the District of Columbia Circuit held that Role Models lacked prudential standing to pursue its NHPA claim, because its motivation in bringing the suit was not within the zone of interests protected by the NHPA—i.e., "the public and private preservation and utilization of all usable elements of the Nation's historic built environment."[14] Stated emphatically by the court, the "Preservation Act does not protect Role Models' right to acquire property for its own use when the use is unrelated to the Preservation act's purpose."[15]

Phased Compliance Under the NHPA and Section 4(f)

National Environmental Policy Act lawyers are quite familiar with the fact that the Council on Environmental Quality's NEPA regulations generally prohibit "segmentation" or "piecemealing."[16] The question before the Ninth Circuit Court of Appeals in *North Idaho Community Action Network v. U.S. Department of Transportation*[17] was whether a similar constraint applies under Section 106 of the National Historic Preservation Act and Section 4(f) of the Department of Transportation Act.

The facts in this case are relatively simple. The Department of Transportation, the Federal Highway Administration, and the Idaho Transportation Department (collectively, the Agencies) proposed a highway construction project on a portion of U.S. Highway 95 located in northern Idaho. The project was designed to improve US-95 in and around the city of Sandpoint. The Agencies designed the project to be funded and constructed in four separate phases. The first, second, and fourth phases involve widening the existing highway to four lanes; the third phase involves realigning a two-mile stretch of the highway to create a byway around downtown Sandpoint.

Because the Agencies deemed the third phase to be the most important, they decided to begin with that phase. To that end, the Agencies approved a final environmental impact statement (EIS) in 1999, which covered all four phases of the project, and issued a record of decision in 2000, selecting the Sand Creek Byway as the preferred alternative for the third phase of the project. In 2005, the Agencies released an environmental assessment (EA) that included various changes to the project design for just the phase-three Byway described in the 1999 EIS. This EA concluded that the changes to the Byway project design would not have significant impacts beyond those already considered in the 1999 EIS; consequently, the Agencies issued a finding of no significant impact. Finally, in 2006, the Agencies prepared an environmental re-evaluation covering additional changes to the Byway project, most of which involved dredging Sand Creek. The re-evaluation concluded that there would be no additional significant impacts associated with the changes and that neither a supplemental EIS, nor another EA were required.

The plaintiff, North Idaho Community Action Network (NICAN), brought suit challenging the Agencies' decision to proceed with the Byway phase of the project. NICAN contended that the Agencies violated the NHPA and Section 4(f) of the Department of Transportation Act by taking a "phased approach" to determining how the Byway project will affect historic properties. The Agencies conceded that they chose a phased approach to identifying and evaluating impacts on historic properties, and that before approving the Byway phase of the project they had completed a detailed Section 106 consultation and Section 4(f) evaluation only on the Sand Creek Byway phase of the project, and not on the remaining three phases.

NHPA Section 106

The court pointed out that the Advisory Council's regulations governing the Section 106 process allow a phased approach to identifying historic properties in some circumstances.[18] Moreover, although an EIS is required to include "discussions" of "historic and cultural resources,"[19] the Agencies' 1999 EIS—which ultimately chose the Sand Creek Byway alternative in part precisely because the through-town alternative would have affected numerous historic sites, whereas the Byway alternative would potentially affect only the historic Burlington Northern Railroad Depot—satisfied this requirement. In addition, the 2005 EA included a more detailed analysis of possible noise and vibration impacts on the Depot, and described and took into account[20] the various mitigation measures the Agencies had agreed to in a Memorandum of Agreement governing the Byway phase of the project developed in consultation with the Idaho State Historic Preservation Officer. The court consequently held that the 1999 EIS, coupled with the 2005 EA and the Agencies' MOA commitments, met the Agencies' NHPA and NEPA requirements with respect to historic properties potentially affected by the Byway phase of the project, and that Section 106 compliance with the other phases of the project could be undertaken later.

DOTA Section 4(f)

The court reached a different conclusion, however, with respect to Section 4(f). Referencing a "markedly similar" case decided by the District of Columbia Circuit in 1999, *Corridor H Alternatives, Inc. v. Slater*,[21] the court determined that Section 4(f) and its regulations required the Agencies to have completed their Section 4(f) evaluation for the entire project prior to issuing a record of decision on any phase of the project.[22] Moreover, because the Agencies are permitted under Section 4(f) to find that a project will have a de minimis impact on historic properties only if that determination has been made pursuant to the Section 106 process,[23] the Section 4(f) evaluation cannot occur until the Section 106 consultation process on the entire project has been completed. While the court consequently found that the Agencies violated Section 4(f) by failing to complete the Section 4(f) evaluation for the entire project before issuing a decision to proceed with the Byway phase, the court declined to enjoin the Byway construction while the Agencies completed the necessary evaluation. Observing that the Section 4(f) evaluation had been completed on the Byway phase of the project, and that the

Byway had independent viability (beginning and ending at points on existing US-95), the court limited the scope of its injunctive relief to precluding the Agencies from commencing construction of the remaining three phases of the project until the Section 4(f) evaluation has been completed in full.

So what conclusions may a cultural property lawyer draw from this case? Stated simply, while phased compliance may be permissible under the NHPA, a practitioner must be mindful of the Council on Environmental Quality's regulations prohibiting segmentation (which can sometimes be overcome when a portion of a larger project has independent utility), and of the Department of Transportation Act requirement that *no portion* of a transportation project may proceed until any required Section 4(f) evaluation has been completed on the *entire* project.

Notes

1. 36 C.F.R. § 800.4(b)(1).
2. *See Pueblo of Sandia v. United States*, 50 F.3d 856 (10th Cir. 1995), and *Muckleshoot Indian Tribe v. Forest Service*, 177 F.3d 800 (9th Cir. 1999), for earlier cases discussing the "reasonable and good faith effort to identify" standard.
3. 547 F.Supp.2d 1033 (D. Ariz. 2008).
4. 16 U.S.C. § 470h-2(*l*).
5. The ACHP had commented that, in its view, the segmentation was improper. With respect to the ACHP's comment, the court pointed out that the BOR's only obligation under 36 C.F.R. § 800.7(c)(4)(i) was to *consider* the ACHP's comment, which the court found the BOR had done.
6. *See* 36 C.F.R. § 800.6(c)(2)(ii).
7. ___F.Supp.2d___, 2008 WL 4425568 (S.D.N.Y.).
8. A "categorical exclusion" refers to a category of actions that do not individually or cumulatively have a significant effect on the human environment, and that have been found to have no such effect in procedures adopted by a federal agency in its NEPA-implementing regulations. *See* 40 C.F.R. § 1508.4 and 23 C.F.R. § 771.117(a).
9. 36 C.F.R. § 800.5(a)(2)(v). *See also* 36 C.F.R. § 800.16(i).
10. *But see* 40 C.F.R. §§ 1502.16(g), 1508.8, and 1508.27(b)(8) (potential impacts to historic properties are effects that must be evaluated in environmental documents prepared pursuant to NEPA).
11. 49 U.S.C. § 303(c).
12. 514 F.3d 1308 (D.C. Cir. 2008).
13. E.g., *Elk Grove Unified School District v. Newdow*, 542 U.S. 1 (2004).

14. 16 U.S.C. § 470-1(5).
15. *Supra* note 12 at 1312.
16. "Segmentation" or "piecemealing" is the forbidden practice of dividing a major federal action into smaller component parts, each with less-significant environmental effects, in order to enable an agency to reach a finding of no significant impact. CEQ regulations expressly prohibit a federal agency from avoiding preparation of an EIS by "breaking [an action] down into small component parts." 40 C.F.R. § 1508.27(b)(7).
17. 545 F.3d 1147 (9th Cir. 2008).
18. *See* 36 C.F.R. § 800.4(b)(2).
19. *See* 40 C.F.R. §§ 1502.16(g), 1508.8, and 1508.27(b)(8).
20. *Supra* note 17 at footnote 5 ("In determining whether the potential construction effects would likely be significant, Agencies are permitted to take into account mitigation measures which reduce the impact of construction. *See Wetlands Action Network v. U.S. Army Corps of Engineers*, 222 F.3d 1105, 1121 (9th Cir. 2000).").
21. 166 F.3d 368 (D.C. Cir. 1999).
22. *Supra* note 17 at 1159.
23. *See* 49 U.S.C. § 303(d)(2).

State and Local

• • •

Section Editor: Kelly Yasaitis Fanizzo

Introduction

This year saw a great deal of activity in the state and local courts, as well as a few noteworthy cases considering federal issues. Interestingly, the due process clause was invoked in a number of instances and the courts reviewed whether the required constitutional tests were met. A violation of the 4th Amendment search and seizure clause was alleged in a case concerning disputed renovations to a historic home. Once more we see the intersection of the Americans with Disabilities Act and historic preservation through a case that provides additional discussion on the determination of what may be "readily achievable." The courts also addressed a challenge arising under the Telecommunications Act and a proposed amendment to a management plan in a National Scenic Area.

Looking broadly at the variety of cases dealing with state and local issues, the courts spent significant time detailing the limited scope of their review in regard to commission, council, or other quasi-judicial decisions. While the cases remain heavily fact specific, it is no surprise that common themes throughout this section include a review of the record for substantial evidence and a determination as to whether the commission or entity exceeded its authority or abused its discretion. We see detailed discussion of state environmental review requirements and analyses of statutory language, plain meaning, and legislative intent. A number of cases include challenges to historic landmark designations and the subsequent restrictions on property use and alterations. Finally, a few cases provide interesting fact patterns involving contract and tax issues relating to historic preservation.

Compliance with Federal Law

Historic Preservation

In the context of considering potential liability insurance coverage and reviewing policy terms, the court in *American Home Assurance Co. v. Oceaneering Int'l, Inc.*[1] recognized the regulatory interest of a federal agency in protecting historic property. A contractor to the corporation seeking a pipeline, Okeanos Gas Gathering Company, LLC, discovered a historic shipwreck in the proposed right of way during the pipeline application process. The discovery was not immediately made known to the Minerals Management Service (MMS). Once MMS learned of the discovery, it began negotiating with Okeanos to protect the site. During this time, the defendant contracted with Okeanos to inspect the pipeline after Hurricane Ivan. The defendant noted a sonar contact and decided to inspect further with a remotely operated vehicle (ROV), not realizing the contact was the shipwreck. Subsequently, the ROV damaged certain artifacts associated with the shipwreck. As a result of these events, Okeanos entered into an agreement with MMS to relieve it of all civil, administrative, and criminal liability in return for a payment of $4.87 million to Texas A&M University for research and preservation of the site. Okeanos sought to recover the costs from the defendant, resulting in the defendant committing to provide $3 million worth of fully crewed ROV time.

The defendant's general liability insurer agreed to indemnify it for $1 million, consistent with the defendant's policy limits. The defendant's excess liability insurer, the plaintiff, denied coverage and filed suit to seek a declaration that its policy did not provide coverage. The court reviewed the terms of the insurance policies and found the plaintiff's policy did provide coverage for the defendant's claim. Noting that the plaintiff's scope of coverage must follow the general liability insurer's scope of coverage, the court found the general liability insurer properly covered the defendant's claim under the "Specialist Operations" provision. Alternatively, the court found the coverage proper under the general liability insurer's provision providing for "loss of, or damage to, or interference with rights in relation to any fixed or movable property."[2] Focusing on the language, "interference with rights in relation to," the court discusses the regulatory interest MMS has in preserving the shipwreck to conclude the defendant, who caused damage to the shipwreck, was properly covered. The court expanded upon MMS' "federally recognized rights that allow it to regulate the conduct of third parties to preserve and protect potentially [historically] significant resources"[3] pursuant to the National Historic Preservation Act (NHPA) and the relationship creating legal interests between MMS and Okeanos as a permit holder. The plaintiff did not establish any exclusion to coverage.

Turning to the scope of coverage, the court found that "the costs associated with protecting the [archaeological] site from additional harm are analogous to costs associated with cleaning up environmental damage caused by the insured. In both cases, the damages reflect the cost of complying with governmental directives in unique contexts . . . in which the government has taken an active role."[4] While the court agreed these costs represent more than "economic losses," and would fall outside the scope of the defendant's coverage, it pointed out the uncertainty in determining how much of the Okeanos-MMS settlement amount could be attributed to the defendant's actions, noting that the settlement provided for more than just protection of the shipwreck.[5] Therefore the court found the extent of the defendant's policy coverage to be a question of fact not resolved by summary judgment.

Due Process

Two courts this year addressed the high threshold needed to succeed on a due process claim. In *Shanks v. Dressel*,[6] private developers were granted a permit to build a duplex addition to a historic house in a historic district listed on the National Register of Historic Places. Logan Neighborhood, a group of homeowners and community organizations, argued the construction caused adverse impacts to the character of the historic district. They alleged a violation of several municipal ordinances, specifically those requiring a certificate of appropriateness for work that affects the exterior of a property, within a historic district, and an administrative special permit for proposed construction in historic districts where development standards have been developed by the landmarks commission. The developers did not seek, nor did the city require them to seek, a certificate of appropriateness or an administrative special permit. Logan Neighborhood brought a due process claim against the city for failure to enforce applicable municipal ordinances, which it alleged resulted in a deprivation of Logan Neighborhood's protected property interests.

The court agreed with Logan Neighborhood that its due process claim was not preempted by the takings clause because it sought to invalidate land use action rather than seek compensation for interference with property rights. However, the court found that Logan Neighborhood did not state a viable procedural or substantive due process claim. As the developers were not "acting under color of law," the court determined the city had no independent duty to protect the neighbors from the adverse impacts of the developers' action.[7] The city's "mere" approval of the building permit did not make it responsible for the developers' actions.[8] Further, the court found "[t]he conduct Logan Neighborhood alleges—a routine, even if perhaps unwise or legally erroneous, executive decision to grant a third-party building permit—falls short of being constitutionally arbitrary."[9] Pointing to Logan Neighborhood's claim as unusual in that it is most often the applicant who argues its due process rights were violated in the denial of a permit, and assuming that "a property owner *ever* could have a constitutionally protected property interest in the proper application of zoning regulations to neighboring properties," the court concluded that Logan Neighborhood's procedural due process claim must fail.[10] There were no mandatory review criteria, or language in the historic preservation ordinances, to significantly restrict the city's discretion in deciding to approve a permit; thus, Logan Neighborhood has no property interest in the denial of the developers' permit. The court took no position with regard to the city's action pursuant to state law.

In response to Logan Neighborhood's claim that the developers violated the NHPA, the court noted that Section 106 of the NHPA creates no private right of action against either federal or private actors, nor does it regulate the use of a federally listed historic property by a private owner. The court also found "[n]othing in this case suggests that a federal forum must be open to hear every claim touching upon the integrity of a federally listed historical landmark."[11]

Again, in *Kuster v. Foley*[12] the question of a property interest sufficient to sustain a due process claim was considered. The court addressed a series of claims arising from the plaintiff's attempt to build a structure on his undeveloped parcel of property. The plaintiff brought a 14th Amendment due process claim based on a property interest. Among other claims, he asserted that his rights were violated by the Department of Planning Director's failure to make a timely decision on his application. The court noted that the plaintiff's application went to review and comment by the State Historic Preservation Division (SHPD). While acknowledging the lengthy time needed for review due to understaffing at the SHPD, the Planning Department argued the plaintiff's application was not complete because it had not received the SHPD's full comment; thus the alleged evaluation time period for the application had not begun. The court found the plaintiff had not raised an issue of fact as to whether his application was complete. Based upon that and other reasons, the court ultimately determined that the plaintiff had not alleged a viable procedural due process claim against the Department Director. Similarly, the court concluded the plaintiff failed to raise a genuine issue of fact regarding arbitrary delay, or an entitlement to have a decision on his application. Therefore no viable substantive due process claim against the Department Director existed.

Americans with Disabilities Act

The court in *Molski v. Foley Estates Vineyard & Winery LLC*[13] heard an appeal from a trial court decision in which the defendant, a historic winery, was ordered to remove all physical access barriers from inside its buildings, in accordance with the American with Disabilities Act, but was not required to build an outside access ramp. The plaintiff, a paraplegic, and an advocacy group asserted that physical barriers prevented the disabled individual from entering the building. The barriers included a sloped ramp, a raised threshold, a round door knob, limited-width doors, and a wine tasting counter that was of more than table height. Before the litigation began, the winery renovated a gazebo on the property to provide wine-tasting services to wheelchair patrons.

The trial court found the removal of exterior barriers, that is, constructing an access ramp to the rear of the building, would have an adverse impact on the winery's architectural significance and therefore, it was not "readily achievable." It found that 28 CFR § 36.405, and the Americans with Disabilities Act Guidelines for Buildings and Facilities, 28 CFR § 36 app. A § 4.1.7, did not apply to barrier removal in existing facilities, and placed the burden of production on the plaintiffs to show the construction of the exterior ramp would not adversely impact the historic significance of the building.

On appeal, the court considered the regulations pertaining to alterations of historic buildings and the provision for alternate procedures, where the alteration would threaten or destroy the historic significance of the building. The court found §4.1.7 can be applied to that which is readily achievable in existing historic facilities. It concluded that 28 CFR §36.405 and §4.1.7 do apply to readily achievable barrier removal in existing facilities. The court further found that the defendant should bear the burden of proof of historic significance of the building and whether it might be impacted by the barrier removal, holding, "Congress relies on private actors, i.e., disabled individuals, to enforce the ADA by filing lawsuits. Thus plaintiffs should not be deterred from filing meritorious claims by an inappropriate allocation of the burden of production."[14]

The court recognized there is diversity among those with disabilities and acknowledged that many disabled individuals would be able to safely traverse a ramp into the building, subsequently finding the lower court properly exercised its discretion in ordering the interior barrier removals. It did not find the gazebo a legally adequate accommodation alternative, when interior barrier removal was readily achievable. The court affirmed the order to remove the interior barriers and remanded to the trial court to apply § 36.405 and § 4.1.7, with the burden of proof on the defendant with regard to whether the exterior ramp would threaten or destroy the historic significance of the building.

Fourth Amendment Search and Seizure

In *Elkins v. D.C.*,[15] the plaintiffs applied and received several permits to complete renovations on their home, which is located within a historic district. Neighbors complained about the construction and the Building and Land Regulation Administration (BLRA) requested a government inspection. When plaintiffs refused, the D.C. Department of Consumer and Regulatory Affairs (DCRA) obtained an administrative search warrant. The warrant allowed the search of the property but did not specify any items to be seized. During the search performed by the D.C. police and representatives of the DCRA and D.C. Historic Preservation Office (HPO), a number of documents relating to, for example, permit and construction records, checking statements, financial records, and construction loan documents were seized.

The District issued a notice for the proposed revocation of the building permits, which the plaintiffs challenged before the District's Office of Administrative Hearings (OAH). The Hearing Officer found the search warrant to be valid and supported by probable cause, as the District had reason to believe the plaintiffs were altering a protected property without Governmental approval and the Government had a legitimate interest in preserving the integrity of the historic building and in enforcing its construction codes. The Hearing Officer found that the warrant did not authorize the seizure of documents, and that the consent and plain view and consent exceptions of the 4th Amendment did not apply; thus he suppressed the admission of all seized items. While noting the potential impacts of the construction to the historic neighborhood, OAH found those concerns to also be present during the original permit application and approval process and sympathized with the plaintiffs about the "nightmare situation in which the [District] officials dueled amongst themselves over the propriety of the project, and they sent out mixed messages."[16] OAH denied the proposed revocation of the permits.

During the OAH proceedings, the plaintiffs filed a complaint in federal court alleging a violation of their 4th, 5th, and 14th Amendment rights under 42 USC § 1983. The federal court stayed the case until the issuance of OAH's final order and then found the doctrine of collateral estoppel applied to the plaintiffs' 4th Amendment claim, which had been litigated and the legality of the search and the seizure of documents resolved. Specifically the court found the plaintiffs estopped from asserting liability of the District officials based on the search, and the defendants estopped from contesting liability based on the seizure. The court allowed the plaintiffs to proceed in their claim for compensatory damages on the 4th Amendment claim of document seizure, noting that punitive damages are not available against the District, but could be available against the individual defendants.

The court found no procedural due process violation as the plaintiffs had an opportunity, albeit "tardy," to appeal the stop work orders and Notice of Violation with the proposed permits revocation.[17] Proceedings are ongoing.[18]

National Scenic Area

In *Friends of the Columbia Gorge, Inc. v. Columbia River Gorge Comm'n*,[19] petitioners challenged a proposed amendment to the Columbia River Gorge National Scenic Area management plan that would allow certain commercial uses of historic properties. Per the terms of the Columbia River Gorge National Scenic Act, the Columbia River Gorge Commission may amend the management plan for the Scenic Area, outside the standard revision process, where conditions in the Scenic Area have significantly changed. At the heart of the dispute was the meaning of "conditions have significantly changed." Any amendment must be consistent with the Scenic Area Act and include a finding that no practicable alternative would be more consistent with the Act.[20] In an effort to provide incentive for pursuing adaptive reuses leading to rehabilitation and maintenance, the Commission desired an amendment to the management plan to allow the Viewpoint Inn, a historic property in the Scenic Area, to reopen the inn and generate enough revenue to support the property restoration, as well as to allow commercial uses of historic properties throughout the Scenic Area.

The Commission gathered information from a survey, consultation with the U.S. Forest Service, the states of Oregon and Washington, Scenic Area counties, Scenic Area tribal governments, the National Trust for Historic Preservation, and others, as well as solicited public testimony, to support its recommendation for the proposed amendment. The Commission felt the Scenic Area had changed significantly, as historic properties were deteriorating or otherwise adversely affected by incompatible alterations. Current owners were unwilling to pay the high costs of rehabilitation. The Commission further found no practicable alternative to the proposed amendment and that it was consistent with the standards of the Act.

The petitioners argued that the Commission did not follow the process to approve the amendment. They argued error in finding changed conditions, because the information relied upon was not "new information or inventory data regarding the land uses or resources that could result in a change of plan designation, classification, or other plan provision,"[21] and the information failed to show the change was "significant" as it did not show a problem with the plan's existing protection for historic properties. The court afforded the Commission deference in interpreting its own administrative rule and did not find the Commission's interpretation of "new," as meaning new to the Commission, plainly erroneous or inconsistent with the regulation.[22] The record was found to support the Commission's determination.

On the necessary finding of most consistent with purposes of the Act, the petitioners argued there were numerous alternatives that would be more consistent. The court noted the Commission was not required to consider each and every imaginable alternative. Finally, the petitioners argued that the Commission's action violated the requirements of the Act because

> it allows commercial use in areas outside urban areas and commercial zones in the general management areas; because it creates the possibility of allowing adverse effects to protected resources in the Scenic Area; because the portions of the amendment pertaining to commercial events on historic properties include no size and scope limitations; because the [C]ommission failed adequately to consider cumulative impacts of the amendment; and because the plan amendments

fails to accomplish its stated purpose of protecting cultural resources such as historic properties.[23]

Treating these arguments as a facial challenge to the validity of the plan amendment, the court reviewed what the Act requires. The court found the Act does not prohibit commercial use outside of urban areas. Protection of cultural resources over that of natural, scenic, and recreational resources was found to be purely speculative. Further, in requiring all commercial events to be "incidental and subordinate" to the property's primary historic use, the amendment provides that those events are still subject to the Act. Cumulative impacts of commercial events are still factored in by the Commission as commercial use would need to meet guidelines in the amendment prior to being approved. Petitioners desired a ruling that revenue generated from use be applied to restoring and maintaining the property, but the amendment did not authorize what the Act prohibits. The Commission action was affirmed.

Telecommunications Act of 1996

In *Southeast Towers, LLC v. Pickens County, GA,*[24] the plaintiffs, wireless telecommunications providers, sought an injunction to compel the county to issue a building permit for the construction of a wireless telecommunications tower. At issue is the location of the tower and its potential effects on the Tate Historic District. The plaintiffs sought and received the necessary approvals from the Federal Communications Commission (FCC) and the Federal Aviation Administration on the determination that the proposed tower would have no visual effect on the nearby historic district. The Georgia State Historic Preservation Office (SHPO) allowed the 30-day review period to lapse without comment. The plaintiffs' consultant conducted a balloon test and showed that no adverse visual effects would occur to the historic district due to "intervening treelines, vegetation, and variable topography."[25]

Photographs from the balloon test were shown to the Planning Commission, at a public hearing, as evidence of the potential direct adverse visual effects the tower would have on certain historic properties, and testimony was given regarding alternative designs for the tower that would create lesser impacts. The Commission subsequently denied the permit.

The court reviewed the intent of the Telecommunications Act (TCA) as finding a balance between the desire to encourage the national expansion of wireless telephone service and to continue significant local control over the siting of such towers. It found the Commissioner had sufficient authority, consistent with the TCA, to deny the permit because of the potential adverse visual impacts to the historic district. Further, the court found that the information given to the SHPO did not accurately characterize the potential effects of the tower to historic properties. The court noted that "nothing in the TCA nor any other federal law to which the [c]ourt has been directed forbids a local government from independently considering compliance with federal law in deciding whether to grant or deny a building permit, particularly where, as here, the local government has before it evidence not considered by the federal agency in rendering its decision."[26] Finally, the court stated that the Commissioner's determination was based on specific and particular evidence meeting the substantial evidence requirement.

Compliance with State Law

Environmental Protection

California courts spent significant time addressing the review requirements of the California Environmental Quality Act (CEQA), and a few cases this year highlight limitations on the use of categorical exemptions. In *Comm. to Save the Hollywoodland Specific Plan and Hollywood Heritage v. City of Los Angeles,*[27] petitioners challenged the city of Los Angeles' decision to approve a plan exception to the Hollywoodland Specific Plan (HSP) and a categorical exemption, per the CEQA, for a wooden fence constructed by a private property owner on top of a historic granite wall. The granite walls were constructed in the 1920s and designated as a Historic-Cultural Monument by the city. The HSP, in part, is intended to protect these walls. The previous homeowners constructed the fence on top of the granite wall without a permit, to which the city responded with a violation and removal order. The homeowners applied for an exception, citing safety reasons. The city subsequently found the exception application to be exempt under CEQA. The Committee to Save Hollywoodland Specific Plan objected to the findings and the use of an exemption under CEQA. The Committee argued that even if an exemption category applied to this situation, it should not be allowed, because of the potential significant effects to a historic property.

During the appeal to the city council, the new property owner argued the existing fence was close to, but did not actually contact the wall; the fence was attached to the curb that sat on top of the wall with drilled poles which did not touch the wall. The city council again found the action to be exempt under CEQA and denied the appeal. The trial court subsequently found substantial evidence supported the city's finding that the "practical difficulties of the property in question warrant the exception" and the exception application did meet a categorical exemption class under CEQA "because there was no substantial change to the historical resources . . . [and] the wall was below grade, not on the public right of way, and a fence on top of the curb supported by the wall would not affect the resource."[28]

The appellate court found substantial evidence supported the city's finding that the exception was needed to allow relief from the 3-foot setback and 42-inch fence height limitation. Additionally, the court did not find the new property owner's hardship to be self-imposed, because he bought the property with knowledge of the fence issues. The hardship in this case is inherent in the property's topography, which does not change with ownership.

The court affirmed the trial court's judgment in reference to the exception to the HSP but reversed and required the city to vacate its approval of the CEQA exemption. Specifically, the court noted "the record is unclear whether fenceposts will be drilled into the curb or the wall; whether the curb is part of the historic resource; and whether the proposed fence will harm the physical stability of the wall,"[29] and the city failed to consider the potential visual impacts due to the height of the fence. The court also found the city did not consider the specific circumstances that may differ from those in the category generally covered by the exemption and that may pose different environmental risks. The court concludes, "the building of a fence atop the wall will significantly impact the environment by altering the historic resource, both as to its physical integrity and its aesthetic appeal from the neighboring streets."[30]

The California courts again considered the proper use of an exemption to CEQA where, in *Valley Advocates v. City of Fresno*,[31] the plaintiffs argued the city violated CEQA in its review of an application to demolish a ninety-year old building. A law firm sought to demolish the apartment building to expand available parking. As the application went through the review process it was referred to the city's historic preservation project manager for consideration of listing in the local register of historic resources and to determine if the listing should be sent to the Historic Preservation Commission. The Commission denied the permit and voted to nominate the building. The city council then voted to deny the listing nomination and found the proposed project to be exempt under CEQA.

Treating an objection to the use of the categorical exemption as an appeal under CEQA, the city council held a meeting to determine whether the project would significantly impact a historic property when the building was not historic under CEQA because the city council has chosen not to treat it so, and heard that "CEQA does not provide direction" when the city council's determination is "second guessed."[32] The court noted in a critical footnote that "[t]his advice misstates law. . . . The prior choice of the City Council regarding listing does not prevent that City Council (or a subsequent council) from choosing differently when addressing whether the property is an historic resource for purposes of CEQA."[33] The city council denied the appeal and confirmed the use of the exemption. The demolition was later approved.

On appeal, Valley Advocates asserted the city violated CEQA by improperly determining whether the building was historic. A building is historic for purposes of CEQA when it is either a mandatory historic resource, that is listed on the California Register of Historical Resources; a presumptive historical resource, that is eligible for listing; or a discretionary historical resource. There was insufficient evidence to support a determination on the first two categories, but the court stopped short of making a discretionary historical resource determination, concluding, "at a minimum, a lead agency has the discretion to address separately whether an object or building is an historical resource for purposes of CEQA's discretionary historical resources category."[34]

The court distinguished the *Valley Advocates* from the circumstances in *Architectural Heritage Assn. v. County of Monterey*,[35] and concluded that the fair argument standard is not applicable to the city's determination regarding the building's historic significance during the preliminary review stage under CEQA. In response to Valley Advocates' argument for the application of the fair argument standard, the court found it "cannot simply leap from the general policy of protecting the environment to the conclusion that a fair argument of historicity is all that is needed to trigger the preparation of an EIR."[36] The court ceded that once a resource is determined to be historic, the fair argument standard would apply to the determination whether the proposed action "may cause a substantial adverse change in the significance of an historical resource,"[37] and thus pose a significant impact to the environment. But the court disagreed with the Valley Advocates' argument that the fair argument standard applies to the determination whether the building is historic to analyze a potential exception to a categorical exemption. The court remanded to the trial court to direct the city to set aside its approval of the application and its finding that the project is categorically exempt, and to conduct a review that considers the discretionary historical resources category.

In *Heritage Fresno v. Redevelopment Agency of the City of Fresno*,[38] the court found a change in the established mitigation measures warranted additional review. The city of Fresno completed an environmental review and adopted a Mitigated Negative Declaration (MND) in 2002, under CEQA, for the site clearance, acquisition, and transfer of land for a proposed downtown redevelopment project. The project consisted of two phases: Phase I as the construction of a new courthouse, and Phase II as the development of office and retail space. A mitigation measure included the relocation of five historic houses from their existing location and allowed for close proximity of the buildings with the remaining historic features of the Old Armenian Town. The city subsequently certified an environmental impact report (EIR) in 2004, for Phase II, which treated the mitigation measure as a mere suggestion to the developer. Heritage Fresno filed a mandamus petition in trial court and succeeded in vacating approval of the 2004 EIR.

On appeal, the court found the city should have completed another environmental review. The court noted that "CEQA requires a lead agency to take steps to ensure that any mitigation measures 'will actually be implemented as a condition of development, and not merely adopted and then neglected or disregarded.'"[39] Further, the court found that "the [mitigation] measure cannot be deleted without a showing that it is infeasible."[40] Treating the deletion of a mitigation measure as a new issue, rather than addressing the change, is not sufficient.

Minnesota In reviewing a quasi-judicial decision, the court's scope of review is rather limited, as it looks to the record for substantial evidence to determine whether a city's decision is unreasonable, arbitrary, or capricious. Through consolidated appeals, the court in *Friends of the Riverfront v. DeLaSalle High School*[41] reviewed whether a city's grant of a Certificate of Appropriateness and a subsequent amended Certificate was arbitrary or capricious. A high school on Nicollet Island, a historic place within the Minnesota National River and Recreation Area, a unit of the National Park System, and the St. Anthony Falls National Historic District, proposed to construct a new athletic facility. The facility would be located on two adjacent parcels of land, which would adversely affect the historic alignment of Grove Street. The city completed an Environmental Assessment Worksheet and determined that an Environmental

Impact Statement would not be required. The high school applied to the Heritage Preservation Commission for a Certificate of Appropriateness because of the project's location in the historic district. The Commission denied the Certificate, finding the project would have "a lasting adverse effect on the [historic] district."[42] Hearing the case pursuant to the high school's appeal and noting the proper intervention of the citizens groups in the proceedings, the city council accepted certain proposals to mitigate the adverse impacts to the historic district and approved the Certificate. While the appeal was pending the high school revised its project and applied for an amended Certificate. Once again, the Commission denied the Certificate and the city council approved it on appeal. The citizens group appealed.

The court reviewed the city's actions in accordance with the Minnesota Environmental Rights Act (MERA). The citizens group argued that the city failed to show no feasible and prudent alternatives to the destruction of historic properties existed as was required by city ordinance. The court found that the no-feasible-and-prudent-alternative standard does not apply in this case and that the city did not arbitrarily or capriciously fail to consider the multiple land use plans and guidelines applicable to the proposed facility site on Nicollet Island in issuing the Certificates. In considering the city's determination regarding feasible and prudent alternatives, the court concluded that the city was not required to analyze alternatives that did not meet a necessary requirement of the proposed facility, that was, to be adjacent to the school.

In a subsequent proceeding, the court in *State of Minnesota by Friends of the Riverfront v. City of Minneapolis*[43] heard the appeal of another challenge to the construction of the athletic facility. This time the court looked at whether collateral estoppel precluded the plaintiff's MERA claim. It found the plaintiffs received a full and fair opportunity to be heard in the city council hearing on the Certificate. In making this determination, the court concluded the appropriate procedural safeguards were present during the city council's hearing, noting that "the purpose of the hearing was to determine whether the development was historically appropriate. In light of the type of evidence that would best address the 'magnitude and complexity of the matter,' a full evidentiary hearing was not required"; neither was the use of an independent hearing examiner.[44] The court did not find the city council to be impermissibly biased or its decision self-serving. The court next looked to whether the plaintiffs were in privity with a party to the city council's determination and found that the Bergs and the Grove Street Flats Association were in privity with the Friends of the Riverfront in the proceedings. As the criteria for collateral estoppel were met, the Plaintiff's were estopped from an independent MERA claim.

New York A number of New York courts this year considered at length the requirements for a review under the New York State Environmental Quality Review Act (SEQRA). The court in *In re Application of John Delvecchio*[45] reviewed the criteria for preparation of an environmental impact statement (EIS) under the SEQRA to find the "may have a significant environmental impact" threshold to be quite low. For instance, due to the project's location contiguous to a historic district and its replacement of an existing historic structure, it was not inappropriate for the City Planning Commission to issue a positive declaration. The court found insufficient evidence to suggest the Commission made the required explanation for its determination; thus the court remanded the matter to the Commission to provide a more complete reasoned elaboration for the basis of its determination.

In another case, the court fleshed out what is meant by a required "hard look." Residents and landowners in *In re Sue Brander*[46] challenged the issuance of two special use permits for the construction of a 68-turbine wind farm as violating SEQRA and the Open Meetings Law. The court disagreed with the petitioners' argument that public participation was required in the scoping process for the development of an EIS. The petitioners argued further that the Town Board did not take the required "hard look" at the potential environmental impacts, because it did not properly evaluate alternatives, or adequately review and mitigate potential adverse impacts, and it improperly delegated its responsibilities to other agencies. Taking each point in turn, the court noted that "to be meaningful, any choice among alternatives must be based on an awareness of all reasonable options, with the degree of detail varying with the circumstances and nature of each proposal."[47] The court concluded that the Town Board did not properly support its determinations regarding alternatives, further requiring boards and commissions to issue complete, judicial type decisions.

Specifically the court found that to deny members of the public input regarding the analysis, mitigation, and tentative mitigation plans included in the SEQRA document was error. The court noted the Town Board issued its findings statement without completing consultation, and that it concluded the SEQRA process without resolving the historic mitigation as required. The Town Board improperly deferred the mitigation issues, resulting in a defective process and a finding that the "granting [of] the special use permits was arbitrary, capricious and unsupported by substantial evidence."[48] In addition, by improperly delegating its SEQRA responsibilities for historic site mitigation to the Public Service Commission and the OPRHP, the Town Board failed to take the required "hard look" at potential environmental impacts. The court vacated the acceptance of the EIS and findings statement and the issuance of the special use permits, and remanded the SEQRA review to the Town Board. The remaining challenges were without merit.

On appeal, the court in *In re Michael Kuzma*[49] found the state conceded its failure to conduct a valid review for the proposed sale of its interests in a former state mental hygiene facility, the J. N. Adam Developmental Center, under SEQRA, the Public Buildings Law, and the Parks, Recreation, and Historic Preservation Law (PRHPL). The court did not find the claims against the state to be premature because in admitting it had yet to comply with those statutes, the state failed to show its determinations were not final. The state's Negative Determination that the Center is not historically significant, and that its sale would have no impact on cultural resources either listed on or eligible for the State Register of Historic Places, was found to be invalid, because it was not based on accurate information. The court further found the state conceded "any minimal consultations" with the OPRHP were insufficient to meet the requirements of the Public Buildings Law or the PRHPL.[50] The court annulled the state's Negative Determination and its determination to enter into a contract for the sale of the Center. Once more addressing a challenge to the validity of a SEQRA review, the court in *Sutherland v. New York City Housing Development Co.*[51] heard petitioners' claim against the New York City Housing Development Corporation's Negative Determination and compliance with the PRHPL for a loan to fund the reservation of 59 out of 269 residential apartments for low income families in a new apartment building. The court noted that without the contested loan, construction would still occur. The petitioners did not seek injunctive relief. The OPRHP had determined that the Cathedral Church of St. John the Divine in the City was eligible for listing on the National Register of Historic Places, and that the construction of the apartment building would have an adverse effect on the Cathedral and the Cathedral Campus, the Close. Petitioners argued the construction would impinge upon their views of the historic Cathedral and Close and impact the character of historic resources in their neighborhood. The court found the petitioners did not have standing to challenge funding for the project.

West Virginia The appellants in *Mountain Communities for Responsible Energy v. Public Service Comm'n of West Virginia & Beech Ridge Energy, LLC; Eisenbeiss v. Public Service Commission of West Virginia and Beech Ridge Energy, LLC*[52] challenged the conditional approval by the Public Service Commission for the construction of a wind-powered wholesale electric generating facility. The Commission set certain conditions in granting the siting certificate, including a requirement to receive any necessary environmental permits or approvals such as a letter from the West Virginia State Historic Preservation Office (SHPO) regarding any cultural resource issues. Pursuant to W.Va. Code § 24-2-11c(c), the Commission must balance the interests of the applicant, the general interests of the state and local economy, and the public interest in evaluating whether to issue a siting certificate. The court found the Commission properly followed its rules and guidelines and properly analyzed the potential impact of the project on historic, scenic, religious, and cultural places prior to issuing the certificate, even though concurrence from the SHPO had not been obtained. The court noted the applicant will need to seek final approvals from the SHPO prior to undertaking construction.

Contracts

Massachusetts The court in *Finbury v. Architectural Heritage Foundation, Inc.*[53] heard a dispute in which the plaintiff, a real estate developer who specialized in the rehabilitation of historic buildings, brought several claims against both Architectural Heritage Foundation and its president, including breach of contract, fraud, promissory estoppels for unjust enrichment, and breach of fiduciary duty, arising from a joint venture agreement to develop properties. Treating each claim in turn, the court dismissed with prejudice the plaintiff's claims for breach of contract and breach of fiduciary duty. The court dismissed with prejudice only to the president the claims for promissory estoppel, unjust enrichment, and violation of G. L. c. 93A, in which plaintiff argued in the alternative that she was a consultant and the Foundation and its president improperly terminated the agreement and excluded her from sharing in the profit. The claims for promissory estoppel, unjust enrichment, and violation of G. L. c. 93A were allowed to stand against the Foundation. The court allowed the fraud claim to stand in regard only to the alleged misrepresentation on the cash bonus for her services and an offer of long-term employment.

Rhode Island In *American Capital Corporation v. Blixseth, C.A.*,[54] the defendant buyers entered into a sales contract for three parcels of real estate in Newport. A mansion was located on one of the parcels and a carriage house was located on another parcel. As required by the Rhode Island Real Estate Sales Disclosure Act, the sellers provided the buyers with a disclosure form but it made no mention of the fact that the parcels were located within the Newport Historic District. When the buyers did not attend the closing or provide the funds to complete the sale, the sellers filed suit. The buyers then requested the sales contract be terminated and their deposit returned as a result of the sellers' failure to disclose certain information.

The court looked at whether the failure to disclose the historic district zoning constituted failure to disclose a "materially deficient condition," so as to entitle the buyer to terminate the pending sale. Finding the historic district zoning to be a "land restriction" and thus a "deficient condition," the court determined the deficient condition was material. "The legislature's attention to detail in this item is a signal as to the importance of this information."[55] The buyers were entitled to terminate the sale and demand the return of their deposit.

Local Zoning and Permits

Colorado In *Kruse v. Town of Castle Rock*,[56] the court heard the appeal of a property owner regarding the designation of her house as a local historic landmark. Shortly after purchasing the property, the owner asked whether the town might be interested in including the house on a walking tour of historic homes and for financial assistance in making certain restoration improvements on the building. The town declined. Subsequently, the owner sought and received a partial demolition permit for outbuildings and additions to the original house. The permit expired without the work being done and was renewed. During that time, the owner spent a considerable sum in renovations. The owner then sought a full demolition permit, at which proceeding the Historic Preservation Board intervened to designate the house as a historic landmark. The Town Council approved the designation, while acknowledging the resulting restrictions it would place on the property.

The court upheld the decision of the Town Council. It found the Council did not exceed its authority in allowing its staff to research the historic significance of the property and make a recommendation for its designation. Concluding the Historic Preservation Commission did not have exclusive jurisdiction over the historic designation process, the court looked to the authority provided in the Town's municipal code and charter as enabling the Town employees to be involved.

On the property owner's argument that terms applied to involuntary historic designations in the municipal ordinance were unconstitutionally vague, the court found the facial constitutional challenge to the ordinance must fail. Reading the criteria for "involuntary historic designation" in context with the "general criteria for historic designation," the court asserted the ordinance "provides property owners with fair notice that their property may be designated a historic landmark if one or more of those criteria are satisfied."[57] While the court noted the terms used in historic preservation ordinances generally are broad, the terms used here are "sufficiently definite" and "persons of common intelligence need not guess at their meaning."[58] The court further found the as-applied constitutional challenge to the municipal ordinance must also fail, noting the "unusual and uncommon" historic significance of the house.[59]

The court considered the record of the public hearings and determined the Town Council's findings were supported by competent evidence, thus, not an abuse of its discretion. Although recognizing the evidence presented by the property owner as to her inability to achieve returns on her property due to the designation, the court did not find the Town Council erred in finding insufficient evidence to support a claim for undue hardship.

Connecticut When reviewing the decisions of a zoning commission, the scope of the court's review was repeatedly limited in several cases in Connecticut this year. The focus was on whether the commission exceeded its authority in making its decision, whether its decision was supported by substantial evidence in the record, and significantly, where the consideration of evidence in the record must occur. The court in *Brenton v. Fairfield Town Plan and Zoning Comm'n; Hess v. Fairfield PZC, Munson Builders, Inc. v. Fairfield PZC*[60] heard a consolidated appeal regarding an approved subdivision, with potential impacts to a historic house. The property owners sought to subdivide 0.8 acres into three building lots. Two of the lots would be sold for new construction to developers, while the remaining lot would continue to contain what was thought to be the oldest house in Fairfield. Neighbors opposed the subdivision application, concerned for the continued integrity of the historic house and site. The commission voted to approve the subdivision, subject to certain conditions including a deed restriction to prohibit the demolition of the house and required review and approval by the Fairfield Historic District Commission for the design and siting for new construction as well as any alterations to the existing house. The neighbors challenged the approval of the subdivision and the developers appealed the imposition of certain conditions on the approval.

Initially, the court noted that no verified pleading to raise environmental issues was filed before the commission and yet the commission considered the historic significance of the property at length. The court indicated that the plaintiffs' argument would have the commission "speculate" as to the environmental issues to address, rather than review specific factual allegations and would circumvent the "deterrence provision contained in Conn. Gen. Stat. § 22a-19a . . . [that] allows a court to tax costs against a party who fails to make a prima facie showing of a likelihood that unreasonable destruction of the public trust in an historic structure will result from the agency's action."[61] Even so, the court concluded that should §22a-19a have been invoked, there was not sufficient evidence in the record to show that the historic house would in fact be subject to "unreasonable destruction" as a result of the approved subdivision. The court found the zoning commission's decision, approving the subdivision, to be supported by substantial evidence.

Turning to whether the commission had the authority to impose the conditions upon the subdivision approval, the court found the commission misread the holding of *Smith v. Zoning Bd. of Appeals of the Town of Greenwich*[62] to justify its action from the "health or public safety" language of the subdivision regulations.[63] The court distinguished this case from *Smith* in stating the subject property is not located in a historic district and the subdivision regulations do not mention "historical factors" or otherwise provide sufficient guidance to the applicant or the commission for such consideration in the review of subdivision applications. The court found the commission exceeded its authority by imposing the prohibition against demolition of the structure and requiring that deed restrictions be included on the subdivision as a condition of filing. Similarly, the condition requiring review and approval for new construction and alterations to the existing house by the Historic District Commission "represents a massive display of overreaching" by the commission as such authority is not provided in the subdivision regulations or the General Statutes.[64] The court also invalidated the condition requiring a certain setback for new construction. The court dismissed the neighbors' appeal and sustained the appeal of the property owners, ordering the commission to approve the subdivision application without the challenged conditions.

The court in *Felician Sisters of St. Francis of Connecticut, Inc. v. Historic District Comm'n of the Town of Enfield*[65] reviewed whether the town historic district commission had the authority to deny the plaintiff's application to replace a gravel parking area with a blacktop driveway and parking lot at an elementary school. In response to the parking problems that have persisted for some time and in accordance with General Statutes § 7-147d(d), the plaintiffs applied for a certificate of appropriateness to redesign and rebuild the driveway and parking area. The historic district commission denied the application on the basis that the added pavement would adversely impact the historic character of the property and surrounding area.

On appeal, the court looked to the language, construction, and broader context of the statute to find the term "occupational parking" applied to the plaintiff's situation and found that parking for a private elementary school is included within the scope of regulation for the historic district and the jurisdiction of the commission. The court noted that while the commission's deliberations followed the appropriate factors, it did not properly assess the size of the parking area to be developed, the movement of the parked cars away from the viewshed of the historic streetscape, and the removal of nonhistoric vegetation and planting of new vegetation. Further, the court found the commission improperly relied on the testimony of nearby landowners which had no factual support and were not relevant to the commission's decision as they did not address the potential impacts to historic properties that would result from the proposal. The court concluded the commission's decision was not supported by substantial evidence and was an abuse of its discretion.

The court in *Gibbons v. Historic District Comm'n of the Town of Fairfield*[66] heard the appeal of a property owner to the denial of a certificate of appropriateness for certain alterations to her property. The property at issue included a historic house with a modern addition and an outbuilding that is not original to the house. The property lies within the boundaries of the Southport Historic District. Because of the visible potential changes, the property owner sought a certificate from the historic district commission. In response to the commission's denial of the certificate, the property owner filed a revised application which would remove the modern addition and deck, relocate and connect the outbuilding to the house, and include other alterations. The commission concluded the effect on the historic district would be adverse and again denied the application.

The trial court concluded the commission's decision was arbitrary and its reasoning was outside its authority. On appeal, the court reviewed the statutory provisions establishing the commission's authority and the process for reviewing applications for certificates of appropriateness. The court found the trial court's opinion to improperly limit the scope of the commission's authority to reviewing the potential preservation value and impacts of proposed alterations only to the building being altered or to the architectural features of surrounding buildings. The court determined that the commission's review authority is broader and includes consideration of "the relationship of a building or structure to a place of historic significance."[67]

Having found the commission to have authority to make the decision, the court turned to whether substantial evidence existed in the record to support its justification. The court noted the scope of its review in that "judicial review of administrative decisions is deferential. A statutory right to appeal, however, must be meaningful."[68] The court noted further that because historic preservation commissioners are empowered to determine what value to place on historic significance in considering the appropriateness of a proposed action, their decisions "must be based on actual knowledge and factual evidence, not solely on personal beliefs or aesthetic preferences."[69] As a case of first impression on this issue, the court determined that its review of the appeal from the historic district commission's decision was limited to only considering whether there was substantial evidence in the record to support the commission's stated justification. The court resolved the potential conflict it identified with the holding in *Stankiewicz v. Zoning Bd. of Appeals,*[70] to conclude the court should not go beyond a commission's stated reason, even if that reason is found to be inadequate, to search the record for any substantially supported reason for the decision. "To go beyond those stated reasons invades the fact-finding mission of the agency by allowing the court to cull out reasons that the agency may not have found to be credible or proven."[71]

Noting the commission's deliberation to be focused on the location and relocation of the outbuilding and not on the potential impacts to the main house, the court found no substantial evidence in the record to support the commission's determination that the relocation of the outbuilding would adversely impact the historic district. The court then found the denial of the certificate to not be "reasonably related to a substantial public purpose,"[72] so as to justify the regulation of private property and thus constitute a valid use of the state's police power. The court concluded by finding the commission's decision to be improperly based upon aesthetic preferences and representing an "unreasonable and arbitrary exercise of its authority."[73] The decision of the trial court was affirmed.

In *Norwalk Preservation Trust, Inc. v. Norwalk Inn and Conference Center, Inc.*,[74] the court granted a temporary injunction against the demolition of a historic building. The defendant owned a hotel on an adjacent property and purchased the subject building to demolish it and expand its hotel operation. Though the property is located within the listed Norwalk Green Historic District, the property owner appeared to not know of any issues relating to the building's historic significance. The defendant sought and received appropriate zoning approvals to expand the hotel, and the plaintiff brought this action in the face of the proposed demolition.

The defendant argued the demolition and hotel expansion were necessary to compete with the market for luxury hotel rooms. The plaintiff gave evidence of alternatives that would meet the need for an increase in a set number of rooms, while preserving either significant elements of, or the entire historic building. The court noted the "paucity of case law exploring what should be the appropriate parameters or methods in weighing feasible and prudent alternatives,"[75] and considered alternatives that would allow for fewer rooms than the suggested number requested by the defendant for profit-efficiency purposes, and on property owned by the defendant rather than the parcel containing the historic building as feasible and prudent. The court acknowledged that some of the alternatives might require additional permits or zoning changes; however, it recognized that it cannot substitute its judgment for that of an administrative reviewer. While sympathetic to the defendant's situation in getting through the regulatory process to a demolition permit before being stopped, the court did not find those circumstances to show a lack of feasible and prudent alternatives to demolition. The court also noted the building's lack of obvious significance, finding that the decision to deny the demolition was not helped by the fact the building "is probably closer to the, say, undistinguished end of the historic spectrum."[76] Nonetheless, the court recognized the value in protecting contributing elements to a historic district to preserving the whole of the district.

The case is a helpful tool for those litigating in Connecticut as the court discussed in footnotes the difficulties that arose in this case, to wit, how a loss of "historic value" in such a building might be treated, how the building's continued deterioration might be monitored, and how the court might weigh feasible and prudent alternatives. The court emphasized that its order was for a temporary injunction and opened the door for additional information to be submitted to clarify whether any feasible and prudent alternative exists.

The court in *Powell v. Zoning Board of Appeals of the Town of New Canaan*[77] dismissed a challenge to the zoning board of appeal's approval of variances to allow a property owner to construct a pool and new principal residence on her property. The owner's residence was a "Modern House," which would be restored to its original 1953 appearance, and subsequently used as a pool house adjacent to the pool, with the primary residence to be constructed on the rear of the property. The variances were required to allow the pool and pool house to be located in the front yard. The court spent some time discussing the intent behind the zoning regulations and the significance of the "Modern House," concluding with a justification of the preservation strategy for this property type and noted, "[w]hile these houses do not represent the mainstream of what many people in New Canaan consider to be a historical resource, their national (and international) importance is expected to increase over time."[78]

The plaintiffs argued that the zoning board lacked the authority to issue the variances, because the property owner had not shown an exceptional difficulty or unusual hardship to warrant their approval. The court described the limits of its review of a decision by the zoning board, referencing *Gibbons v. Historic District Commission*, and noted repeatedly that a hardship warranting a variance must not be self-imposed or self-created. Thus focusing its review jurisdiction, the court found substantial evidence supported the board's determination that an unusual hardship existed on the property due to the presence of wetlands and the historic property. Acknowledging "the purchase with knowledge rule" that would implicate the hardship to be self-imposed, the court found it did not apply here as the property owner was not attempting to put her property to a use not contemplated under the zoning regulations. Rather, the property owner was seeking the variances only for the location of the otherwise permitted placement of a pool, pool house, and primary residence on the property. The hardship existed because of the application of the ordinance to certain conditions on her property that are outside any property owner's control. The court further found no support in the record for the plaintiffs' allegation that the board premised its approval on the assumption that the necessary wetland approvals would be given from the Environmental Commission. The court ruled the board did not act arbitrarily, illegally, or unreasonably in issuing the variances and dismissed the plaintiffs' appeal.

In *Tripp v. New Milford Zoning Comm'n*,[79] the defendant sought to modify a barn and construct an addition to a historic house consisting of four residential condominium units. The plaintiffs, whose property was located within 100 feet from the subject parcel, appealed the zoning commission's approval of the applications. Among other challenges, the plaintiffs argued the commission failed to follow mandatory rehabilitation requirements in applicable zoning regulations and failed to find the proposed use and alterations compatible with the surrounding neighborhood. The court, in looking to the actual language of the regulations, determined that "[t]hese rules [for rehabilitation] providing direction without the possibility of invalidation based on noncompliance appear to be precise examples of discretionary guidelines."[80] The court went on to note that it found evidence of the commission's consideration of the zoning regulations in reviewing the application, but concluded that guidelines are not mandatory. The court found the commission did consider and discuss the conformity of the proposed use and alterations with the surrounding neighborhood and the character of the Town Landmark District. The conclusion was reasonably supported in the record and therefore the court would not insert its judgment in place of the commission's decision. Plaintiff's appeal was dismissed.

Delaware The petitioners in *Brown v. City of Wilmington Zoning Board of Adjustment*[81] challenged the grant of a use variance to construct an office complex on property zoned primarily for residential use. The property at issue contained a historic walled estate, which is subject to a conservation easement, that was placed on the property as a condition of its sale to Preservation Delaware, Inc. (PDI). After unsuccessfully seeking to develop the estate into a bed and breakfast and restaurant, PDI sought to develop the property into office space. Reviewing the developer's application for a use variance for the commercial use, the zoning board of adjustment heard evidence from PDI that office space was the only viable reuse alternative proposal that arose from its search, that would generate sufficient funds to maintain and restore the property. In addition to hearing about the deteriorating condition of the mansion, the zoning board was told that because of the easement's restrictions on the property, residential development was not economically viable. The zoning board approved the variance, finding "circumstances of hardship or exceptional practical difficulty."[82]

Noting the requirements to "meet the more onerous 'unnecessary hardship' test"[83] for a use variance, as opposed to seeking an area variance, the court held "a landowner has no right to a use variance when the hardship is self-imposed. The hardship will be deemed self-imposed if it results from a voluntary, affirmative act of the landowner."[84] The court concluded that where, as here, the landowner has created a self-imposed hardship for which he sought the use variance, he cannot meet all the requirements to satisfy the "unnecessary hardship" test. The court was sympathetic, stating "[t]his unfortunate circumstance cannot be remedied by a use variance,"[85] and suggested alternative methods of resolving the issue. The court found the zoning board committed legal error in its grant of the use variance and reversed.

The petitioners in *Calagione v. City of Lewes Planning Comm'n*[86] challenged the approval of a subdivision of two parcels in the Old Town Residential District and historic district, where the subsequent adoption of an amended zoning code set a minimum lot requirement larger than the subdivided lots. The court found the petitioners had standing but did not demonstrate the requisite harm for injunctive relief. The court noted that there had been no construction, nor any plans for construction, on the subdivided properties, other than work on an underground storm water management system and a sidewalk. Thus, any harm was speculative. Further, the court found the case was not ripe as any construction on the parcels would need to go through appropriate reviews with the city's Building Inspector and the city's Historic Preservation Commission, to obtain a building permit. The court dismissed the petition without prejudice.

District of Columbia Two cases this year examined the permit review process under the Historic Preservation Act and delineated the authority of the Historic Preservation Review Board (HPRB) and the Mayor's Agent for Historic Preservation. In *Embassy Real Estate Holdings, LLC v. District of Columbia's Mayor's Agent for Historic Preservation*,[87] the court considered the impacts of an application for historic landmark designation on pending construction permits. The petitioner proposed to convert the former Italian Embassy into a condominium building through partial demolition and a new addition. The petitioner was told the building was most likely historic and that he could either attempt to designate it himself or, at some risk, attempt to develop private agreements with certain preservation organizations who would be likely to apply for its designation. The petitioner met with the District of Columbia Historic Preservation Office (HPO) and other community groups to present a design plan for the renovation. After some delay, the petitioner met again with the HPO and presented a revised design plan to which the HPO expressed concern over potential adverse effects to the building and viewsheds. The petitioner did not believe the HPO intended to designate the building at that time. The petitioner entered into an agreement with the D.C. Preservation League, in which the Preservation League agreed to file for a landmark designation in exchange for certain design changes and preservation commitments.

The petitioners applied to the D.C. Department of Regulatory and Consumer Affairs (DCRA) for the appropriate permits. After the permits for construction staging and sidewalk usage were granted, but while the permits for excavation, sheeting, shoring, alteration/renovation, and new construction were still pending, the HPO applied to designate the property as a historic landmark. The HPRB designated the property as a historic landmark and, as a result, found the permits for excavation and new construction, which had been issued after the application for landmark designation had been filed, to be inconsistent with the purposes of the Historic Landmark and Historic Preservation Act. The HPRB found the DCRA issued the permits in error, because permits for the property require historic preservation review, and argued that the permits should be voided. On appeal, the Mayor's Agent affirmed the HPRB's determination regarding the permits and voided them. The Mayor's Agent did not find the project to be of "special merit" or the petitioner to have shown economic hardship amounting to a taking.

The court found the protections in the Historic Landmark and Historic Preservation Act to apply to properties subject to a pending application for historic landmark designation, as well as those already designated. The court also found the law to apply to properties for which permit applications have already been filed, and that the regulations require an expedited review of a landmark application in such circumstances. The HPRB must both hold a hearing and decide whether to make the designation within ninety days, counted from the date the designation application is official.[88]

The court concluded the Mayor's Agent and the HPRB had proper jurisdiction to review the permit applications in accordance with the Historic Landmark and Historic Preservation Act. The court declined to "entertain [the] petitioner's arguments for equitable relief based on laches," takings, or estoppel.[89]

Also pursuant to the Historic Preservation Act, the petitioner in *N Street Follies L.P. v. D.C. Board of Zoning Adjustment*,[90] was required to seek approval from the Board of Zoning Adjustment (BZA) and the Mayor, because of the nature and location of its project in the Dupont Circle Overlay District. The petitioner applied for three special exceptions and three variances from the zoning regulations to construct a hotel on several lots. The HPRB rejected the design plans, and BZA granted the motion of intervenor Tabard Corporation and dismissed petitioner's application as moot based on the lack of HPRB approval for the plans submitted. BZA noted that the HPRB's review was informal, but that the HPRB was unlikely to recommend the plans for approval even after formal review.

While acknowledging the BZA has the authority to dismiss an application as moot, the court found the BZA erred as a matter of law. The petitioner's plans were not formally rejected by the Mayor's Agent, the entity under the Historic Preservation Act with the authority to make the final determination regarding such applications. Conceptual design reviews by the HPRB are not binding. Further, the court, "assuming without deciding that attenuation is sufficient grounds to dismiss an application,"[91] found no substantial evidence to support the BZA's decision. The court reversed.

Florida In *Friends of the Great Southern, Inc. v. City of Hollywood*,[92] the court considered the constitutionality of the evaluation criteria, used to review an application for a certificate of appropriateness, in the City of Hollywood Land Development Code. Challenging the approval of a certificate of appropriateness for the partial demolition of the Great Southern Hotel, a contributing element of the Historic Hollywood Business District, and the proposed new construction of a condominium, retail, and parking complex, the appellants argued the code lacked sufficient standards and provided improper discretion to the city commission. The court found the code's instruction that the city commission "shall consider the following criteria" to be mandatory, thus not allowing for criteria other than those listed to be considered, and those listed to be objective and appropriately specific. The court concluded that the code is constitutional and affirmed the trial court.

The court in *Stranahan House, Inc. v. City of Fort Lauderdale*[93] heard an appeal relating to the proposed development of a downtown Fort Lauderdale property, the Hyde Park Market site, which is adjacent to the historic Stranahan House. While the Stranahan House is in a historic preservation district, the Hyde Park Market site is zoned to allow significant use. Coolidge-South Markets Equities, L.P. (Coolidge) purchased the Hyde Park Market site and proposed to construct a large condominium tower. The city sought to put a public park on the property through an eminent domain proceeding. The city, Stranahan House, Inc., and Friends of the Park at Stranahan House, Inc. (Stranahan) made an agreement in which Stranahan would contribute funds toward the purchase of the property. The trial court granted summary judgment against the city's eminent domain petition, and later approved a Consent Final Judgment between the city and Coolidge in which Coolidge agreed to provide an alternative site plan for the property to include the creation of a park-like plaza area. Stranahan challenged the city commission's subsequent approval of the alternative site plan and argued the development order was inconsistent with the comprehensive plan's protection of historic properties and neighborhood compatibility. The trial court dismissed, finding the issues to have been adjudicated by the court.

In reviewing the trial court's decision, the court noted that the Consent Final Judgment addressed the original site plan but did not address, nor did any other ruling by the court, whether the alternative site plan was consistent with the comprehensive land use plan. The court then determined that neither the Consent Final Judgment nor the agreement between the city and Stranahan prevented Stranahan from seeking declaratory and injunctive relief. The court noted the limitations on the scope of the agreement between the city and Stranahan as to the city's eminent domain proceedings and found it "sufficiently separate"[94] from the claim here, so as not to act as a waiver of Stranahan's ability to challenge the alternative site plan. The court concludes Stranahan and the Friends group had standing and reversed the trial court.

In the companion case, the court in *Stranahan House, Inc. v. City of Fort Lauderdale*[95] heard Stranahan's consolidated petition for certiorari review of the city's approval of the settlement agreement and through it, the original site plan and the city's approval of the alternative site plan. In both instances, Stranahan argued the city did not follow the appropriate procedures to approve the plans. The trial court found the settlement agreement did not constitute improper contract zoning and afforded all parties due process, and that the city's decision was supported by substantial evidence. The court noted the limits of its certiorari review and excluded consideration of Stranahan's claims regarding the alternative site plan's inconsistency with the comprehensive plan. The court went on to find the trial court's dismissal of Stranahan's challenge to the settlement agreement to be proper. Stranahan did not intervene in the circuit court proceedings, thus it cannot challenge the settlement agreement. In regard to Stranahan's second petition, the court, once again very aware of its limited review, found the trial court applied the correct law in resolving Stranahan's due process claim, its contention that the wrong regulations were applied to review the alternative site plan, and its allegation that the city failed to obtain a certificate of appropriateness. The court denied the petition.

Georgia Challenging the denial of a certificate of appropriateness for proposed subdivisions, property owners in *DeKalb County v. Buckler*[96] argued that the decision was void, because it lacked the input of all seven required members of the historic preservation commission and the public hearing on the application was not properly noticed. The court noted that "[i]n Georgia, '[a] substantial compliance with any statutory requirement, especially on the part of public officers, shall be deemed and held sufficient, and no proceeding shall be declared void for want of such compliance, unless expressly so provided by law.'" [97] Looking to the language of the Georgia Historic Preservation Act, requiring a local governing body to establish a historic preservation commission, and the DeKalb County's historic preservation ordinance, the court found no basis to invalidate a decision as a result of having only four members present. The court reversed the superior court's grant of a partial summary judgment.

Indiana The owner of a historic property in *Pressley v. Newburgh Town Council*[98] challenged the town council's adoption of an ordinance designating her property within an historic preservation district and, as a result, causing her property to be subject to certain use and development limitations. As to her allegation that the town did not comply with required statutory criteria in adopting the ordinance, the court found that generally boards "speak or act officially only through the minutes and records made at duly organized meetings,"[99] but here the affidavit properly supplemented the meeting minutes.

The property owner alleged the town's designation of her property in the historic district was erroneous as a matter of law, because the meeting minutes lacked evidence of any new study after the 1997 ordinance, creating the historic preservation commission, which would warrant such designation. In reviewing the trial court's judgment, the court noted the town established the commission and set forth a process for the recommendation and implementation of historic preservation district designations. While noting further that an additional survey was in fact conducted in this case, as shown in the zoning administrator's affidavit, the court found the commission has discretion to determine the need for supplemental surveys or maps, in recommending designations for historic preservation districts in areas that have been previously surveyed. The court concluded that the property owner failed to show that the town did not follow the appropriate procedures in designating her property for inclusion in the historic preservation district and affirmed the trial court.

Maryland The owner of a historic house in *Hamza Halici v. City of Gaithersburg, Maryland*[100] challenged the denial of his permit to demolish his property on the basis of substantial financial hardship. Prior to that time, the owner had filed a petition to have the house designated as a local historic site, which it was, and received tax credits for renovations on the property. The owner used it as a hair salon for years. While the Historical Preservation Advisory Committee (HPAC) recommended the application for demolition be denied, the Historic District Commission (HDC) conditionally approved the application and required that a site plan for new construction be awarded prior to issuing the permit. Years later, when the work had not been done and the approval expired, the property owner filed an application for a new permit. After public hearings, the HPAC again recommended denying the permit. The HDC held a public meeting, and later a failed application.

The circuit court found the HDC's decision to be supported by substantial evidence and rejected the property owner's challenge to the qualifications of one of HDC's members. On appeal, the court found the owner's challenge of the HDC member's qualifications to constitute an attack on the HDC's application of a statute and not a question of subject matter jurisdiction. Viewing this as a question of fact that would require an inquiry beyond its limited scope of review and noting that the property owner did not raise this issue during the administrative proceedings, the court found the claim not properly before it. The court found the HDC did not apply a heightened or erroneous legal standard in reviewing and denying the demolition permit and its determination that the property owner failed to show retention of the building would cause "substantial financial hardship" was based on substantial evidence. The court affirmed.

Missouri In a strongly worded judgment, the court in *Missouri v. Missouri Dep't of Natural Resources*[101] considered the protection of a National Historic Landmark and other historic properties from the adverse effects, namely odors and dangerous airborne pollutants, of a proposed Concentrated Animal Feeding Operation (CAFO). The Department of Natural Resources granted a permit for the construction of the CAFO, despite receiving a protest and opposition from the National Trust for Historic Preservation objecting to the construction due to the potential impacts to air and water quality. The court cited the significant amount of animal waste that would be produced by the CAFO, as well as the related airborne pollutants and human health risks. The court noted the duty of the Department of Natural Resources to protect the state's historic properties and found the Department of Natural Resources and its director failed to meet their historic preservation obligations. Bound to protect the National Historic Landmark, the Village of Arrow Rock, the Department and the director should have ensured the historic properties were taken into consideration in all planning and development relating to the permit application. The court declared that the proposed construction and operation of the CAFO within two miles of the Village of Arrow Rock would deny residents and visitors to the area their Constitutional rights, because of threats to their health, and would result in "irreparable damage" to the National Historic Landmark and other historic properties, severely impacting the tourist industry. The court found further that this action is the plaintiffs' only available remedy, noting the Department's failure to enforce previous Stay Orders of the Administrative Hearing Commission.

The court concluded that no CAFO may be allowed within at least a fifteen mile radius of the Village of Arrow Rock and nearby historic sites, that no CAFO may transport, spread, or deposit any waste from its operation within the same distance, and that the Department of Natural Resources must revoke the permit issued for this specific CAFO construction. Emphasizing the Department's duty to protect historic properties in the state, the court elected to maintain jurisdiction over permits to construct or operate other CAFOs, to ensure an adequate remedy is available should such operations similarly threaten the Village of Arrow Rock and other nearby historic sites.

New York The court in *Berkoski v. The Board of Trustees of the Incorporated Village of Southampton*[102] found the intended use of park property, to include an outdoor hiring site, to constitute an unlawful alienation of parkland without proper authority and in violation of certain provisions of the Town Law and Southampton Town Code. Such a commercial use would be incompatible with the intent to maintain this property's natural, scenic, historic, and open space characteristics.

The petitioner in *Downey Farms Development Corp. v. Town of Cornwall Planning Board*[103] sought to subdivide his property into single family lots. While his application was pending, the town amended its zoning code and up-zoned the area in which the petitioner's property was located. Prior to the zoning change, the petitioner had been following through with the application process, including the development of plan revisions, visual impact studies, an archaeological study, and other items, and had only received preliminary subdivision approval. The petitioner alleged bad faith delays on the part of the town board and filed an Article 78 proceeding in which he argued that he had vested rights, such that his application should proceed under the prior zoning code. Among other actions the board required of the petitioner, the court questioned the need for two visual studies, to determine the potential effects on the historic Bethlehem Church, and to ascertain the potential impacts on residents' views of the historic Salisbury Trestle. The court found sufficient evidence of improper delays on behalf of the board to support a "special facts exception" finding in this case and concluded that the petitioner obtained vested rights to proceed with the subdivision in accordance with the pre-amendment zoning code.

Ohio The appellant in *Greenbelt Advocates v. Division of Mineral Resources Management*[104] challenged the denial of a Lands Unsuitable Petition (LUP) by the Chief of the Division of Mines and Reclamation. The court explained that in certain situations, including where the operations could significantly damage important historic or cultural properties, a discretionary "lands unsuitable designation" may be sought to prevent all or some coal mining in that area. The Village of Barnesville and the Warren Township Trustees filed such a petition to protect fragile and historic lands, as well as land use plans and water supplies, and designate an area of over four thousand acres outside the Barnesville Village limits as unsuitable for surface mining. After the petition was denied, a citizens group, not including the petitioners, appealed. The Reclamation Commission affirmed the decision.

Reviewing the Commission's decision, the court found the Commission did consider relevant land use plans and that those plans were not "necessarily *incompatible* with mining."[105] Further, the court found the Commission's decision with regard to protecting water reservoirs was not arbitrary, capricious, or inconsistent with the law. The appellant argued the blasting of the surface mining would threaten the Barnesville Historic District and the court again found the Commission's decision with regard to historic resources was not arbitrary, capricious, or inconsistent with the law. The court qualified its decision in reiterating its limited scope of review in this case and stated, "[e]ven though we affirm the Commission's decision, it is important to remember that doing so would not per se authorize mining within the petition area."[106]

The court in *State of Ohio, Ex. Rel. v. Seneca County Board of Commissioners*[107] found the Seneca County Board of Commissioners has the authority from the General Assembly to approve the demolition of a historic courthouse.

Eminent Domain and Takings

Florida In *City of Hollywood Community Redevelopment Agency v. 1843, LLC,*[108] a community development agency attempted to take a parcel of property, containing a single story commercial building, from the Mach family, for use at the core of its redevelopment plan. Also located in the area, and separated from the Mach property by an alley, was the Great Southern Hotel, a historic building. The planners proposed a parking garage entrance that would allow for the preservation of important elements of the Great Southern Hotel, spurring the need to take the Mach property. A member of the Broward Trust for Historic Preservation and chair of the Hollywood Preservation Board testified that "[w]ithout the Mach property, from 16 to 25 feet of the west façade would be lost."[109] The city commission voted to condemn the Mach property and the community redevelopment agency brought an unsuccessful petition in eminent domain.

On appeal, the court reviewed the requirements a condemning authority must meet to prove a reasonable necessity for a taking. The first prong was met by showing some evidence of reasonable necessity, for which there is broad discretion in the condemning authority. "A landowner cannot complain simply because some other location might have been made or some other property obtained which would have been suitable for the purpose."[110] The court found that historic preservation serves a public purpose and is a legitimate reason upon which to dismiss an alternate site plan. Finding no evidence that the community redevelopment agency's condemnation action was a result of fraud, bad faith, or an abuse of discretion, the second prong of the reasonable necessity test, the court reversed the trial court's decision and remanded for entry of an order of taking. The dissent cautioned that, "[a] condemning authority is not permitted to acquire through eminent domain a greater quantity of property than is necessary to serve the particular public use for which the property is sought."[111]

Taxes

North Carolina In *The Lynnwood Foundation v. North Carolina Department of Revenue,*[112] at issue was whether the Lynnwood Foundation, a charitable organization incorporated for the purpose of preserving and restoring the historic White Oaks Mansion and promoting an appreciation for its historic and architectural features, was still entitled to a tax refund after the assumption of certain civic functions. The Department of Revenue argued the Lynnwood Foundation did not meet the requirements for the refund in the North Carolina statutes because "it (1) does not aid a charitable class, (2) does not operate for public use, (3) operates for a profit, and (4) does not use the taxed property for charitable purposes."[113] The court disagreed.

In addition to preservation of the mansion, the Lynnwood Foundation also operates the Lee Institute, which offers leadership programs and training at the mansion. The Department of Revenue argued that the Lynnwood Foundation no longer qualified as a charitable organization because it did not aid a charitable class. In reviewing the definitions provided in precedent, the court determined that the Lynnwood Foundation falls within another type of defined charitable organization, that is, "created and maintained for the purpose of dispensing public good or benevolence."[114] The court noted the Lynnwood Foundation restored the mansion and its grounds and allowed public viewing at no charge, and emphasized the value of historic preservation in understanding our country's heritage and promoting the general welfare of all people.

Notes

1. *American Home Assurance Co. v. Oceaneering Int'l, Inc.*, No. H-06-2105, 2008 U.S. Dist. LEXIS 41750 (S.D. Tex. May 22, 2008).
2. *Id.* at 24.
3. *Id.* at 26.
4. *Id.* at 38-39.
5. *Id.* at 39-40.
6. *Shanks v. Dressel*, 540 F.3d 1082 (9th Cir. 2008).
7. *Id.* at 1087-88.
8. *Id.* at 1088.
9. *Id.* at 1089.
10. *Id.* at 1090.
11. *Id.* at 1093.
12. *Kuster v. Foley*, Civ. Nos. 07-00264 SOM/BMK, Civ. Nos. 07-00265 SOM/BMK (Consol.), 2008 U.S. Dist. LEXIS 39658 (D. Haw. May 13, 2008).
13. *Molski v. Foley Estates Vineyard & Winery LLC*, 531 F.3d 1043 (9th Cir. 2008).
14. *Id.* at 1049.
15. *Elkins v. D.C.*, 527 F. Supp. 2d 36 (D.D.C. Dec. 12, 2007).

16. *Id.* at 43.
17. *Id.* at 49.
18. *Elkins v. D.C.*, 250 F.R.D. 20 (D.D.C. May 28, 2008).
19. *Friends of the Columbia Gorge, Inc. v. Columbia River Gorge Comm'n*, 179 P.3d 706 (Or. Ct. App. Feb. 27, 2008).
20. *Id.* at 710.
21. *Id.* at 713 (quoting OAR 350-50-0030[1][b] [Nov. 15, 1999]).
22. *Id.* at 715.
23. *Id.* at 718.
24. *Southeast Towers, LLC v. Pickens County, GA*, No. 2:06-CV-0172-RWS, 2008 U.S. Dist. LEXIS 38767 (N.D. Ga. May 13, 2008).
25. *Id.* at 8.
26. *Id.* at 24.
27. *Comm. to Save the Hollywoodland Specific Plan and Hollywood Heritage v. City of Los Angeles*, No. B197018, 2008 Cal. App. LEXIS 501 (Cal. Ct. App. March 12, 2008).
28. *Id.* at 24.
29. *Id.* at 37.
30. *Id.* at 38.
31. *Valley Advocates v. City of Fresno,* No. F050952, 2008 Cal. App. LEXIS 368 (Cal. Ct. App. Feb. 15, 2008), *modified by* No. F050952, 2008 Cal. App. LEXIS 367 (Cal. Ct. App. March 17, 2008).
32. *Id.* at 12.
33. *Id.* at 12-13, FN 5.
34. *Id.* at 37.
35. *Architectural Heritage Assn. v. County of Monterey*, 122 Cal. App.4th 1095 (Cal. Ct. App. 2004).
36. *Valley Advocates*, 2008 Cal. App. LEXIS at 59.
37. *Id.* at 63 (citing CEQA, Public Resources Code § 21084.1).
38. *Heritage Fresno v. Redevelopment Agency of the City of Fresno*, No.C055298, slip op. 2008 Cal. App. Unpub. LEXIS 4341 (Cal. Ct. App. May 28, 2008).
39. *Id.* at 21-22 (quoting *Napa Citizens for Honest Government v. Napa County Bd. of Supervisors*, 91 Cal. App.4th 342, 358-59 [Cal. Ct. App. 2001]).
40. *Id.* at 24 (quoting *Napa Citizens for Honest Government v. Napa County Bd. of Supervisors*, 91 Cal App.4th 342, 359).
41. *Friends of the Riverfront v. DeLaSalle High School*, No.A06-2222, A07-944, 2007 Minn. App. Unpub. LEXIS 1118 (Minn. Ct. App. Nov. 20, 2007).
42. *Id.* at 4.
43. *State of Minnesota by Friends of the Riverfront v. City of Minneapolis*, 751 N.W.2d 586 (Minn. Ct. App. 2008).

44. *Id.* at 590.
45. *In re* Application of John Delvecchio, 856 N.Y.S.2d 497 (N.Y. Sup. Ct. 2007).
46. *In re* Sue Brander, 847 N.Y.S.2d 450 (N.Y. Sup. Ct. 2007).
47. *Id.* at 454.
48. *Id.* at 457.
49. *In re* Michael Kuzma, 45 A.D.3d 1308 (N.Y. App. Div. 2007).
50. *Id.* at 1310.
51. *Sutherland v. New York City Housing Development Co.*, No.114415/07, 2008 N.Y. Misc. LEXIS 4047 (N.Y. Sup. Ct. July 8, 2008).
52. *Mountain Communities for Responsible Energy v. Public Service Comm'n of West Virginia & Beech Ridge Energy, LLC; Eisenbeiss v. Public Service Commission of West Virginia and Beech Ridge Energy, LLC*, 665 S.E.2d 315 (W.Va. June 23, 2008).
53. *Finbury v. Architectural Heritage Foundation, Inc.*, No. 07-2416-BLS2, 2007 Mass. Super. LEXIS 577 (Mass. Super. Ct. Nov. 19, 2007).
54. *American Capital Corporation v. Blixseth, C.A.*, 563 F.Supp. 2d 316 (D.R.I. June 11, 2008).
55. *Id.* at 321.
56. *Kruse v. Town of Castle Rock*, 192 P.3d 591 (Colo. Ct. App. July 24, 2008).
57. *Id.* at 599.
58. *Id.*
59. *Id.* at 601.
60. *Brenton v. Fairfield Town Plan and Zoning Comm'n; Hess v. Fairfield PZC, Munson Builders, Inc. v. Fairfield PZC*, CV064016627S, CV064016811S, CV064016881S, 2008 Conn. Super. LEXIS 247 (Conn. Super. Ct. Jan. 31, 2008).
61. *Id.* at 16, 16-17.
62. *Smith v. Zoning Bd. of Appeals of the Town of Greenwich*, 629 A.2d 1089 (Conn. 1993).
63. *Brenton*, 2008 Conn. Super. LEXIS at 18.
64. *Id.* at 23.
65. *Felician Sisters of St. Francis of Connecticut, Inc. v. Historic District Comm'n of the Town of Enfield*, 937 A.2d 39 (Conn. 2008).
66. *Gibbons v. Historic District Comm'n of the Town of Fairfield*, 941 A.2d 917 (Conn. 2008).
67. *Id.* at 924.
68. *Id.* at 925 (referencing in this discussion *Felician Sisters of St. Francis of Connecticut, Inc. v. Historic District Comm'n of the Town of Enfield*, 937 A.2d 39).
69. *Id.* at 926.
70. *Stankiewicz v. Zoning Bd. of Appeals*, 556 A.2d 1024 (Conn. 1989).
71. *Gibbons*, 941 A.2d at 928 (quoting *Fonfara v. Reapportionment Comm'n*, 610 A.2d 153, 173 FN 12 [Conn. 1992]).

72. *Id.* at 931.
73. *Id.*
74. *Norwalk Preservation Trust, Inc. v. Norwalk Inn and Conference Center, Inc.*, No. FSTCV074010609S, 2008 Conn. Super. LEXIS 286 (Conn. Super. Ct. Feb. 6, 2008).
75. *Id.* at 8-9.
76. *Id.* at 17.
77. *Powell v. Zoning Board of Appeals of the Town of New Canaan*, No. FSTCV064008859S, 2008 Conn. Super. LEXIS 895 (Conn. Super. Ct. April 11, 2008).
78. *Id.* at 7.
79. *Tripp v. New Milford Zoning Comm'n*, No. LLICV064005391, 2008 Conn. Super. LEXIS 115 (Conn. Super. Ct. Jan. 17, 2008).
80. *Id.* at 11.
81. *Brown v. City of Wilmington Zoning Board of Adjustment*, C.A. No. 06A-10-005 JRS, 2008 Del. Super. LEXIS 252 (Del. Super. Ct. July 21, 2008).
82. *Id.* at 10.
83. *Id.* at 15.
84. *Id.* at 17.
85. *Id.* at 28.
86. *Calagione v. City of Lewes Planning Comm'n*, No. 2814-CC, 2007 Del. Ch. LEXIS 157 (Del. Ch. Nov. 13, 2007).
87. *Embassy Real Estate Holdings, LLC v. District of Columbia's Mayor's Agent for Historic Preservation*, 944 A.2d 1036 (D.C. Ct. App. 2008).
88. *Id.* at 1048.
89. *Id.* at 1050.
90. *N Street Follies L.P. v. D.C. Board of Zoning Adjustment*, 949 A.2d 584 (D.C. Ct. App. 2008).
91. *Id.* at 590.
92. *Friends of the Great Southern, Inc. v. City of Hollywood*, 964 So. 2d 827 (Fla. Ct. App.2007).
93. *Stranahan House, Inc. v. City of Fort Lauderdale*, 967 So. 2d 427 (Fla. Ct. App. 2007).
94. *Id.* at 432.
95. *Stranahan House, Inc. v. City of Fort Lauderdale*, 967 So. 2d 1121 (Fla. Ct. App. 2007).
96. *DeKalb County v. Buckler*, 654 S.E.2d 193 (Ga. Ct. App. 2007).
97. *Id.* at 195 (quoting Official Code of Georgia Annotated § 1-3-1[c]).
98. *Pressley v. Newburgh Town Council*, 887 N.E.2d 1012 (Ind. Ct. App. 2008).
99. *Id.* at 1016.

100. *Hamza Halici v. City of Gaithersburg, Maryland*, 949 A.2d 85 (Md. Ct. Spec. App. 2008).
101. *Missouri v. Missouri Dep't of Natural Resources*, No. 07AC-CC00923 (Cir. Cole Cty. 2008).
102. *Berkoski v. The Board of Trustees of the Incorporated Village of Southampton*, 856 N.Y.S.2d 496 (N.Y. Sup. Ct. 2008).
103. *Downey Farms Development Corp. v. Town of Cornwall Planning Board*, 858 N.Y.S.2d 542 (N.Y. Sup. Ct. 2008).
104. *Greenbelt Advocates v. Division of Mineral Resources Management*, 893 N.E.2d 230 (Ohio Ct. App. June 26, 2008).
105. *Id.* at 235.
106. *Id.* at 244.
107. *State of Ohio, Ex. Rel. v. Seneca County Board of Commissioners*, 889 N.E.2d 153 (Ohio Ct. App. 2008).
108. *City of Hollywood Community Redevelopment Agency v. 1843, LLC*, 980 So. 2d 1138 (Fla. Ct. App. 2008).
109. *Id.* at 1141.
110. *Id.* at 1142.
111. *Id.* at 1144.
112. *The Lynnwood Foundation v. North Carolina Department of Revenue*, 660 S.E.2d 611 (N.C. Ct. App. 2008).
113. *Id.* at 614.
114. *Id.*

Tribes, Tribal Lands, and Indian Arts

• • •

Section Editor: Rob Roy Smith

Introduction

This past year offered reasons for optimism and pessimism for tribal cultural resource protection advocates seeking to expand the scope of protections for sacred sites. This section focuses on cultural property issues involving Indian tribes in the courts, legislation in the United States Congress, tribes, state legislatures, and on a programmatic level, as well as Indian Arts and Crafts Act matters.

Tribes

Native American Graves Protection and Repatriation Act

The year 2008 saw litigation and regulatory and legislative activity concerning the Native American Graves Protection and Repatriation Act (NAGPRA).[1] NAGPRA is a federal law that recognizes cultural property rights of individual Indians, Indian tribes, and Native Hawaiian organizations and enables these groups to make claims to seek the return of ancestors and items of cultural property. NAGPRA provides the opportunity for the return of human remains and artifacts; ultimately, those with standing to make the claims determine what action to take.

Litigation The only NAGPRA litigation of note in 2008 involved a complex set of claims by the Quechan Indian Tribe against the United States under the Federal Tort Claims Act, and other statutes, concerning the government's actions in placing utility electrical lines on reservation lands that allegedly damaged numerous cultural sites.[2] The case involves some novel uses of NAGPRA. Among the claims was an allegation that NAGPRA provides the standard of care applicable to actors accused of committing gross negligence for failure to protect tribal sacred sites during construction activities. The court denied the government's motion to dismiss, concluding that NAGPRA could impose a standard of care for persons conducting ground-disturbing activities on reservation lands in a negligent manner. In addition, the court agreed with the tribe that NAGPRA applies to "tribal lands" that are "within the exterior boundaries of an Indian reservation," but refused to extend NAGPRA to support an idea that the federal law creates in the tribe a beneficial title to a right of way held in fee by the United States to protect in situ cultural properties. The court recognized that NAGPRA does not establish rights in real property, but does acknowledge rights to human remains of ancestors exhumed.

Tort claims for negligence in the treatment of human remains formed the basis of an action in *Lummi Nation v. Golder Associates*.[3] The case resolved in a settlement after the court ruled that the tribes were a third-party beneficiary to a contract for exhumation of a Native American burial site, between a city and an archaeology firm.

At the close of the year, the Western Shoshone Nation and others filed an action against the U.S. Bureau of Land Management seeking to revoke a permit to Canadian Barrick Gold for hardrock mining on Mount Tenabo, within the territory of the Western Shoshone Nation. The action alleges "Western Shoshone religious and cultural uses of the mine will be permanently eliminated."[4]

Regulatory Action: Disposition of Culturally Unidentifiable Human Remains Rules The Department of the Interior published a proposed rule on October 16, 2007, relating to the ultimate disposition of culturally unidentifiable remains recently discovered or held by federal agencies.[5] The process to create the rule started in 1994. Current regulations implementing NAGPRA require museums and federal agencies to retain possession of culturally unidentifiable human remains until final regulations are promulgated, or the Secretary of the Interior recommends otherwise. The disposition of funerary objects associated with culturally unidentifiable human remains is not specifically addressed in NAGPRA, and is voluntary under the proposed rule.[6]

In addition to certain record keeping and information sharing provisions, the proposed rule establishes three choices for the disposition of culturally unidentifiable human remains. First, the rules would require a museum or federal agency to offer to transfer control of culturally unidentifiable human remains for which it cannot prove right of possession to Indian tribes or Native Hawaiian organizations according to three priority categories. A museum or federal agency can maintain right of possession to Native American human remains, where the acquisition occurred with the full knowledge and consent of the next of kin or the official governing body of the appropriate culturally affiliated Indian tribe; that is, those with authority to grant a transfer. The next of kin or tribe can expressly relinquish the right to control human remains under the law.

The first priority of return would be to the Indian tribe or Native Hawaiian organization on whose tribal land, at the time of recovery, the human remains were recovered. The second priority would be to the Indian tribe or tribes that are recognized as aboriginally occupying the area in which the human remains were recovered. The third priority would be to Indian tribes and Native Hawaiian organizations with a cultural relationship to the region from which the human remains were removed or, for human remains lacking geographic affiliation, a cultural relationship to the region in which the museum or Federal agency with control over the human remains is located. The concept of cultural relationship is addressed in NAGPRA Section 3, Ownership, but has not been defined in law or regulations. In addition, the rule proposes a process for the voluntary transfer of control of culturally unidentifiable human remains that are not transferred under the priority provisions, under state or other law, upon recommendation from the United States Secretary of the Interior. Thus far, Iowa and Colorado have received authorization from the Secretary to use state protocols.[7]

The rule was strenuously opposed by a number of groups and a member of Congress, among them the Society of American Archaeology (SAA) which argued, among other things, that the Interior Department does not have the authority to issue the new rules; the rules are impractical because they do not allocate implementation funding; the rules could lead to results antithetical to the SAA's view of intent of NAGPRA; and the rules assert control over material not covered by NAGPRA. The SAA claimed that the proposed rule could result in the transfer of all unaffiliated human remains to tribes or other "Native American" groups having only a "weakly" demonstrated relationship to them. These cries were echoed by Representative Doc Hastings (R-WA) who has introduced numerous amendments to NAGPRA, which have not passed, seeking to expand the act's scientific study provisions. The regulations proposed by the Department of Interior are an "obvious attempt to end-run congressional intent and a federal court ruling in the long-fought Kennewick Man case," he wrote in a letter to Interior Secretary Dirk Kempthorne. In that case, the 9,200 year old human remains were desired by eight individuals for study. The United States Court of Appeals for the Ninth Circuit found that the remains were not "Native American" as defined by NAGPRA because, among other things, the remains lacked a "present day" connection to the claimant Indian tribes. NAGPRA, however, does not contain an age limitation for its application.

The SAA and Representative Hastings overstate the reach of the proposals. The unclaimed remains regulations appear to present a reasonable approach to the treatment of human remains and are 18 years overdue. The proposed regulations merely create a process for such remains to be returned to tribes, as descendant guardians; they do not preordain a result. The rules remain in the proposed rule stage of the rulemaking process.

Federal Legislation The bipartisan Native American Omnibus Technical Corrections Act of 2007, introduced on September 25, 2007 by Senators Byron L. Dorgan (D-ND) and John McCain (R-AZ), was left stranded on the Senate Calendar for action at the conclusion of the 110th Congress.[8] The bill passed out of committee in 2007. The bill sought to amend various federal laws addressing Indian affairs. The second section of the bill would have amended Section 2(9) of NAGPRA, 25 U.S.C. § 3001(9), by "(1) by inserting 'or was' after 'is'; and (2) by inserting after 'indigenous to' the following: 'any geographic area that is now located within the boundaries of'" so that the new definition of "Native American" under NAGPRA would read: "'Native American' means of, or relating to, a tribe, people, or culture that is or was indigenous to any geographic area that is now located within the boundaries of the United States." The bill would have effectively served as a technical fix to the limitations of the definition of "Native American" highlighted by the Ninth Circuit's *Bonnichsen v. United States* decision in 2004, and would have clarified that cultural connection, not present-day tribal membership of the deceased, is necessary for cultural affiliation.[9] Under NAGPRA, Indian tribes have standing to bring claims. The claims brought may be for human remains or cultural artifacts, determined to be "Native American," for which the tribe has cultural affiliation, unless the claim arises from a new discovery on tribal land, or the tribe requests disposition of culturally unidentifiable Native American human remains in collections. More than one present-day tribe may be descendants of ancient ancestors.

NAGPRA Review Committee Actions In October 2008, the Native American Graves Protection and Repatriation Act Review Committee voted 6-0 to recommend the return of the remains of 180 ancestors to the Onondaga Nation of New York. The remains were removed from a burial site 41 years ago, when New York State was building Route 17, and a worker driving a bulldozer uncovered an ancient burial site near the village of Nichols. The burial mound, about 105 miles south of Syracuse and 60 miles from the present Onondaga Nation's reservation, contained the remains of persons believed to have died between A.D.1000 and 1500. After the remains were shifted between a few owners, they wound up in boxes in the collection of the New York State Museum in Albany, which holds the remains.

The tribe wanted to rebury the ancestors, but the museum claimed they were too old to be culturally affiliated with the Onondaga and had opposed a return of the remains to the tribe. The tribe sought relief from the NAGPRA Review Committee. The NAGPRA Review Committee heard the dispute and determined that the remains should be returned to the tribe based on the tribe's affiliation with the remains and the site.

The NAGPRA Review Committee's recommendations are not binding. The State University of New York at Binghamton continues to possess the burial artifacts—pottery and other objects—that were excavated from the site where the remains were found. The New York State Museum also possesses another 880 sets of culturally unidentifiable remains.[10]

Other Congressional Action On September 26, 2008, the Senate Committee on Indian Affairs supported a call for a Government Accountability Office (GAO) investigation to explore federal government compliance and enforcement of NAGPRA. The scope of the report would be to study whether the NAGPRA process has been accountable to Indian tribes. The call for a study is in response to an August 2008 report released by the Makah Indian Tribe and the National Association of Tribal Historic Preservation Officers, funded by a NAGPRA grant, and three years of recommendations from the NAGPRA Review Committee.

State Measures In Colorado, 45 tribes, the Colorado Commission of Indian Affairs, and the Colorado Historical Society developed a NAGPRA protocol approved by the Department of Interior that might prove to be a blueprint for similar plans across the country.[11] The group created the protocol to ensure the repatriation of remains and funerary objects discovered on Colorado State lands or private lands that cannot be culturally affiliated with a specific Indian tribe. The protocol works within the boundaries of state and federal cultural resource laws by shortening the time frame for repatriating inadvertently discovered remains and funerary objects on Colorado State lands and private lands, and addressing a gap in federal law by making it possible for the repatriation and reburial of culturally unidentifiable "Native American" human remains and associated funerary objects that come into the state's possession. The protocol should provide tribes with an improved process to recover remains.

Tribal Lands, Sacred Sites, and Cultural Properties

Religious Freedom Restoration Act

The 2008 *Yearbook* introduced readers to the Religious Freedom Restoration Act of 1993 (RFRA),[12] which was passed by Congress to buttress the protections afforded by the Free Exercise Clause of the First Amendment to the United States Constitution to "better protect . . . all Americans of all faiths in the exercise of their religion."[13] RFRA provides that federal government activities "shall not substantially burden a person's exercise of religion" unless the government can demonstrate that "application of the burden to the person (1) is in furtherance of compelling governmental interest; and then (2) is the least restrictive means of furthering that compelling interest."[14]

Free Exercise: San Francisco Peaks Litigation On March 12, 2007, the Navajo Nation, Hopi Tribe, and other southwest tribes scored a major sacred sites victory before the Ninth Circuit Court of Appeals (*Navajo Nation, et al. v. U.S. Forest Serv.*) by stopping certain activities of a ski resort in the San Francisco Peaks of Arizona, including the resort's planned use of reclaimed wastewater for snowmaking at the environmentally sensitive and spiritually important site.[15] The Ninth Circuit panel decision was the first case to hold that RFRA was available to Indian tribes to use religious beliefs to block certain land use practices that threaten Indian sacred sites. However, the victory for the Indian tribes was short lived.

On August 8, 2008, a twelve judge *en banc* panel of the Ninth Circuit issued a 9–3 opinion vacating the prior opinion and reversing the prior holding that

RFRA barred use of reclaimed wastewater at the ski resort.[16] The opinion found that the Indian tribes failed to show that the government's approval of the use of reclaimed wastewater placed a "substantial burden" on the Indian tribes' exercise of their religion, essentially reverting to pre-RFRA standards.[17] The majority decision concluded that "[n]o plants would be destroyed or stunted; no springs polluted; no places of worship made inaccessible, or liturgy modified" and that the Indian tribes would continue to have "virtually unlimited access to the mountain."[18] Thus, the majority concluded, "the sole effect of the artificial snow is on the Plaintiffs' subjective spiritual experience," and that protection from offending their "feelings" and decreasing "spiritual fulfillment" are not rights under the RFRA.[19] The majority further noted that the reclaimed wastewater would contain only "0.0001% human waste."[20] With the case so structured, the majority concluded that RFRA does not protect against "damaged spiritual feelings" of a subjective nature because the government has not "compelled" the Indian tribes to "act contrary to their religious tenets" because the Indian tribes could "otherwise practice their religion using whatever resources they may choose."[21]

The three-judge dissent took offense at the majority's rejection of the Indian tribes' testimony as to the importance of the Peaks and the harm that the use of reclaimed wastewater would cause. The dissent likened the use of artificial snow using the reclaimed wastewater to the government "permit[ing] only" baptismal water contaminated with recycled wastewater for Christians, or "permit[ing] only" non-Kosher food for Orthodox Jews.[22] The dissent concluded with a rare judicial apology: "RFRA was passed to protect the exercise of all religions, including the religions of American Indians. If Indians' land-based exercise of religion is not protected by RFRA in this case, I cannot imagine a case in which it will be. I am truly sorry that the majority has effectively read American Indians out of RFRA."[23]

Much as the 2007 panel decision temporarily established the scope of RFRA, the *en banc* opinion may have limited RFRA's reach within the courts of the Ninth Circuit by severely limiting what can constitute a "substantial burden on [the] free exercise of religion." As RFRA now stands, at least in the Ninth Circuit, the fundamental altering of a religious system does not suffice under RFRA to block destructive land use practices at a sacred site. Likewise, the *en banc* decision calls into question the potency of tribal religious elder testimony to prove harm to the resources and the places upon which tribes rely for their religious practices. More than a rejection of protections for "land based" religions that might not resemble non-Indian religions, the *en banc* panel has called into question the value of Indian religious beliefs by suggesting that the only harm suffered was "subjective" and somehow not real enough to trigger a RFRA violation. The statement by the majority that the Indian tribes could simply practice their religion elsewhere, using other resources, ignores testimony about the importance of this site and the exact resources at stake. Whether it is a fundamental misunderstanding of the differences between religious practices, or a call for assimilation of tribal religious practices, the majority's reasoning is troubling from the perspective of tribal resource advocates. Perhaps nothing short of the razing of the Peaks, akin to the government-sanctioned destruction of all church structures related to a specific religion, would satisfy RFRA's high bar.

Religious Freedom Restoration Act—*Snoqualmie Indian Tribe v. FERC* In the first case to be adversely affected by the *Navajo Nation* decision discussed above, the Ninth Circuit denied the petition of the Snoqualmie Indian Tribe for review of the Federal Energy Regulatory Commission's (FERC) grant to Puget Sound Energy of a renewal of a license to operate a hydroelectric project for 40 years at Snoqualmie Falls.[24] The tribe brought the petition under RFRA, claiming a substantial burden to the tribe's free exercise of religion and for failure to consult with the tribe on a government-to-government basis as required by the National Historic Preservation Act (NHPA). The falls are a spiritually and culturally important site to the Snoqualmie people. As to RFRA, the Ninth Circuit found that the tribe failed to meet the *Navajo Nation* standard. The court also rejected the tribe's NHPA claims based on the fact that the tribe was not federally recognized until 1999, two years after the first consultation ended in 1997. That circumstances had materially changed since the prior license authorization was not found to require further consultation action. Snoqualmie Falls and the cycle of flowing water has played a part in ancient sacred experiences including vision quests and treating mist as an integral part of religious experiences. The hydroelectric project denied the tribe access to the falls and eliminated the associated religious experiences. The Ninth Circuit applied the pre-RFRA test of loss of government benefit, or criminal or civil sanctions, for practicing religion, as the basis of their decision.[25]

Free Exercise—Medicine Bluffs In stark contrast to the San Francisco Peaks litigation, on September 23, 2008, the United States District Court for the Western District of Oklahoma provided a substantial victory to the Comanche Nation, under RFRA, to protect the Medicine Bluffs sacred site.[26] The court granted a preliminary injunction barring the United States and Fort Sill military reservation from erecting a new building directly south of the Medicine Bluffs, a natural landform that has historic importance, as well as religious importance, to the Comanche Nation.[27] The tribe claimed that the proposed building violates RFRA because the construction would substantially interfere with their religious practices; because the area is a place where religious leaders gather to pray, gather plants for use in healing and ceremonies, and engage in sacred observances; and because the construction would also block a viewscape of the area.[28] The United States responded by noting that the building was not to be constructed on the Bluffs and that the tribal religious leaders could go elsewhere.[29]

The trial court disagreed with the United States. Noting the substantial testimony in the record from several Comanche leaders expressing the singular importance of the site, the court found that the site is of "great cultural and religious significance" and that the area is the "situs" of traditional religious practices for "perhaps hundreds" of Comanches.[30] Because the practice of the ceremonies is "private," the court found that the intrusion of the building and increased traffic amounted to a potential violation of RFRA, and, therefore, the tribe had met its burden to obtain a preliminary injunction under RFRA to bar the construction that would substantially burden the exercise of the tribe's religious practices at the site.[31] The court rejected the United States' claims because it had not demonstrated that the current proposed location was the least restrictive means of furthering the project.

The *Comanche Nation* decision begs the question, what makes this case different from the *Navajo* case in the Ninth Circuit? Of the many similarities, the most important is the fact that both cases involve substantial testimony from tribal religious leaders demonstrating the importance of the site as part of their land-based religion. The obvious difference, that one case arises in Oklahoma and the other in Arizona, is not sufficient as a matter of legal analysis. The most glaring difference is the United States' failure to demonstrate in *Comanche Nation* that they could not simply relocate the construction of the building to some other place. This option was not available to the ski resort in *Navajo*. Moreover, the United States in *Comanche Nation* admitted that they did not take the tribe's interests into account because they did not believe the construction would impact a sacred site. Thus, it is not the tribe's evidence of need in *Comanche* that distinguishes this case from *Navajo* but, rather, what the defendant United States failed to show in a lack of viable options. This does not provide much comfort to tribal sacred site advocates, or the drafters of RFRA. The singular importance of a site for tribal religious purposes, by itself, remains insufficient to secure RFRA protections. Rather, the court's determination will likely rest upon whether the United States considers all of its options, and whether suitable alternatives for the proposed project exist.

Establishment Clause—Cave Rock The 2008 *Yearbook* discussed a challenge brought by recreational users against a United States Forest Service decision protecting a sacred site in Nevada. The Ninth Circuit Court of Appeals upheld the decision of the Forest Service to ban "the recreational activity of rock climbing" at Cave Rock, issued by the agency in 2003.[32] On February 29, 2008, the United States Forest Service issued a final rule to protect Cave Rock by banning all climbing. The Washoe Tribe views Cave Rock as the site of important mythological events that are central to their cosmology.[33] The Ninth Circuit based its decision on the historic, nonreligious features of the rock and noted the destructive impact of climbers to the site's historic integrity.

Other Sacred Site Protection Efforts

Last year saw a return to tribal ownership of various sites held sacred to Indian tribes. In Oregon, the Confederated Tribes of the Coos, Lower Umpqua, and Siuslaw Indians of Oregon received a federal transfer of 24 acres of ancestral land by Congressional act.[34] The transfer included a return to tribal ownership of an abandoned lighthouse that includes an ancestral village and burial grounds.

Indian Arts and Crafts

Indian arts and crafts are a culturally and commercially important part of the lives of many tribal people. This section discusses efforts pertaining to Indian artisans and their craft, including the Indian Arts and Crafts Act (IACA).

Congressional Action

On May 1, 2007, Senator John McCain introduced S. 1255, "The Indian Arts and Crafts Amendments of 2007," designed to protect Indian arts and crafts through the improvement of applicable criminal proceedings to provide for the investigation and punishment of individuals misrepresenting Indian produced goods and products.[35]

This bipartisan legislation would amend the IACA to authorize any federal law enforcement officer (not just the Federal Bureau of Investigation as is currently the case), including an officer under the Indian Law Enforcement Reform Act acting in coordination with a federal law enforcement agency on a violation outside Indian Country, to investigate offenses involving the sale of arts and crafts that are misrepresented as Indian products. The bill would also revise the requirements for initiating civil actions for the misrepresentation of Indian produced goods to make it easier for the enforcement of IACA.

On September 23, 2008, the bill was passed by the U.S. Senate with amendments by unanimous consent. On September 24, 2008, the bill was referred to the U.S. House Committee on Natural Resources and Committee on the Judiciary, for a period to be subsequently determined by the Speaker of the House. The U.S. House of Representatives did not take any action on the proposed legislation before the 110th Congress adjourned.

Litigation

A trial began in June 2008 alleging violations of the Archaeological Resources Protection Act (ARPA) by an Albuquerque, New Mexico dealer who was charged with illegally buying, selling, or transporting Navajo gray-ware pots that allegedly were unlawfully taken from federal lands. The jury acquitted Robert V. Gallegos, a well-known dealer in tribal artifacts, of one count of violating ARPA and hung on four other counts. On September 3, 2008, the United States filed a motion asking the court to dismiss the remaining four counts, noting that Gallegos had agreed to relinquish the collection of 42 items. The pots are utilitarian items, used for cooking and storage, dating from 1500 to 1750, found in the Largo Camp area of the Four Corners. The collection was considered to have great scholarly value. The agreement preserves a significant and valuable collection while conserving judicial and prosecutorial resources of a retrial, the U.S. Attorney's Office said, in seeking dismissal of the remaining charges. See Practice Area 8, Enforcement, for additional analysis.

Tribal Courts and Tribal Codes

The Cherokee Nation adopted its own version of the Indian Arts and Crafts Act in January 2008. The act, Truth in Advertising for Native Art Act, requires anyone selling Indian art within Cherokee Nation lands to be a member of a federally recognized Indian tribe. The act's main purpose is to foster authentic Indian art and combat non-Indians selling art as Indian art. It defines an

"Indian" as a federally recognized tribal citizen. The definition is more limited than that of the IACA. The Cherokee Nation act expands the definition of "art" beyond IACA, to include all art forms, such as performance art, as well as physical acts. "Art" is defined as "an object or action that is made with the intention of stimulating the human senses as well as the human mind/and or spirit regardless of any functional uses," including crafts, handmade items, traditional storytelling, contemporary art or techniques, oral histories, other performing arts, and printed materials.

The passage of the act by the Cherokee Nation represents an important step in the development of tribal protection for Indian arts and crafts that takes into account specific tribal cultural values and fills gaps in the IACA. This law may provide a model for other tribes.

Conclusion

Tribal cultural resource and sacred site protection continues to present new challenges and opportunities for protection advocates. While the *Navajo Nation* case represents a setback for sacred site protection efforts, the *Comanche Nation* decision provides new promise for RFRA's application to the protection of tribal religious sites. The efforts of states and tribes, as well as the NAGPRA Review Committee, with respect to culturally unidentifiable human remains may yield advances in the ability of tribes to recover and protect the remains of their ancestors.

Notes

1. Native American Grave Protection and Repatriation Act ("NAGPRA"), 25 U.S.C. §§ 3001 *et seq*.
2. *Quechan Indian Tribe v. United States*, 535 F. Supp.2d 1072 (S.D. Cal.2008).
3. *Lummi Nation v. Golder Assoc., Inc.*, 236 F. Supp. 2d 1183 (W.D. Wash. 2002).
4. Shoshone Indians Sue to Stop Barrick's Nevada Gold Mine, Environmental News Service (Nov. 24, 2008).
5. 72 Fed. Reg. 58582 (Oct. 16, 2007).
6. 25 U.S.C. § 3006(c)(5).
7. www.nps.gov/history/NAGPRA/RevCom
8. S. 2087, 110th Cong. (2007). H.R. 4027, 110th Cong. (2007) Rep. Hastings (R-WA) to amend the definition of "Native American" to require a "significant relationship to be found between remains discovered on federal lands and pres-

ently existing Native American tribe" authored in response to S. 2087 to make it more difficult for tribes to protect remains from unwanted study.

9. *Bonnichsen v. Corps of Engineers*, 357 F. 3d 962 (9thCir. 2004), as amended, 367 F. 3d 864 (9th Cir. 2004).
10. Decisions of the NAGPRA Review Committee, Id. n. 7.
11. Tribes gain faster access to remains, DENVER POST (June 4, 2008).
12. 42 U.S.C. §§ 2000bb – 2000bb-4.
13. President W. J. Clinton, Religious Freedom Restoration Act Signing Ceremony, Fed. News Service (Nov. 16, 1993).
14. 42 U.S.C. §§ 2000bb-1(a) and (b).
15. *Navajo Nation, et al. v. U.S. Forest Serv.*, 479 F.2d 1024 (9th Cir. 2007) (vacated by *en banc* decision).
16. *Navajo Nation, et al. v. U.S. Forest Serv.*, 535 F.3d 1058 (9th Cir. 2008) (*en banc*). On October 5, 2008, the Ninth Circuit issued an order staying the decision to allow the Indian tribes to seek a writ of certiorari to the United States Supreme Court. As of the date of this writing, no petition for a writ of certiorari had been filed.
17. *Id.* at 1063.
18. *Id.*
19. *Id.*
20. *Id.*
21. *Id.* at 1070 n.12; *id.* at 1078 n.25.
22. *Id.* at 1097.
23. *Id.* at 1114.
24. *Snoqualmie Indian Tribe v. FERC*, 545 F.3d 1207 (9thCir. 2008).
25. *Id.* at 1213.
26. *Comanche Nation v. United States*, No. 08-849, 2008 WL 4426621. (W.D. Okla., Sept. 23, 2008) (Federal Reporter citation unavailable).
27. *Id.*, Slip Op. at 2.
28. *Id.*, Slip Op. at 6.
29. *Id.*, Slip Op. at 6-7.
30. *Id.*, Slip Op. at 12, 28.
31. *Id.*, Slip Op. at 29.
32. *The Access Fund v. USDA*, 499 F.3d 1036 (9th Cir. 2007).
33. *Id.* at 1039.
34. H.R. 6370 (signed into law Oct. 12, 2008).
35. S. 1255, 110th Cong. (2007).

Marine Environment

• • •

Section Editor: Nathaniel R. Orpen

The Griffin

In September of 1679, a crew of six Frenchmen set sail from an island near what is now Green Bay, Wisconsin in a crudely made vessel packed with 6,000 pounds of fur and other goods. The 40- to 60-foot sailboat was named *The Griffin*, and was built by the French explorer Robert Cavelier, Sieur de la Salle near Niagara Falls. *The Griffin* is believed to be the first European trading ship to sail the waters of Lake Huron and Lake Michigan. Packed with its fur cargo and a six-man crew, *The Griffin* was caught in a violent storm and sank while sailing across northern Lake Michigan on its way back to Niagara.

In 2004, Great Lakes Exploration Group, LLC (GLEG), a private marine exploration company, found a wreck in the cold and murky depths of northern Lake Michigan. GLEG believes that this wreck is *The Griffin*. A bow tip and mussel-covered mast can be seen protruding from the bottom of the lake, but investigation of the wreck has been difficult because visibility at the site is very poor.[1] Since the discovery, GLEG has refused to disclose the location of the wreck to protect its legal claim and to avoid possible damage from sport divers and looters.

On June 7, 2004, GLEG filed an *in rem* admiralty action in the United States District Court for the Western District of Michigan to request that they be appointed guardian of the wreck, and that the court arrest the vessel in order to establish jurisdiction in federal court. The district court found that

GLEG had not met the pleading requirements because it had not included the wreck's precise location and therefore had not described the wreck with the requisite "reasonable particularity."

GLEG filed an amended complaint, but before the court could act, the State of Michigan intervened, claiming ownership of the wreck under the Abandoned Shipwreck Act (ASA).[2] Under the ASA, the federal government asserts title to all abandoned wrecks that are (1) embedded in state submerged lands; (2) embedded in state-protected coralline formations; or (3) on state submerged lands and included in or determined eligible for inclusion in the National Register. Title to such wrecks are then, by means of a legal fiction, transferred to the state in or on whose submerged lands the shipwreck is located. The district court ordered GLEG to disclose the location of the wreck so that Michigan could investigate whether the wreck is "embedded." GLEG refused to identify the precise location of the wreck out of a fear that Michigan would try to obtain actual possession of *The Griffin*. With legal possession, Michigan could invoke the Eleventh Amendment to take away federal jurisdiction, which would prevent GLEG from obtaining salvage rights in federal court. The Eleventh Amendment interacts with the ASA to bar federal jurisdiction over a salvor's *in rem* admiralty action if a state has actual possession of a wreck or has otherwise satisfied the title requirements under the ASA. When GLEG failed to disclose the location of the wreck, the district court dismissed the claim without prejudice. GLEG appealed to the Sixth Circuit Court of Appeals.

The Sixth Circuit held that GLEG did not need to disclose the location of the wreck until federal jurisdiction was perfected to support its claim. Federal jurisdiction in an admiralty case involving a shipwreck is often obtained by the court seizing the *res* through issuing a warrant of arrest over a specific physical part of the wreck, such as an artifact brought up from the wreck. The arrest protects the salvage rights of the salvor by securing possession of the wreck with the court.

While legal ownership of the wreck is being worked out in the legal system, GLEG is trying to authenticate the find as *The Griffin*. GLEG has hired an expert from the Field Museum in Chicago to visit the find, and in July 2008, submitted a sliver of wood from the wreck for testing.

GLEG has predicted that France may desire to file a claim, but to date France remains uninvolved. The wreck's value is mostly historical.

"The Black Swan"

In May 2007, an American salvage company, Odyssey Marine Exploration, Ltd., announced that they had discovered a shipwreck off the coast of Portugal. Odyssey claimed to have recovered 500,000 silver coins from the find, but refused to comment on the mysterious wreck's identity, referring to it only as "The Black Swan." The value of this find (estimated at $500 million) has attracted the attention of media across the world, and has caused both Spain and Peru to contest the salvage rights action filed by Odyssey in U.S. district court.

Spain and Peru believe that the "Black Swan" is really the *Nuestra Señora de las Mercedes*, a Spanish frigate that sank off the coast of Portugal in 1804. The location of the "Black Swan" wreck, 180 nautical miles west of the Strait of Gibraltar, is consistent with this theory. The *Mercedes* and three other Spanish frigates—the *Fama*, the *Medea*, and the *Santa Clara*—were returning to the port city of Cádiz, laden with gold and silver coins from Peru. On October 5, 1804, the *Mercedes* and its sister ships encountered British war vessels off the coast of Portugal at Cape Santa Maria. A battle ensued, and the *Mercedes* was destroyed by British cannon fire and sank to the bottom of the Atlantic. The three remaining Spanish ships were captured, brought to England, and conscripted into service with the British Royal Navy. Two months later, Spain entered the Napoleonic War by declaring war on Great Britain.

Spain has now entered a modern-day legal battle over what could be the same ship that brought them to war over 200 years ago. In April 2007, Odyssey filed an admiralty lawsuit in the United States District Court for the Middle District of Florida to arrest "The "Black Swan" and establish federal jurisdiction for its salvage claim. Convinced that the wreck is of Spanish origin, and is probably the *Mercedes*, Spain filed a verified claim in the case in May 2007. Spain asserts that its kingdom has never expressly abandoned any of its vessels lost at sea, and that the wreck and its cargo remain the property of the Spanish government. In January 2008, the court ordered Odyssey to share its information concerning the wreck with Spain, but also ordered that Spain must keep the records confidential.

The Spanish government is taking its claim to "The Black Swan" very seriously. In 2007, Spanish gunboats twice temporarily detained Odyssey's salvage vessels in the Mediterranean, and the Spanish media ran an editorial likening Odyssey to plundering pirates. Spain has announced that no compensation will be paid for recovered items, arguing that no treasure hunters have salvage rights in any Spanish wreck, and that anything recovered must be returned to Spain.

More recently, a third player has emerged. In August 2008, the Republic of Peru filed a Verified Conditional Claim in the "Black Swan" case. Peru's position is that the gold and silver were likely made of metal taken by Spaniards from the Incas, and that the treasure rightfully belongs to the modern-day government of Peru as part of its cultural heritage. Peru's claim seeks further information about the wreck and its treasure. This is an especially noteworthy event as this is the first time that Peru has come forward to claim cargo previously taken by Spain.

In September 2008, Spain filed a motion to dismiss, arguing that the district court lacked jurisdiction over "The Black Swan." Odyssey filed its response on November 17, 2008, and asserted that sovereign immunity does not apply to the "Black Swan" site or its cargo, even if it is determined to be the *Mercedes*. Additionally, Odyssey argues that almost all of the cargo aboard "The Black Swan" was privately owned commercial property, and that its recovery was made without disturbing the wreck. It is the opinion of Odyssey's legal counsel that even if a legitimate claim to the treasure is made, Odyssey will still be entitled to a "significant majority" of the recovery.

UNESCO Convention on the Protection of the Underwater Cultural Heritage

The Convention on the Protection of the Underwater Cultural Heritage enters into force on January 2, 2009. The Convention, which was adopted by the United Nations Educational, Scientific and Cultural Organization (UNESCO) at the 2001 General Conference, binds States Parties to the preservation and protection of underwater cultural heritage, such as shipwrecks and ruins. The treaty was triggered into effect through its ratification by twenty States Parties, the last being Barbados on October 2, 2008.[3]

The States Parties will hold their first meeting March 26–27, 2009, at UNESCO Headquarters in Paris, France. In accordance with Article 23, the States Parties will meet no less than once every two years thereafter as convened by the Director-General of UNESCO. At the March 2009 meeting, the States Parties are expected to adopt rules of procedure, further determine the functions and responsibilities of States Parties, and establish a Scientific and Technical Advisory Board to assist the States Parties in the implementation of the Convention's "rules concerning activities directed at underwater cultural heritage" (explained below) and other matters. While these matters of procedure remain to be decided, that is not to say that the Convention lacks form or substance.

The Convention is based on four central principles: (1) the obligation to preserve underwater cultural heritage, (2) a preference for *in situ* ("in the original place") preservation, (3) preventing commercial exploitation, and (4) cooperation among States to protect cultural property, to promote training in underwater archaeology, and to encourage public access to underwater heritage and raise awareness of the importance of underwater cultural heritage.[4] These principles can be found throughout the Convention, but also take the explicit form of rules in the Annex.

The Annex of the Convention contains the aforementioned "rules concerning activities directed at underwater cultural heritage": thirty-six rules governing all manner of human undertakings upon submerged cultural heritage sites. These rules cover project planning, safety precautions, documentation and reporting, funding, the competence of project directors, and many other details. Many of these rules reflect practices that are widely recognized by archaeologists. For example, Part I, Rule 2 of the Annex bars the commercial sale of artifacts; Rule 4 mandates nondestructive techniques for surveying and recovery; Rule 5 prohibits unnecessary disturbance of human remains; Rule 6 ensures proper recording of cultural, historical, and archaeological information; and Rule 7 promotes public access to sites unless it is incompatible with protection and management concerns.[5] Not all of the Convention's provisions convey such assertiveness, however.

For what progress the Convention and its strengthened protections for underwater cultural heritage offer, it is mindful of its place with respect to more established international legal authority. Under Article 3, the Convention describes itself as subservient to international law and the United Nations Convention on the Law of the Sea, proclaiming that it should not be interpreted to "prejudice the rights, jurisdiction and duties" of nations under existing international laws. Additionally, Article 2 specifically disallows the use of the Convention's provisions as claims against the jurisdiction or laws of sovereign nations.[6]

Over time, this deferential position will be judged by the importance of the Convention: an overly cautious approach for compiling ratification instruments, or a reflection of patience for the Convention's gradual expansion into broader influence. Regardless, the Convention's coming to force will positively impact the way that the twenty State Parties manage underwater cultural property. The Convention is a good effort toward filling existing gaps in international law with protections for underwater cultural heritage, but its potential will not be realized until more States agree to be bound by its terms.

Defining Abandonment Under The Abandoned Shipwreck Act[7]

As explained earlier, under the Abandoned Shipwreck Act (ASA),[8] the federal government takes title to all abandoned wrecks embedded in state submerged lands or state-protected coralline formations, or located on state submerged lands and included in or determined eligible for inclusion in the National Register. Interestingly, the ASA—despite the use of the word in its title—does not define what is meant by "abandoned."[9] This lack of guidance has resulted in litigation, and was finally addressed but not solved, more than a decade after the ASA's enactment, by the Supreme Court in *California v. Deep Sea Research, Inc.*[10] The Court held that the definition of abandonment supplied by maritime law should be used in ASA inquiries to determine the disposition of shipwrecks.[11] Unfortunately, this decision did not solve the quandary, as maritime law has struggled with differing abandonment standards for many years. The question of abandonment has caused confusion and controversy among the courts as they attempt to honor maritime law precedent while settling present ownership disputes.

Below is an explanation of the competing theories of abandonment: express and inferential. It is this editor's opinion that the inferential abandonment standard is preferential. Justifications for this conclusion will follow an explanation of the two theories.

Abandonment has been described as the act of "leaving or deserting property without hope of recovering it and without the intention of returning to it."[12] Under modern maritime law, abandonment is demonstrated by proving "(1) intent to abandon, and (2) physical acts carrying that intent into effect."[13] The difficulty courts have encountered in applying this test is that it is unclear whether express proof or inferential proof will suffice to prove intent to abandon.

The present maritime law test for abandonment grew out of the historic view that "[w]hen articles are lost at sea the title of the owner in them remains, even if they be found floating on the surface or cast upon the shore."[14] As a result, the law has been hesitant to assume abandonment of property involuntarily taken from the control of an owner.[15] Yet, in circumstances where enough evidence supports an inference that the owner intended to abandon the property, some courts are willing to find that the property has been abandoned.[16] As a result, courts now struggle to articulate clear and consistent standards for determining abandonment.[17]

There are two competing standards for classifying a shipwreck as abandoned. The first and strictest standard is the traditional view that original owners of property lost at sea maintain good title to the property until they expressly renounce ownership of title in the property. This reasoning is referred to as the express abandonment standard.[18] Under express abandonment, an example of sufficient proof would be a written document that expressly states the owner's intention to abandon the property.[19] The second and more lenient standard allows the traditional presumption of continued ownership to be overcome by marshalling enough facts and circumstantial evidence to establish an inference of abandonment.[20] This is referred to as the inferential abandonment, or implied abandonment, standard.[21] Whether enough circumstantial evidence has been demonstrated by the finder to support an inferential abandonment is a question for the finder of fact, and is made on a case-by-case basis.

Under either test, abandonment is a question of fact.[22] Most circuit courts addressing abandonment under the ASA have concluded that the "clear and convincing" evidentiary standard should be applied.[23] The Sixth Circuit held that each factor did not need to be proved by clear and convincing evidence individually.[24] Rather, the overarching question of abandonment needed to be proved through clear and convincing evidence.[25] This distinction between the evidentiary standard for abandonment and the standard for its individual factors is explained by the Sixth Circuit through a discussion of lapse of time and nonuse. "[N]either lapse of time nor an owner's failure to return, standing by themselves, will necessarily establish abandonment. Instead, these may be a part of a combination of facts that may support a finding of abandonment if, taken together, they clearly and convincingly show that abandonment occurred."[26]

Additionally, the Sixth Circuit instructed that courts should not engage in balancing tests wherein the probability of theories supporting ownership would be weighed against a theory of abandonment.[27] Rather, under the ASA, the burden is put upon the state to prove clearly and convincingly that the owner abandoned the ship.[28]

As was explained above, there are two standards for proving abandonment, express and inferential. To this editor's knowledge, all circuit courts that have heard an abandoned shipwreck case have recognized the express abandonment test, but there is a split among the circuit courts as to whether abandonment can also be shown by inference. The Fourth, Fifth, and Eleventh Circuits clearly allow only the express abandonment test.[29] The Sixth and Ninth Circuits have recognized the inferential abandonment standard.[30] The Second Circuit, in *Dluhos v. Floating and Abandoned Vessel, Known as "New York,"* expressly declined to decide upon the validity of inferential abandonment, and other circuit courts have not addressed the question.[31]

Express Abandonment

In *Columbus-America Discovery Group, Inc. v. Unidentified, Wrecked and Abandoned Sailing Vessel* (*Columbus III*), the Fourth Circuit refused to find property to have been abandoned absent an express declaration of intent to abandon made by the owner.[32] The court held that abandonment requires a voluntary, clear, and unmistakable affirmative act indicating renunciation of ownership.[33] Similarly, the Eleventh Circuit has held that to effectuate abandonment, the owner must leave the property "with a positive intent to part with ownership, and without coercion or pressure."[34]

Despite the stringency of this express rule, the Fourth Circuit allowed an exception for abandonment to be proven by inference when dealing with ancient shipwrecks where no owner steps forward to claim ownership.[35] The court clearly explained, however, that even for ancient shipwrecks, once a previous owner steps forward to claim title, inferential proof will no longer suffice, and the express abandonment standard is applied.[36] The Fourth Circuit reviewed its *Columbus II* decision in 2000 and declined to reexamine the issue of abandonment, leaving its earlier holding intact.[37] This exception has also been recognized by the First Circuit, which reasoned that inferential abandonment is appropriate when a shipwreck is "so long lost that time can be presumed to have eroded any realistic claim of original title."[38] Rationale for this exception is easy to comprehend, as is explained by the Fifth Circuit: "[d]isposition of a wrecked vessel whose very location has been lost for centuries as though its owner were still in existence stretches a fiction to absurd lengths."[39]

In *Sea Hunt, Inc. v. The Unidentified Shipwrecked Vessel or Vessels*, a 2000 case, the Fourth Circuit applied the express abandonment test, but was unable to consider inferential abandonment because the case involved a sunken ship that had served under the Spanish navy, and the court was required to follow a treaty from 1902 between the United States and Spain that required express abandonment:[40]

> Appellees' attempts to glean a broad inferential abandonment standard from circuit law overlooks one salient point—none of the cases they rely upon involved an original sovereign owner's claim to its shipwrecked vessels. To adopt an inferential abandonment standard in this context would casually divest sovereigns of ships which sank against their will and to which they still lay claim.[41]

As the court references, there are compelling policy reasons to treat vessels owned by a sovereign nation differently from vessels owned by private individuals.[42]

Inferential Abandonment

Some courts have rejected an exclusive use of express abandonment, finding that traditional maritime law authority and good public policy also necessitate the recognition of an inferential abandonment standard.[43] Inferential abandonment is proven when circumstantial evidence creates an inference of intent to abandon.[44]

Although there is no definitive test for inferential abandonment, the Sixth Circuit looked to eight factors in its 2001 decision, *Fairport International Exploration, Inc. v. The Shipwrecked Vessel Known as The Captain Lawrence* (*Fairport VI*): (1) whether the wreck occurred recently; (2) the depth of the water in which the wreck lies; (3) the technological feasibility of recovery; (4) any records regarding the ship after it sank, such as value estimates, or presence of a write-off for "total loss"; (5) whether there is an insurance policy on the ship; (6) whether lifesaving assistance was accepted or declined; (7) whether the owner ever attempted to salvage the wreck; and (8) whether the owner died with or without a will.[45] In addition to these eight factors, the *Fairport VI* court also considered whether the owner ever intended to return to salvage the wreck—a query somewhat related to factors (3) and (7).[46] In discussing this additional question, the court looked to the affordability of recovery attempts and the potential concern for secreting the wreck from others.[47] This secreting theory lends itself to a line of reasoning that is impossible to prove, for if the owner intended to recover the wreck, yet kept this fact secret to protect its existence and whereabouts, it is likely that no proof of intent would survive the owner's death. Perhaps for this reason, the court did not seriously address this argument. Under factor (2), depth of the water, the court also considered the degree to which the wreck has been scattered over time by natural physical forces, such as underwater currents.[48]

Different circuit courts have considered other factors as well. Two common considerations are lapse of time and nonuse. While lapse of time alone or a lone showing of nonuse by the owner will not support a finding of abandonment, these two facts combined with other supporting evidence can demonstrate abandonment.[49] The Fourth Circuit, in *Columbus-America Discovery Group v. Atlantic Mutual Ins. Co.*, ("*Columbus III*") held that an owner's nonuse of the property over a long period of time coupled with the owner's failure to act or assert any claim to the property are, by themselves, insufficient to prove abandonment.[50] Nevertheless, these two factors when coupled with other evidence can be used to add weight to an inference of abandonment.

In its examination of a shipwreck case under the ASA, a district court in New York considered yet more factors in its determination of abandonment. The court found it relevant that the association that owned a wrecked tugboat failed to "return to the tug" after the wreck allegedly caused environmental damage.[51] This indicated to the court that the owner intended to establish that it had abandoned the wreck out of a fear of potential litigation.[52] Also considered by the court was whether the owning association still existed, and whether its failure to return to the wrecked tugboat, even though it was in an easily accessible body of water, indicated intent to abandon.[53]

Any of the above factors can be used for abandonment determinations under the inferential test because there is no set list of factors that must be satisfied. That the factors outlined above have been considered by courts in examinations of inferential abandonment validates their use for future inquiries but does not discourage the use of other considerations likely to assist a determination in future cases.

Conclusion

There exists incongruence between congressional intent and a strict application of the express abandonment standard under the ASA. An inferential abandonment standard ensures a broader application of the ASA, and furthers Congress' intended policies of protection and preservation because more shipwrecks would fall under the control of the ASA. Therefore, the logical conclusion is that implied abandonment should be allowed under the ASA. The Sixth Circuit explains: "[c]ommon sense makes readily apparent that the statute did not contemplate a court's requiring express abandonment; such explicit action is obviously rare indeed, and application of such a rule would render the ASA a virtual nullity."

Inferential abandonment is the better and more responsible standard to apply under the ASA, for it will give government control over a greater number of shipwrecks. Federal and state governments are already equipped with (and have the means to obtain more of) the resources needed to deal with the many different and competing interests the public has in shipwrecks. Under an exclusive use of the express abandonment standard, fewer shipwrecks would transfer to the government, and therefore more historical artifacts could slip out of the public's view and into the private hands of treasure hunters and private collectors. It is possible that important pieces of historical significance would end up in private homes, hidden away from researchers and the public. It is a better public policy to preserve and protect our past, and to ensure access for all to the artifacts of world history. For these reasons, the inferential abandonment standard is the better interpretation of abandonment under the ASA.

Notes

1. A GLEG diver described bumping into a portion of the wreck on one dive because visibility was only a few inches.
2. 43 U.S.C. §§ 2101-2106 (2008).
3. The ratifying "States Parties" have consented to be bound by the Convention; they are, in order of ratification, Panama, Bulgaria, Croatia, Spain, Libyan Arab Jamahiriya, Nigeria, Lithuania, Mexico, Paraguay, Portugal, Ecuador, Ukraine, Lebanon, Saint Lucia, Romania, Cambodia, Cuba, Montenegro, Slovenia, and Barbados. Nonparty States and territories can become States Parties to the Convention by their own instrument of ratification, acceptance, approval, or accession. Three months after the deposit of such an instrument with UNESCO, the Convention will take effect for that State.
4. UNESCO, *Convention on the Protection of the Underwater Cultural Heritage will enter into force in January 2009*, Press Release No. 97-2008, available at http://portal.unesco.org/culture/en/ev.php-URL_ID=37965&URL_DO=DO_TOPIC&URL_SECTION=201.html (last visited Dec. 11, 2008).

5. UNESCO Convention on the Protection of the Underwater Cultural Heritage, Annex, I, Nov. 2, 2001, http://portal.unesco.org/en/ev.php-URL_ID=13520&URL_DO=DO_TOPIC&URL_SECTION=201.html
6. UNESCO Convention on the Protection of the Underwater Cultural Heritage, art. 2(10), Nov. 2, 2001, http://portal.unesco.org/en/ev.php-URL_ID=13520&URL_DO=DO_TOPIC&URL_SECTION=201.html
7. Below I have used abbreviations or nicknames for cases as they have been cross-cited within one another. These names often refer to the wrecked vessel from the case. However, the roman numerals following such abbreviations are mostly of my own designation, and were my best attempt at organizing the dizzying array of appeals and remands with respect to each case.
8. 43 U.S.C. §§ 2101-2106 (2008).
9. "Embedded" is defined by the ASA in 43 U.S.C. § 2102(a): "the term 'embedded' means firmly affixed in the submerged lands or in coralline formations such that the use of tools of excavation is required in order to move the bottom sediments to gain access to the shipwreck, its cargo, and any part thereof."
10. 523 U.S. 491. (1998).
11. *Id.* at 508. The Supreme Court remanded: "we decline to resolve whether the *Brother Jonathan* is abandoned within the meaning of the ASA. We leave that issue for reconsideration on remand, with the clarification that the meaning of 'abandoned' under the ASA conforms with its meaning under admiralty law." *Id.* While the precise words used by the Supreme Court are "admiralty law," Black's Law Dictionary lists "admiralty law" as a synonym of "maritime law," and most, if not all of the cases cited in this section refer to "maritime law" cases for precedent on the issue of abandonment. Black's Law Dictionary 988 (8th ed. 2004). Therefore, I will refer to the case-law body of precedent I cite as "maritime law" throughout this section.
12. *Columbus-America Discovery Group, Inc. v. Unidentified, Wrecked and Abandoned Sailing Vessel*, 742 F.Supp. 1327, 1335 (E.D. Va., 1990) (hereinafter *Columbus II*) (citing 3A *Benedict on Admiralty* § 134 (7th Ed., 1980).
13. *Zych v. The Unidentified, Wrecked and Abandoned Vessel, Believed to be the SB "Lady Elgin,"* 755 F.Supp. 213, 214 (N.D. Ill. 1990) (hereinafter *Lady Elgin*) (citing *Chemical Sales Co. v. Diamond Chemical Co.*, 766 F.2d 364, 368 (8th Cir. 1985); *Columbus II*, 742 F.Supp. at 1335; *Hoelzer v. City of Stamford*, 722 F.Supp. 1106, 1111 (S.D. N.Y. 1989); *State of Idaho v. Oregon Short Line R.R. Co.*, 617 F.Supp. 213, 217 (D. Idaho 1985)).
14. *The Akaba*, 54 F. 197, 200 (4th Cir. 1893); *Sea Hunt, Inc. v. The Unidentified Shipwrecked Vessel or Vessels*, 221 F.3d 634, 641 (4th Cir. 2000).
15. *Columbus III*, 974 F.2d 450, 467-68 (4th Cir. 1992).
16. *See Fairport Intern. Exploration, Inc. v. The Captain Lawrence*, 245 F.3d 857, 862 (6th Cir. 2001) (hereinafter *Fairport VI*).

17. Kevin Berean, Sea Hunt, Inc. v. Unidentified Shipwrecked Vessel or Vessels: How The Fourth Circuit Rocked the Boat, 67 BROOK. L. REV. 1249, 1253 (2002).
18. Seena Foster, Annotation, *Validity, application and construction of Abandoned Shipwreck Act of 1987 (43 U.S.C.A. §§ 2101 et seq.)*, 163 A.L.R. Fed. 421, § 4[a] (2007).
19. *Columbus III*, 974 F.2d at 461 ("The proof that need be shown must be 'strong . . . , such as the owner's express declaration abandoning title.'" (citing T. Schoenbaum, *Admiralty and Maritime Law* § 15-7, at 512 (1987))); *See Fairport VI*, 245 F.3d at 865 (though this is an implied abandonment case, a written casualty report was considered by the court in determining abandonment because it included a section wherein the ship was written off as a total loss).
20. *Lady Elgin*, 755 F.Supp. 213, 214 (N.D. Ill. 1990) (citing *U.S. v. Sylvester*, 848 F.2d 520, 525 (5th Cir. 1988); *Katsaris v. U.S.*, 684 F.2d 758, 762 (11th Cir. 1982); *Columbus II*, 742 F.Supp. 1327, 1335 (E.D. Va., 1990)).
21. Foster, *supra* note 63, at § 4[b].
22. *Fairport VI*, 245 F.3d 857, 862 (6th Cir. 2001).
23. *Fairport Intern. Exploration, Inc. v. The Shipwrecked Vessel Known as The Captain Lawrence*, 177 F.3d 491, 499 (6th Cir. 1999) (hereinafter *Fairport III*); *See Columbus III*, 974 F.2d 450 461(4th Cir. 1992) (citing *Lady Elgin*, 755 F.supp. at 214 ("A finding of abandonment must be supported by strong and convincing evidence")).
24. *Fairport VI*, 245 F.3d at 860 n.2, 862.
25. *Id.* at 860 n.2.
26. *Id.* at 862.
27. *Fairport VI*, 245 F.3d 857, 863 (6th Cir. 2001).
28. *Id.*
29. *See Columbus III*, 974 F.2d 450 (4th Cir. 1992); *Treasure Salvors I*, 569 F.2d 330 (5th Cir. 1978); *Katsaris v. U.S.*, 684 F.2d 758 (11th Cir. 1982).
30. *See Fairport II*, 105 F.3d 1078 (6th Cir. 1997); *Deep Sea, Inc. v. The Brother Jonathan*, 102 F.3d 379 (9th Cir. 1996) (hereinafter *Brother Jonathan II*).
31. *Dluhos v. Floating and Abandoned Vessel, Known as New York*, 162 F.3d 63, 74 (2nd Cir., 1998) ("This case, however, does not provide us with an opportunity to reexamine the blanket application of the nonabandonment fiction.").
32. 974 F.2d 450, 461, 464 (4th Cir. 1992).
33. *Id.* at 461 (citing *The Port Hunter*, 6 F. Supp. 1009, 1011 (D. Mass. 1934)).
34. *Katsaris*, 684 F.2d at 762.
35. *Columbus III*, 974 F.2d at 461, 464-65.
36. *Id.*
37. *Columbus-America Discovery Group v. Atlantic Mutual Insurance Co.*, 203 F.3d 291, 304 (4th Cir. 2000) (hereinafter *Columbus VIII*) ("Our en banc court has declined to reexamine our panel holding in 974 F.2d 450 [*Columbus III*] as to the proof necessary for abandonment, although two members of the panel favored reexamination.").

38. *Martha's Vineyard Scuba Headquarters, Inc. v. Unidentified, Wrecked and Abandoned Steam Vessel*, 833 F.2d 1059, 1065 (1st Cir. 1987).
39. *Treasure Salvors I*, 569 F.2d 330, 337 (5th Cir. 1978).
40. 221 F.3d 634 (4th Cir. 2000) (The treaty said that Spanish vessels and U.S. vessels may only be abandoned by express acts). Under Art. IV, §3 of the Constitution: "Congress shall have power to dispose of and make all needful Rules and regulations respecting the Territory or other Property belonging to the United States." Therefore under our Constitution, implied abandonment is not allowed regarding federal property, only an express act authorized by Congress can abandon federal property.
41. *Sea Hunt* 221 F.3d 634, 642 (4th Cir. 2000).
42. *Id.* at 647 (By extending Spain a presumption of non-abandonment, the U.S. is insuring that its "sunken vessels and lost crews are treated as sovereign ships and honored graves, and are not subject to exploration, or exploitation, by private parties seeking treasures of the sea.").
43. *Fairport III*, 177 F.3d 491, 499 (6th Cir. 1999) (citing *Fairport II*, 105 F.3d 1078, 1085 (6th Cir. 1997)).
44. *Deep Sea Research, Inc. v. Brother Jonathan*, 89 F.3d 680, 688 (9th Cir. 1996) (hereinafter *Brother Jonathan I*); *See Lady Elgin*, 755 F. Supp. 213, 214 (N.D. Ill. 1990) ("A finding of abandonment must be supported by strong and convincing evidence, but it may, and often must, be determined on the basis of circumstantial evidence.").
45. 245 F.3d 857, 865 (6th Cir. 2001).
46. *Id.* at 860.
47. *Id.*
48. *Id.* at 866.
49. *See Sea Hunt*, 221 F.3d 634, 647 (4th Cir. 2000) (passage of time alone is not sufficient to support abandonment); *Lady Elgin*, 755 F. Supp. at 216 (court held that absence of any salvage attempts during 130 year period did not establish abandonment, especially when such efforts would have had minimal chance for success); *Hatteras, Inc. v. The U.S.S. Hatteras,* 1984 A.M.C. 1094, 1097 (S.D. Tex. 1981) (nonuse alone does not establish abandonment); *Wiggins v. 1100 Tons, More or Less, of Italian Marble*, 186 F.Supp. 452, 456 (E.D. Va. 1960) (lapse of time and nonuse are insufficient by themselves, but when coupled with a failure to attempt recovery efforts an inference of abandonment was found).
50. *Columbus III*, 974 F.2d 450, 462 (4th Cir. 1992) (citing *Hatteras,* 1984 A.M.C. at 1097 n. 5); *See also Wiggins*, 186 F. Supp. at 456.
51. *Trueman v. Historic Steamtug New York*, 120 F. Supp.2d 228, 234-35 (N.D.N.Y., 2000).
52. *Id.*
53. *Id.*

Museum

• • •

Section Editor: Lucille A. Roussin

Introduction

The year 2008 might be called "the year of the museum," a year in which many museum policies changed regarding both accession and deaccession of works of art. The legal issues in museum acquisitions of stolen antiquities and art looted during World War II continued to be in the headlines of international news.

Museum Policies and Politics

Both the American Association of Museums (AAM) and the Association of Art Museum Directors (AAMD) issued new policy statements on the acquisition of antiquities in June and July, respectively. The AAMD is the leading professional organization of museum directors from the United States, Canada, and Mexico. Their new guidelines recognize the 1970 UNESCO Convention on the Means of Prohibiting and Preventing the Illicit Import and Export and Transfer of Ownership of Cultural Property as "providing the most pertinent threshold date for the application of rigorous standards to the acquisition of archaeological material and ancient art."[1] The guidelines are not binding on member museums, but several museums have issued statements indicating that they will follow the AAMD's recommendations. One important change in the language is the use of the term "country of modern discovery" rather than "country of origin," which has given rise to a whole polemic on what "country of origin" means. Unfortunately, the term "country of modern discovery" is modified by the word "probable," which might give rise to whole new qualifications.

The guidelines state that a museum should not normally acquire a work unless research substantiates that the object was out of its probable country of modern discovery before 1970, or was legally exported from its country of modern discovery after 1970. Such research should include thorough provenance research and an effort to obtain written documentation, including import and export documents. Such documentation should also be required not only of sellers, but donors as well. There is, however, a major loophole that allows museums to acquire antiquities when there is no provenance information if they deem that the "benefit of collecting, presenting, and preserving the work in trust for the educational benefit of present and future generations" outweighs the harm of acquiring a possibly looted antiquity.[2] The AAMD has also posted an Object Registry on its website, which is searchable by a number of rubrics, including Cultures, Institutions, Object Types, Countries, and Materials and Techniques. The Registry, which should be a useful tool, requires museums to post an image and all information about the work, including provenance and "all facts relevant to the decision to acquire it."[3] The new guidelines have been met with approval by the Archaeological Institute of America, which has expressed the hope that decisions by museums to acquire antiquities will take into consideration "the rights of the country of origin and the potential harms to the world's cultural heritage."[4]

The AAM's *Standards Regarding Archaeological Material and Ancient Art* were approved by the AAM Board of Directors and went into effect as of August 2008. These standards go beyond the requirement that museums "comply with all applicable U.S. law, including treaties and international conventions of which the U.S. is a party, governing ownership and title, import and other issues critical to acquisitions decisions."[5] The AAM Standards include a provision that states that "beyond the requirements of U.S. law, museums should not acquire any object that, to the knowledge of the museum, has been illegally exported from its country of modern discovery or the country where it was last legally owned."[6] The Standards also require documentation that the object was out of the probable country of modern discovery by November 17, 1970, the date on which the 1970 UNESCO was signed. As in the AAMD guidelines, there is a loophole allowing acquisition of unprovenanced antiquities, only requiring that the museum acquiring such an object be "transparent about why this is an appropriate decision in alignment with the institution's collection policy and applicable ethical codes."[7] The AAM Standards again go a step further than the AAM guideline in stating that claims should be respectfully and diligently addressed and that each claim, "whether based on ethical or legal considerations, should be considered on its own merits." They also suggest that such claims should be resolved through voluntary discussions with the claimant or facilitated by a third party.[8]

The news from the University of Pennsylvania Museum of Archaeology and Anthropology is mixed. On the benefit side, the Museum announced the creation of The Penn Cultural Heritage Center, which will be dedicated to education and outreach on issues of cultural heritage. Dr. Richard M. Leventhal, Professor of Anthropology at the University, as well as former Williams Director of Penn Museums, is founder and director of the new Center. The Center's initiatives include education and outreach programming for diverse audiences, offering law enforcement, customs officers, lawyers, policymakers, as well as outreach to the general public. On the international level the Center is already consulting with agencies in Mali, Montenegro, and Honduras. The Center will also sponsor conferences and publications. The goals of this new Center are certainly timely and much needed—as Dr. Leventhal said, "In a rapidly changing global world cultural heritage has become an important topic, playing an increasingly critical role in the identity politics of communities, the economic growth of world tourism, and the rules and regulations governing the international antiquities trade."[9]

On the disappointing side of the news, from the University of Pennsylvania Museum there are reports that the Museum has fired 18 research fellows and effectively shut down the Museum's Science Center. The Center is renowned for the breadth and quality of its research scientists and their contributions to the field of archaeology. The importance of the Center Newsletter as a vehicle for the dissemination of the results of scientific analysis is considered crucial to the field.[10]

The Los Angeles County Museum, the Mingei International Museum in San Diego and Escondido, California, the Pacific Asia Museum in Pasadena, California, and the Bowers Museum in Santa Ana, California were all caught in an investigation by the Internal Revenue Service, Immigration and Customs Enforcement, and the National Park Service into stolen antiquities from Burma, Thailand, and China and tax fraud.[11] Among the antiquities are many from the Ban Chiang Culture in northeast Thailand, named a World Heritage

Site in 1992, and considered to be among the most important sites in Southeast Asia.[12] The investigation, carried out by an undercover agent, involved criminal activity by Jonathan and Cari Markell, who were accused of purchasing, transporting, receiving, and selling Chinese and Thai antiquities that they knew to be stolen from those countries. Mrs. Markell admitted to an undercover agent that they knew the antiquities they were importing were stolen and that "Chinese millionaires were trying to buy back their history but she had no compunction at all because the Communists who run the country are not nice people."[13] Indeed, the case has all the makings of a good movie.

The couple were charged with violating the California Penal Code; the Archaeological Resources Protection Act; Thailand's Act on Ancient Monuments, Antiques, Objects of Art and National Museums; the 1982 People's Republic of China on the Protection of Cultural Relics; Burmese Sanctions Regulations (Executive Order 13310, issued on July 28, 2003); and Conspiracy to Aid and Assist in the Preparation of False Tax Returns (18 U.S.C. §371 and 26 U.S.C. §7206(2)). The museums are involved only to the extent that many of the stolen antiquities were donated to them by the Markells, their agents, and clients under false tax declarations. An individual taxpayer who claims a charitable deduction for donations of property valued between $500 and $5,000 must report the donation on his or her tax return. Any gifts of property valued at $5,000 or more must have received a qualified appraisal. Part of the scheme involved appraisals of the antiquities to be donated to the museums at values below $5,000.[14] Under the search warrant, the federal authorities were granted permission to seize all records from the Los Angeles County Museum from 1998 to the present pertaining to the acquisition of antiquities from the Ban Chiang Culture obtained from the Markells, their relatives, or clients.[15]

In other Los Angeles museum news the Museum of Contemporary Art (MOCA), in a financial crisis, was in danger of having to close its doors after having spent much of its endowment over the last eight years. The Board of MOCA declined to accept an offer to merge with the Los Angeles County Museum of Art, and has instead accepted a $30 million bailout from art collector and philanthropist Eli Broad. Under the terms of the bailout the Eli and Edythe Broad Foundation will match contributions to MOCA's endowment up to $15 million and give an additional $3 million a year for five years for exhibitions. The MOCA Trustees have also pledged more than $20 million since the museum's financial difficulties became known. Further terms of the agreement include a provision that the museum must restrain operating expenses within an annual budget between $13 million and $16 million. The museum must strengthen its board of trustees, engage investment advisers to manage its endowment, and cooperate fully with the investigation into its finances by the California Attorney General. UCLA Chancellor Emeritus Charles E. Young has been appointed the museum's first chief executive and will work with a newly appointed advisory committee of arts leaders.[16]

Another major museum in financial difficulties, the National Academy Museum in New York City, took a more drastic step and deaccessioned two of its most important works. Frederic Edwin Church's *Scene on the Magdalene* (1854) and Sanford Robinson Gifford's *Mt. Mansfield* (1859) were sold to a private foundation through an unnamed dealer. The sale was approved by the Academy's membership of artists by a vote of 181 to 1, with one abstention.[17]

Carmine Branagan, interim director, said two other works, which she refused to identify, are also being considered for sale. The National Academy Museum houses one of the largest public collections of 19th and 20th century American art in the country, with holdings of more than 5,000 works, according to its website.[18] In response to this sale the AAMD censured the National Academy, reiterating its professional principle that works may be deaccessioned only to provide funds to acquire other works of art and enhance a museum's collection. In response to the AAMD's censure, the National Academy voluntarily withdrew its membership in the association. Ms. Branigan said that the National Academy has a chronic operating deficit of about $800,000, on a $3 million budget, and may not use any of its $10 million endowment for operating expenses.[19]

In response to this situation, and the possibility of several other museums currently considering deaccessioning to finance operating expenses, the New York State Board of Regents was considering a proposed amendment to allow other New York State museums and historical societies to deaccession works. The amendment states that deaccession would be permitted "with the approval of the Board of Regents, to sell or transfer items or material in its collections for purposes of obtaining funds to pay outstanding debt, and thereby provide an alternative to the institution's bankruptcy or dissolution and the possible loss or liquidation of a collection because of debt."[20] The proposed amendment was withdrawn until a more thorough review of museum policies, rules, and regulations can take place next year.[21]

A bill permitting deaccession of "undocumented property" did pass the New York State Legislature in June 2008. The bill is intended to help museums deal with property that was lent to them years or decades ago, by lenders who can no longer be located or identified. The minimum period of time after which a museum may seek to deaccession a work is five years after the definite term of a loan has expired, or 10 years if the loan was for an indefinite period. "Undocumented property" is defined as objects with "intrinsic historic, artistic, scientific or cultural value for which the museum cannot determine the lender, donor, or owner by reference to its records."[22] The Museum Bill provides for explicit notice and publication procedures pursuant to which a museum may acquire the full title, and mandates that the proceeds from the sale of such "undocumented property" shall be used only for acquisition, conservation, protection, or preservation purposes and not to defray operating expenses.[23] Henceforth museums must provide potential donors with its mission statement, and collection and deaccession policies.[24] The legislation provides a specific exemption for any property created before 1945 and having changed hands due to "theft, seizure, confiscation, forced sale or any other involuntary means in Europe during the Nazi era (1933–1945).[25] New York is the first state to not only provide museums with statutory guidelines to responsibly deal with "undocumented property," but also to preserve the rights of claimants to recover objects involuntarily lost, looted, or sold under duress during the Nazi period. Although silent on the repatriation of Native American items, the state legislation does not take priority over federal law, including the Native American Graves Protection and Repatriation Act.

In England, the government has decided to enact legislation that would permit institutions to restitute Nazi-looted art to the families or the heirs that once owned them. Under current legislation all national museums and galleries are forbidden to dispose of any of their works. The Spoliation Advisory Committee, created in 2000, has advised on eight separate cases and is considering a ninth. The Tate, the British Museum, and the British Library are all known to hold looted art, and experts estimate that several hundred looted artworks may be in British galleries and museums.[26]

International

Claims to Antiquities in U.S. Institutions

The Cleveland Museum of Art and Italy reached an agreement by which the Museum will return 14 artworks to Italy. The objects were proven by Italy to have been illegally excavated or stolen. Among the objects are an Apulian red-figured krater by the Dorias painter, which stands approximately four feet tall. Other antiquities to be returned include a red-figured terra cotta Donkey-Head rhyton, Etruscan silver bracelets, and a Corinthian column krater. Also being returned is a 14th century processional cross from a small town near Sienna.[27] Two important works that are still under discussion are the bronze statue of Apollo Sauroktonos (the Lizard Slayer) and an ancient Puglian ceramic vase, known as the Medea vase. In return for this restitution Italy has agreed to loan the Cleveland Museum 14 works of equivalent value for 25 years, which could be renewed. Italy will also work with the Cleveland Museum on an exhibition of artworks from Italian museums on a subject yet to be determined.[28]

Egypt is claiming an ancient mummy mask unearthed more than 50 years ago at the Saqqara pyramids and now in the St. Louis Art Museum. The mask, a golden image of a noblewoman named Ka Nefer Nefer, is said to have been deposited by the archaeologist who discovered it in the storeroom at Saqqara and was still there in 1959. The St. Louis Art Museum acquired it in 1998. Zahi Hawass, head of Egypt's Antiquities Authority, claims that there is no record of the mask ever leaving Egypt legally and its restitution is his number one priority. The museum's director, Brent Benjamin, contends that Egypt does not have sufficient proof that it was stolen and that an inquiry to the Egyptian Museum in Cairo did not elicit a response that it was stolen. The museum's provenance, however, is patently false because it puts the mask in the possession of a Belgian art dealer in 1952 when the Egyptians can prove clearly that it was in the Saqqara storeroom in 1959.[29]

Peru has reneged on its Memorandum of Understanding with Yale University on the Machu Picchu antiquities, excavated by Hiram Bingham in 1912, and has instead decided to sue. Peru and Yale University had negotiated and agreed on a Memorandum of Understanding in September 2007, in which Yale recognized Peru's title to the artifacts from Machu Picchu and the two parties agreed on collaborative projects. Yale and Peru's National Institute of Culture were to collaborate on an international traveling exhibition, after which some 400 museum-quality objects would be displayed in a new museum to be built in Cuzco. Yale has stated that Peru's claims are barred by the statute of limitations and that it will defend itself against the claims vigorously.[30]

Korea is seeking restitution of an ancient reliquary stolen during Japanese occupation; a "Silver-plated Lamaist Stupa" in the shape of a pagoda is thought to have been made during the Goryeo Kingdom (918–1392) and is said to contain the relics of Buddha and other high-ranking monks. A Seoul

Metropolitan Council member and a Buddhist monk will visit the U.S. in early January to request restitution of the reliquary. The Boston Museum allegedly bought the piece from Japan. The Koreans have been actively seeking restitution of cultural assets that were taken by the Japanese colonial authorities.[31]

Antiquities

Greece is gradually getting back small pieces of the Parthenon sculptures. In September Italy returned a 14 by 13 inch fragment of the foot of the goddess Artemis that was originally a part of the Panathenaic Procession on the frieze of the Parthenon. The fragment was given by Lord Elgin to a friend in Sicily during a stop on his way back to England.[32] The Vatican's Museo Gregoriano Etrusco has made a one year loan of the marble head of a youth from the frieze of the Parthenon's Panathenaic Procession. Greece hopes that this will serve as a model for returning other ancient treasures.[33]

Hungary has offered to return ancient artifacts to Greece. The Museum of Fine Arts in Budapest bought the pieces several years ago from a private collector. The Hungarians realized only recently that some of the pieces are certainly from excavations in Greece and illegally brought to Hungary. Greek and Hungarian officials will meet to discuss which of the 22 pieces will go back to Greece.[34]

Some 230 priceless antiquities stolen from Iraqi museums in the aftermath of the United States–led invasion five years ago have been recovered. They were found in a sting operation just as they were about to be smuggled abroad. During the investigation, conducted by Iraqi and British security forces, antiquities destined for private collectors in the Middle East and the West were found buried in gardens and hidden under floors in houses in the suburbs of Basra. The objects recovered include Sumerian and Babylonian sculptures, gold jewelry, decorative silverware, and ceramics. Seven members of a gang said to have specialized in trafficking in looted antiquities were arrested. [35]

Holocaust-Era Looted Art

After protracted litigation in the District Court of the District of Columbia the heirs of Kazimir Malevich and the Stedelijk (City) Museum of Amsterdam came to a settlement. In 2005, when 14 Malevich paintings were on display at the Guggenheim Museum in New York and the Menil Collection in Houston, the heirs brought suit for restitution of the paintings. In 2007, the City renewed its motion to dismiss on several grounds, including the Act of State and, significantly, the court rejected the City's motion to dismiss under the purview of the FSIA, finding that sufficient contacts existed to establish jurisdiction under the FSIA's expropriation exception and that the City's loan of the artworks to U.S. institutions was commercial in nature, thus constituting a basis for jurisdiction under the FSIA.[36] Under the terms of the settlement, five of the 14 were deemed the property of the heirs and the museum received title to all of the many Malevich paintings remaining in the museum. The most famous of the restituted paintings, *Suprematist Composition* sold on November 3, 2008, at Sotheby's for over $60 million.

The Goudstikker Collection

Jacques Goudstikker was among the most renowned Jewish art dealers in Europe in the 1930s. Forced to flee when the Nazis invaded Holland, he died in a tragic accident when he fell through an uncovered hatch on the deck of the ship that was taking him and his wife and young son to freedom in England. But in his pocket was a small notebook inventorying most of his collection of over 1,000 paintings. In 2006, his heirs, Marei and Charlene von Saher, recovered 200 paintings from the Dutch government, many of which were exhibited this year at the Bruce Museum in Greenwich, Connecticut and will be at the Jewish Museum in New York in the spring of 2009.[37] Marei von Saher filed a claim in the Central District of California to recover Lucas Cranach the Elder's life-size paintings of Adam and Eve from the Norton Simon Museum in Pasadena, California. A motion to dismiss by the Museum was granted on the grounds that the statute of limitations had expired. The court held, among other things, that California's statute extending the statute of limitations for the recovery of Holocaust-era looted art was unconstitutional.[38] Oral argument was held before the Ninth Circuit on December 8, 2008.[39]

The Max Stern Collection

The Max Stern Collection, which in 2008 recovered two of the paintings that were sold in a forced sale at the Lempertz Auction House in Cologne, has recovered another two paintings from this important collection. One painting, *Girl from the Sabiner Mountains*, by Franz Xaver Winterhalter, has been in the possession of Maria-Louise Bissonnette who inherited it from her stepfather, a high ranking member of the Nazi party. The district court in Rhode Island awarded the painting to the Stern estate in 2007, and Bissonnette appealed on the grounds of laches.[40] On appeal, the court recounted Max Stern's efforts to recover his confiscated art, beginning in the immediate postwar years with a claim to the military government in the British zone of occupied Germany and continuing for many years thereafter. Upon his death in 1987, he bequeathed his art collection, specifically including any works of art that might yet be recovered, to McGill University, Concordia University, and Hebrew University of Jerusalem.

In 2004, the Stern Estate contacted the Art Loss Register and listed the painting with Germany's Lost Art Internet Database. The court found that Bissonnette had failed to carry the burden of proving she had been in any way prejudiced by the delay necessary for a finding of laches and awarded the painting to the Stern estate. A second painting from the Stern Collection, Jan Wellens de Cock's *Flight Into Egypt* (16th C.), was recovered from the former collection of German Chancellor Konrad Adenauer, who died in 1967. The whereabouts of the painting since then were not disclosed.[41]

The Museum of Modern Art and the Guggenheim Foundation v. Julius S. Schoeps et al.

This case concerns two iconic paintings by Pablo Picasso, *Boy Leading a Horse* (1906) in the Museum of Modern Art and *Moulin de la Galette* in the Guggenheim (the Paintings).[42] When the museums received a demand seeking restitution of the paintings on November 1, 2007, which they refused on December 7, 2007, the museums filed a Complaint for Declaratory Judgment in the Southern District of New York. The paintings were in the collection of Paul von Mendelssohn-Bartholdy until his death in 1935. Julius Schoeps is the grandson of one of von Mendelssohn–Bartholdy's sisters. MoMA acquired *Boy Leading a Horse* from William S. Paley as a gift in 1963. Paley acquired the painting through art dealer Justin Thannhauser in August 1935. *Moulin de la Galette* was in the possession of Justin Thannhauser when he emigrated to New York in 1940 and bequeathed and transferred to the Guggenheim in 1963 as part of a larger gift, which became permanent upon Thannhauser's death in 1978.

In their First Amended Counterclaim, Schoeps, joined by the heirs of Mendelssohn-Bartholdy's second wife, assert that Mendelssohn-Bartholdy sold the painting under duress after sustaining catastrophic financial losses under Nazi persecution. The case is expected to go to trial in 2009.

The Museum of Fine Arts, Boston v. Dr.Claudia Seger-Thomschitz

This is another peremptory suit filed to quiet title to a painting by Oskar Kokoschka, *Two Nudes (Lovers)*, which the Museum of Fine Arts, Boston, acquired in 1973 by bequest of Sarah Reed Platt, who acquired it from an art gallery in 1948 or 1949.[43] Claudia Seger-Thomschitz is the sole heir of Oskar Reichel, a Jewish doctor and art collector/gallerist in Vienna who was forced by the Nazis to file a property declaration in June 1938 and whose assets were confiscated by 1939. The painting was acquired by Viennese art dealer Otto Kallir in or about 1939 in what Seger-Thomschitz characterizes as a forced sale.

Seger-Thomschitz, a nurse with no connection to or knowledge of the art world, was unaware of the artworks and other property confiscated from Oskar Reichel until 2003, when she was contacted by a Vienna museum about four paintings that had been confiscated by the Nazis. A number of prominent historians of the Holocaust have criticized the museum for its stance on the claim for restitution. Deborah E. Lipstadt, a prominent historian of the Nazi era, has said, "To suggest, at that period in Vienna, that there was no pressure is ridiculous. . . . It's ludicrous."[44]

Restitution of Looted Artworks

The Jewish Museum in Prague, acting on a proposal of the National Gallery in Prague, will restitute 32 paintings and drawings to the heirs of Emil Freund, who died in the Lodz Ghetto in Poland after being deported from Prague. The collection includes valuable works by André Derain, Paul Signac, and Maurice Vlaminck. Thirteen of the works have been declared national treasures under Czechoslovakia's Heritage Protection Act and may not be taken out of the country. The fate of the rest of the collection is the subject of negotiations between the museum and the American heirs. The Jewish Museum actually appealed the decision of the National Gallery, but the appeal was denied by the National Gallery.[45]

The Minneapolis Institute of Arts will restitute Ferdinand Leger's painting *Smoke Over Rooftops* to the heirs of Alphonse Kann. The painting was donated to the museum in 1961 by Minneapolis businessman Putnam Dana McMillman, who acquired it from the Buchholz Gallery in New York; it is valued at $2.8 million. The heirs of Alphonse Kann made the demand in 1997. The provenance research took 10 years, and was the subject of a French lawsuit. One of the issues was that this is not one of the Kann paintings confiscated by the Nazis and moved to the Jeu de Paume in 1940, for which the Nazis kept lists. The painting remained in Kann's house until 1942, when the French government auctioned the house's contents at the behest of the

Nazis. It is not known what the heirs intend to do with the painting, but the Minneapolis Museum has said it would not seek to buy it back if it were to be offered at auction.[46]

The heirs of Jewish artist Eduard Einschlag have received restitution of one or more works painted by him before his deportation and death in the Treblinka death camp. The family's lawyer, Yoel Levi of Tel Aviv, said this restitution took years of wrangling with the Leipzig officials, who claimed that the paintings might even have been a gift of the artist.[47]

A Matisse painting stolen by the Nazis will be restituted to Israel's Magen David Adom (Israel's "Red Cross"). The painting, *Le Mur Rose*, was stolen in 1941 from Henry Fuld, Jr., who had fled Nazi Germany in 1937. The painting was found among the possessions of an SS officer in 1948 and was given to the Centre Pompidou in 1949, where it remained among the unclaimed artworks restituted by the Allies. Fuld died in 1963 and bequeathed his estate to a woman named Gisela Martin, about whom nothing more is known. She in turn left her estate to the Magen David Adom, which is now working to find and recover parts of the Fuld collection.[48]

Through the auspices of the Holocaust Claims Processing Office of the New York State Banking Department, eight works of art held by the Albertina Museum and the Vienna Museum were restituted to Monique Goss, the granddaughter and sole surviving heir of Ignatz Pick, who died in Vienna in 1941. Pick's assets were sold by the administrator of his estate to pay the punitive taxes of the Nazi regime. His wife and daughters had managed to flee to New York. The restituted works include portraits by Johann Baptist Lampi and other works by Austrian artists.[49]

Museum Exhibitions

"Orphaned Art: Looted Art from the Holocaust in the Israel Museum" was on exhibition at the Israel Museum from February until June 2008. Exhibited in conjunction was "Looking for Owners: Custody, Research, and Restitution of Art Stolen in France during World War II," drawn from the collection of unclaimed art in the collection of the Musées Nationaux Récupération in France. The collection of the Musées Nationaux Récupération was thereafter on exhibition at the Museum of Jewish Art and History in Paris.

The Israel Museum's catalogue, written by curator Shlomit Steinberg, with introductions in both English and Hebrew, is amply illustrated.[50] The French catalogue, *À qui appartenaient ces tableaux?* (Looking for Owners), is also well documented and well illustrated.[51] There are an astounding number of works by major artists such as André Derain, Egon Schiele, Petrus Christus, Simon Vouet and Cezanne among other notable artists. Although it would not be possible to exhibit all the objects in either of these collections, the two publications are thorough and well illustrated and should be of great service to anyone doing provenance research.

The Leopold Museum, Vienna, is embroiled in claims that its benefactor bought art that was stolen by the Nazis from Jewish owners. Both the Israelitische Kultusgemeinde, the official representative of Austria's Jews, and the Green Party, have issued statements that the museum is holding at least 14 paintings from Jewish families.[52] According to University of Salzburg law professor Georg Graf, who wrote a legal opinion for the Jewish community, "He knew or he must have known, that these paintings belonged to people who were persecuted by the Nazis." Until now, the Austrian restitution law governed only state museums and the Leopold Museum is technically a private foundation, but the government funded its construction, subsidizes it, and gave it the funds to purchase Dr. Leopold's collection. Culture Minister Claudia Schmied said she expected the foundation to "open up" and approve an independent examination of its collection by two researchers paid by the federal government. She also said the Austrian government planned to change Austrian law to facilitate the restitution of other looted property, and the proposed changes would cover the period from 1933 to 1945, rather than the current period of 1938 to 1945.[53]

General Observations for the Year

This year marks the tenth anniversary of the "Washington Principles" that were a result of the 1998 Washington Conference on Holocaust Era Looted Assets,[54] by which nations agreed to the research and restitution of Nazi-era looted artworks, and to opening a central registry of information and means for a "just and fair" resolution of claims. A number of conferences have been scheduled to review what has been accomplished since 1998, but whether these meetings will advance the cause of restitution without the full cooperation of governments is questionable. As one prominent author has written, "unless governments are prepared to aggressively investigate the provenance of artworks in public collections, locate owners and heirs, and establish functioning mechanisms to fairly adjudicate art claims, additional conferences will be academic exercises of no meaningful value to Nazi victims the Washington Principles were intended to aid."[55] Indeed, the legal strategy now practiced by museums to file to quiet title the minute they become aware of a claim in cases of Holocaust-era art is in direct contradiction to the Washington Principles.

The subject of Judaica recovered by the Allies, chiefly in the American zone of occupation, is becoming a major topic among Jewish museums in Europe. In the aftermath of the Holocaust it was assumed that Jewish life in Europe was not viable, but time has proven that is not so. In the immediate post-war years the Jewish Restitution Successor Organization and Jewish Cultural Reconstruction were assigned by U.S. military law, which was valid only in the American sector of occupation, to take control of all unclaimed Torahs (scrolls), Jewish books, and ritual objects to be inventoried and distributed for "the benefit of the Jewish people." Most of the objects were sent to the U.S. and Israel, with the rest distributed to Britain and South Africa. In November 2008, at the meeting of the Association of European Jewish Museums, one of the topics of discussion was how to recover the cultural works removed from Europe.

The economic crisis will certainly affect the art world and the museum community—we have already seen the move to deaccession works of art to make up the loss in operating expenses. Whether we will see an increase in negotiated settlements, rather than litigation, of Holocaust era looted art remains to be seen.

Notes

1. 823 U.N.T.S. 231, 10 I.L.M. 289 (1971); www.aamd.org .
2. Guidelines, II.F. *See also* Erin Thompson, *What Effect Will the AAMD Guidelines Have on the Antiquities Markets?* ART & CULTURAL HERITAGE LAW NEWSLETTER, A Publication of the Art & Cultural Heritage Law Committee of the American Bar Association Section of International Law, available at http://www.abanet.org/dch/committee.cfm?com=IC936000
3. Available at http://aamdobject registry.org
4. Helen Stoilas, *New guidelines for U.S. museums acquiring antiquities,* THE ART NEWSPAPER, Issue 193, July, 2008.
5. AAM Standards Regarding Archaeological Material and Ancient Art, available at http://www.aam-us.org/museumrosources/ethics/standards_ancientart.cfm .
6. *Id.*

7. *Id.*
8. *Id.*
9. Press Release, Penn Museum Launches Penn Cultural Heritage Center, Aug. 18, 2008, available at http://www.museum.upenn.edu/new/news/fullrelease.php?which=342
10. E-mail from professor Irene Winter, Harvard University, available at http://www.flckr.com/photos/imperial_fora_of_rome/3096516520
11. *United States of America v. Los Angeles County Museum*, Search Warrant on Written Affidavit Docket No. 08-0100M (C.D. CA., Jan. 19, 2008)
12. *Id.* at 10.
13. *Id.* at 25.
14. *Id.* at 13.
15. *Id.* at 33.
16. MOCA Accepts Broad's Offer, Appoints CEO, Dec. 23, 2008, available at http://www.artinfo.com/news/story/29886/moca-accepts-broads-offer-appoints-ceo
17. Lee Rosenbaum, Stealth Deaccessions: National Academy Sells Major Works by Church and Gifford," available at http://www.artsjournal.com/culturegrrl/2008//12/stealth_deaccessions_at_nation_html
18. http://www.ny.com/museums/national.academy.museum.html
19. AAMD Censures National Academy Museum, Dec. 5, 2008, available at http://www.artinfo.com/news/story/29702/aamd-censures-national-academy-museum 20. NY Board of Regents to Vote on "Desperate Deaccessioning," Dec. 12, 2008, available at http://www.artinfo.com/news/story/29790/ny-board-of-regents-to-vote-on-desperate-deac
21. Richard Richtmyer, NY museums may be able to sell work to pay debt, Dec. 13, 2008, available at http://www.newsday.com/local/wire/newyork/by-bc-ny-museum collections1213
22. An Act to amend the education law, in relation to property of other museums, NYS Education law §233-aa(d). The author was a member of the Art Law Committee of the New York City Bar Association, which suggested and helped draft the legislation.
23. Museum Law, §233-aa(g).
24. *Id.* §233-aa(i)(3).
25. *Id.* §233-aa(9)(a).
26. Jasper Copping, National galleries to hand back Nazi art, THE TELEGRAPH, Oct. 18, 2008.
27. Cleveland Museum of Art strikes deal with Italy to return 14 ancient artworks, Nov. 19, 2008 available at http://blog.cleveland.com/plaindealer/2008/11/cleveland_museum_of_art1.html

28. *Id.* This arrangement is similar to that made by Italy and the Getty Museum, where a loan exhibition of some 60 works by Bernini opened on August 5, 2008. Elisabetta Povoledo, *Getty is Lent a Bounty of Berninis,* NY TIMES, Feb 2, 2008 at B7.
29. *St. Louis museum proud of its ancient mask purchase but Egypt calls it a steal,* INTERNATIONAL HERALD TRIBUNE, Nov. 24, 2008, available at http://iht.com/articles/2008/11/24/mideast/loot.php ; Tom Finkel, *The Saint Louis Art Museum Ka-Nefer-Nefer Egyptian Mask Saga Continues,* RIVERFRONT TIMES, Nov. 26, 2008.
30. Press release, *Yale Seeks Collaborative Relationship with Peru,* Dec.9, 2008, available at http://opa.yale.edu/news/article.aspx?id=1997 ; Press Release, Statement by Yale University, Dec. 9, 2008, available at http://opa.yale.edu/news/article.aspx?id=6279
31. Bae Ji-sook, *A Mission to Get 'Stolen'Art Back from U.S. Museum,* THE KOREA TIMES, Dec. 15, 2008, available at http://www.koreatimes.co.kr/news/nation/2008/12/117_36149.html
32. Nicholas Paphitis, *Italy returns piece of Parthenon Marbles to Greece,* INTERNATIONAL BUSINESS TIMES, Sept. 23, 2008, available at http://www.ibtimes.com/articles/2008923
33. *Vatican returns Parthenon fragment to Greece,* The Associated Press, Nov. 5, 2008.
34. Nicholas Paphitis, Hungary to return looted antiquities to Greece, Associated Press, Sept. 12, 2008.
35. Kim Sengupta, *Looted ancient treasures recovered in Basra "sting,"* THE SUNDAY INDEPENDENT, Dec. 23, 2008, available at http://www.independent.co.uk/news/world/middleeast/looted-ancient-treasures/1208500.html
36. *Malewicz v. City of Amsterdam,* 362 F. Supp. 2d 298 (D.D.C. 2005). *Malewicz v. City of Amsterdam,* 517 F. Supp. 2d 322 (D.D.C. 2007; *See* Gerstenblith and Roussin, Art and International Cultural Property, 42 The International Lawyer 741 (Summer 2008). David D'Arcy, *If This Picture Could Talk: A Malevich painting's long route to the auction block,* WALL STREET JOURNAL, Nov. 1, 2008.
37. Peter C. Sutton, *Reclaimed: Paintings from the Collection of Jacques Goudstikker*, Yale University Press, 2008.
38. *Marei von Saher v. Norton Simon Museum of Arts at Pasadena*, 2007 U.S. Dist LEXIS 95757 (C.D. Cal. 2007); Suzanne Muchnic, *Norton Simon to keep pair of prized paintings,* LA TIMES, Oct. 19, 2007 at B3.
39. Kenneth Ofgang, *Ninth Circuit Urged to Revive Suit Over Art Looted by Nazis,* METROPOLITAN NEWS-ENTERPRISE, Dec. 9. 2008.
40. *Vineberg v. Bissonnette,* 529 F.Supp.2d 300 (D.R.I. 2007); *Vineberg v. Bissonnette,* 2008 U.S. App. LEXIS 24043 (1st Cir. Nov. 19, 2008).
41. Janice Arnold, *Adenauer painting returned to Stern estate,* THE CANADIAN JEWISH NEWS, Dec. 18, 2008.

42. Southern District of New York, 07 Civ. 11074. Roussin is an expert witness in the litigation.
43. U.S. District Court of Massachusetts, Civil Action No. 08-10097, filed May 29, 2008.
44. Geoff Edgers, *Holocaust historians blast MFA stance in legal dispute,* THE BOSTON GLOBE, May 28, 2008 at A1.
45. Artworks from the former collection of Dr. Emil Freund, http://www.jewishmuseum.cz/en/arestit.html
46. Mary Abbe, *MIA send Nazi 'loot' home to Paris,* MINNEAPOLIS STAR TRIBUNE, Oct. 30, 2008, available at http://www.startribune.com/templates/Print_This_Story?sid=33551004
47. Moti Katz, *Leipzig Mayor hand delivers Nazi-era art to painter's heirs,* HA'ARETZ, Oct. 28, 2008, available at http://www.haaretz.com/hasen/spages/1031942.html
48. *Matisse Painting Stolen by the Nazis to be returned,* Nov. 25, 2008, available at http://www.artinfo.com/news/story/29607/matisse-painting-stolen-by-the-nazis-to-be-returned
49. Press Release, Holocaust Claims Processing Office, Oct. 2, 2008.
50. Shlomit Steinberg, *Orphaned Art: Looted Art from the Holocaust in the Israel Museum,* Jerusalem, 2008.
51. *À qui appartenaient ces tableaux? (Looking for Owners),* Musées d'art et d'histoire du Judaisme, Paris, 2008.
52. Martha Lufkin, *Leopold Museum in Vienna accused over Nazi-looted art,* THE ART NEWSPAPER, April 24, 2008, Issue 190. The Associated Press, *Austrian Minister calls for clarity on 'looted' art allegations,* available at http://iht.com/bin/printfriendly.php?id-11444011
53. Washington Conference on Holocaust-Era Looted Assets, 1998, available at http://www.state.gov/regions/eur/wash_conf_material.html
54. Marilyn Henry, Metro Views: *Talking looted art,* THE JERUSALEM POST, Aug. 23, 2008.
55. Marilyn Henry, Metro Views: *Back to Context,* THE JERUSALEM POST, Nov. 16, 2008.

Art Market

• • •

Section Editors:
Thomas R. Kline and L. Eden Burgess

This past year was another eventful one for the art market. The message to market participants to proceed with caution is finally being received, particularly by the antiquities trade. Antiquities, in fact, strongly dominated 2008's headlines, with Holocaust-related issues also appearing frequently. Two trends were most pronounced in 2008. First, American museums and private collectors returned a significant number of objects—most of which had passed through the art market at one time or another—to European nation claimants. The flow of artifacts to their countries of origin to the east has been slowly increasing over the past few years, as source countries, especially Italy and Greece, have ramped up efforts to document, locate, and reclaim their cultural property; 2008 in particular has been a busy one for international antiquities shippers. New museum association acquisition guidelines, announced in 2008 in an effort to halt the practices that contributed to these many returns, are already being felt by the marketplace as poorly provenanced objects have become less desirable, while well-documented pieces now sell for a considerable premium.

Second, U.S. courts took up several cases in 2008 whose outcomes seem destined to influence art market practices. In the Holocaust claims arena, this year has seen a significant increase in preemptive lawsuits brought against claimants by possessors of objects subject to dispute. Museums and collectors, who have typically acquired such artwork after a series of market transactions in Europe and the U.S., have been unwilling to let claimants dictate the pace of research, negotiation, and litigation. Instead, museums and collectors are increasingly seizing the initiative by filing their own lawsuits for declaratory judgment concerning title in an effort to control the claim-resolution process, as well as to force a law-oriented, as opposed to an ethical-moral, approach to Holocaust restitution claims.

In 1998, the Washington Conference on Holocaust Assets issued the Washington Principles,[1] calling on museums and collectors to seek "just and fair" solutions to art restitution claims based on allegations of Nazi looting—signaling the interest of Western governments in seeing ethical and moral solutions, not just legalistic ones. Both the American Association of Museums (AAM) and Association of Art Museum Directors (AAMD) issued guidelines for handling restitution claims based on allegations of Nazi art looting and, in the case of the AAM, authorizing museums to waive claims if necessary and appropriate to help reach a just and fair solution. In 2008, such claims on museums, auction houses, and collectors became more frequent, and were often made on the eve of a potential sale. No authoritative data can be found on the number of such claims, especially in light of the many quick settlements, and only anecdotal information is available on numbers of claims and trends. Although settlements are by far the most common outcome of these claims, litigation seems to be on the rise.

Ban Chiang Objects and Past Lapses in Diligence

2008 opened with a dramatic—if not entirely unanticipated—bang for a Southern California importer and an art dealer, and the museums the dealer had been supplying. In a movie-like scene, several hundred federal agents raided Bobby O. Imports of Cerritos, California; Silk Roads Gallery in Los Angeles in January 2008; and at the same time, Los Angeles County Museum of Art (LACMA); the Charles S. Bowers Museum in Santa Ana; Mingei International Museum in San Diego; and Pasadena's Pacific Asia Museum. U.S. agents sought looted antiquities, Native American objects, and evidence of tax fraud. Culminating a five-year investigation by Immigration and Customs Enforcement, the National Park Service, and the criminal investigation division of the Internal Revenue Service, federal agents came to suspect that the owners of Silk Roads and their clients were dealing in artifacts smuggled from Asia (primarily from the fairly new Ban Chiang site in Thailand), objects looted from Native American archaeological sites in the United States, and tax fraud, as the objects appear to have been donated to museums with inflated values. One account noted, "In cases involving at least two institutions, the Bowers and the Pacific Asia museums, the affidavits say curators appeared to be aware that the objects that they were accepting as donations had been looted or illegally imported."[2]

Notably, the FBI warrant alleges that LACMA knew one particular object had been illegally exported from Thailand, but sought to acquire it anyway.[3] After the raids, the AAMD issued a statement condemning the looting of works of art, commending the museums for cooperating with authorities, and recognizing that the investigations are ongoing.[4] AAMD took no position on whether, if the allegations were substantiated, AAMD guidelines had been violated and if so, whether member museums would be in danger of losing their AAMD affiliations if shown to have been engaged in knowing violation of AAMD policies and procedures. About a month after the raids, the *New York Times* reported that many other museums could be affected by the investigation—such as the Metropolitan Museum of Art in New York, the Freer and Sackler Galleries in Washington, D.C., the Museum of Fine Arts, Boston, the Cleveland Museum of Art, the Minneapolis Institute of Arts, and the Asian Art Museum in San Francisco—since the government's filings imply that all objects being sold from the Ban Chiang site, which was not discovered until after Thailand enacted its antiquities law, may be owned by Thailand and could, therefore, be considered stolen property under U.S. law.[5]

The investigation was going forward midyear, with the May 2008 arrest of Roxanna M. Brown, director of the Southeast Asian Ceramics Museum at Bangkok University in Thailand. Brown was alleged to have allowed her signature to be used on appraisal forms that inflated the values of antiquities donated to several Southern California museums; the Silk Roads Gallery affidavit alleges that Brown provided an undercover agent with an overvalued appraisal.[6] However, Brown died at a federal detention center in Seattle days after her May arrest, which may affect the progress of the investigation.[7]

The January raids emphasize the increased risks to museums caused by market circulation of unprovenanced antiquities, particularly those in the hands of private collectors whose past acquisitions cannot be completely verified for legality. According to the *Los Angeles Times*, on the same day as the raids in California, authorities searched the private Chicago museum of Barry MacLean, a trustee of the Art Institute of Chicago.[8] Warrants authorized federal agents to seize artifacts from Thailand and related documents. Pieces from MacLean's collection were traveling on tour at the time of the search, including a stop at the Honolulu Academy of Arts. According to the Academy's director, Stephen Little, the institution had since "made a conscious decision not to show private collections anymore," apparently due in large part to the problems with independently vetting every piece in an exhibition.[9] Little's comment demonstrates the present impact of past lapses in diligence in building private collections through market purchases: private collectors may not be welcome to exhibit their collections in museums anymore, losing out on these prestigious opportunities to show off their antiquities. The *Los Angeles Times* also reported that Dartmouth's Hood Museum cancelled its exhibition of MacLean's traveling collection.

Improving Museum Acquisition Policies and Practices Raise Standards for the Marketplace

The year 2008 was a breakwater, both for better and worse, in the development of museum acquisition guidelines that are intended to head off scandals like the trade in Ban Chiang objects. The International Council of Museums (ICOM) Code of Ethics has long stated that an acquiring museum's due diligence "should establish the full history of the item since discovery or production,"[10] but ICOM's standard is viewed as excessively constricting by museums in this country. It is therefore generally ignored by American collecting museums in favor of the more lenient policy of the AAMD, although the AAM has issued an antiquities collections policy that is somewhat stricter than AAMD's, as discussed below.

Culminating a lengthy and partly successful attempt to coordinate their efforts, the AAMD issued its Report on Acquisition of Archaeological Materials and Ancient Art in June 2008,[11] and the AAM adopted its Standards Regarding Archeological Material and Ancient Art in July 2008.[12] Small but significant differences between these policy statements may now fuel confusion in museum board rooms and uncertainty in the art market concerning what the governing requirements are for safe antiquities trading. The AAMD Report states that "museums normally should not acquire a work unless provenance research substantiates that the work was outside its country of probable modern discovery before 1970 or was legally exported from its probable country of modern discovery after 1970." Using similar language, AAM also establishes 1970 as the critical cutoff; both organizations thereby accept the ethical and moral significance of the date UNESCO adopted for its Convention on the

Means of Prohibiting and Preventing the Illicit Import, Export and Transfer of Cultural Property, which sought to prevent pillage of archaeological sites by limiting international trade in illegally obtained objects.[13]

For purposes of acquiring poorly documented objects, however, a gap appears between the two standards, with AAMD appearing to be more forgiving if only incomplete information is available. Both guidelines contain a savings clause that will allow museums to acquire antiquities whose provenance cannot be assured back to export from country of origin before 1970, or lawful import into the United States after 1970. AAMD provides a lengthy explanation of the various rationales available to museums wanting to acquire antiquities without full provenance, such as that even in the absence of adequate documentation, "an informed judgment can indicate that the work was outside its probable country of modern discovery before 1970 or legally exported from its probable country of modern discovery after 1970, and therefore can be acquired." A museum is also justified in relying on "the cumulative facts and circumstances resulting from provenance research, including, but not limited to, the independent exhibition and publication of the work, the length of time it has been on public display and its recent ownership history. . . ."

AAMD's guidelines warn museums that if they are following this lesser standard to acquire objects with incomplete provenance documentation, they should "carefully balance the possible financial and reputational harm of taking such a step against the benefit of collecting, presenting, and preserving the work in trust for the educational benefit of present and future generations." AAMD further calls for the immediate posting of such objects on the museum's website, along with an image and relevant information, including "all facts relevant to the decision to acquire it, including its known provenance." AAMD also provides its own website, which currently shows one object, for this purpose.[14] It is at precisely this point that AAM's standards are significantly stricter than the AAMD's Report guidelines; when a museum acquires an object without full documentation that it was exported from the country of origin before 1970 or, if exported after 1970, that it was exported legally and imported legally into the U.S., the AAM Standards insist that the member museum document its reasons for acquiring the object by being "transparent about why this is an appropriate decision in alignment with the institution's collections policy and applicable ethical codes." Since most major antiquities-collecting institutions are members of both organizations (directly in the case of AAM and through their directors in AAMD), it will be interesting to see whether the AAM's more demanding savings clause will promote greater transparency or will be ignored in favor of the AAMD's lower standard.

In spite of these differences, the overall direction of both policy statements is undoubtedly towards requiring far more provenance documentation for museum antiquities acquisitions than has been the norm to date, a change that is destined to be event-forcing on the art market. Because the market had anticipated these changes, the antiquities trade felt the impact of the AAMD and AAM reports almost contemporaneously with final issuance of the new policies, as antiquities auctioned at Sotheby's and Christie's with provenance dating back to the early 1900s sold at premium prices in summer 2008. Both auction houses saw objects collected and exported from their countries of origin in the early part of the 20th century sell far above projected estimates. In contrast, works with limited provenance information that could not establish export from the country of origin pre-1970 did not sell as well.[15] These trends continued in the December antiquities sales, where objects with pre-1970 export documentation garnered high sale prices, and those without—like a rare silver paten (communion plate) described by Christie's as entering a "European private collection" in 1978—often fell short of estimate or failed to sell.[16]

In a well-timed step towards ensuring that U.S. government-owned museums are not encouraging trade in illicitly obtained objects, the Smithsonian Institution, perhaps responding to the problems at the Getty and other museums, the AAM and AAMD development of their policies, and related news about inadequate diligence in the art market, adopted a Statement of Values and Code of Ethics "to reaffirm its longstanding commitment to the public trust and the highest standards of professional conduct, both individually and collectively."[17] The statement does not directly address acquisitions, but should amplify the impact of AAM and AAMD guidelines by declaring, with respect to managing its collections, that "the Smithsonian conducts [its] activities in accordance with professional standards and practices and ensures that legal requirements are observed and compliance is documented."[18]

Specific Antiquities Disputes Demonstrate Risks from Past Diligence Failures

Further helping to warn collectors about the risks of acquiring unprovenanced antiquities on the art market, in November, the Cleveland Museum of Art agreed to return thirteen ancient artifacts and an early-Renaissance cross to Italy.[19] After months of negotiations—and a mistaken announcement in September by Italy's former minister of culture Francesco Rutelli that a deal had been reached[20]—the museum and Italy reached an accord settling several, but not all, Italian claims: a committee will be set up to discuss two other objects sought by Italy, a first-century chariot attachment and a fourth-century B.C. bronze statue of Apollo slaying a lizard.[21] In 2007, the Louvre withdrew a request to borrow the Apollo statue, which the Cleveland Museum obtained in 2003 from the notorious dealers Hicham and Ali Aboutaam.[22] According to the *New York Times*, "Greek pressure on the Louvre drew applause from many in the art world, particularly academics who have long criticized antiquities trading as fraught with corruption."[23]

Two ancient Greek acroliths, apparently stolen from Italy decades ago and funneled here through Switzerland and a London dealer, then donated anonymously to the University of Virginia's art museum, will be returning to Italy. The sculptures, which had been exhibited at the University's art museum since their anonymous donation in 2002, were originally displayed inside a temple near the modern-day city of Aidone, Italy.[24] According to the University's student newspaper *The Cavalier Daily*, the school's Associate General Counsel Richard Kast stated that the University agreed with the donor not to publicize the acroliths or reveal the identity of the donor: "Under the agreement that is in place, the University is not supposed to openly publicize the fact that they have the acroliths."[25] Such an agreement, pursuant to which a museum (associated with a public university) does not publicize its ownership of certain antiquities, is likely not in compliance with the AAMD (¶ II.E)[26] or AAM Guidelines (¶ 3).[27] The University's museum has made other returns of recently acquired objects as well; in 2007, the University returned to Sicily a terra cotta antefix (roof ornament) in the shape of a leopard that had been purchased at auction two years earlier.[28]

Adding to the increasing flow of antiquities back to their countries of origin,[29] Shelby White, who established the Institute for the Study of the Ancient World at New York University, returned numerous objects to Italy and Greece this year. In July, she reached an agreement with Greece to return two antiquities from her collection;[30] she returned several objects to Italy earlier this year in the first negotiated agreement between Italy and a private collector in the United States.[31] So far, White has not been accused of wrongdoing, having consistently claimed that she and her late husband Leon Levy made purchases only from dealers they "believed to be reputable."[32]

U.S. museums are not, however, wholeheartedly embracing the need for restitution of claimed antiquities: Yale University has resisted returning antiquities allegedly looted from Peru, according to a complaint filed in D.C. federal court in December. Peru seeks the return of objects and artifacts currently in the possession of Yale and the National Geographic Society (NGS) that it alleges were taken without permission in the early 1900s.[33] Peru's complaint cites an 1893 decree that prohibits "the exploration or excavation of archaeological objects . . . due to the 'absolute disregard for national rights' and the 'dishonor of [Peru's] national civilization and culture.'"[34] If Peru can prove that the export of archaeological finds violated the 1893 and related decrees,[35] Yale and NGS may have to return those objects, although Peru failed to make a similar showing in litigation in California in the early 1990s.[36] Yale has commented that it is "disappointed" that Peru did not honor a 2007 agreement under which the two would have jointly financed a museum to house many returned artifacts; Peru responded that it already has suitable museums and that the agreement contained "unacceptable" terms that would have let Yale keep objects for research "for 99 more years."[37]

Issues concerning ancient coins continue to reverberate in the antiquities market ever since the United States and Cyprus agreed to trade restrictions on coins from Cyprus in the 2007 Memorandum of Understanding under the 1970 UNESCO Convention and the 1983 U.S. Convention on Cultural Property Implementation Act. Early this year, a tomb raider in Cyprus gave a rare and frank interview about why he repeatedly and knowingly breaks the Cyprus cultural property protection laws, using a metal detector to find rare artifacts, then keeping, selling, or giving them away. "Achilleas" says that he became interested in detecting when he found some interesting coins. He sent them to Nicosia, the capital of Cyprus, as the law requires, where the coins should have become part of a collection. When he went to Nicosia to view the coins, however, he was told they had been "mislaid." Since then, Achilleas keeps whatever he finds, believing that there is a black market operating in Nicosia that sends anything of value out of the country. Achilleas now has a treasure trove of objects hidden in his home, yet claims that he wants to work with the government to stop the destruction and export of Cypriot culture.[38]

That's unlikely: the Director of Cyprus' Antiquities Department, Dr. Pavlos Flourentzos, was "shocked and outraged" by Achilleas' story. He told the *Cyprus Mail* that private citizens are unqualified to excavate archaeological sites; only an archaeologist may conduct excavations. He also pointed to the 2007 Memorandum of Understanding (MOU) reached between Cyprus and the U.S., which imposed import restrictions on Cypriot coins that date from the end of 600 B.C. to 235 B.C.[39]

Other dealers remain unconvinced of the need for raising diligence standards. A U.S. Army pilot sought to market almost 100 ancient artifacts he stole from the Ma'adi Museum in Cairo when he was stationed there in 2002.[40] Around 2003, the pilot sold the stolen pieces to an art dealer who in turn consigned them to various galleries around the world. The dealer apparently bought the pieces although the pilot had no documentation of ownership; he claimed that his grandfather collected the pieces while working in Egypt in the 1930s–1940s.[41] The U.S. government returned approximately 80 of the objects to Egypt in early December 2008, "reunit[ing] the people of Egypt with an important piece of their cultural heritage," according to Peter J. Smith, head of U.S. Immigration and Customs Enforcement's New York office.[42] Not all of the stolen pieces have been recovered. Here, even minimal diligence by the art dealer who paid the pilot for the undocumented pieces probably would have revealed the theft at an early stage and prevented risk to the dealer and his clients, as well as the worldwide dissipation of the stolen artifacts.

A seizure in December shows how diligence at the highest levels, such as by one of the world's leading auction houses, can affect small-time but numerous looters and smugglers. Authorities filed a suit in federal court in New York seeking to take ownership of two Byzantine artifacts—a bronze Polycandelon (lamp) and a mosaic panel—that had been consigned to Christie's with falsified documents after having been smuggled into the United States. When questions arose about the objects' origins, the auction house contacted authorities and London police arrested a man connected with the falsified records, who confessed that he lied on the papers to get the objects into the U.S.[43] In addition, the provenance papers were "bogus."[44] According to the complaint, the man said that the objects were smuggled out of Yugoslavia and Turkey in pieces, and the lamp was later reassembled.[45]

This year also saw what may be the final chapter of the *United States v. Schultz*.[46] A UK antiquities dealer and a U.S. antiquities dealer (the latter, President of the National Association of Dealers in Ancient, Oriental and Primitive Art) were both sent to prison approximately ten years ago for knowingly dealing in stolen Egyptian objects, which they had covered in plastic and painted black to look like tourist-quality items. The exports violated Egypt's law banning the export of antiquities more than 100 years old. At the close of 2008, one of the objects finally went back to Egypt.[47]

Holocaust/World War II Disputes Also Air Issues from Past and Current Market Transactions

Several current cases in the U.S. courts, including some 2008 decisions, address issues of standards and practices for diligence and transparency in the art market. In February 2008, Northfield Auctions in Massachusetts became the target of the FBI's seizure of six landscape paintings upon the request of the Free State of Bavaria, Germany.[48] The Bavarian State Paintings Collection (BSPC) then pursued a claim for restitution of the paintings based on a wartime or immediate postwar theft. The paintings had been consigned to the auction house for sale by the estate of a U.S. Army officer who acquired them in Germany after World War II, then brought them home to the United States. The auction house's paintings report plainly stated, "The six works being offered from the estate of a former U.S. Army officer were bought in Germany, just after the close of W.W.II, and brought back to the United States in 1947."[49] Despite the obvious implications of this history, the auction house appears to have accepted the paintings (at least one of which was not on stretchers) for sale without question, using the colorful history as part of its marketing effort. BSPC and the consignor promptly settled the case on confidential terms, and the paintings have since been returned to Bavaria.

The first U.S. case to hold a sale ordered by the Nazis to be the equivalent of a confiscation and, therefore, a theft was affirmed by the First Circuit Court of Appeals in November 2008, in *Vineberg v. Bissonnette*.[50] The First Circuit relied upon the lower court's factual finding that the National Socialist government ordered Jewish art gallery owner Dr. Max Stern to liquidate his entire inventory, including the disputed work, Franz Xaver Winterhalter's *Girl from the Sabiner Mountains*—a fact not contested by the defendant. Like the District Court, the First Circuit applied Rhode Island law because the defendant did not challenge that aspect of the District Court's decision.

Although she had tried to sell the painting on the market in Rhode Island and, apparently, in Germany, and had also indicated her disagreement that the forced sale was the equivalent of a theft, in the end Bissonnette relied primarily on her laches defense, claiming that delay in pursuing recovery of the painting by Dr. Stern and later by his estate had prejudiced her. The Court of Appeals rejected this argument. Bissonnette could not show prejudice, in part because she had inherited the object. Accordingly, the Court of Appeals held the 1937 forced sale to be invalid and affirmed the writ of replevin issued by the court below:

> A de facto confiscation of a work of art that arose out of a notorious exercise of man's inhumanity to man now ends with the righting of that wrong through the mundane application of common law principles. The mills of justice grind slowly, but they grind exceedingly fine.

On the other hand, Swiss law of good faith acquisition featured heavily in a 2008 decision in the Southern District of New York in which Judge William H. Pauley ruled that the possessor of an Egon Schiele drawing had acquired title and right to possession through a 1950s purchase in Switzerland, and that the heirs of Holocaust victim Fritz Grunbaum could not, therefore, establish superior ownership rights (*Bakalar v. Vavra*).[51] Judge Pauley, applying Swiss law to a purchase that he found took place in Switzerland in the 1950s, concluded that a predecessor buyer to Bakalar had exercised sufficient diligence (although the buyer only asked the seller where the drawing came from, learning that it came from family in Vienna).

Even though, as is now well-known, Austria was occupied and Jewish-owned property there was comprehensively looted by the Nazis in the late 1930s and early 1940s, Judge Pauley did not believe the overall circumstances or the information provided by the seller obligated the purchaser to inquire further about the painting's origin under Swiss standards applicable to art purchases at that time. The Court further reasoned that, if the buyer had been required to conduct further research, "it would have been highly unlikely that he would have been able to conclude that the Nazis, or anyone else, had taken the Drawing from [the original owner]"; even with the benefit of modern-day research tools, the parties had been unable to produce "concrete evidence" of looting or spoliation.[52] The Court concluded on that basis that the preceding buyer purchased the drawing in good faith in 1956, thus had received title and had authority to pass title to the gallery that sold it to the plaintiff in 1963.[53]

The issue of what kind of transaction would constitute a forced sale in the context of the Third Reich is the subject of two museum declaratory judgment suits brought together in the U.S. District Court for the Southern District of New York. In 2008, the court allowed the cases to go forward, rejecting Julius Schoeps' attempt to avoid litigation of his claim regarding two Picasso paintings, *Boy Leading a Horse* and *Le Moulin de la Galette*, currently in the collections of the Museum of Modern Art and the Guggenheim Foundation, respectively. Schoeps, who also has restitution litigation concerning a Picasso pending in New York against Andrew Lloyd Webber, had demanded return of the paintings in letters to the museums in November 2007, based on his allegation that the paintings were sold under duress in 1934–1935. After "provid[ing] access to [their] records and encourag[ing] Mr. Schoeps to share . . . any factual support for his claim,"[54] the museums asserted that Schoeps had no evidence of forced sales and sued him for a declaratory judgment that Schoeps does not have a valid claim to the works.[55] Schoeps moved to dismiss on the ground that he had not yet been appointed as the representative of the estate, but the judge denied his motion and allowed the case to go forward. In October 2008, the museums moved for summary judgment on their declaratory judgment claim, arguing that laches bars Schoeps' restitution claim under New York law, that sales of the paintings were not forced, and that good faith purchases occurred under Swiss law (and on other grounds).[56] The court can be expected to rule on the motion before the end of 2009.

In another case involving allegations that a painting was lost to the Nazis through a forced sale, Museum of Fine Arts, Boston, followed a path similar to MoMA and Guggenheim in filing suit in January 2008, seeking an order declaring it to be the proper owner of Oskar Kokoschka's *Two Nudes* (*Lovers*). MFA acquired the painting by bequest from a donor, who apparently acquired it in a market transaction in 1947 or 1948. The claimant, Dr. Claudia Seger-Thomschitz—identified as the "select niece" of the son of Dr. Oskar Reichel[57]—claims that the painting was sold under coercion or duress in 1939. MFA disagrees, based upon a considerable volume of provenance research, saying that "The painting was never confiscated by the Nazis, was never sold by force as a result of Nazi persecution, and was not otherwise taken from Dr. Reichel."[58] More specifically, MFA asserts that when Reichel sold the painting to Otto Kallir in 1939, after previously consigning the painting to Kallir for sale several times,[59] he did so voluntarily, as the two "had known each other and traded in art for many years."[60]

Seger-Thomschitz has countersued MFA in conversion and replevin, as well as bringing her own counterclaim seeking a declaratory judgment of ownership of the painting (and other claims). Among her supporting evidence: Dr. Reichel's June 1938 property declaration, which lists *Two Nudes*, and a 2003 report by Viennese authorities describing forced sales to Kallir's gallery.[61] MFA's case has sparked controversy in the art restitution community. The museum has taken hits in the press over its lawsuit, with the *Boston Globe* reporting in May 2008 that a number of Holocaust historians are "particularly critical of one of MFA's main arguments: that Reichel's sale to an art dealer who later moved to New York was, as the MFA suit contends, not 'by force as a result of Nazi persecution,'" and stating their view that in 1939 Vienna, a voluntary sale by a Jewish person simply was not possible.[62] Other researchers remain impressed with the amount of work done by MFA and the quality of its court presentations, with one leading expert saying, "It certainly seems that the museum has been sort of thorough in examining the facts here."[63] The forced sale issue may never be resolved in court, however; based on a long history of public exposure of the painting and Seger-Thomschitz's knowledge of where it was, MFA filed a motion for summary judgment in late 2008 solely on statute of limitations grounds, which is pending as of the date of this publication.[64]

In a case brought by a collector related to MFA's suit, Sarah Blodgett Dunbar filed a complaint in federal court in Louisiana against Seger-Thomschitz the same week that MFA commenced its suit against her, claiming to be the sole heir of the legal owner of Kokoschka's *Portrait of a Youth*, which Seger-Thomschitz also claims.[65] Similarly to MFA, Dunbar alleges that the 1939 sale of the painting "was just one of many instances in which the parties [the Reichels and Kallir] consigned, lent, sold, or otherwise voluntarily dealt with each other as Viennese art collectors and dealers."[66] As with the *Bakalar* case, Dunbar's mother bought the painting from Kallir's gallery in 1946.

Seemingly emboldened by the recent trend of preemptive possessor lawsuits, a South Korean art collector who purchased a Marie Laurencin painting from Christie's in 1991 filed suit against the auction house in December 2008, claiming that it was negligent in selling her the artwork.[67] The collector claims that she tried to sell the painting through Sotheby's in 2006, but Sotheby's told her that the Nazis stole the painting from famed Paris art dealer Paul Rosenberg during World War II. According to the collector, Sotheby's refuses to sell or return the painting because of the cloud on title.[68] As of this writing, Christie's has not made a filing in the case.

Conclusion

The need for transparency and diligence in art market transactions has been increasingly apparent in recent years, even more so in 2008 due to the many returns of looted objects to Italy and Greece, and the volume of Holocaust- and World War II-looted artworks that surface on the market or can be tracked back to market transactions. In addition, 2008 saw antiquities auction prices feeling the effects, with only well-provenanced pieces selling at or above estimates. Art market participants should expect to see these trends continue.

At the same time, claim recipients are establishing a new pattern of preemptive declaratory judgment suits to resolve claims, particularly those based on allegations of loss through forced sales during the Holocaust. A common theme in these cases is the clash between the claimants' stated goal of achieving a "just and fair" solution under the soft law of the Washington Principles and museum guidelines, versus the museum perception that it should not surrender property held in trust unless faced with a valid legal claim. All of these disputes indicate a growing need for participants in art market disputes to decide what constitutes a strong claim, and what claims are appropriate for settlement.

Notes

1. Available at http://www.lootedartcommission.com/Washington-principles
2. Edward Wyatt, *Four California Museums Are Raided*, N.Y. TIMES, Jan. 25, 2008; Stacey Silberman, *Hollywood Today*, Jan. 26, 2008; Amy Taxin, Doug Irving, Laura Bleiberg and Richard Chang, *Federal agents raid Bowers Museum for smuggled antiquities*, ORANGE COUNTY REGISTER, Jan. 24, 2008. Search warrants available at www.ocregister.com/articles/museum-irs-bowers-1966311-asked-criminal
3. Wyatt, *Four California Museums Are Raided*, *supra* note 2.
4. AAMD, *Statement in Response to Allegations Concerning Some California Museums*, Feb.1,2008,available at http://www.aamd.org/newsroom/documents/Statement_on_California_Museums.pdf.
5. Jori Finkel, *Thai Antiquities, Resting Uneasily*, N.Y. TIMES, Feb. 17, 2008.
6. Richard Chang, *Asian antiquities expert arrested*, ORANGE COUNTY REGISTER, May 12, 2008.
7. Mike Carter, *Asian-antiquities expert held in SeaTac dies in custody*, SEATTLE TIMES, May 15, 2008.
8. Jason Felch and Mike Boehm, *Federal probe of stolen art goes national*, L.A. TIMES, Jan. 29, 2008.
9. *Id.*
10. *ICOM Code of Ethics for Museums*, 2006, http://palimpsest.stanford.edu/icom/ ethics.html
11. AAMD, *Report on Acquisition of Archaeological Materials and Ancient Art*, June 4, 2008, available at http://www.aamd.org/newsroom/documents/2008ReportAndRelease.pdf
12. AAM, Standards Regarding Archaeological Material and Ancient Art, July 2008, available at http://www.aam-us.org/museumresources/ethics/upload/Standards%20Regarding%20Archaeological%20Material%20and%20Ancient%20Art.pdf

13. 1970 UNESCO Convention available at http://portal.unesco.org/en/ev.php-URL_ID=13039&URL_DO=DO_TOPIC&URL_SECTION=201.html
14. At http://aamdobjectregistry.org/Object-Types
15. Souren Melikian, *A wake-up call for the antiquities market*, INTERNATIONAL HERALD TRIBUNE, June 12, 2008.
16. Souren Melikian, *Rare antiquities show remarkable success*, INTERNATIONAL HERALD TRIBUNE, Dec. 13–14, 2008.
17. SI Announcement, May 13, 2008.
18. The Smithsonian Institution Statement of Values and Code of Ethics, available at http://www.si.edu/about/policies/values-code-of-ethics.asp
19. Elisabetta Povoledo, *Pact Will Relocate Artifacts to Italy From Cleveland*, N.Y. TIMES, Nov. 19, 2008.
20. Steven Litt, *The Cleveland Museum of Art still has no deal with Italy on returning allegedly looted antiquities*, PLAIN DEALER, Sept. 10, 2008.
21. Povoledo, *Pact Will Relocate Artifacts*, *supra* note 19.
22. In December 2003, Hicham Aboutaam was arrested and charged with smuggling, a felony, and with making false statements related to a silver drinking vessel. In June 2004, he pled guilty to a federal charge of falsifying customs documents related to the same object. Also in 2004, Egypt tried Ali Aboutaam *in absentia* for antiquities smuggling and sentenced him to 15 years in prison. Barry Meier, *Art Dealer Pleads Guilty In Import Case*, N.Y. TIMES, June 24, 2004.
23. Ron Stodghill, *Do You Know Where That Art Has Been?*, N.Y. TIMES, March 18, 2007.
24. *U.Va. to Return Looted Greek Statues to Italy*, DAILY PROGRESS, Jan. 4, 2008.
25. Laura Hoffman and Thomas Madrecki, *Greek sculptures spark controversy*, CAVALIER DAILY, Sept. 5, 2007.
26. "The museum should promptly publish acquisitions of archaeological materials and ancient art, in print or electronic form, including in these publications an image of the work (or representative images in the case of groups of objects) and its provenance, thus making this information readily available to all interested parties."
27. "Existing Collections . . . [M]useums should make available the known ownership history of archaeological material and ancient art in their collections. . . ."
28. Elisabetta Povoledo, *Two Marble Sculptures to Return to Sicily*, N.Y. TIMES, Sept. 1, 2007.
29. In March, the Palazzo Poli in Rome opened an exhibit of illicitly excavated antiquities returned to Italy by American museums, dealers, and collectors. Elisabetta Povoledo, *Repatriated Art in Rome*, N.Y. TIMES, March 29, 2008. Rome is celebrating "Nostoi" (Greek for "return home") to mark the homecoming of Italian artworks. PBS interviewed Francesco Rutelli about the looting and return of Italian

artworks in February 2008, available at http://www.culturalheritagelaw.org/news-issues/news-issues-in-cultural-heritage/pbs-interview-with-francesco-rutelli/

30. Press Release, The Greek Ministry of Culture and Shelby White Conclude Agreement on Return of Two Antiquities to Greece, July 11, 2008.
31. Elisabetta Povoledo, *Collector Returns Art Italy Says Was Looted*, N.Y. TIMES, Jan. 18, 2008.
32. Povoledo, *Repatriated Art in Rome*, *supra* note 29.
33. Complaint, *Republic of Peru v. Yale Univ.*, Case No. 08-cv-02109 (D.D.C.); *Peru Sues Yale for Return of Inca Treasures*, COURTHOUSE NEWS, Dec. 8, 2009.
34. Complaint ¶ 8.
35. Complaint ¶¶ 9, 11, 22–23.
36. *Peru v. Johnson*, 720 F. Supp. 810 (C.D. Cal. 1989), *aff'd by unpubl. order*, 933 F.2d 1013 (9th Cir. 1991).
37. *Peru foreign minister defends lawsuit against Yale*, YAHOO! NEWS, Dec. 11, 2008.
38. Jill Campbell Mackay, *Tomb raider opens crypt on why he's breaking the law*, CYPRUS MAIL, Jan. 27, 2008.
39. Leo Leonidou, *'All antiquities belong to the state, and that's that,'* CYPRUS MAIL, Jan. 27, 2008.
40. Tom Hays, *Artifacts stolen by US Army pilot return to Egypt*, AP PRESS, Dec. 3, 2008.
41. David Glovin, *U.S. Army Officer Charged in Egyptian Artifacts Theft*, BLOOMBERG, Feb. 6, 2008.
42. Hays, *Artifacts stolen by US Army pilot return to Egypt*, *supra* note 40.
43. Bruce Golding, *Feds Call Artifacts Bad "Byz,"* N.Y. POST, Dec. 5, 2008.
44. *Feds Seize Smuggled Ancient Art*, Courthouse News Service, Dec. 5, 2008.
45. *Id.*
46. 178 F. Supp. 2d 445 (S.D.N.Y. 2002).
47. Sarah Knapton, *Smuggled ancient sculpture returns to Egypt*, LONDON TELEGRAPH, Dec. 19, 2008.
48. *United States v. Six Paintings Seized From Paul Gorzocoski III, d/b/a Northfield Auctions, Route 63/105 Main Street, Northfield, Massachusetts, on October 1, 2007*, Case No. 08-10161 (D. Mass.). The authors represented the Free State of Bavaria in this case.
49. U.S. Verified Complaint for Forfeiture *in Rem*, Feb. 1, 2008, Ex. 5.
50. *Vineberg v. Bissonnette*, 2008 WL 4924929 (1st Cir. Nov. 19, 2008). The authors represent the Trustees of the Max Stern Estate in this case.
51. 2008 U.S. Dist. LEXIS 66689, Case No. 05-cv-3037 (S.D.N.Y. Sept. 2, 2008).The authors represented a third-party witness called by the defendants in the *Bakalar* case.
52. *Id.* at *18–22.

53. *Id.* at *24.
54. *Statement Regarding Claims on Two Picasso Paintings*, Dec. 7, 2007, available at http://www.guggenheim.org/guggenheim-foundation/foundation-press/1918-statement-regarding-claims-on-two-picasso-paintings
55. *The Museum of Modern Art and the Solomon R. Guggenheim Fdtn. v. Schoeps*, Case No. 07-11074 (S.D.N.Y.).
56. Oral argument was held on December 18, 2008.
57. MFA Boston Press Release, "The Museum of Fine Arts, Boston, Asserts Rightful Ownership of Kokoschka Painting, *Two Nudes (Lovers)*," Jan. 24, 2008, available at http://www.mfa.org/dynamic/sub/ctr_link_url_5980.pdf
58. Geoff Edgers, *MFA sues to bolster claim to disputed 1913 painting*, BOSTON GLOBE, Jan. 24, 2008.
59. *Id.*
60. MFA Boston Press Release, *supra* note 57.
61. Dr. Claudia Seger-Thomschitz's First Amended Answer and Counterclaim, filed July 3, 2008.
62. Geoff Edgers, *Holocaust historians blast MFA stance in legal dispute*, BOSTON GLOBE, May 28, 2008.
63. *Id.*
64. *The Museum of Fine Arts, Boston v. Seger-Thomschitz*, Case No. 08-10097 (D. Mass.).
65. *Dunbar v. Seger-Thomschitz*, Case No. 08cv711 (E.D. La.).
66. *Id.*, Complaint, Jan. 22, 2008.
67. The authors have been retained to represent Christie's in this case, *Doss Inc. v. Christie's*.
68. *Doss Inc. v. Christie's*, Case No. 08-cv-10577 (S.D.N.Y.); *$235,500 Demanded For Nazi-Looted Art*, COURTHOUSE NEWS SERVICE, Dec. 8, 2008.

International Cultural Property

Section Editors:
Patty Gerstenblith and Laina Lopez

Introduction

In 2008, major steps were taken toward wider acceptance of the 1954 Hague Convention on the Protection of Cultural Property in the Event of Armed Conflict with the vote of the U.S. Senate to ratify the main Convention and the drafting of legislation by the United Kingdom and New Zealand that would implement the Convention and both Protocols. Recoveries of cultural objects that were brought into the United States illegally continued, as did also voluntary restitutions of classical antiquities from American collections to Italy and to Greece. Litigation by the victims of terrorist attacks to attach cultural objects on loan from Iran to U.S. institutions was further complicated by legislation enacted in early 2008. This legislation amended the Foreign Sovereign Immunities Act to make it easier for victims to attach the property of a state sponsor of terrorism to satisfy judgments that they had previously obtained.

International Conventions and Agreements

The 1954 Hague Convention on the Protection of Cultural Property in the Event of Armed Conflict

The 1954 Hague Convention was the first international treaty to address cultural property exclusively. Adopted in the aftermath of the cultural devastation of World War II, the Hague Convention is intended to establish principles for protecting cultural property, including sites, monuments, and repositories of cultural objects, during armed conflict and for preventing looting and smuggling of such objects from occupied territory. The First Protocol, which aims to prohibit illegal export of cultural objects from occupied territory and to facilitate return of such objects at the end of occupation, was also adopted in 1954. The Second Protocol was finalized in 1999 and came into effect in 2004. The Second Protocol clarifies and strengthens several sections of the main Convention and, among other provisions, requires States Parties to create a criminal offense for violation of the Second Protocol and of the main Convention. At this time, there are 121 States Parties to the main Convention, 100 States Parties to the First Protocol, and 51 States Parties to the Second Protocol. All three instruments received significant attention during the 2003 Gulf War, particularly because two of the central military powers involved in the conflict, the United States and the United Kingdom, were not parties to the Convention, although they had signed it in 1954.

In May 2004, the United Kingdom announced, on the fiftieth anniversary of the Convention, that it would move toward ratification of the main Convention and both the First and Second Protocols.[1] After release of a consultation paper and a period for comment, the Department for Culture, Media and Sport presented to Parliament a draft Cultural Property (Armed Conflicts) bill in January 2008.[2] This legislation proposes, in one action, to implement the main convention and both protocols.

The most significant feature of the draft bill is the creation of two new criminal offenses. Creation of a criminal offense under Article 15 is perhaps the most fundamental requirement of the Second Protocol. The first offense created by the U.K. draft bill is for serious breaches of the Second Protocol by intentionally committing one of the acts listed in Article 15, § 1(a)-(e) of the Second Protocol,[3] knowing that the property fits the Article 1 definition of cultural property in the main Convention.[4] Second, the draft bill would create a criminal offense for someone who deals in cultural property unlawfully exported from occupied territory knowingly or with reason to suspect that the property has been unlawfully exported.[5] The bill creates forfeiture provisions for illegally exported cultural objects, either in connection with a criminal proceeding[6] or without.[7] Finally, the bill includes broad provisions for immunity from seizure or forfeiture under any enactment or rule of law[8] while the cultural objects are in the United Kingdom. These provisions apply to objects being transported from outside or through the United Kingdom, and protected under Article 12 of the Hague Convention, and objects for which the United Kingdom is acting as depository under Regulation 18 of the main Convention.[9]

In September 2008, the New Zealand Parliament considered draft legislation that seems modeled on that proposed for the United Kingdom.[10] The Cultural Property (Protection in Armed Conflict) Bill 2008 establishes the criminal offenses, required by the Second Protocol, for knowing, serious violations of the Second Protocol, including "making enhanced protection property the object of attack; using enhanced protection property, or its immediate surroundings, in support of military action; the extensive destruction or the extensive appropriation of cultural property; making cultural property the object of attack; stealing, appropriating, or vandalizing cultural property (vandalizing includes marking, tagging, and defacing)." The First Protocol would be implemented through creation of an offense for the illegal removal from occupied territory of cultural property and of "enhanced protection property" as defined by Articles 10–14 of the Second Protocol.[11] This provision seems more limited than the U.K.'s proposed implementation of the First Protocol, which includes the offense of dealing in cultural property illegally removed from occupied territory.

Like the United Kingdom, the United States signed the main Convention in 1954 but did not ratify it, because of objections from the military as Cold War tensions increased. Only with the fall of the Soviet Union did the military review the Convention and withdraw its objections. President Clinton transmitted both the main Convention and the First Protocol to the Senate Foreign Relations Committee (SFRC) in March 1999. The transmittal was accompanied by a recommendation from the State Department that the United States opt out of the first part of the First Protocol. In early 2007, the State Department listed the Convention and First Protocol on its treaty priority list. In April 2008, the SFRC held hearings on the Convention and unanimously recommended ratification to the full Senate. On September 25, 2008, the Senate voted to give its advice and consent to ratification to the main Convention. The SFRC and the Senate did not consider the First Protocol.

United States ratification was subject to four understandings and one declaration.[12] The First Understanding states that the level of protection to be accorded to property under special protection is consistent with existing customary international law.[13] The Second Understanding clarifies that the action of any military commander or other military personnel is to be judged based on the information that was reasonably available at the time an action was taken. The Third Understanding clarifies that the rules of the Convention apply only to conventional weapons and do not affect other international law concerning other types of weapons, such as nuclear weapons. The Fourth Understanding states that the provisions of Article 4(1) requiring Parties "to respect cultural property situated within their own territory" means that the "primary responsibility for the protection of cultural objects rests with the Party controlling that property, to ensure that it is properly identified and that it is not used for an unlawful purpose." The Declaration states that the Convention is self-executing, meaning that it operates "of its own force as domestically enforceable federal law." It does not require any implementing legislation, but the Declaration also notes that the Convention does not confer any private rights enforceable in U.S. courts.

Ratification of the Convention may have relatively little direct impact on the conduct of the U.S. military because the U.S. government took the position that its military already complies with the core provisions of the Convention. However, ratification raises the status and awareness of cultural property within the military and concerns for preservation should therefore be incorporated into earlier stages of military planning. Article 7 of the Convention also requires States Parties to train their military in cultural preservation and to maintain cultural heritage professionals within their military forces. This could lead to greater military efforts by the United States to recruit cultural resource professionals. Finally, ratification demonstrates to other nations that the United States will take cultural heritage preservation more seriously in the planning and conduct of future military operations.

UNESCO Conventions

Four new nations ratified the 2001 UNESCO Convention on the Protection of the Underwater Cultural Heritage. This brings the total number of States Parties to twenty, paving the way for the Convention to come into force on January 2, 2009, for those nations that have deposited their instrument of ratification or acceptance by October 2, 2008.[14]

The United States renewed and broadened its Memorandum of Understanding (MOU) with Cambodia under the Convention on Cultural Property Implementation Act (CPIA), the U.S. legislation that implements the 1970 UNESCO Convention on the Means of Prohibiting and Preventing the Illicit Import, Export and Transfer of Ownership of Cultural Property.[15] Such agreements, which impose import restrictions on designated categories of archaeological and ethnological materials, must be renewed every five years.

In renewing the agreement with Cambodia, the United States broadened the agreement to cover earlier archaeological materials of the Bronze and Iron Ages, while continuing protection for the Khmer period sculptures, architectural fragments, and ceramic and metal artifacts of the sixth through sixteenth centuries A.D., which were covered under the earlier MOU.[16]

In April 2008, the United States imposed import restrictions under the CPIA and the Emergency Protection for Iraqi Cultural Antiquities Act[17] on illegally exported Iraqi cultural materials,[18] consonant with UNSCR 1483, which requires nations to prohibit trade in Iraqi cultural materials illegally removed from Iraq any time after August 1990. The special legislation broadens the definitions of cultural materials to which these import restrictions can apply. The CPIA allows protection only for archaeological materials, defined as objects of archaeological interest that are at least two hundred and fifty years old, and ethnographic materials, defined as the products of a tribal or preindustrial society. In contrast, the special legislation allows import restrictions for objects of "archaeological, historical, cultural, rare scientific, and religious importance," without any age requirement or other limitation.[19]

Recoveries, Restitutions, and Claims

Restitutions

The United States Department of Homeland Security Immigration and Customs Enforcement (ICE) returned several groups of seized archaeological artifacts to their country of origin. The largest restitution was a group of over one thousand Iraqi antiquities that were seized in four separate investigations conducted by ICE dating back to 2001.[20] In addition, ICE returned to Colombia sixty pre-Columbian artifacts that had been seized in Miami.[21] Eight items illegally excavated at burial sites in northern Afghanistan and recovered in 2005 during an undercover investigation conducted by the television show *Dateline NBC* were returned to the Afghan national museum director.[22] In January 2008, a marble sculpture of the Roman Emperor Marcus Aurelius was returned to Algeria. The statue had been stolen, along with eight other sculptures, from an Algerian museum in the town of Skikda, in 1996. The sculpture of Marcus Aurelius was seized from Christie's auction house where it had been offered for sale.[23]

Edward George Johnson, a U.S. Army pilot, was arrested on charges of selling 370 Egyptian antiquities that had been stolen from the museum storeroom at the predynastic-era (ca. 3900–3600 B.C.E.) site of Ma'adi near Cairo, Egypt. Johnson was an active duty chief warrant officer in the U.S. Army assigned to the U.S. Embassy in Cairo, when, using his diplomatic status, he smuggled the items out of Egypt, brought them to the U.S. and sold them to a dealer, claiming that they had been in his family since the early twentieth century. Johnson was charged with one count of transportation of stolen property and one count of wire fraud. He later pled guilty to possession of stolen property, was sentenced to eighteen months of probation and was ordered to make restitution to the antiquities dealer to whom he sold the objects.[24] On December 3, seventy-nine of the artifacts were returned to the Government of Egypt.

Italy and Greece have claimed classical antiquities that are in the collections of several U.S. museums based on evidence relating to the commercial dealings of an Italian dealer, Giacomo de Medici, whose Geneva warehouse was raided by Swiss and Italian authorities in 1995. Over the past few years, the J. Paul Getty Museum in Malibu, California, the Metropolitan Museum of Art in New York, the Boston Museum of Fine Arts, and the Princeton Museum of Art have returned artifacts to both countries.[25] This year, the private collector Shelby White returned nine antiquities to Italy, with a tenth to be returned in 2010,[26] and two objects to Greece, including the upper part of a 4th century B.C.E. grave stele, the lower part of which was excavated in Greece, and a bronze calyx krater.[27] Finally, the Cleveland Museum of Art agreed to return thirteen antiquities and a late Gothic processional cross to Italy. Italy agreed to lend comparable objects to the museum for renewable periods of twenty-five years, and the museum and Italy will establish a commission to study the origins of a bronze sculpture of Apollo, acquired by the museum in 2004, and of a small bronze chariot ornament.[28]

Two sixth century B.C.E. marble sculptures that had been in the collection of New York businessman Maurice Tempelsman were returned to Italy. The sculptures were likely looted from the Greek settlement site of Morgantina in Sicily. Tempelsman turned the sculptures over to the University of Virginia in 2002, which then returned them to Italy after gaining full title under an agreement with Tempelsman.[29]

In a joint action carried out by ICE and FBI agents, four paintings—one by Claude Monet, one by Alfred Sisley, and two by Jan Breughel the Elder—stolen in France were recovered in Miami in 2007. A French citizen was sentenced in Miami in 2008 to sixty-two months in prison and an order of restitution, for conspiracy to transport four stolen paintings and visa fraud.[30]

Peru's Claim against Yale

Yale University has held, for close to a hundred years, Incan artifacts recovered from the site of Machu Picchu in Peru by Hiram Bingham. In 2001, Peru's president, Alejandro Toledo, presented a claim to Yale for the return of the artifacts. In 2007, Peru and Yale reached a tentative agreement that called for Yale to return approximately 400 of the artifacts, while recognizing Peru's title to all of the objects.[31] However, negotiations and relations between the two deteriorated over the past year, and on December 5, Peru filed a claim in Federal District Court in the District of Columbia to recover all of the artifacts, seeking "the immediate return of all such property as well as damages that it has suffered on account of Yale's persistent breach of its obligations and profit at the expense of the people of Peru."[32]

Claim for Neo-Assyrian Earrings

At its December antiquities sale of ancient jewelry, Christie's planned to auction a pair of Neo-Assyrian earrings of the 8th to 7th centuries B.C.E. from northern Iraq. Donny George, former director of the Iraq Museum, recognized the earrings as likely coming from one of the royal graves discovered and excavated at Nineveh in 1989.[33] The only provenance information given in the Christie's catalogue was the year "1969." A few days before the planned auction, the earrings were removed from sale.[34] While Iraq is pursuing its claim for the earrings, the sparse provenance history given in the catalogue seems to display a lack of concern for the significance of provenance.

Settlement of *Malewicz v. City of Amsterdam*

The heirs of the artist Kazimir Malevich allege that Malevich left a group of his paintings in the possession of a friend in Germany who, after World War II, wrongfully transferred them to the Museum of the City of Amsterdam and that the paintings rightfully belong to them. Fourteen of these paintings were loaned to the Guggenheim and deMenil Museums in 2003 as part of an international exhibition.[35] The State Department granted these paintings immunity from seizure under the Immunity from Seizure Act (ISA).[36]

While the paintings were in the United States, attorneys filed suit on behalf of the heirs against the museum to recover the value of the paintings (or, in the alternative, the paintings themselves) under the Foreign Sovereign Immunities Act (FSIA).[37] The plaintiffs alleged that the City of Amsterdam is not immune from suit under the FSIA because the paintings were present in the United

States as part of a commercial activity. The U.S. District Court for the District of Columbia published two decisions, both favorable to the plaintiffs, holding that the loan exhibition constituted a sufficient commercial activity to establish jurisdiction for suit against the City in the United States under the FSIA.[38] While the appeal was pending, the parties settled and agreed that the City of Amsterdam would give five of the disputed paintings to the plaintiffs. The settlement leaves unanswered the interesting questions of how to reconcile an apparent conflict between the FSIA and ISA, and the status of loans of art to United States institutions, when it is claimed that the works themselves are stolen property. One of the returned paintings, *Suprematist Composition*, was auctioned at Sotheby's for $60 million, setting a record for sales by this artist and for Russian art.

Max Stern Estate Recovery of Painting

The estate of a Canadian art collector Max Stern succeeded in recovering through litigation a painting by Franz Xaver Winterhalter, *Madchen aus den Sabiner Bergen (Girl from the Sabiner Mountains)*.[39] Dr. Stern inherited the painting from his father in 1934, as part of the inventory of a gallery located in Dusseldorf, Germany. After the rise of the Nazis, Dr. Stern was persecuted and forced to liquidate the gallery and its inventory, which was sold off by the Lempertz Auction House. The eventual possessor of the painting, the defendant Bissonnette, was the stepdaughter of the person who purchased it at the Lempertz sale. The Art Loss Register identified the painting as belonging to the Stern Estate, when it was put up for sale in 2004. After negotiations failed, the Stern Estate sued Bissonnette, who relied on a laches defense. Both the trial and appellate courts, however, rejected this defense, noting that a key element of the defense, that the plaintiff's delay caused either evidence-based or expectations-based prejudice to the defendant, was lacking. The defendant failed to show that she had suffered any prejudice, or a link between the potential loss of evidence and the issues in controversy. In addition to clarifying the causal element in the relationship between a plaintiff's delay and prejudice to a defendant, the other significant aspect of these decisions is the courts' equation of a forced sale with a theft.[40] Because many artworks that were appropriated during the Holocaust were taken as a result of forced sales, this judicial determination opens the door to future recoveries.

Investigations of Antiquities Smuggling and Museums in Southern California

An undercover investigation carried out over several years by several U.S. federal agencies culminated in a series of search warrant executions on four southern California museums. They were the Los Angeles County Museum of Art, the Pacific Asia Museum in Pasadena, the Bowers Museum in Santa Ana, and the Mingei International Museum in San Diego. Also implicated were the Malter Gallery in Encino; the Silk Road Gallery, owned by Jonathan and Cari Markell in Los Angeles; and Barry MacLean, a private collector in Chicago and a trustee of the Art Institute of Chicago.[41] The affidavits submitted to obtain the warrants alleged an elaborate scheme in which the undercover agent, posing as a collector, was taken to the storerooms of an alleged smuggler who sold artifacts stolen and smuggled out of several Asian and Southeast Asian countries, including China, Thailand, Cambodia, and Myanmar. The artifacts were given a valuation just below the IRS $5000 threshold, which would have required more documentation of an object's value for tax purposes and which could also trigger a violation of the National Stolen Property Act.[42] The "collector" then donated the objects to various museums for a charitable gift deduction. The low value attributed to the artifacts prompted the investigation to consider the trafficking provision of the Archaeological Resources Protection Act (ARPA),[43] which requires no minimum monetary value as a threshold for a misdemeanor and $500.00 for a felony. Under ARPA the items must be over 100 years old regardless of value. The U.S. law enforcement agencies involved in the investigation include the Internal Revenue Service, Immigration and Customs Enforcement of the Department of Homeland Security, and the National Park Service. As of the end of the year, no indictments were issued.

Museum Policies for Acquiring Antiquities

Museums in the United States have come under criticism for acquiring antiquities that were possibly looted and obtained in violation of national ownership laws. The two main U.S. museum associations, the Association of Art Museum Directors (AAMD) and the American Association of Museums (AAM), both adopted guidelines this year for their members, concerning the acquisition of antiquities.[44] While sharing some similarities, the two sets of guidelines differ in some of their important and more interesting details.

Both guidelines offer a sharp contrast to the positions previously taken by many U.S. museums. The most significant change from past operations is that museums are expected to trace the ownership history of any potential acquisition back to 1970. However, both guidelines permit an acquisition to proceed under varying circumstances even if this standard cannot be attained. Both policies require that a museum make publicly available its acquisition policy and that it make publicly accessible information about new acquisitions, including provenance background and an image of the object.

In a somewhat novel step, the AAMD established a website where any object whose provenance history cannot be traced back either to 1970 or to legal export from the country of origin should be posted with available documentation and an image.[45] The first, and so far only, object to be listed on the registry is a Ganesha Stele of the 11th century from the area of modern Bangladesh, which was purchased by the Portland Art Museum.[46] The only provenance history given is a sale at Sotheby's in 2000 and the Christie's sale in 2008, when the museum purchased it. This incident raises the possibility that what appeared intended to be a narrow and rarely used loophole in the AAMD guidelines could become, through the mechanism of the registry, an exception that largely swallows the whole. If museums feel that they can acquire artifacts that do not have a documented provenance back to 1970, so long as the museum posts information about the artifact on the AAMD registry, then museums may be *encouraged* to acquire such unprovenanced objects, despite the apparent intent of the guidelines to inhibit such acquisitions. In contrast to the AAMD, in addition to focusing on new acquisitions that do not have provenance history that can be traced back to 1970, the AAM guidelines expect museums to research the background of artifacts currently in a museum's collection for possible restitution to the country of origin.

International Application of the National Historic Preservation Act

The National Historic Preservation Act (NHPA)[47] applies primarily to federal undertakings within the United States that might have an adverse impact on historic properties listed or eligible for listing on the National Register of Historic Places.[48] A provision added when the United States ratified the 1972 UNESCO Convention concerning the Protection of the World Cultural and Natural Heritage makes the NHPA applicable to federal undertakings that may have an adverse impact on historic properties that are World Heritage Sites or that are listed on a foreign nation's equivalent to the U.S. National Register of Historic Places.[49] In an earlier decision, the District Court for the Northern District of California held that this provision of the NHPA is applicable to a decision of the U.S. Department of Defense, when constructing a naval base near Okinawa, Japan, that might have an adverse impact on the *dugong*, a sea mammal that is listed on Japan's Register of Cultural Properties.[50] In a further decision this year,[51] the District Court held that the Department of Defense failed to follow the appropriate procedures laid out in the NHPA for determining whether the new naval facility would have an adverse impact and for failing to take those adverse effects into account for the purpose of avoiding or mitigating adverse effects to the dugong. At issue is the desire of the Navy to build a dock, which would have a direct physical impact on the habitation site of the dugong. Previously, the court found that impact to a habitation site is an impact to the life of the animal, clearing the way for the Navy to perform a NHPA Section 106 analysis at the site.

Litigation Concerning Iranian Artifacts on Loan to U.S. Institutions and Related Developments[52]

In *Rubin v. Iran,*[53] a group of plaintiffs are attempting to attach ancient Persian artifacts currently housed at various U.S. museums in satisfaction of a multimillion dollar default judgment against Iran for allegedly providing material support to Hamas to carry out an act of terrorism in Israel.[54] Iran has opposed these attempts, arguing that Iran's assets are immune from attachment. There were several significant developments in 2008 in the *Rubin* case and in the area of foreign sovereign immunity generally.

The *Rubin* Proceeding in Chicago

In Chicago, the *Rubin* plaintiffs sued the University of Chicago's Oriental Institute (OI) and the Field Museum (FM)[55] alleging that those institutions had in their possession Iranian artifacts which were subject to attachment under the Foreign Sovereign Immunities Act (FSIA)[56] and/or §201 of the Terrorism Risk Insurance Act (TRIA).[57] In 2006, after the court ruled that the OI and the FM could not raise the defense of immunity on Iran's behalf,[58] Iran entered the case and moved for summary judgment to declare the artifacts immune from attachment.[59] The plaintiffs opposed, citing the need to take discovery pursuant to Fed. R. Civ. P. 56(f).[60] The court granted the plaintiffs' requested discovery, but Iran continued in 2008 to contest two issues.

First, Iran contests discovery related to one of the artifact collections, the Chogha Mish Collection. To prove that there is a title contest[61] between Iran and the OI (or the United States, on the OI's behalf) regarding the Chogha Mish Collection, plaintiffs requested production of documents from the arbitration pending before the Iran-U.S. Claims Tribunal.[62] The magistrate permitted this discovery even though Iran and the United States agree that there is no such title contest, and even though the Tribunal's Co-Registrars stated that arbitration documents cannot be produced to third parties.[63] In August 2008, Iran filed objections to the magistrate's ruling before the district court judge.[64] Those objections remain pending.

Second, Iran contests plaintiffs' request for documents and a deposition as to all of Iran's assets nationwide. Iran moved to quash this "general assets" discovery on three main grounds: the Algiers Accords, comity, and foreign relations. The United States generally agreed with Iran, as stated in the United States' Third Statement of Interest.[65] In 2008, Iran appealed the district court's order requiring Iran to produce general assets discovery pursuant to 28 U.S.C. §1291,[66] arguing that, under the collateral order doctrine, the court could review the order as an infringement on Iran's sovereign immunity. The Seventh Circuit has not yet ruled whether it has jurisdiction to hear the appeal.

Also in 2008, the plaintiffs in *Peterson v. Iran*[67] successfully intervened in the Chicago *Rubin* proceedings.[68] The *Peterson* plaintiffs argued that their alleged right to attach the artifacts supersedes any rights of the *Rubin* plaintiffs.[69] That issue also remains pending before the district court.

The *Rubin* Proceedings in Massachusetts and the First Circuit

The *Rubin* plaintiffs also sued Harvard University (HU) and the Museum of Fine Arts (MFA) in Boston, asserting that those institutions too possess Iranian artifacts which are subject to attachment.[70] HU and MFA argue that they, not Iran, own the artifacts. Earlier this year, the district court certified three questions to the First Circuit: (1) whether certain properties may be considered "blocked assets" pursuant to TRIA,[71] (2) whether a foreign sovereign's immunity may be asserted only by the sovereign,[72] and (3) whether the "commercial use" exception under FSIA §1610(a)(7) applies only when the sovereign itself has used the property in the United States.[73] The First Circuit declined to hear the appeal because of the factual questions that exist as to whether Iran actually owns any of the artifacts at issue.

National Defense Authorization Act §1083 and the *Rubin* Proceeding in the District of Columbia

In 2008, as a result of lobbying by victims of terrorism, including especially the *Peterson* plaintiffs, Congress passed the National Defense Authorization Act, which President Bush signed into law on January 28, 2008.[74] Section 1083 of that Act *inter alia* created a new "terrorism exception to immunity" in the FSIA[75] and amended §1610, the FSIA's exception to immunity from attachment and execution.[76]

The Act is landmark for several reasons, a few of which are highlighted here. First, §1605A, which replaced old §1605(a)(7), now provides a private right of action against a "state sponsor of terror" for materially supporting an act of terrorism, and permits an award of punitive damages against that nation. Second, filing under §1605A automatically establishes a lien of *lis pendens* upon "any real property or tangible personal property" that is subject to execution under the amended §1610. Iran has argued that such a lien, to the extent it covers Iranian assets pending before the Tribunal, violates the Algiers Accords.[77] Third, the Act broadens the definition of victim to include, in addition to U.S. nationals, members of the Armed Forces and employees and contractors of the U.S. government, regardless of whether they are U.S. nationals.

Fourth, under new §1610(g), property of foreign states and of their agencies and instrumentalities is subject to attachment regardless of the foreign state's level of economic control over the property, including profits, day-to-day management, and other factors. Certain plaintiffs—such as the *Peterson* plaintiffs—have argued that there is no requirement that the property be used for "commercial activity" at all, and that all assets, including those with no U.S. connection, may be attached.

The Act also includes a waiver provision, permitting the President to waive the application of §1083 to Iraq. President Bush issued such a waiver on January 28, 2008, in an effort to protect and promote Iraq's reconstruction.

In 2008, the *Rubin* plaintiffs convinced the federal court in Washington, D.C.—which issued the underlying default judgment against Iran—to amend their judgment to include a claim for §1605A relief.[78] However, the four institutions with claims pending against them—the OI, the FM, HU, and the MFA—later moved to intervene in that proceeding and for reconsideration,[79] arguing that such retroactive application of §1605A should not permitted based on *Plaut v. Spendthrift Farm, Inc.*[80] The court has not yet decided whether to permit intervention.

The FSIA amendments also have affected the museum community outside of the courtroom. Recently, Syria was unable to lend fifty-five ancient cultural objects to the Metropolitan Museum of Art, fearing possible attachment proceedings by plaintiffs who hold multimillion dollar "terrorism" judgments against the nation. The objects were going to be included in the Met's exhibition, *Beyond Babylon: Art, Trade, and Diplomacy in the Second Millennium B.C.*, and in fact already had been listed in the exhibition catalogue. On one of the exhibit's wall labels, the Met wrote, "We express our deep regret that recent legislation in the United States has made it too difficult and risky for these planned loans to proceed."[81]

Conclusion[82]

Probably the greatest threat to the free international exchange of cultural objects is the continued whittling away at the concept of foreign sovereign immunity. In addition to general principles of foreign sovereign immunity, additional immunity from seizure provisions specific to cultural objects on loan were enacted in 1966 to allow the continued international loan of cultural artifacts without threat of legal action. Such cultural interchange is crucial if we are to understand and learn about different cultures, different peoples, and different histories.

The *Malewicz* litigation raised the question of how to resolve a conflict between the Immunity from Seizure Act and the Foreign Sovereign Immunities Act in the context of allegedly stolen artworks. In one sense, the ISA was vindicated because the paintings were not seized or otherwise subjected to judicial process while they were in the United States, but the District Court opinions that were favorable to the claimants foreshadow that lenders of artworks may need to be concerned as to potential liability. Although there is no appellate court decision that definitively resolves the apparent conflict between these statutes, imposing liability on a foreign lender for the value of the loaned artworks may be justified when the artworks are themselves stolen property.

However, the continued whittling away of foreign sovereign immunity, particularly for those nations deemed to be state sponsors of terrorism, has already had its impact on one proposed international loan where there is no allegation of theft. This whittling is most apparent in the attachment proceedings against Iranian artifacts on loan to U.S. institutions. The Iranian artifacts were loaned to the Oriental Institute before immunity from seizure was available. In that sense, the fate of these artifacts is not directly applicable to future loans for which immunity can now be obtained. However, the fact that Syria could not lend objects to the Metropolitan Museum of Art, even though the immunity from seizure protection is (at least theoretically) available to it, presents a much graver threat to future loans. A clear distinction needs to be made between artworks on loan that may themselves be stolen property (as in *Malewicz*) and artworks that are being sought solely to satisfy a judgment that has no connection to the artworks other than that they are owned by a foreign sovereign that has an outstanding judgment against it.

To achieve this distinction and to protect artifacts and artworks on loan from attachment may require a carefully delineated amendment to the ISA, the FSIA, or both statutes. Such an amendment would need to make an exception from attachment for cultural objects on loan to U.S. institutions whose purpose is to increase cross-cultural understanding. With such a provision in place, international loans of cultural objects would once again receive the protection they merit.

Notes

1. *See* http://www.culture.gov.uk/global/consultations/2005+current+consultations/hauge_convention.htm?properties=2005+current+consultations%2C%2Fglobal%2Fconsultations%2Fdefault%2C&month=. For the Consultation Paper released in September 2005, *see* Department for Culture, Media and Sport, "Consultation Paper on: The 1954 Hague Convention on the Protection of Cultural Property in the Event of Armed Conflict and its two Protocols of 1954 and 1999 (September 2005)," available at: http://www.culture.gov.uk/NR/rdonlyres/C234A6B1-3178-4350-8C72-C354F24D1CF9/0/HagueConvention.pdf. *See also* Patty Gerstenblith, *International Cultural Property*, *in* YEARBOOK OF CULTURAL PROPERTY LAW 2008, 119, 120 (Sherry Hutt & David Tarler eds 2008).
2. Department for Culture, Media and Sport, Draft Cultural Property (Armed Conflicts) Bill, January 7, 2008, available at http://www.culture.gov.uk/images/publications/culturalpropertyarmedconflictsdraftbill.pdf [hereinafter "Armed Conflicts Bill"].

3. Article 15 of the Second Protocol states:
   1. Any person commits an offence within the meaning of this Protocol if that person intentionally and in violation of the Convention or this Protocol commits any of the following acts:
      a. making cultural property under enhanced protection the object of attack;
      b. using cultural property under enhanced protection or its immediate surroundings in support of military action;
      c. extensive destruction or appropriation of cultural property protected under the Convention and this Protocol;
      d. making cultural property protected under the Convention and this Protocol the object of attack;
      e. theft, pillage or misappropriation of, or acts of vandalism directed against cultural property protected under the Convention.

   Paragraph 2 of this article requires the creation of a criminal offense and extension of criminal responsibility even to those who did not directly commit the criminal act. The U.K. Armed Conflicts Bill does this in Sections 5 and 6.
4. Armed Conflicts Bill, § 3(1). The criminal offense can be committed by a non-U.K. national if the act fits within Article 15, paragraph 1(a), (b) or (c). *Id.* § 3(3). Article 15 of the Second Protocol clarified and strengthened Article 28 of the main Convention, which called for the establishment of "penal or disciplinary sanctions" for those who commit a breach of the convention. Both the U.S. and the U.K. objected to this provision, in particular for calling for criminal punishment when they considered the definition of "cultural property" under Article 1 to be vague. The U.K. Bill cures this problem by adding a second knowledge requirement—that the person knew the property fit the Article 1 definition.
5. *Id.* § 18(1). This provision carries a semi-retroactive effect in that it applies only to property imported into the United Kingdom after the provision goes into effect but apparently will apply to property illegally exported before the effective date. *Id.* § 18(2). Dealing includes acquisition, disposal, importation, and exportation of cultural property. *Id.* § 18(3)(a).
6. *Id.* § 19.
7. *Id.* § 22.
8. Seizure or forfeiture includes reference to Schedule 12 to the Tribunals, Courts and Enforcement Act 2007. The Tribunal, Courts and Enforcement Act provides immunity from seizure in any criminal or civil proceeding for objects that are on temporary loan for exhibition from collections in foreign nations. Tribunals, Courts and Enforcement Act 2007, ch. 15, Part 6, Protection of Cultural Objects on Loan, ss. 134-38. *See* Gerstenblith, *supra* note 1, at 124.
9. Armed Conflicts Bill, § 27.

10. *See* Cultural Property (Protection in Armed Conflict) Bill 2008, Research Publications Bills Digests No. 1642, available at: http://www.parliament.nz/en-NZ/PubRes/Research/BillsDigests/7/e/6/48PLLawBD16421-Cultural-Property-Protection-in-Armed-Conflict-Bill.htm
11. *Id.*
12. 110TH CONG. 2D SESS. EXEC. REP. 110-26 (Sept. 16, 2008), http://frwebgate.access.gpo.gov/cgi-bin/getdoc.cgi?dbname=110_cong_reports&docid=f:er026.pdf
13. The Convention in Articles 8–11 provides that cultural property may be placed under special protection. However, special protection was sought for very few properties and so this provision is considered to be of relatively little importance.
14. Convention on the Protection of the Underwater Cultural Heritage States Parties, available at: http://portal.unesco.org/la/convention.asp?KO=13520&language=E
15. 19 U.S.C. §§ 2601-13.
16. Extension of Import Restrictions Imposed on Archaeological Material from Cambodia, 19 C.F.R. Part 12, Fed. Reg. 73,183 at 54309-13 (Sept. 19, 2008), available at: http://culturalheritage.state.gov/Cambodia2008FRN.pdf
17. Miscellaneous Trade and Technical Corrections Act of 2004, P.L. 108-429, §§ 3001-03, 118 Stat. 2434 (2004); *see also* Patty Gerstenblith, *International Cultural Property*, *in* YEARBOOK OF CULTURAL PROPERTY LAW 2006 (Sherry Hutt & David Tarler eds 2006) 91, 93.
18. 73 Fed. Reg. 23334-42 (Apr. 30, 2008).
19. *Id.*
20. Dept. of Homeland Security, ICE returns more than 1,000 artifacts to Iraq, Sept. 15, 2008, available at: http://www.ice.gov/pi/nr/0809/080915washington.htm
21. U.S. Immigration and Customs Enforcement, Fact Sheet: Cultural Heritage Investigations, available at http://www.ice.gov/pi/news/factsheets/cultural-artifacts-repatriation.htm
22. *Id.*
23. *Id.*
24. *Id.*
25. Lucille A. Roussin, *Museum*, *in* YEARBOOK OF CULTURAL PROPERTY LAW 2008 (Sherry Hutt & David Tarler eds 2008) 87, 87-89.
26. Elisabetta Povoledo, *Collector Returns Art Italy Says Was Looted*, N.Y. TIMES, Jan. 18, 2008, at B1.
27. Julie Bloom, *Collector to Return Antiquities to Greece*, N.Y. TIMES, Jul. 12, 2008, at B8.
28. Steven Litt, *Museum Returns Artwork to Italy*, CLEVELAND PLAIN DEALER, Nov. 20, 2008, at 1.
29. Elisabetta Povoledo, *Tempelsman Sculptures Return to Italy*, N.Y. TIMES, Feb. 26, 2008, at E2.

30. U.S. Immigration and Customs Enforcement, Fact Sheet, *supra* note 20.
31. Gerstenblith, *supra* note 1, at 123-24.
32. Paul Neeham, *Peru Sues Yale over Artifacts*, YALE DAILY NEWS, Dec. 9, 2008.
33. Jane Arraf, *Iraq bids to stop Christie's sale of ancient earrings*, CHRISTIAN SCIENCE MONITOR, Dec. 4, 2008, at 7.
34. Jane Arraf, *Christie's takes disputed earrings off auction block*, CHRISTIAN SCIENCE MONITOR, Dec. 5, 2008, at 25.
35. *See* Gerstenblith, *supra* note 17, at 100-02.
36. 22 U.S.C. § 2459.
37. 28 U.S.C. §§ 1602 *et seq.*
38. *Malewicz v. City of Amsterdam*, 362 F. Supp. 2d 298 (D.D.C. 2005); 517 F. Supp. 2d 322 (D.D.C. 2007).
39. *Vineberg v. Bissonnette*, 529 F. Supp. 2d 300 (D.R.I. 2007), *aff'd*, 2008 U.S. App. LEXIS 24043 (1st Cir. 2008).
40. 529 F. Supp. 2d at 307 (stating that "[t]he Nazi party's actions in this instance are therefore properly classified as looting or stealing.").
41. Bruce Zagaris, *U.S. Tax Investigation Turns Up Apparently Stolen Cultural Artifacts*, 24 INT'L LAW ENF. REP. Apr. 2008; Edward Wyatt, *Four Museums Are Raided in Looted Antiquities Case*, N.Y. TIMES, Jan. 25, 2008, at A14; Edward Wyatt, *Papers Show Wider Focus in Inquiry of Artifacts*, N.Y. TIMES, Jan. 30, 2008, at A11.
42. 18 U.S.C. §§ 2314-15.
43. 16 U.S.C. § 470ee(c), which provides that "no person may sell, purchase, exchange, transport, receive, or offer to sell, purchase, or exchange, in interstate or foreign commerce, any archaeological resource excavated, removed, sold, purchased, exchanged, transported, or received in violation of any provision, rule, regulation, ordinance, or permit in effect under State or local law."
44. The AAMD principles are available at: http://aamd.org/newsroom/documents/2008ReportAndRelease.pdf. The AAM standards are available at: http://www.aam-us.org/museumresources/ethics/upload/Standards%20Regarding%20Archaeological%20Material%20and%20Ancient%20Art.pdf
45. The AAMD Object Registry can be found at: http://aamdobjectregistry.org/
46. *See* Object Registry, available at: http://aamdobjectregistry.org/node/28
47. 16 U.S.C. §§ 470-470w-6.
48. 16 U.S.C. § 470(f).
49. 16 U.S.C. § 470a-2.
50. Okinawa Dugong v. Rumsfeld, No. 03-4350, 2005 U.S. Dist. LEXIS 3123 (N.D. Cal. Mar. 1, 2005). *See also* Gerstenblith, *supra* note 17, at 97–98.
51. Okinawa Dugong (Dugong Dugon) v. Gates, 543 F. Supp. 2d 1082 (N.D. Cal. 2008).

52. This section is based upon an article that will be published in *International Legal Developments in Review: 2008*, 43 INT'L LAW. (2009).
53. *Rubin v. Islamic Republic of Iran*, Case No. 03-cv-9370 (N.D. Ill.) (hereinafter "*Rubin* Chicago proceeding"). *See also* Patty Gerstenblith, *International Cultural Property*, *in* YEARBOOK OF CULTURAL PROPERTY LAW 2007, 109, 113-15 (Sherry Hutt & David Tarler eds 2007).
54. *Campuzano v. Islamic Republic of Iran*, 281 F. Supp. 2d 258 (D.D.C. 2003).
55. *Rubin v. Islamic Republic of Iran*, 349 F. Supp. 2d 1108 (N.D. Ill. 2004).
56. 28 U.S.C. §§1330, 1602-1611.
57. Pub. L. No. 107-297, Title II, §201, 116 Stat. 2322 (Nov. 26, 2002).
58. *See Rubin v. Islamic Republic of Iran*, 436 F. Supp. 2d 938 (N.D. Ill. 2006).
59. *See* Dkt. 199, *Rubin* Chicago proceeding.
60. Rule 56(f) provides in relevant part that, if an opponent of a summary judgment motion can show that it requires fact-finding to justify its opposition, the court may continue the motion to allow for discovery.
61. Plaintiffs claim that, if there is a title contest, the artifacts are attachable under TRIA §201 as "blocked assets."
62. The Tribunal, located in The Hague, was created in 1981 by the Algiers Accords, the agreement which resolved the 1979 hostage crisis.
63. *See* Dkt. 379, *Rubin* Chicago proceeding.
64. *See* Dkt. 410, *Rubin* Chicago proceeding.
65. *See* Dkt. 300, *Rubin* Chicago proceeding.
66. Section 1291 provides for appellate jurisdiction over "appeals from all final decisions of the district courts of the United States. . . ."
67. *See* Dkt. 429, *Rubin* Chicago proceeding.
68. *See* Dkt. 429, *Rubin* Chicago proceeding.
69. *See* Dkt. 429 at 2-3, *Rubin* Chicago proceeding.
70. *Rubin v. Islamic Republic of Iran*, 456 F. Supp. 2d 228 (D. Mass. 2006).
71. *Id.* at 235.
72. *Id.* at 231-32.
73. *Id.* at 234-35.
74. 110 P.L. 181, 122 Stat. 3 (2008).
75. 28 U.S.C. §1605A.
76. Section 1605A applies to those nations designated by the U.S. Department of State as "state sponsors of terrorism"—Cuba, Syria, Iran, and Sudan. In fall 2008, the United States removed North Korea from the list and achieved a settlement with Libya (removed in 2006) regarding all terrorism cases pending against that nation.
77. *See* Dkt. 288, *Rubin* Chicago proceeding.
78. *See* Dkt. 81 at 2.3, *Rubin v. Islamic Republic of Iran*, Case No. 01-1655 (D.D.C).

79. *See* Dkt. 82, *Rubin v. Islamic Republic of Iran*, Case No. 01-1655 (D.D.C.).
80. 514 U.S. 211, 225 (1995).
81. This information was gathered from a November 21, 2008, post on http://www.artsjournal.com/culturegrrl/
82. The views in this Conclusion are solely those of one of the authors, Patty Gerstenblith.

Enforcement Actions

Section Editor: David Tarler[1]

Introduction

Plus ça change, plus c'est la meme chose might be one theme for this year's review of federal enforcement actions. Every volume of the *Yearbook* has reported on new federal prosecutions involving the theft of rare books, manuscripts, letters, maps, illustrations, illuminations, autographs, and other documents and ephemera from libraries and archives. This year is no different (*Renehan; Brubaker; Weber*). The new cases also remind us that a significant number of offenses involving the theft of library, archival, and museum items are committed by employees and others entrusted with particularized access to and knowledge about the fruits of their crimes (*Malatare; Renehan; Weber*), and, in addition, that crimes involving cultural heritage resources from these institutions often are not detected until the items are offered for sale through the internet, an auction house, or a gallery, and someone—most often a member of the public—recognizes the items' provenance (*Ary; Malatare; Johnson; Weber; Renehan*).

Last year, this section noted that the nonimposition of an advisory U.S. Sentencing Guideline range, nonuse of all the 2B1.5 Guideline-specific offense characteristics, or the Government's decision to charge a crime allowing for a considerably lower maximum sentence all have resulted in some sentences that appear to be lower than otherwise would be indicated by strict use of U.S. Sentencing Guideline § 2B1.5 to sentence defendants convicted of a crime involving a cultural heritage resource.[2] As several of the sentencings in 2008 continue that thread (*Allen; Johnson; Garihan; Mardirosian*), a hard look at this phenomenon might still be warranted. By contrast, this year did see one departure upward from the advisory guideline range (*Weber*).

The year 2008 witnessed the use of several laws that have not often been used as statutes of conviction in cases involving cultural heritage resources offenses. They include destruction of veterans' memorials (18 U.S.C. 1369) (*Elibosang*); theft concerning programs receiving Federal funds (18 U.S.C. 666) (*Malatare; Weber*); receipt of stolen property within a special maritime jurisdiction (*Johnson*); and making and subscribing a false tax return (*Weber*).

Two enforcement cases involving cultural heritage resources were decided by federal appellate courts (*Ary; Allen*). The United States Court of Appeals for the Tenth Circuit held that "auction value" could be used to measure fair market value and, thus, satisfied the criteria for determining "loss" for purposes of applying Federal Sentencing Guideline 2B1.1 (*Ary*). Meanwhile, in a case of first impression, the United States Court of Appeals for the Sixth Circuit first determined that the Sentencing Guidelines' definition of "loss" was the key to identifying which cultural heritage resources to value for purposes of applying Federal Sentencing Guideline 2B1.5, and then found that the definition of "loss" to be used for this purpose was not always the same one. This interesting opinion merits attention and critical review.

The Archaeological Resources Protection Act

The Archaeological Resources Protection Act (ARPA; 16 U.S.C. §§ 470aa-mm) prescribes criminal punishment (at 16 U.S.C. § 470ee) for persons who:

(a) excavate, remove, damage, or otherwise alter or deface any archaeological resource located on public lands or Indian lands, or attempt to do so, without a permit (16 U.S.C. § 470ee (a));

(b) sell, purchase, exchange, transport, or receive, or offer to sell, purchase, or exchange any archaeological resource removed from public lands or Indian lands in violation of (a), or any provision, rule, regulation, ordinance, or permit in effect under any other provision of federal law (16 U.S.C. § 470ee (b));

(c) sell, purchase, exchange, transport, receive, or offer to sell, purchase, or exchange, in interstate or foreign commerce, any archaeological resource excavated, removed, sold, purchased, exchanged, transported, or received in violation of any provision, rule, regulation, ordinance, or permit in effect under state or local law (16 U.S.C. § 470ee (c)); or

(d) counsel, procure, solicit, or employ another to violate (a), (b), or (c) (16 U.S.C. § 470ee (d)).

An ARPA offense is a general intent crime. The government must prove that the defendant knowingly committed the offense conduct.[3]

ARPA also provides for the assessment of civil penalties for violations on public lands and Indian lands (16 U.S.C. § 470ff). In the case of a second or subsequent violation of ARPA, the amount of a civil penalty may be double the amount that would have been assessed if such violation were the first violation (16 U.S.C. § 470ff (a); 43 C.F.R. § 7.16 (a)(2); 36 C.F.R. § 296.16 (a)(2); 32 C.F.R. § 229.16 (a)(2); and 18 C.F.R. § 1312.16 (a)(2)). Intent is not an element of a civil violation of ARPA.[4]

United States v. Kenneth Spry[5]

Kenneth Spry pled guilty to one misdemeanor count of violation of ARPA (16 U.S.C. 470ee (a)). Originally, he had been charged in an indictment with one felony count of violation of the Act. Spry was sentenced to 36 months of probation, and was ordered to pay a fine of $500 and restitution to Ozark-St. Francis National Forest in the amount of $3,288.

In 2007, a Forest Service officer observed Spry walking out of a wooded area within Ozark National Forest, in Arkansas. Spry's hands were dirty and his back pockets were bulging. During a search of Spry, the officer recovered twelve stone projectile points and a piece of metal. Spry admitted he had been digging for artifacts, stated that he knew he was excavating within Ozark National Forest, and showed the officer the holes he had dug while looking for the artifacts.

The archaeological value of the archaeological resources involved in the offense conduct is not known; their commercial value was $84. The cost of restoration and repair of the archaeological resources involved in the offense was at least $3,288. In a separate proceeding, in State court, Spry pled guilty to possession of a controlled substance (methamphetamine).

United States v. Robert V. Gallegos, Jack Beasley, and Peter Lewis Hester[6]

Robert V. Gallegos was acquitted by a jury on one felony count of aiding and abetting the violation of ARPA (16 U.S.C. 470ee (b) and 18 U.S.C. 2). On four other felony counts charging Gallegos with the same violations, the jury was hung. Following the mistrial on the remaining counts, the Government moved to dismiss those charges, as well as a Forfeiture Allegation, as applied to Gallegos, and the judge dismissed them with prejudice. In the same case, Jack Beasley and Peter Lewis Hester were charged with the same five felony counts as Gallegos. Beasley pled guilty to one misdemeanor count of aiding and abetting the violation of ARPA (16 U.S.C. 470ee (b) and 18 U.S.C. 2), and Peter Lewis Hester pled guilty to the five felony counts of aiding and abetting the violation of ARPA (16 U.S.C. 470ee (b) and 18 U.S.C. 2) charged in the indictment. Beasley was sentenced to 12 months of probation, and Hester was sentenced to three months of imprisonment followed by 24 months of supervised release.

Gallegos is a dealer in, and collector of, antique tribal arts from the American Southwest, based in Albuquerque, New Mexico. He also has served as Treasurer (2007–2008) of The Antique Tribal Art Dealers Association, Inc. In 2002, Gallegos purchased 42 Navajo grayware pots dating between 1500 and 1700 from Orion Allen and Larry Moore, a school principal and a gas pipeline company supervisor, for $25,950. Beasley and Hester brokered the deal, for which Hester received $1,250 from Gallegos.

In the 1950s and 1960s, at a time when they were employed as oil camp workers, Allen and Moore had removed the pots from caves and crevices in the Canyon Largo region, near Bloomfield, New Mexico. The area from which the pots were taken is known as the Dinetah region, on public lands managed by the Bureau of Land Management, and Allen and Moore's acts had been committed in violation of the Antiquities Act of 1906.[7]

A five-felony count indictment charged the three defendants with purchasing, transporting, and receiving archaeological resources with a commercial value exceeding $500. The Forfeiture Allegation sought the entire 42-piece collection for the United States.

Gallegos argued that, in order for him to be convicted, the Government would have to prove he knew both that he was purchasing archaeological resources and that the archaeological resource had been removed from public land. The United States, on the other hand, contended that it need only prove Gallegos knew that he was purchasing archaeological resources and, consequently, it filed a *motion in limine* asking that Gallegos not be allowed to present evidence, or argue as a defense, that he did not know the Navajo grayware pots he purchased came from public land. The court denied the motion, reasoning that to read the "knowing" requirement out of the "removed from public lands" element of a 16 U.S.C. 270ee (b) violation would criminalize a broad range of apparently innocent conduct. After all, Gallegos's purchase of the grayware pottery would have been legal had Moore and Allen lawfully removed it from Canyon Largo, as not every purchase of pottery legally defined as an archaeological resource amounts to a criminal act.

At trial, Allen and Moore testified under a grant of immunity from prosecution. In his defense, Gallegos asserted that he had believed the pots came from private land.

United States v. William Paul Rogers[8]

William Paul Rogers pled guilty to one misdemeanor count of violation of ARPA (16 U.S.C. 470ee (a)). He was sentenced to 12 months of probation, and ordered to perform 10 hours of community service. In addition, Rogers agreed to forfeit the Yamaha Rhino all terrain vehicle he used to access the archaeological site, transport digging tools, and transport archaeological resources in committing the offense conduct, and whose value was estimated to be $8,000.

In 2006, Tennessee Valley Authority Police, acting on a complaint that someone had been digging on the lake bottom of Normandy Reservoir, in Coffee County, Tennessee, observed Rogers digging at a documented archaeological site. Rogers admitted to the officers that he was looking for arrowheads, that he had been digging at the site over the course of two weeks, and that he had been helped by his wife, mother-in-law, and juvenile nephew. When apprehended, Rogers was in possession of numerous Native American artifacts. Subsequently, Rogers voluntarily escorted the TVA officers to his home, where he showed them additional archaeological resources that he admitted had come from the site in question, as well as archaeological resources that he admitted had been removed from other lands managed by TVA. All the artifacts, along with the ATV found at the crime scene—containing a Remington Model 700 rifle—were seized. The commercial value of the archaeological resources involved in the offense conduct was less than $500.

Neither the archaeological value of the approximately 120 x 60 foot area disturbed by Rogers, nor the cost of restoration and repair of the archaeological resources involved in the offense is known. These values, though, as well as the absence of signage indicating that the site of the offense was an archaeological site, were of apparent concern to the judge during Rogers' initial sentencing hearing.

United States v. Robert Gee[9]

Robert Gee pled guilty to one misdemeanor count of violation of ARPA (16 U.S.C. 470ee (a)). Originally, he had been charged in a criminal information with three misdemeanor counts of violation of the Act. Gee was ordered to pay a fine of $2,000 and restitution to Mesa Verde National Park in the amount of $1,000. In addition, he was banned from entering any National Park unit for a period of three years, and required to write a letter to the *Cortez Journal* newspaper describing what happened and why what he did was wrong.

While investigating an unrelated case involving employees of Kirkland Construction, which had been engaged in a repaving project at Mesa Verde National Park, National Park Service investigators learned through a confidential informant that Gee, a company employee, had been removing archaeological resources from locations near the construction site, had been seen with a bag of pot sherds, and had been overheard talking about removing sherds, a mano and a metate (stone tools) from the park. A search of Gee's residence revealed 252 pre-contact period archaeological resources; drug paraphernalia also was found. When interviewed, Gee admitted to having removed the archaeological resources from Mesa Verde National Park over a month-long period.

United States v. Tina Todd[10]

Tina Todd pled guilty to one felony count of violation of ARPA (16 U.S.C. 470ee (a)). She was sentenced to time served followed by 12 months of supervised release, and ordered to participate in a program of testing and treatment for substance abuse.

Bryan Keith Gary, Kristi L. Hendricks, and Tina Todd excavated, disturbed, and removed archaeological resources from a site located in the Long Cane Ranger District of the Sumter National Forest, in South Carolina, which had been occupied during the Early Archaic, Middle Archaic, Late Archaic, Early Woodland, and Mississippian cultural periods. A site damage assessment found that approximately 93 square yards of the site were disturbed to a depth of up to 12 inches. The cost of restoration and repair of the site was determined to be $19,985 and the archaeological value of the archaeological resources involved in the offense conduct was calculated to be $49,632.

All three defendants were charged in an indictment with one felony count of violation of ARPA.[11] Gary and Hendricks each pled guilty to that count. Gary was sentenced to 24 months of imprisonment and Hendricks was sentenced to 12 months and one day of imprisonment. In addition, Gary and

Hendricks each were ordered to pay restitution to the Francis Marion and Sumter National Forests in the amount of $800. At the time of Gary and Hendricks's sentences, Tina Todd had been approved for entry into the pretrial diversion program. As a result, her trial was continued until the July 2008 term of the court.

United States v. Carl Henderson[12]

Carl Ray Henderson, also known as Carlos, pled guilty to one felony count of violation of ARPA (16 U.S.C. 470ee (a)). He was sentenced to 21 months of imprisonment followed by 12 months of supervised release, with periodic drug testing. Also, he was ordered to pay restitution to Buffalo National River in the amount of $2,720.

In 2006, National Park Service rangers at Buffalo National River, Arkansas received a report of possible illegal excavation in the Lower Wilderness area of the park. An investigation by rangers and the park archaeologist revealed 45 disturbances at a known archaeological area. Altogether, 2,000 cubic feet at the six-acre site had been excavated. Evidence discovered at the site and patrol logs placing Henderson in the area tied him to the site within a three-month span. When confronted with the evidence, Henderson confessed to having excavated at the site in question. Over the next six months, he returned archaeological resources he had taken from the Lower Wilderness site, with archaeological resources, including human remains, removed from other sites.

On the date he was to be sentenced, Henderson failed to appear. The judge issued an arrest warrant, and Henderson was arrested and held in Fort Smith until sentencing.

Theft and Embezzlement of Government Property

The first paragraph of 18 U.S.C. § 641 creates the crime of theft of Government property, which is the unlawful taking of "a thing of value of the United States." The second paragraph of the statute concerns the unlawful possession of that property after it has been stolen.

In order to prove theft of Government property, the Government must prove that, at the time of the alleged unlawful act, the United States owned, or had possession of and control over, the property in question; that the defendant stole that property; and that the defendant intended to deprive the Government of the use and benefit of that property.[13]

The law provides for both a felony and a misdemeanor offense, depending on the value of the property stolen, with less than $1,000 a misdemeanor and above a felony offense. "Value" is defined in the statute. It means "face, par, or market value, or cost price, either wholesale or retail, whichever is greater" (18 U.S.C. § 641).

United States v. Kirby Loren Amlee[14]

Kirby Loren Amlee pled guilty to one felony count of violation of 18 U.S.C. 641, one felony count of interstate transportation of stolen goods (18 U.S.C. 2314), and one felony count of transporting ammunition in interstate commerce by a prohibited person (18 U.S.C. 922 (g)(1) & (6)). He was sentenced to 63 months of imprisonment. This sentence is to run consecutively with the sentence imposed by the United States Court for the Middle District of North Carolina in another conviction. Amlee also was ordered to pay, jointly and severally with Joey Kenneth Priddy, restitution in the amount of $22,451.75 ($21,809.99 to the National Park Service and $641.76 to Lajitas International Airport). Following release, Amlee will be on 36 months of supervised release. The court recommended to the Bureau of Prisons that Amlee receive the benefits of drug abuse treatment programs, and that he participate in a mental health program.

Amlee and Joey Kenneth Priddy committed burglaries at Fort Davis Historical Site, the Hallie Stillwell Museum, and the Lajitas International Airport during April 2006. The items they stole from the Stillwell Museum included an 1895 Winchester rifle, a revolver with holster, a double barrel shotgun, two bandoliers, a box of ammunition, arrowheads, a bone-handled knife in a sheath, a tomahawk, and a wooden butter mold. At the Fort Davis Historical Site Museum, the defendants gained access by smashing the transom over the back door, then smashed several glass display cabinets and removed museum items that included an Allen & Thurber bar hammer percussion pistol, a Colt Model 1849 revolver, a Colt Model 1851 Navy revolver, a Colt Model 1860 Army revolver, a Colt Model 1873 SAA revolver, a converted Colt SAA revolver, a U.S. Model 1842 percussion pistol, and a Bowie knife. (The theft from the airport did not involve cultural property.)

The double barrel shotgun and the two bandoliers were recovered in Texas. The defendants took the other items to North Carolina, where they were recovered. The recovered firearms were sent to the Springfield Armory, in Massachusetts, for stabilization and restoration.

Fort Davis, a National Park Service unit, is one of the best surviving examples of a frontier military post in the southwest United States. From 1854 to 1891, the fort protected migrants, mail coaches, and freight wagons on the Trans-Pecos portion of the San Antonio-El Paso Road and the Chihuahua Trail, and controlled activities on the southern stem of the Great Comanche War Trail and Mescalaro Apache war trails. Fort Davis also housed the 24th and 25th U.S. Infantry and the 9th and 10th U.S. Cavalry, which were African American regiments established after the Civil War.

Amlee and Joey Kenneth Priddy each pled guilty to the three identical felony counts with which they were charged in the indictment.[15] In 2006, Priddy was sentenced to 46 months of imprisonment, followed by 36 months of supervised release, and ordered to pay, jointly and severally with Amlee, the restitution amount of $22,451.75.

U.S. v. Max L. Ary[16]

Max L. Ary, the former president and chief executive officer of the Kansas Cosmosphere and Space Center (1976–2002), was convicted by a jury of two felony counts of violation of 18 U.S.C. 641, three felony counts of interstate transportation of stolen goods (18 U.S.C. 2314), two felony counts of wire fraud (18 U.S.C. 1343), three felony counts of mail fraud (18 U.S.C. 1341), and two felony counts of money laundering (18 U.S.C. 1956 (a)). He was sentenced to 36 months in prison, followed by 36 months of supervised release, and ordered to pay restitution in the amount of $132,374 ($50,000 to an insurer; $33,359 to the Kansas Cosmosphere and Space Center; $30,400 to the National Aeronautics and Space Administration; and $18,615 to other artifact owners) and $1,200 to the Federal Crimes Victims' Fund, and to forfeit $124,140.

Ary was the President and Chief Executive Officer of the Kansas Cosmosphere and Space Center, a space museum in Hutchinson, Kansas. He was hired to manage the museum in 1976, and was continuously employed by the Cosmosphere until he resigned in 2002, and moved to Oklahoma City, Oklahoma. The Cosmosphere is home to a significant collection of United States and Soviet space artifacts. Many of the artifacts in the Cosmosphere collection are owned by the museum and were either purchased by or provided to the museum by private donation. Others are provided to the museum on loan from institutions such as the Smithsonian Institution, the United States Air Force, the National Air and Space Museum, the International Space Hall of Fame, and the National Aeronautics and Space Administration ("NASA").

Evidence presented at trial showed that, in 2000 and 2001, Ary knowingly sold at auction, through Superior Galleries, an auction house located in California, at least 25 items—including astronaut gear, spacecraft hardware, and a tape recording of the Apollo 15 mission—that either belonged to the Cosmosphere or were on loan to the Cosmosphere from the Smithsonian Institution, the Air Force, the National Air and Space Museum, or the National Aeronautics and Space Administration. Further, as director, Ary had signed the loan agreements, which prohibited loaned items from being sold without their owners' permission. The court determined that the loss caused by Ary's offenses was more than $200,000.

Ary appealed his conviction and sentence. He argued that the district court erred by concluding that he had waived the work-product protection and attorney-client privilege, and by allowing the introduction of hearsay evidence at trial. Also, he claimed that the lower court erred in its calculation of loss for purposes of determining his offense level.

The United States Court of Appeals for the Tenth Circuit affirmed Ary's conviction and sentence. The Tenth Circuit reviewed the district court's rulings on Ary's attorney-client privilege and work-product doctrine claims for abuse of discretion, and found that, while the disclosures in question were involuntary—two boxes of materials had been seized pursuant to a search warrant—Ary had waived work-product protection and attorney-client privilege. In his communication with the U.S. Attorney, Ary never identified the contents of the boxes of materials as protected. Also, by waiting six weeks after the meeting between Ary's counsel and the U.S. Attorney to review discovery materials[17] in order to assert protection, he did not assert protection in a timely fashion. Consequently, the district court permissibly concluded, and the Tenth Circuit agreed, that this delay was sufficient to constitute a waiver.

The Tenth Circuit, likewise, reviewed the district court's admission into evidence of the Cosmosphere's computer and paper inventory records for an abuse of discretion. The Court found that, while the inventory records offered by the Government were hearsay—they were out-of-court statements offered by the Government for the truth of the matter asserted, namely that either the United States Government or the Cosmosphere owned the items sold by Ary—nevertheless, they were properly admitted because they were business records that fall under an exception to the hearsay rule[18] and because the Government laid foundation for their admission under the business records exception.[19]

The district court's loss calculation at sentencing was a factual question that the Tenth Circuit reviewed for clear error. At sentencing, the district court relied on facts stated in the presentence report (PSR), to which Ary objected. First, Ary argued the PSR took into account 19 items he sold at auction that were not included in the indictment, and whose ownership was not proved at trial or at sentencing. Second, Ary objected to the U.S. Probation Office's use of an $88,947 "auction value," based on estimated prices published in auction catalogs, to fix the loss for artifacts delivered to the Government by his lawyer, from Ary's residence, which Ary characterized as speculative and inadequate to measure the harm. At sentencing, the district court had overruled Ary's objections, and adopted the PSR's calculation of loss.

The Tenth Circuit held that the use of "auction value" was appropriate as a measure of fair market value and, therefore, satisfied the criteria for determining loss prescribed by the U.S. Sentencing Guidelines.[20] Further, the record demonstrated that the auction value of the items seized at Ary's house and those turned over to the government exceeded $88,947. As to the issue of ownership, the Tenth Circuit found that the Government had met its burden of proving ownership by a preponderance of the evidence as to 15 of the 19 artifacts in question. With respect to the other four items, the Court held that the Government had not proved ownership and that, consequently, $37,050 must be deducted from the loss calculation. Nonetheless, the amount of loss still remained greater than $200,000 and, thus, still lay within the U.S. Sentencing Guidelines' range for the 12-level enhancement of Ary's offense level applied by the district court.[21] Consequently, the district court's error in calculating the amount of loss was harmless.

Had Ary committed the crimes for which he was convicted after November 1, 2002, his sentence of imprisonment could have been much longer than 36 months. As the items involved in the offense conduct were "cultural heritage resources,"[22] the sentencing judge could have used Sentencing Guideline 2B1.5 to sentence Ary, and, at minimum, could have placed Ary at an offense level of 24.[23] Given a Category I criminal history, the Guidelines prescribe a sentence of 51–63 months of imprisonment for an offense level of 24. In fact, the judge calculated Ary's offense level to be 22, for which the Guidelines prescribe a term of imprisonment of 41–51 months, and then the judge departed downward from the Guideline range, imposing the 36-month sentence.

***United States v. Joseph U.R.M. Elibosang*[24]**

Joseph Umiich Rosario Mafnas Elibosang pled guilty to one felony count of violation of 18 U.S.C. 641, one felony count of destruction of veterans' memorials (18 U.S.C. 1369), and one felony count of conspiracy to transport stolen goods in interstate or foreign commerce (18 U.S.C. 2314). He was sentenced to 21 months of imprisonment followed by 36 months of supervised release, with participation in a program for substance abuse, and ordered to pay restitution to the Department of the Interior in the amount of $58,800.

The three-charge indictment to which Elibosang pled stemmed from his theft and sale, in 2007, of at least 23 metal plaques secured to the wall of the War in the Pacific National Historical Park, in Asan Bay Overlook, Guam. Constructed for the 50th Anniversary of the liberation of Guam, the park commemorates the 16,000 Chamorros who were tortured or died on Guam during the Japanese occupation and the more than 2,500 U.S. servicemen who died there during World War II; the plaques contain their names. Each plaque weighs 18 kilograms and has a value of $1,700. Elibosang admitted to having sold 23 of them to Xiong's Family Recycling Center, as scrap, for $54 each. Xiong's, in turn, was shipping the plaques to a recycling firm in Hong Kong. Information from an informant led to the recovery of seven plaques from Xiong's; others were found in Hong Kong.

The U.S. Sentencing Guidelines consider the plaques to be a cultural heritage resource for purposes of applying Sentencing Guideline 2B1.5. They are a "commemorative work."[25]

Theft of Major Artwork

The offense of Theft of Major Artwork (18 U.S.C. 668) is the act of obtaining from a "museum" by theft or fraud an "object of cultural heritage," or receiving, concealing, exhibiting, or disposing of such an object, knowing that the object has been stolen or obtained by fraud. An "object of cultural heritage" is an object that either is over 100 years old and worth in excess of $5,000, or is of any age and worth at least $100,000. A "museum" is an organized and permanent institution situated in the United States whose activities affect interstate or foreign commerce and whose essential purpose is educational or aesthetic, has a professional staff, and owns, utilizes, and cares for tangible objects that are exhibited to the public on a regular schedule. Theft of major artwork is a general intent crime. The government must prove that the stolen property came from a museum, and that the defendant knew the item was stolen (or obtained by fraud), but need not prove that the defendant knew the item came from a museum.

United States v. Charles Thomas Allen II and United States v. Warren Christopher Lipka, Spencer Wilson Reinhard, Eric Joseph Borsuk, and Charles Thomas Allen II[26]

Eric J. Borsuk, Warren C. Lipka, Charles T. Allen II, and Spencer W. Reinhard each pled guilty to six counts of a nine-count indictment, including two felony counts of violation of 18 U.S.C. 1951(a) (both conspiracy to unlawfully obstruct, delay, and affect commerce by robbery and the robbery itself), and one felony count each of theft of major art work, interstate transportation of stolen property (18 U.S.C. 2314), possession of stolen property (18 U.S.C. 2315), and conspiracy to commit the last three offenses (18 U.S.C. 371). The charges stemmed from their theft of rare books, art books, manuscripts, and sketches from the Special Collections Library at Transylvania University, in Lexington, Kentucky. Each defendant was sentenced to 87 months in prison. U.S. Sentencing Guideline 2B1.5, cultural heritage resources, was used to calculate the sentences.

All the defendants were 20 years old and college students at the time of the robbery, in 2004. Using color-coded nicknames for themselves inspired by the movie *Reservoir Dogs*, they first attempted to steal the items while dressed in various costumes. Calling off that attempt, the next day Lipka and Borsuk gained access to the Special Collections Library. They wrestled the Special Collections Librarian to the ground, zapped her in the arm with a pen-type stun gun, and took the materials, which included four multivolume publications, a first edition of Charles Darwin's *The Origin of Species*, an illuminated manuscript from the 15th century, and twenty sketches by John James Audubon done in the 1850s. Altogether, Lipka and Borsuk prepared to carry from the library seven "objects of cultural heritage," valued at $5,760,000. Because Lipka and Borsuk had underestimated the sizes and weights of all the items, they abandoned some of them in the Special Collections Library and dropped others in a library stairwell while fleeing.

Allen drove the getaway van and Reinhard, while not participating in the robbery, was in contact with the other three defendants by cellular phone. Before the theft, the defendants had sent electronic messages to Christie's auction house, in New York, expressing a desire to obtain an appraisal of and sell various rare books through a private sale. Following the theft, they drove from

Kentucky to New York with the stolen items, where they displayed them for viewing by a representative of Christie's. Ultimately, no deal was struck with Christie's. The books were returned to Transylvania University.

All four defendants appealed their sentences on the grounds that the district court erred in finding that the stun pen was a dangerous weapon[27] and, consequently, increasing their offense level by two levels.[28] In addition, Allen claimed two additional errors peculiar to his sentence. First, he argued that the Government breached a cooperation agreement and that, as a remedy for the breach, he was entitled to a downward departure in his sentence.[29] Second, Allen argued that his participation in the offense fell somewhere between "minimal" and "minor" and that, as such, his offense level should be decreased by three levels.[30]

The United States cross-appealed, claiming an identical error in all four sentences. For its part, the Government contended that, at sentencing, the district court erred in omitting from its loss computation the books that Lipka and Borsuk dropped in the library stairwell while fleeing. Had the court included those items, together with the items actually removed from the library, the enhancement of the defendants' offense level would have been, at minimum, 16 levels, rather than the 14 levels calculated by the lower court.[31] Consequently, even if the defendants' own value estimates were used, the total offense level should have been at least 31, with a sentencing range of 108–135 months of imprisonment, instead of level 29, with 87–108 months of incarceration.[32]

With respect to Allen's two claims, the United States Court of Appeals for the Sixth Circuit held that, regardless of whether or not the Assistant U.S. Attorney breached the cooperation agreement, Allen could not show any harm, inasmuch as the information he provided was neither included in the presentence report nor relied upon by the district court in calculating and imposing Allen's sentence. Further, as there was no plea agreement in this case, there was no *quid pro quo* to Allen's entry of his plea, hence, there was no sentencing recommendation for the Government to offer. As to Allen's role in the offense, the degree of participation and culpability is a factual determination reviewed for clear error. As Allen visited the library prior to the robbery to gather intelligence, such as staffing and security; conducted a stake-out of the library to gather additional intelligence; developed the escape route; obtained and drove the escape vehicle; arranged hotel accommodations in New York; helped to finance the operation; went to the library in costume as part of the initial robbery plan; helped to hide the stolen items in his residence; disposed of the instrumentalities of the crime from his residence; and helped transport the stolen items to Christie's in New York and back to Kentucky, the Sixth Circuit found no basis for Allen's claim that the district court clearly erred in finding that he was just as culpable as the other three defendants.

The Sixth Circuit reviewed for clear error the district court's application of the dangerous weapon enhancement to increase all four defendants' offense levels by two levels. The test used in applying the enhancement is "whether a reasonable individual would believe that the object is a dangerous weapon under the circumstances."[33] The Sixth Circuit held that, based on the testimony of the Special Collections Librarian, the district court did not clearly err in finding that a reasonable person would have believed that the stun pen, as brandished and used by Lipka and Borsuk during the robbery, was capable of inflicting serious bodily injury.

The Sixth Circuit agreed with the Government that the district court erred when it considered only the items actually removed from the library building in tabulating the loss for its sentencing calculation. The lower court had held that "loss" constitutes things that have been "taken," that "taken" means removed from "the zone of control," and that the "zone of control" was the library building proper. Determining that the district court was interpreting and applying the U.S. Sentencing Guidelines when it calculated loss, the Sixth Circuit reviewed the lower court's action *de novo*.

The Sixth Circuit's reasoning that all the targeted items could be included in the calculation of loss is interesting. U.S. Sentencing Guideline 2B1.5 uses the term "value" for cultural heritage resources involved in an offense, and refers to the table of enhancements in Sentencing Guideline 2B1.1(b)(1), which deals with theft of property and receipt of stolen property, to determine the offense level that correlates with the value determination. The table in 2B1.1(b)(1) is used to determine the enhancement that correlates with the "loss" determination. "Loss" is defined in Application Note 2 to Sentencing Guideline 2B1.1 as the greater of actual or intended loss. The Sixth Circuit held that the definition of "loss" used to determine the increase in offense level provided by the loss table in Sentencing Guideline 2B1.1(b)(1) depends on the circumstances of the offense. Thus, if the offense constitutes theft of property or receipt of stolen property, "loss" will mean the greater of actual or intended loss. On the other hand, if the offense constitutes robbery, then "loss" will mean "the value of the property taken, damaged, or destroyed," as that term is defined in Application

Note 3 to Sentencing Guideline 2B3.1. Reasoning that "robbery," an offense sentenced under Guideline 2B3.1, is a more specific offense than "offenses involving stolen property," which is sentenced under Guideline 2B1.1, and that this case involved a robbery, the Sixth Circuit held the definition of "loss" for purposes of this particular sentencing to be the value of the property taken, damaged, or destroyed. In the Court's words, "the crime of Robbery implicates 2B3.1, which defines loss as the value of the property *actually taken*; and the fact that the property taken consisted of 'cultural heritage resources' implicates 2B1.5, which instructs the district court to apply the table in 2B1.1(b)(1), though without regard to its application note."[34]

Based on a reading of cases from other circuit courts of appeal and the Sentencing Guidelines, the Sixth Circuit held that a robber "takes" an object when the robber exercises dominion and control over that object, such that the robber has completed the acts necessary to seize that object. Applying the holding to the facts, the Sixth Circuit concluded that Lipka and Borsuk exercised control over the items they dropped in the stairway of the library, as well as the items they removed from the library.

The Court also made a point of saying that the items left in the Special Collections Library were "taken," too, but were being excluded from consideration because the Government had not pressed this position on appeal, and the Court declined to act on its own initiative. As the sentence enhancement should have been 16, rather than 14, based on the Sixth Circuit's measure of loss, the Court remanded the case to the district court to reconsider its sentence.

Although the Sixth Circuit found the advisory guideline range to be 108–135 months of imprisonment, on remand, the district court resentenced all four defendants to the same 87 months of imprisonment to which they had originally been sentenced, to be followed by 36 months of supervised release. The court also ordered the defendants to pay restitution to Transylvania University in the amount of $2,130.

United States v. Steven Lee Olson and United States v. Roman Szurko[35]

Steven Lee Olson and Roman Szurko each pled guilty to one felony count of conspiracy to steal an object of cultural heritage from a museum (18 U.S.C. 371 and 668 (b)(1)). Olson was sentenced to 60 months of imprisonment followed by 36 months of supervised release. In sentencing Olson, the district court judge noted Olson's role as the mastermind of the theft and his criminal record that included 23 prior arrests and nine convictions, four of which were for weapons offenses. Szurko was sentenced to 12 months and one day of imprisonment followed by 36 months of supervised release.

In November 2007, New Jersey residents Olson, a self-employed truck driver, and Szurko, a restaurant worker, took the 1778 painting *Children with a Cart,* by Francisco de Goya from an unmarked, climate-controlled moving truck being used to transport the painting from the Toledo Museum of Art, in Ohio, which owns the painting, to the Solomon R. Guggenheim Museum, in New York. The crated work was in the care of professional art transporters who had stopped overnight at a Howard Johnson Inn off Route 80, in Bartonsville, Pennsylvania. Olson and Szurko broke the lock on the back of the truck, removed the painting, which the Toledo Museum of Art had insured for $1.1 million, and hid the painting at Olson's residence.

After the Toledo Museum of Art offered a $50,000 reward for information leading to the recovery of the painting, and hoping to collect the reward, Olson, through an attorney, turned over the painting to the FBI, claiming he had discovered it in his basement wall. Further investigation revealed that Olson and Szurko had taken the painting. The piece was returned undamaged to the Toledo Art Museum.

Receipt of Stolen Property from an Indian Tribal Organization

The first paragraph of 18 U.S.C. § 1163 creates the crime of theft of property belonging to an Indian tribal organization or in the custody of a tribal organization official. The second paragraph of the statute concerns the unlawful receipt or possession of that property after it has been stolen. The statute defines "Indian tribal organization" as any tribe, band, or community of Indians that is subject to the laws of the United States relating to Indian affairs, or any corporation or other group organized under such laws.

In order to prove receipt of stolen property from an Indian tribal organization, the Government must prove that, at the time of the alleged unlawful act, the property in question "belonged" to an Indian tribal organization or was in the custody of a tribal organization official; that the defendant received, concealed, or retained that property; that the defendant knew the property was stolen; and that the defendant intended to deprive the Indian tribal organization of the use of that property. The law provides for both a Class D felony and a Class A misdemeanor offense, depending on the value of the property stolen, with the dividing line between a misdemeanor and a felony offense being

$1,000. Thus, in order to prove felony receipt of stolen property from an Indian tribal organization, the Government also must prove that the value of the property in question was greater than $1,000. Interestingly, while "value" is defined in the theft and embezzlement of Government property statute, the term has been left undefined here.

A defendant who has been found guilty of embezzlement and theft from an Indian tribal organization also may be sentenced to pay a fine. For a felony offense, an individual may be fined up to $250,000 and an organization may be fined up to $500,000. For a misdemeanor, the maximum fine is $100,000, and $200,000 for an organization.

United States v. Steven Stewart Farmer[36]

Steven Stewart Farmer pled guilty to one felony count of receiving stolen property belonging to an Indian tribal organization. He was sentenced to 41 months of imprisonment followed by 36 months of supervised release, with a substance abuse and counseling program. Farmer also was ordered to pay $4,000 restitution to a victim.

In January 2005, a burglary occurred at the Cultural Museum of the Cabazon Band of Mission Indians, in Indio, California. The Cabazon Band is a federally recognized Indian tribal organization. During the burglary, eight California Indian-made reed baskets and nine ceramic Zuni and Hopi pots on loan to the museum, and over 40 pieces of retail jewelry were stolen. That same year, Farmer received seven of the pots and seven of the baskets, which he knew to have been stolen from the Cabazon Band and which he intended to convert to his use. The value of the pots was $73,000 and the value of the baskets was $79,500. Farmer was arrested after trying to sell the artifacts to an FBI informant for $4,000, to feed a methamphetamine addiction.

United States v. Marilyn Skahan Malatare and Colette Julia Malatare[37]

Colette Julia Malatare pled guilty to one felony count of embezzlement and theft from an Indian tribal organization. She was sentenced to six months of imprisonment followed by 36 months of supervised release, to include periodic drug tests. She had been charged in an indictment with 21 felony counts of the same offense. Colette's mother, Marilyn Skahan Malatare, pled guilty to one felony count of theft concerning programs receiving federal funds (18 U.S.C. 666(a)(1)(A)). She was sentenced to nine months of imprisonment followed by 36 months of supervised release, to include periodic drug tests. Marilyn had been charged in an indictment with 15 counts, including 4 counts of the offense of her conviction and 11 counts of embezzlement and theft from an Indian tribal organization. In addition Colette and Marilyn were ordered to pay restitution to Bowlby's Pawn Shop in the amount of $1,164.72.

Over a six-month period in 2006 and 2007, Marilyn, the curator and program manager at the Yakama Nation Museum for more than ten years, stole cultural items worth $49,507 from the museum; her daughter Colette stole cultural items having a value of $62,457. Marilyn and Colette subsequently sold many of the pieces to pawn shops. The Yakama Nation is a federally recognized Indian tribal organization, and each year receives funds from the federal government.

Most of the stolen pieces were from the Nipo Strongheart collection. Strongheart, a 1920s movie actor and adopted member of the Yakama Nation, gave his collection to the tribe. At the time of his death, in 1966, the collection was valued at $200,000.

Receipt of Stolen Property within a Special Maritime Jurisdiction

Whoever buys, receives, or conceals stolen property within the special maritime and territorial jurisdiction of the United States is guilty of violating 18 U.S.C. § 662. In order to prove the offense, the Government must prove that, at the time of the alleged unlawful act, the property in question had been stolen from another; that the defendant bought, received, or concealed that stolen property; that the defendant knew the property was stolen; and that the defendant's act occurred within the special maritime and territorial jurisdiction of the United States. The law provides for both a Class E felony and a Class A misdemeanor offense, depending on the value of the property stolen, with the dividing line between a misdemeanor and a felony offense being $1,000 of value of the items. For a felony offense, an individual may be fined up to $250,000 and an organization may be fined up to $500,000. If the offense is a misdemeanor, the maximum fine is $100,000 for an individual and $200,000 for an organization.

The term "special maritime and territorial jurisdiction of the United States" is defined at 18 U.S.C. § 7. It includes locations such as the high seas, any place outside the jurisdiction of any nation, and any aircraft owned by the United States, or a U.S. citizen or corporation while in flight over the high seas.

United States v. Edward George Johnson[38]

Edward George Johnson, also known as "Dutch," pled guilty to one count—whether a felony or a misdemeanor is unknown—of receiving stolen property within a special maritime jurisdiction. He was sentenced to 18 months of probation, the first six months as home detention subject to electronic monitoring. In addition, Johnson was ordered to pay restitution to Susan McGovern-Huffman, a dealer in antiquities, in the amount of $21,200. Johnson originally had been charged in an indictment with interstate transportation of stolen property (18 U.S.C. 2314) and wire fraud (18 U.S.C. 1343), both of which are felonies.

Johnson, an Army attack- and scout-helicopter pilot and chief warrant officer from Fayetteville, North Carolina, was deployed to Egypt in 2002, when about 370 archaeological artifacts were stolen from the Ma'adi Museum. The items had been excavated from the Ma'adi site in the 1920s and 1930s. In 2003, Johnson contacted Susan McGovern-Huffman, President of Sands of Time Antiquities, Inc., in Texas, and offered to sell her a group of Egyptian antiquities. Johnson told the dealer that he had identified her through an Internet search, and saw that her website offered for sale items similar to his. Johnson represented that he inherited his antiquities from his father, whose own father had originally acquired them while working for a mineral company in Egypt in the 1930s or 1940s. Johnson stipulated, though, that he had no documentation to establish either the artifacts' origin or chain of title. McGovern-Huffman purchased approximately 90 artifacts from Johnson, paying him a total of $21,200. Subsequently, she consigned some of the antiquities to galleries or collectors in New York, London, Zurich, and Montreal, among other places, and sold approximately ten of the pieces to three galleries or collectors in New York. Later, experts determined that the majority of the antiquities that Johnson sold were part of the group stolen from the Ma'adi Museum.

The elements of the charge to which Johnson pled remain unclear. Presumably, he concealed the stolen antiquities belonging to the Government of Egypt while on or over the high seas, knowing that they were stolen.

If Johnson pled guilty to a felony offense, then the sentencing magistrate could hardly have followed advisory Sentencing Guideline 2B1.5 in sentencing Johnson. A base offense level of 8, a 4-level increase because the offense involved a cultural heritage resource having a "value" of more than $10,000 and less than $30,000, a 2-level increase because the offense involved a cultural heritage resource from a museum, a 2-level increase because the offense involved a cultural heritage resource constituting "cultural property," a 2-level increase because the offense was committed for pecuniary gain, and a 3-level reduction for acceptance of responsibility would have resulted in an offense level of 15, for which the Sentencing Guidelines prescribe 18–24 months of imprisonment. Perhaps in the end, the Government, after initially charging Johnson with two felony counts, allowed him to plead to a misdemeanor.

Making and Subscribing a False Tax Return

Any person whose return, statement, or other document to the Internal Revenue Service is accompanied by a written declaration that it is made under the penalties of perjury, but who does not believe the document to be true and correct as to every material fact is guilty of fraud and making false statements to the IRS, in violation of 26 U.S.C. § 7206 (1). This violation is a Class E felony. A defendant who has been found guilty of making and subscribing a false tax return also may be sentenced to pay a fine. An individual may be fined up to $250,000 (18 U.S.C. § 3571 (b)(3)) and an organization may be fined up to $500,000.

United States v. Lester F. Weber and Lori E. Childs[39]

Lester F. Weber pled guilty to one felony count of making and subscribing a false tax return (18 U.S.C. 7206(1)), one felony count of theft from an organization receiving Federal funds (18 U.S.C.666 (a)(1)(A)), and one felony count of mail fraud (18 U.S.C. 1341). He was sentenced to 48 months of imprisonment, with a recommendation that, while incarcerated, he undergo a mental health evaluation and receive appropriate counseling and treatment for any mental health conditions. Following release from imprisonment, Weber is to be on supervised release for a term of 36 months with periodic drug tests, and to continue participation in mental health counseling and treatment; is prohibited from engaging in any employment where he has access to archived material; must file amended tax returns for 2002 through 2005, to reflect the income received from sales on eBay, and pay all taxes, interest, and penalties; and must fully cooperate with the Mariners' Museum to value and recover the items that are the subject of his prosecution. Weber also was ordered to pay restitution to the Mariners' Museum, in Newport News, Virginia in the amount of $172,357.39. In addition to the three counts to which he pled, Johnson was charged in a 26-count indictment with one count of conspiracy to commit mail fraud (18 U.S.C. 1349), 11 counts of wire fraud (18 U.S.C. 1343), eight additional counts of mail fraud, and three additional counts of making and subscribing a false tax return.

Lori E. Childs, Weber's wife, pled guilty to one felony count of making and subscribing a false tax return. She was sentenced to 15 months of imprisonment, with a recommendation that, while incarcerated, she, likewise, undergo a mental health evaluation and receive appropriate counseling and treatment. Following release from imprisonment, Childs is to be on supervised release for 12 months, with drug tests, and must file amended tax returns for 2002 through 2005, to reflect the income received from sales on eBay, and pay all taxes, interest, and penalties. In addition to the one count to which she pled, Childs originally was charged in a 25-count indictment with one count of conspiracy to commit mail fraud, 11 counts of wire fraud, nine counts of mail fraud, and three additional counts of making and subscribing a false tax return.

Weber and Childs used the mail to fraudulently sell documents stolen from a museum receiving Federal funds. Also, under penalty of perjury, they failed to disclose on their income tax returns that they were engaged in the operation of a business activity from which they derived income, knowing that they were required to disclose this business activity and the income they derived from it.

Weber, the former chief archivist at the Mariners' Museum in Newport News, Virginia, stole thousands of documents from the collections he oversaw. The museum has the world's third-largest maritime library. From 2002 until 2006, when he was dismissed, he sold at least 3,500 documents on eBay under Childs's name. The sales included materials from the Aks Collection, compiled by a mother and son who survived the 1912 sinking of the *R.M.S. Titanic*. The museum had purchased the collection for $80,000, in 2001. Weber and Childs made over $172,000 on the fraudulent sales, but the Mariners' Museum estimated that the worth of the stolen items exceeded $500,000.

Weber and Childs's scheme was uncovered by a collector in Switzerland who found a reference to the Mariners' Museum on a document he bought on eBay while examining the document with an infrared light. The collector investigated the sender's name on the envelope used to mail the document, Lori Childs, and found an article that linked Childs to Weber and the Mariners' Museum. The collector then alerted the museum, and an investigation by Newport News police, the Internal Revenue Service, the U.S. Postal Service, and the Secret Service ensued.

Eventually, the museum recovered nine of 12 stolen items from the *Titanic* collection, but most of the 3,500 documents are still missing. In April 2007, the museum filed a $1.35 million civil suit against Weber and Childs.

The district court judge computed Weber's offense level to be 20, for which the U.S. Sentencing Guidelines prescribe a sentence of 33–41 months of imprisonment. Instead, citing Weber's breach of the public trust and the repetitive nature of the crime over a long period of time, Judge Rebecca Beach Smith departed upward from the Guidelines' recommendation and sentenced him to a term of 48 months of imprisonment.

National Stolen Property Act

Interstate Transportation of Stolen Property

Part of the National Stolen Property Act is codified at 18 U.S.C. § 2314. Some of the prohibited acts in this section include the transportation or transfer in interstate or foreign commerce of stolen goods having a value of $5,000 or more. In addition, the Government must prove that the defendant knew the goods had been stolen or obtained by fraud. Interstate transportation of stolen property is a Class C felony.

United States v. Maxwell Garihan and Gary Paul Garihan[40] Maxwell Garihan and his brother, Gary Paul Garihan, each pled guilty to two felony counts of interstate transportation of stolen property. Maxwell was sentenced to 70 months of imprisonment, with a recommendation that, during his incarceration, he undergo a mental health assessment and receive any mental health treatment as is appropriate. Gary Paul was sentenced to 29 months of incarceration. Following their imprisonment, Maxwell and Gary Paul will be on supervised release for a period of 36 months. While on supervised release, Maxwell and Gary Paul Garihan have been ordered to submit to one drug test within 15 days of release and periodic drug tests thereafter, to participate in a program of testing and treatment for drug abuse and abstain from the use of alcohol or other intoxicants during the course of that treatment, and to participate in a program of mental health treatment. Maxwell's conditions of supervision also require him to remain medication compliant and take all medications prescribed by his treating psychiatrist. Both Maxwell and Gary Paul will be barred from visiting any national park unit during the period of their supervised release. They also must pay, jointly and severally, a total of $86,147 in restitution to Ganado Glory Temple Ministries, in Ganado, Arizona ($2,155), Hubbell Trading Post National Historic Site, in Ganado, Arizona ($4,750), Lewis Bobrick Antiques, in Denver, Colorado ($15,500), David Cook Fine Art, in Denver, Colorado ($3,500), Native American Trading Company, in Denver, Colorado ($2,000), and Agate Fossil Beds National Monument, in Harrison, Nebraska ($58,242).

In May 2007, the defendants transported from Arizona to Colorado 10 antique Navajo rugs that they knew had been stolen from Hubbell Trading Post National Historic Site. In July 2007, they transported from Nebraska to Colorado approximately 20 American Indian cultural items from the James Cook-Red Cloud Collection, including moccasins, war clubs, war shirts, and other late 19th century Plains Indian artifacts traced to the Oglala Sioux chief Red Cloud that they knew had been stolen from Agate Fossil Beds National Monument. Before their arrests, the Garihans sold four of the stolen rugs in Colorado and contacted five museums specializing in American Indian cultural items, as well as nine antiques dealers, trying to sell the stolen artifacts.

All of the stolen items were recovered undamaged. The National Park Service determined the commercial value of the stolen items to be $200,000 and the repair costs for National Park Service property damaged to be $63,000.

At sentencing, the district court judge determined that the value of the cultural heritage resources was more than $120,000 but less than $200,000, and calculated both defendants' total offense level to be 21. She adopted a criminal history of V for Maxwell Garihan and a criminal history of III for Gary Paul Garihan. The advisory guideline range for Maxwell was thus 70–87 months of imprisonment, and the range for Gary Paul was 46–57 months of imprisonment. The district court judge imposed the advisory guideline range with respect to Maxwell, sentencing him to 70 months of imprisonment. With Gary Paul, the judge departed below the advisory guideline range, sentencing him to 29 months of imprisonment. In doing so, the judge granted the motion of the Government for downward departure—part of the Government's plea agreement with Gary Paul—due to Gary Paul's substantial assistance in the prosecution of another person who had committed an offense.[41]

United States v. Edward J. Renehan, Jr.[42] Edward J. Renehan pled guilty to one felony count of interstate transportation of stolen goods. He was sentenced to 18 months of imprisonment followed by 24 months of supervised release. While on supervised release, Renehan has been ordered to participate in a program of mental health treatment, and to continue to take any prescribed medications. Renehan also was ordered to pay restitution in the amount of $86,700 to Swann Galleries, Inc., in New York

Renehan, a historian who served as Interim Executive Director of the Theodore Roosevelt Association between March 2005 and May 2006, stole from the Association a letter written by Abraham Lincoln on March 1, 1840, and two letters written by George Washington on August 9, 1791 and December 29, 1778, respectively. The letters had been stored in a vault at the Theodore Roosevelt Birthplace National Historic Site, in New York. Renehan then sold the three letters through Swann Galleries, in New York, for approximately $97,000, of which he received $86,700. Presumably, he transported the stolen letters from New York to his residence in Rhode Island, and subsequently transported them from his residence back to New York, to Swann Galleries.

In a separate case, Renehan pled guilty in Nassau County Court, in New York, to grand larceny in the third degree for stealing from the Theodore Roosevelt Association's Muttontown office a letter written by Theodore Roosevelt about his son Quentin's death in World War I. It was the discovery of that theft which led the Association to check for items that might be missing from their collection and, ultimately, led to the Federal investigation and prosecution of Renehan.

United States v. James Lyman Brubaker[43]

James Lyman Brubaker pled guilty to one felony count of interstate transportation of stolen property and one felony count of sale or receipt of stolen property which has crossed a State or United States boundary (18 U.S.C. 2315). He was sentenced to 30 months of imprisonment followed by 36 months of supervised release. As a condition of his supervised release, Brubaker must participate in a program for mental health/anger management treatment. Brubaker also was ordered to pay a total of $23,162 in restitution to Western Washington University, in Bellingham, Washington ($21,600); Bozeman Public Library, in Bozeman, Montana ($5); Jamestown College, in Jamestown, North Dakota ($15); University of Minnesota Libraries, in Minneapolis, Minnesota ($60); University of Wyoming Libraries, in Laramie, Wyoming ($175); University of Lethbridge Library, in Lethbridge, Alberta, Canada ($465); University of Washington Libraries, in Seattle, Washington ($140); Central Washington University Brooks Library, in Ellensburg, Washington ($192); Colorado State University—Pueblo Library, in Pueblo, Colorado ($30); Great Falls Public Library, in Great Falls, Montana ($90); Park County Library, in Cody, Wyoming ($60); Utah State University Library, in Logan, Utah ($175); and University of San Francisco Gleeson Library, in San Francisco, California ($155).

Brubaker, a 74-year old resident of Great Falls, Montana, is believed to have stolen 832 books from 109 libraries and universities in the United States and Canada, and to have removed 20,000 individual pages of maps and colored plates from other books with a razor or Exacto knife. To date, 338 books have been confirmed to have been stolen from 51 libraries and universities. The victim libraries were found in Arizona, California, Colorado, Idaho, Iowa, Michigan, Minnesota, Montana, Nebraska, North Dakota, Oregon, South Dakota, Texas, Utah, Washington, Wyoming, as well as in Alberta, Canada (Calgary, Edmonton, and Lethbridge). The 338 books confirmed to have been stolen had an aggregate value of $89,110; the total loss amount represented by the 832 books was $220,000. These values did not take into account either the value of the pages removed from books or the damage to the books whose pages had been removed.

Brubaker offered stolen items for sale on eBay, claiming that they were part of a personal collection he had amassed. Records seized at Brubaker's residence suggest that, in 2007 alone, he completed more than 9,000 transactions on eBay, and grossed almost $500,000.

In 2006, a librarian at Western Washington University's Wilson Library discovered that fold-out maps had been cut out of books with a sharp instrument. A complete inventory revealed that 108 volumes of governmental books had been mutilated in this manner, and 648 pages of maps and colored plates were missing. Realizing that the thefts had likely been for resale, the librarian started searching the eBay website and discovered that several of the missing pages were listed for sale under the seller name "montanasilver." The librarian arranged with investigators for third parties to bid on and purchase two documents which the librarian recognized as matching items stolen from Wilson Library. The items were purchased and sent to the Washington State Patrol Crime Lab, where an examination showed conclusively that they were taken from the books belonging to the university. Montanasilver, the eBay seller, was Brubaker. A check of the university's parking records showed that Brubaker's vehicle was issued a citation on February 17, 2006, while parked in the university parking lot closest to Wilson Library.

Sale or Receipt of Stolen Property Which Has Crossed a State or United States Boundary

Another part of the National Stolen Property Act is codified at 18 U.S.C. § 2315. Some of the prohibited acts in this section include possessing, concealing, storing, bartering, selling, or disposing of stolen goods having a value of $5,000 or more, or pledging or accepting as security for a loan stolen goods having a value of $500 or more. In addition, the Government must prove that the goods crossed a State or United States boundary after being stolen or unlawfully converted, and that the defendant knew the goods had been stolen or unlawfully converted. Sale or receipt of stolen property is a Class C felony.

United States v. Robert Mardirosian[44]

Robert Mardirosian was convicted by a jury of one felony count of possession of stolen property that had been transported interstate after having been stolen. He was sentenced to 84 months of imprisonment followed by 36 months of supervised release, and ordered to pay a fine in the amount of $100,000 and return six paintings to Michael Bakwin, from whom they were stolen in 1978.

In 1978, seven paintings, including *Bouilloire et Fruits* by Paul Cezanne, were stolen from the home of Michael Bakwin, in Stockbridge, Massachusetts, allegedly by David Colvin, then a client of Boston lawyer Mardirosian. Colvin allegedly told Mardirosian that the paintings were stolen. Colvin was shot to death in 1979, but he left the paintings behind in an office loft owned by Mardirosian, who discovered them in 1980. Mardirosian did not try to return the stolen paintings. Instead, in 1988, he moved them from Massachusetts to Monaco and then to Switzerland. Allegedly, Mardirosian wanted a finder's fee of $1 million or 10% of the paintings' value in exchange for returning them to Bakwin.

Mardirosian was able to keep his possession of the paintings secret by working through lawyers in London, Monaco, and Switzerland, as well as a Panamanian shell company he created, Erie International Trading Company. Using the cover of Erie, Mardirosian allegedly tried to sell the paintings in London, in 1999, but an investigation by the Art Loss Register determined that the artwork was stolen. ALR alerted Bakwin that his stolen paintings had surfaced and, ultimately, brokered a deal between Bakwin and Erie, whereby Erie handed over the Cezanne in exchange for Bakwin's relinquishing all claims to the other six paintings.

In 2006, Mardirosian tried to sell four of the stolen paintings at Sotheby's, in London, through intermediaries. Bakwin sued to rescind the "contract" with Erie on the grounds that it was made under duress. The British court agreed with Bakwin. The court also revealed that the client for whom the intermediaries were trying to sell the paintings was Mardirosian. Mardirosian was arrested in February 2007 at Logan International Airport, in Boston, upon his arrival in the U.S. from France.

The district court's sentence of Mardirosian to 84 months of imprisonment was below the advisory guideline range. The sentence was imposed pursuant to a defense motion for a sentence outside the advisory guideline range to which the Government did not object. Before the downward departure, the district court had calculated Mardirosian's total offense level to be 32, for which the Sentencing Guidelines prescribe an imprisonment range of 121–151 months.

Notes

1. The section editor wishes to thank Elise Foster, Attorney, and Janet Thorsted, Paralegal, U.S. Department of Agriculture, Office of the General Counsel for their technical assistance.
2. For a complete and reader-friendly history, presentation, and explanation of U.S. Sentencing Guideline § 2B1.5, see Paula J. Desio, *Crimes and Punishment: Developing Sentencing Guidelines for Cultural Heritage Resources Crimes*, in LEGAL PERSPECTIVES ON CULTURAL RESOURCES 61–84 (Jennifer R. Richman & Marion P. Forsyth eds., 2004).
3. For a discussion of the intent, or *mens rea*, required to be proved in an ARPA criminal prosecution, see Marion P. Forsyth & David Tarler, *Model Jury Instructions in ARPA Prosecutions: Removing the "Lynch-Pins"*, in PRESENTING ARCHAEOLOGY IN COURT 127-142 (Sherry Hutt, Marion P. Forsyth & David Tarler eds., 2006).
4. For a detailed treatment of ARPA civil penalties, see Elise Foster, U.S. Dep't of Agric., USING ARPA CIVIL PENALTIES TO PROTECT ARCHEOLOGICAL RESOURCES ON PUBLIC AND INDIAN LANDS (Sherry Hutt & David Tarler, Nat'l Park Serv., eds., 2007).
5. *United States v. Kenneth Spry*, No. 5:08CR50031-001 (W.D. Ark. sentence Nov. 24, 2008).
6. *United States v. Robert V. Gallegos, Jack Beasley, and Peter Lewis Hester*, No. 1:07CR01166-MCA (D.N.M. acq. June 18, 2008 and remaining counts and for-

feiture allegation dismissed Sept. 3, 2008 (Gallegos), and sentence Aug. 21, 2008 (Hester) and Dec. 8, 2008 (Beasley)).

7. Among other things, the Antiquities Act prescribes criminal punishment for persons who "appropriate, excavate, injure or destroy any historic or prehistoric ruin or monument, or any object of antiquity, situated on lands owned or controlled by the Government of the United States, without the permission of the Secretary of the Department of the Government having jurisdiction over the lands on which said antiquities are situated" (16 U.S.C. § 433). A split of authority exists among the circuits on whether or not the criminal enforcement section of the Antiquities Act is unconstitutionally vague in violation of the due process clause of the Constitution. In *U.S. v. Diaz* (368 F. Supp. 856 (D. Ariz. 1973)), the trial judge admitted the testimony of a witness qualified as an expert, who offered an opinion on the meaning of "object of antiquity," a legal term that was left undefined in the Act. The witness testified that the term has reference not only to the age of an object but also to the use for which the object was made and to which it was put, and that, consequently, three- or four-year-old face masks removed from a medicine man's cave on the San Carlos Indian Reservation were objects of antiquity. As a consequence of the opinion testimony, Diaz was convicted of violation of the Antiquities Act. On appeal of the conviction (499 F.2d 113 (9th Cir. 1974)), rather than hold that the trial court judge had committed reversible error in admitting opinion testimony on the meaning of a legal term, which is a matter of law for the judge to decide, the United States Court of Appeals for the Ninth Circuit held that the criminal enforcement provision of the Antiquities Act, by use of undefined terms of uncommon usage, was fatally vague in violation of the due process clause of the Constitution. By contrast, in *U.S. v. Smyer* (596 F.2d 939 (10th Cir. 1979)), the United States Court of Appeals for the Tenth Circuit upheld the convictions of the defendants under the Antiquities Act for looting 800–900-year-old archaeological resources belonging to the Mimbres culture from the Gila National Forest. Disagreeing with the Ninth Circuit's holding that the term "object of antiquity" was unconstitutionally vague, the Tenth Circuit judges relied on Webster's International Dictionary to determine that the legal term meant "times long since past" and to hold that, when measured by common understanding and practice, the challenged language conveys a sufficiently definite warning as to the proscribed conduct.
8. *United States v. William Paul Rogers*, No. 4:07-CR-22-001 (E.D. Tenn. sentence Mar. 31, 2008).
9. *United States v. Robert Gee*, No. 07-MJ-00143-DLW (D. Colo. sentence Jan. 8, 2008).
10. *United States v. Tina Todd*, No. 8:07-19 (3) (D.S.C. sentence Aug. 20, 2008).

11. *United States v. Byran Keith Gary, Kristi L. Hendricks, and Tina Todd*, No. 8:07-CR-19-HFF (D.S.C. sentence June 20, 2007 (Gary and Hendricks), and continuance order June 27, 2007 (Todd)).
12. *United States v. Carl Henderson*, No. 3:07CR30002-001 (W.D. Ark. sentence Feb. 27, 2008).
13. Leonard Sand, John S. Siffert, Walter P. Loughton, Steven A. Reiss & Nancy Batterman, MODERN FEDERAL JURY INSTRUCTIONS—CRIMINAL VOLUMES § P 23A.01 (Theft of Government Property) (2005).
14. *United States v. Kirby Loren Amlee*, No. 4:06-CR-172-01 RAJ (W.D. Tex. sentence May 21, 2008).
15. *United States v. Kirby Loren Amlee and Joey Kenneth Priddy*, No. P06-CR-172 (W.D. Tex. sentence Oct. 19, 2006 (Priddy)).
16. *U.S. v. Max L. Ary*, 518 F.3d 775 (10th Cir. 2008), *aff'g* No. 05-CR-10053-01-JTM (D. Kans. sentence May 15, 2006 and order of restitution Aug. 24, 2006).
17. Fed. R. Crim. P. 16 (a)(1)(E).
18. Fed. R. Evid. 803(6).
19. *U.S. v. Max L. Ary*, 518 F.3d 775, 786 (10th Cir. 2008) (citing *U.S. v. Samaniego*, 187 F.3d 1222, 1224 (10th Cir. 1999)).
20. U.S.S.G. 2B1.1 comment. (n.2(C)(i)).
21. U.S.S.G. 2B1.1(b)(1)(G).
22. The items were "objects of cultural heritage," as defined by 18 U.S.C. 668 (a)(2), because they belonged to a "museum" and were worth more than $100,000. *See* U.S. Sentencing Commission, *Guidelines Manual*, § 2B1.5, comment. (n.1 (F)) (Nov. 2002).
23. This offense level is reached by taking the base offense level (8), and increasing it on the basis that the value of the cultural heritage resources was more than $200,000 (12 levels), the offense conduct involved cultural heritage resources from a "museum" (2 levels), and the offense was committed for pecuniary gain (2 levels). *See* U.S. Sentencing Commission, *Guidelines Manual*, § 2B1.5 (Nov. 2002).
24. *United States v. Joseph U.R.M. Elibosang*, No. CR-07-00062-001 (D. Guam sentence Apr. 9, 2008).
25. *See* U.S. Sentencing Commission, *Guidelines Manual*, § 2B1.5, comment. (n.1 (E)) (Nov. 2002).
26. *United States v. Charles Thomas Allen II*, 516 F.3d 364 (6th Cir. 2008), *cert. denied sub nom. Allen v. United States* 2008 U.S. LEXIS 4837 (U.S. June 9, 2008); *United States v. Warren Christopher Lipka, Spencer Wilson Reinhard, Eric Joseph Borsuk, and Charles Thomas Allen, II*, No. 5:05-CR-39-JBC (E.D. Ky. correction of sentence on remand Oct. 30, 2008).

27. *See* U.S. Sentencing Commission, *Guidelines Manual*, § 2B1.5 comment. (n.7) (Nov. 2002).
28. *See* U.S. Sentencing Commission, *Guidelines Manual*, § 2B1.5(b)(6) (Nov. 2002).
29. *See* U.S. Sentencing Commission, *Guidelines Manual*, § 5K1.1 (Nov. 2002).
30. *See* U.S. Sentencing Commission, *Guidelines Manual*, § 3B1.2 (Nov. 2002).
31. In calculating an advisory guideline range for inclusion in the presentence report, the U.S. Probation Office had included in its loss computation the books that Lipka and Borsuk dropped in the library stairwell, and used the defendants' value estimate of all the items in question ($1,985,000), which resulted in a 16-level enhancement. Had the presentence report used the Government's value estimate for those same items ($3,285,000), the result would have been an 18-level enhancement. In any event, the district court did not concur with the PSR's loss computation.
32. On appeal, the Government did not argue for inclusion of the items abandoned in the Special Collections Library as part of the loss computation.
33. *U.S. v. Rodriguez*, 301 F.3d 666, 668 (6th Cir. 2002).
34. *United States v. Charles Thomas Allen II*, 516 F.3d 364, 379 (6th Cir. 2008).
35. *United States v. Steven Lee Olson*, No. 2:7cr847-01 (D.N.J. sentence June 11, 2008); *United States v. Roman Szurko*, No. 2:7cr999-01 (D.N.J. sentence June 11, 2008).
36. *United States v. Steven Stewart Farmer*, No. ED CR 06-107 VAP (C.D. Cal. sentence Jan. 2, 2008).
37. *United States v. Marilyn Skahan Malatare and Colette Julia Malatare*, No. 2:08CR02002 (E.D. Wash sentence June 5, 2008).
38. *United States v. Edward George Johnson*, No. 08CR00491-01(KNF) (S.D.N.Y. sentence Sept. 16, 2008).
39. *United States v. Lester F. Weber and Lori E. Childs*, No. 4:08cr17 (E.D. Va. sentence Dec. 17, 2008).
40. *United States v. Maxwell Garihan and Gary Paul Garihan*, No. 07-cr-00335-MSK (D. Colo. sentence Mar. 31, 2008).
41. *See* U.S. Sentencing Commission, *Guidelines Manual*, § 5K1.1 (Nov. 2002).
42. *United States v. Edward J. Renehan, Jr.*, No. 1:08 CR 00444-001(DC) (S.D.N.Y. sentence Sept. 19, 2008).
43. *United States v. James Lyman Brubaker*, No. 4:08-cr-00042-GF-SEH (D. Mont. sentence Sept. 15, 2008).
44. *United States v. Robert Mardirosian*, No. 1:07 CR 10075-001-MLW (D. Mass. sentence Dec. 15, 2008).

International Mediation of Cultural Property Ownership Issues —It's the Right Thing to Do!

Marilyn Phelan

International Council of Museums' Mediation Process

The International Council of Museums (ICOM) finalized a formal mediation process in 2007, as a means to settle disputes regarding the return/restitution of stolen and/or illegally exported cultural property held in museum collections.[1] In December 2005, the ICOM Executive Council formally adopted the recommendation of the ICOM Legal Affairs Committee—which had cosponsored a discussion of the legal and ethical considerations associated with questions of ownership of cultural properties at the 2004 annual ICOM meeting in Seoul, Korea—that ICOM should establish a formal mediation process in which museums could participate to resolve some of the possession and ownership issues without their having to resort to costly litigation. Through its initiation of a new written mediation procedure, ICOM has revitalized its ongoing policy, which it had espoused at least since its 1983 (London) General Conference, of seeking voluntary settlements to disputes regarding the ownership of objects in museum collections that allegedly were stolen or illegally exported from the country of origin.[2] Through this formal mediation process, ICOM will offer practical assistance and advice on mediation as an alternative to court proceedings.[3] As John McAvity, the current chair of the ICOM Legal Affairs Committee, has affirmed, museums and those who have disputes with museums can begin to utilize ICOM's formal mediation process after ICOM completes its training for approved mediators in 2009.[4] Patrick

Boylan, the first chair of the ICOM Legal Affairs Committee, emphasized that ICOM would not want to choose sides between museums and has no desire to be a party to litigation.[5] Boylan characterized the ICOM mediation process as one wherein ICOM "will help willing parties get to the table" so as to move them "a step closer to a reconciliation."[6]

As John McAvity articulated, the difficult and costly procedure when courts attempt to decide questions of ownership of cultural property, by applying the individualized laws of different countries, as well as the ethical questions inherent in museums having continuing possession of looted and/or illegally exported artifacts in their collections, should persuade members of the museum community to do "the right thing," and attempt to resolve disputes over cultural property through utilization of the ICOM mediation process.[7] Alissandra Cummins, the current President of ICOM, commented in her statement promoting the use of mediation in the resolution of ownership disputes,[8] that the possibility of "a former generation of staff and trustees" applying "less strict acquisition rules to those applicable today" could "cause even those museums that follow strict rules requiring positive evidence of legal ownership and title to acquisitions to face claims for return of objects."[9]

When ICOM announced its policy to provide a panel to assist museums in mediating issues relating to cultural property ownership, it issued a document citing its policy of many years to "encourage the negotiated resolution of disputes regarding the ownership of objects in museum collections that allegedly were stolen or illegally exported from the country of origin" and articulated its current position that there should be "the early settlement of such disputes through voluntary settlement procedures rather than through lengthy and expensive litigation or through political decisions."[10] The document provides guidance notes on the ICOM mediation process and refers to ICOM's panel of international mediators "who can be nominated to consider issues relating to the return/restitution of cultural property in museum collections that was stolen, illegally exported, illegally confiscated, or otherwise wrongfully expropriated."[11] The Executive Council of ICOM will appoint members of the Mediation Panel after taking appropriate specialist advice. The ICOM mediation process provides that upon request "from a museum, some other entity, or an individual, for assistance in establishing a mutually agreed mediation procedure, the President of ICOM, after due consultation, may refer a dispute to a mediation forum in which an impartial person or persons, the mediator or mediators, facilitate communication between parties to the dispute to promote reconciliation, settlement, or understanding among them."[12] The ICOM mediation process is "applicable to restitution, repatriation, and return cases."[13]

Legal Principles Relating to Stolen and/or Illegally Exported Cultural Property

Unfortunately, in addressing mediation of issues relating to stolen and/or illegally exported cultural property in museum collections, there are limited and often confusing legal principles to guide participants in the mediation process. Further, there are differing views among members of the museum community regarding the approach to difficult ownership and return/restitution issues. Mediation of these demanding issues is almost mandated because, while there are international treaties that seek to protect and preserve cultural property and that present international precepts associated with the repatriation of stolen and illegally exported objects, there is no adequate legal regime in place to address ownership and return/restitution issues.

There are five major international conventions, discussed herein,[14] that were drafted to protect cultural property and that address issues relating to stolen and/or illegally exported cultural property. However, these conventions will provide an international law regarding possession and ownership of cultural property only where, and to the extent that, countries involved in ownership disputes have adopted the conventions into their domestic law. Because several countries have not ratified all or some of the conventions and/or their provisions, some, if not all, of the principles set out in the conventions are not law in many countries. This paper summarizes briefly the laws relating to cultural property for informational purposes, but also to demonstrate that while these laws are inadequate to resolve ownership and return/restitution issues, museums, countries, and mediators must nonetheless consider the differing legal principles as they set about to mediate issues that often involve multiple countries, as well as citizens of different states.

Stolen Cultural Property

Although there is no international law, nor a forum with international jurisdiction to decide questions relating to the ownership of cultural property with questionable provenances, courts in the United States have provided some judicial remedies to foreign governments and to individuals who seek to recover cultural property in museum collections.[15] These remedies are based on the common law principle, the English *nemo dat* rule,[16] which provides that one who purchases property from a thief, no matter how innocently, acquires no title in the property. Title remains with the true owner.[17] This common law principle has been codified into express law in the United States Uniform Commercial Code,[18] and, thus, is recognized statutory law in all the states. One U.S. court commented that this law "stands as a bulwark against the handiwork of evil, to guard to rightful owners the fruits of their labors."[19] The effect of this rule is that museums as purchasers and donees of stolen cultural property may be exposed indefinitely in U.S. courts to claims of original owners.

While U.S. courts must recognize that a seller cannot convey good title to property that was previously stolen, a few courts earlier imposed a due diligence requirement upon the original owners as a prerequisite to proving their claim to their stolen artworks.[20] More recently, U.S. courts have recognized the unfortunate results of such a mandate and have shifted the due diligence requirements to potential purchasers of valuable artifacts.[21] In balancing the equities between purchasers and the original owners, courts more often will tip the scale in favor of the rightful owners who have faced difficult and often unfair burdens in meeting a due diligence requirement.[22]

A purchaser of stolen cultural property can acquire good title to stolen property at the expiration of a statute of limitations on the actual owner's claim.[23] As courts in the United States earlier had expressed a concern about protecting innocent purchasers, when the original owner had not exercised due diligence to recover stolen property,[24] with the exception of New York courts[25] and California, because of its statute relating to a true owner's discovery of the location of stolen property,[26] U.S. courts have ruled that the statute of limitations on suits to recover stolen property begins to run when the rightful owner knew "or reasonably should know" of her or his cause of action and the identity of the possessor of the property.[27] Thus, there can be a cutoff of a victim's title after a certain number of years, if a court decides an owner has not exercised due diligence in pursuing the owner's claim.[28] Still, with courts more recently shifting the due diligence requirement to a potential purchaser of valuable artworks, the "reasonably should know" component of the discovery rule possibly may be applied more favorably to original owners who have been innocent victims of the illicit trade in valuable cultural treasures. In New York, limitation on the time during which suit may be brought to recover stolen property does not begin until the rightful owner asserts a claim to the property and the possessor refuses to return the property.[29] Courts in New York have determined that the claim rule is better than the discovery rule applicable in other states because it "gives the owner relatively greater protection and places the burden of investigating the provenance of a work of art on the potential purchaser."[30]

In Porter v. Wertz,[31] a New York State Attorney General wanted a court to rule that it was a departure from reasonable standards for a purchaser of a valuable painting to fail to inquire about title to a painting or to question the credentials of the seller as an art dealer. According to the State Attorney General, good faith among art merchants requires an inquiry as to ownership of an object d'art.[32] The Art Dealers Association of America (ADAA), on the other hand, contended that such a rule of law would cripple the art market.[33] The court in Wertz declined to rule on the good faith question.[34] However, in Autocephalous Greek-Orthodox Church v. Goldberg,[35] the court decided that a potential purchaser must make a formal search of records and a full background search of the seller and the seller's claim of title.[36] Courts now are more likely to conclude that a purchaser of cultural property was not an "innocent purchaser" if the potential buyer failed to conduct an adequate search of the artifact's provenance.

The common law principles noted above contrast with the principles in most civil law countries, wherein a purchaser of stolen property often can obtain title through a limitations period.[37] Countries whose legal systems are based on Roman law, or civil law, generally permit a period of five years after a theft for a legal owner to recover the goods from an innocent purchaser. After that period of time, the purchaser has good title to the property. In civil law countries the person or entity who purchased the stolen property must have been a "good faith" or "innocent" purchaser for the limitations period to begin to run.[38] Further, if a State determines that a current possessor of stolen cultural property has good title to such property, the rightful owners or their heirs may be successful in bringing a claim for return of the property, or payment of the property's value, in a court in the United States.[39]

Illegally Exported Cultural Property

In contrast to stolen property, laws in the United States have not in the past prevented purchasers from acquiring good title to illegally exported artifacts.[40] A purchaser's possession of an illegally exported artifact generally was not disturbed in the past if the artifact was not stolen.[41] Now many countries have patrimony laws that declare state ownership of all property found at their archaeological sites.[42] If a government asserts title to artifacts located within its boundaries, courts in the United States may apply the National Stolen Property Act (NSPA)[43] to the removal without permission of such artifacts, even though the artifacts may never have been physically possessed by agents of the country of origin. In *United States v. McClain*,[44] a court upheld the conviction, under NSPA, of individuals who sold pre-Columbian artifacts in Texas. The court determined that there was clear Mexican ownership in the artifacts.[45] A U.S. court again applied the National Stolen Property Act to punish encroachments upon legitimate and clear State ownership rights to imported artifacts from Egypt in the recent case, *United States v. Schultz*,[46] discussed below.[47]

Museums and those who have acquired illegally exported cultural property may be subject to an action brought by the country of origin, including criminal indictments, against the possessors of such property. For example, Italy has brought a criminal indictment against a prior curator for the J. Paul Getty Museum on charges of conspiring to export looted antiquities from Italy.[48] Although the Getty agreed to return forty ancient artifacts in its collection to Italy, Italy has not dropped the criminal charges against the curator. Italy has agreements with the Metropolitan Museum of Art, the Boston Museum of Fine Arts, and the Princeton University Art Museums for return of some of the objects in their collections.[49] Greece also brought criminal action against the former Getty curator, but dropped the charges when the Getty agreed to return to Greece forty artifacts in its collections.[50]

International Conventions

Concern for the protection of cultural property evolved in the mid-19th century,[51] but the first significant international legislation to protect cultural property was the 1954 Hague Convention for the Protection of Cultural Property in the Event of Armed Conflict. The Hague Convention seeks to protect cultural property during wartime.[52] The 1954 Hague Convention prohibits the destruction or seizure of cultural property during armed conflict, whether international or civil in nature, and during a period of belligerent occupation, but it also applies to peacetime international trafficking in cultural property unlawfully seized during an armed conflict.[53] Its preamble provides that "damage to cultural property belonging to any people whatsoever means damage to the cultural heritage of all mankind," since, as the Preamble states "each people makes its contribution to the culture of the world."[54] Although the United States did not become a signatory to the Hague Convention until 2008, armed forces of the United States follow and receive training on its provisions.

The second international agreement, the 1970 UNESCO Convention on the Means of Prohibiting and Preventing the Illicit Import, Export and Transfer of Ownership of Cultural Property[55] focuses on private conduct, primarily during peacetime.[56] The international community became concerned in the 1960s about the importation into various countries of artifacts unlawfully obtained from the country of origin. This concern led to the drafting in 1970 of an international agreement by the General Conference of UNESCO, wherein the parties to the convention agreed to oppose all illicit import, export, and transfer of ownership of cultural property with whatever means at their disposal.[57] At the meeting of the General Conference in Paris in 1970, the several nations in attendance recognized that the illicit trade in cultural property of various nations had become a primary cause of the impoverishment of the cultural heritage of originating countries. It concluded that international cooperation constituted one of the most efficient means of protecting each country's cultural property against the dangers resulting from the illicit transfer of such properties.[58] The Preamble to the 1970 UNESCO Convention declares that "cultural property constitutes one of the basic elements of civilization and national culture and its interchange increases the knowledge of the civilization of man, enriches the cultural life of all people, and inspires mutual respect and appreciation among nations."

The United States Congress enacted the Cultural Property Implementation Act[59] in 1982, effective in 1983, to implement a few of the provisions of the 1970 UNESCO Convention into domestic law.[60] At that time, members of Congress noted that the demand for cultural artifacts had resulted in the irremedial destruction of archaeological sites and articles and was depriving the situs countries of their cultural patrimony and important knowledge of the past.[61] Members of Congress were concerned that the United States had become a principal market for articles of archaeological or ethnological interest and of art objects, and that the discovery of stolen or illegally exported artifacts in the United States had in some cases severely strained relations with the countries of origin, some of which were close allies of the United States.[62]

The Convention on Cultural Property Implementation Act provides that when a participating nation makes a request to the United States for import restrictions on cultural property from that nation, because the requesting nation contends the cultural patrimony of the nation is in jeopardy from the pillage of its cultural properties, the President of the United States may enter into a bilateral agreement with that nation to apply import restrictions.[63] The import restrictions would provide that no designated archaeological or ethnological material exported from the requesting nation can be imported into the United States unless the requesting nation has issued a certificate that the exportation was not in violation of that nation's laws.[64] The term "archaeological material" refers to an object of cultural significance that is at least 250 years old and has been normally discovered as a result of scientific excavation, clandestine or accidental digging, or exploration on land or underwater.[65] The term "object of ethnological interest" refers to an object that is the product of a tribal or nonindustrial society and is important to the cultural heritage of a people because of its distinctive characteristics, comparative rarity, or its contribution to the knowledge of the origin, development, or history of that people.[66]

The Convention for the Protection of the World Cultural and Natural Heritage, which was adopted by UNESCO in 1972, [67] addresses the need for international protection of cultural property.[68] It recognizes that a "heritage of all nations of the world" often remains incomplete at the national level and places the responsibility squarely upon the international community to provide "collective assistance" to individual countries in protecting their cultural properties that have universal value.[69] The Convention was adopted to establish "an effective system of collective protection of the cultural and natural heritage of outstanding universal value, organized on a permanent basis and in accordance with modern scientific methods."[70] The 1972 Convention established an Intergovernmental Committee for the Protection of the Cultural and Natural Heritage of Outstanding Universal Value, called the "World Heritage Committee."[71] Each party State to the Convention submits to the World Heritage Committee an inventory of property forming part of the cultural and natural heritage in its territory. The World Heritage Committee must maintain an up–to-date and published list of these properties in its "World Heritage List."[72] The World Heritage Committee also assembles from the World Heritage List a List of Heritage in Danger for which major operations are necessary and for which assistance has been requested.[73] The 1972 Convention established a fund for the protection of cultural property of outstanding universal value, called the "World Heritage Fund," but it also encourages the establishment of national, public, and private foundations whose purposes are to invite donations for the protection of the cultural and natural heritage.[74] The U.S. Senate approved the 1972 UNESCO Convention in 1973, but implementing legislation for U.S. participation in the 1972 UNESCO Convention was not enacted until 1980.[75]

In 1995, the UNIDROIT Convention on Stolen or Illegally Exported Cultural Property was adopted in Rome. Parties to the UNIDROIT Convention avowed that they wereconvinced "of the fundamental importance of the protection of cultural heritage and of cultural exchanges for promoting and understanding between peoples, and the dissemination of culture for the well-being of humanity and the progress of civilisation."[76] The UNIDROIT Convention mandates the return of a stolen cultural object to the original owner.[77] Further, any cultural object that was excavated unlawfully, or excavated lawfully but retained unlawfully, is deemed to be stolen.[78] In addition, a party nation to the UNIDROIT Convention may demand that a court of another party country to the convention order the return of a cultural object illegally exported from territory of the requesting nation.[79]

The UNIDROIT Convention provides for time limitations on claims for restitution but does not require due diligence on the part of claimants.[80] A claim for restitution must be brought within a period of three years from the time the claimant knew of the location of the cultural object and the identity of its possessor, and in any case within a period of fifty years from the time of the theft.[81] A cultural object forming an integral part of an identified monument or archaeological site, or belonging to a public collection, is not subject to time limitations, other than the three-year limitation period from the time when the claimant knew the location of the cultural object and the identity of its possessor.[82] However, each nation may declare that a claim is subject to a time limitation of seventy-five years or a longer period as provided in its law.[83] The Convention includes as a "public collection," which is not subject to time limitations other than the three-year limitation period, inventoried or otherwise identified cultural objects owned by religious institutions and other institutions established for "an essentially cultural, educational or scientific purpose" and recognized by a nation as serving the public interest.[84]

The notion of an innocent purchaser has relevance under the UNIDROIT Convention only with respect to the issue of whether a current possessor of stolen or illegally exported cultural objects is entitled to compensation. The Convention provides for compensation to a possessor of a stolen cultural object who is required to return the object if the possessor "neither knew nor ought reasonably to have known that the object was stolen" and can prove "due diligence when acquiring the object."[85] Thus, while the UNIDROIT Convention does not impose due diligence upon a claimant of cultural property, it does impose a due diligence requirement upon a bona fide possessor who seeks compensation after being required to return a cultural object. In determining whether a possessor exercised due diligence, the Convention provides that the following circumstances regarding the acquisition must be considered:[86]

> character of the parties, the price paid, whether the possessor consulted any reasonably accessible register of stolen cultural objects, and any other relevant information and documentation which it could reasonably have obtained, and whether the possessor consulted accessible agencies or took any other steps that a reasonable person would have taken in the circumstances.

In determining whether a possessor knew or reasonably ought to have known that a cultural object had been illegally exported, one must consider the absence of an export certificate required under the law of the requesting nation.[87]

Although the UNIDROIT Convention dictates the repatriation of cultural objects, provisions of this Convention only apply prospectively. Required restitution under the UNIDROIT Convention does not apply to cultural objects that were stolen before the Convention was in force in a country in which a claim is brought,[88] nor to cultural objects that were illegally exported before the Convention was in force in the requesting country, or in the country in which the claim is brought.[89] While the UNIDROIT Convention provides for the return of all stolen or illegally exported cultural property, albeit only from the effective date of the Convention in the country in which a claim is brought,[90] it provides that a claim for restitution of stolen or illegally exported cultural objects may be brought before the courts of the country in which the cultural object is located.[91] The Convention contains a provision stating that it does not in any way legitimize any illegal transaction that occurred before the Convention was in force nor does it limit the right of any country or person to make a claim under remedies available outside the framework of the Convention for the restitution or return of a cultural object stolen or illegally exported before the effective date of the Convention.[92]

To date thirty-nine countries have ratified the 1995 UNIDROIT Convention, but the United States is not one of them.[93] However, as noted previously, courts in the United States have provided avenues for the restitution of stolen cultural objects under general property law.[94] In addition, Congress gave formal recognition to the concept of the restitution of cultural objects when it enacted the Native American Graves Protection and Repatriation Act (NAGPRA).[95] The enactment of NAGPRA attests to congressional recognition that common law restitution provisions have merit, in that NAGPRA requires federal agencies and museums, which receive federal funds and which have possession or control over collections of Native American human remains and associated funerary objects, to compile an inventory of such items and, to the extent possible, based on information possessed by such entities, to identify the geographical and cultural affiliation of such items.[96] If the cultural affiliation of Native American human remains and associated funerary objects is determined, then, upon the request of a lineal descendant of the Native American individual, or the tribe, a museum or federal agency must expeditiously return such remains and associated funerary objects.[97] NAGPRA also contains a similar process for other cultural items, wrongfully removed from the tribe, to which the museum cannot show right of possession.

Concern for the protection and preservation of the underwater cultural heritage led to the enactment in 2001 of the Convention on the Protection of the Underwater Cultural Heritage. In the 2001 Convention, UNESCO acknowledged the importance of underwater cultural heritage and recognized that all States must accept responsibility for protecting and preserving this heritage. The Convention on the Protection of the Underwater Cultural Heritage acknowledges that the importance of underwater cultural heritage is "an integral part of the cultural heritage of humanity and a particularly important element in the history of peoples, nations, and their relations with each other concerning their common heritage."[98] It notes the importance of protecting and preserving the underwater cultural heritage and the responsibility of all States and considers that "survey, excavation and protection of underwater cultural heritage" necessitates the availability and application of special scientific methods and the use of suitable techniques and equipment. It requires member parties to "cooperate in the provision of training in underwater archaeology, in techniques for the conservation of underwater cultural heritage, and on agreed terms in the transfer or technology relating to underwater cultural heritage."[99] It recognizes the need to codify and develop rules relating to the protection and preservation of underwater cultural heritage and expresses the value of public education to contribute to "awareness, appreciation and protection of that heritage." The Convention requires each member party to "take all practicable measures to raise public awareness regarding the value and significance of underwater cultural heritage and the importance of protecting it."[100] It expresses concern for the increasing commercial exploitation of underwater cultural heritage, and in particular of certain activities directed to the sale, acquisition, or barter of underwater treasures. For further updates on the convention, *see* Practice Area 4: Marine Environment, in this volume.

Conflicting Positions of the Museum Community on Return/Restitution Issues

There are conflicting positions among members of the museum community regarding cultural property ownership and return/restitution questions. Some museum officials have sanctioned "universal" museums accessioning cultural treasures that have questionable provenances.[101] Others consider this highly controversial posture to be unethical, if not illegal. The arguments presented in two important U.S. cases, *Schultz* and *An Antique Platter of Gold*, illustrate the perspective of those members of the museum community who make allowances for museums acquiring artifacts that were illegally exported from the country of origin.

The first of the two cases is *United States v. An Antique Platter of Gold,*[102] wherein the American Association of Museums (AAM) submitted an *amicus curiae* brief supporting the actions of an art collector, who also was a benefactor of the New York Metropolitan Museum of Art, in importing into the United States a looted third-century B.C. phiale. The phiale was taken from an archaeological site in Sicily, was exported in violation of Italian laws, and was imported into the United States in violation of its customs laws.[103] A 1939 Italian law presumes that an archaeological item belongs to the State unless its possessor can show private ownership prior to 1902.[104] The Italian government sought the assistance of the U.S. government in investigating the circumstances of the phiale's exportation and requested that it confiscate the Phiale for return to Italy.[105] The district court ruled that the phiale must be returned to Italy.[106] On appeal, the AAM filed an *amicus* brief wherein it urged the appellate court not to give effect to the cultural patrimony laws of other countries.[107] The AAM asserted, "American museums have a deep and longstanding interest in, and commitment to, the responsible collection and exhibition of cultural objects of all countries and civilizations."[108] It further stated that "American museums have supported, and will continue to support, all responsible efforts to further the preservation and conservation of cultural objects, and to combat their destruction, looting and theft."[109] However, it then postulated that the decision of the district court (that ordered the forfeiture of the phiale and its return to Italy) "threatens the ability of U.S. museums to collect (through purchase, gift and bequest) and make available for public exhibition objects from around the world that have *not* been stolen or been the object of looting" but that "may have been the subject of sweeping foreign cultural patrimony laws."[110] It declared that these cultural patrimony laws "are, in significant respects, antithetical to fundamental principles of U.S. law and public policy" and expressed concern that if the decision of the court below was not reversed, "countless objects" in museum collections would be in peril.[111] The AAM maintained that the decision of the court would "have a profound impact on the law governing all museums and their ability to collect and exhibit cultural objects."[112] It then declared that American museums were "compelled" to urge the court to reverse the decision of the court below.[113] The AAM took the position that the district court committed "fundamental error" in "its automatic enforcement of Italy's patrimony law."[114] It contended that the U.S. government" became a "surrogate for the Italian government" when U.S. customs used a "civil forfeiture law in tandem with the NSPA,"[115] and described the "efforts of some nations to claim ownership of all objects discovered within their borders" as a "more parochial view of cultural property," one that would "directly challenge the 'common cultural heritage' philosophy" upon which, it stated, "our museums and society are founded."[116]

The AAM declared in its *amicus* brief that "cultural patrimony laws are fundamentally inconsistent with the United States' treatment of its own cultural property and with our underlying system of private property."[117] It further stated that "the effect of the indiscriminate application of these laws will be to jeopardize existing museum collections and the future ability of our museums to continue to collect and exhibit cultural objects for the public."[118] The AAM avowed in its *amicus* brief that, if the appellate court affirmed the decision of the district court that the phiale must be returned to Italy, the decision "will amount to a judicial fiat . . . that often will preclude *responsible* museums from acquiring cultural objects from other countries."[119] (Emphasis added.) The Second Circuit Court of Appeals disagreed with the AAM's position and affirmed the district court's ruling that the phiale had to be returned to Italy.[120]

The second and more recent case is *United States v. Schultz,*[121] in which some members of the museum community filed an *amicus curiae* brief supporting a well-known art dealer who was convicted for knowingly transporting stolen Egyptian antiquities.[122] Schultz was indicted for "conspiring to receive stolen Egyptian antiquities that had been transported in interstate and foreign commerce" in violation of the National Stolen Property Act,[123] discussed above. Schultz contended that the objects he had taken were not stolen within the meaning of NSPA, because they were not owned by anyone and, thus, could not be stolen.[124] The prosecution, on the other hand, successfully demonstrated that the Egyptian government owned the antiquities pursuant to a patrimony law known as "Law 117," which provides that all antiquities found in Egypt after 1983 are property of the Egyptian government.[125] Evidence in the case showed that a co-defendant, Parry, smuggled an ancient Egyptian sculpture, the head of Pharaoh Amenhotep III, out of Egypt by disguising the figure in plastic and plaster to take it out of Egypt. Schultz later paid Parry a substantial fee to serve as the agent to sell the sculpture.[126] The two men then created a false provenance for the sculpture, claiming that it had been brought from Egypt in the 1920s and had been maintained since that time in an English private collection, which they called the "Thomas Alcock Collection."[127] They prepared fake labels for the sculpture, which were designed to appear as if they had been printed in the 1920s.[128] After a jury trial in the U.S. District Court for the Southern District of New York, Schultz was convicted of conspiring to receive stolen property that had been transported in interstate or foreign commerce under NSPA. The case was appealed to the Court of Appeals for the Second Circuit.[129] Dealer groups and a newly formed "Citizens for a Balanced Policy with Regard to the Importation of Cultural Property" filed *amicus curiae* briefs supporting Schultz.[130] The organization was a group of twenty-seven individuals that included a curator emeritus of the Department of Egyptian Art for the Museum of Fine Arts in Boston; a then-member of the Board of Trustees of the Metropolitan Museum of Art, and the then-Chairman of its Acquisitions Committee; a member of the Board of Trustees of the Freer-Sackler Museum in Washington, D.C.; a former Executive Vice President and Counsel to the Trustees of the Metropolitan

Museum of Art; a former curator of Egyptian, Classical and Near Eastern Art at the Brooklyn Museum of Art; a Director Emeritus of the Princeton University Art Museum; a then-Chair of the Advisory Committee of the Princeton University Art Museum and former Chairman of the Jacksonville Art Museums; the former curator of Pre-Columbian Art at the Princeton University Art Museum; the former curator of Ancient Art at the Tampa Museum of Art; and the then-consulting curator at the Denver Art Museum.[131] This twenty-seven member group of individuals stated that their interest in the case was their "abiding commitment to the preservation of cultural heritage and the continued existence of a national policy with regard to international trade in cultural property that balances the legitimate but often conflicting interest of archaeologists, art dealers, collectors, museums and our national government."[132] In their brief, the group asserted that Schultz's indictment "shook the American art world," and with it, members of the group.[133] The group contended that if the NSPA reaches claims of ownership based on foreign patrimony laws, "our nation's cultural policy is at stake."[134] The Second Circuit Court of Appeals disagreed and affirmed Schultz's conviction.[135] The Court ruled that NSPA applies to property that is stolen in violation of a foreign patrimony law and that the Cultural Property Implementation Act is not the exclusive means of dealing with stolen artifacts and antiquities, as Schultz and the twenty-seven member group had contended.[136]

Facts in the above noted cases and the conflicting opinions expressed by different members of the museum community regarding the return/restitution of illegally exported cultural property in museum collections accentuate the importance of museums mediating ownership and return/restitution issues relating to the retention of such artifacts in their collections.

Holocaust Looted Art in Museum Collections

Ownership and return/restitution problems relating to artworks in museum collections that may be Holocaust looted art, that is, pieces with ambiguous provenances acquired between 1933 and 1945, are, like questions relating to illegally exported artifacts in museum collections, especially appropriate issues for mediation. Many of the artworks with 1933–1945 provenance gaps became a part of the collections of some museums either as a result of the museums having purchased the artworks through the international market, or having received such property through donations from art collectors who purchased the property on the international market. Although many members of the museum community have offered to open their collections to the Jewish community to determine what works were indeed stolen and, thus, should be restituted, the process of returning looted Jewish cultural property has been slow. Most civil law countries provide a means for a good faith purchaser to obtain good title to stolen merchandise, facilitating validation of ownership of Holocaust looted art. While property laws in the United States and other common law countries do not recognize a good faith purchaser in the context of stolen goods, victims of Holocaust looting still face burden of proof and statute of limitation problems as they seek redress in the courts.

There are numerous international agreements in place, some prior to World War II and after, that prohibit pillage during military conflicts. Museums and mediators should consider the provisions of these agreements as they mediate ownership and return/restitution issues regarding museums' acquisitions of artworks that have questionable provenances and that were sold on the international art market during the years 1933 to 1945.

One of the early international conventions directed at cultural treasures acquired during a military conflict is the 1907 Hague Convention on the Laws and Customs of War on Land. It provides that an enemy's property cannot be seized unless the seizure is imperatively demanded by the necessities of war. Another is the 1919 Treaty of Versailles, which required Germany to make restitution of objects taken during the war where it could identify them in territory belonging to Germany or its allies. Several laws were enacted during and after World War II that specifically address the issue of property taken illegally by the Nazis. In 1943, the United States government issued the Inter-Allied Declaration Against Acts of Dispossession Committed in Territories under Enemy Occupation or Control,[137] known as the "London Declaration," that set the stage for the postwar restitution policy in Europe. In the 1943 London Declaration, the Allies cautioned nations that all transfers of, or dealing with, property taken by Axis powers could be declared invalid. In 1946, the Provisional Government of Austria enacted a federal law that declared void all acts of dispossession which occurred in connection with the National Socialist accession to power during the period of the occupation of Austria, from 1938 through 1945.[138] This law provided that dispossession was assumed if a person acquired property from persons who were subjected to Nazi persecution. The Nuremberg Charter included as a war crime the plunder of public or private property during a military conflict. The Nuremberg Tribunal ruled that Germany had engaged in an illegal war of aggression and branded the looting of Jewish property as part of the persecution, thus a crime against humanity. The United Nations General Assembly later passed a resolution recognizing the Nuremberg Charter and Judgment as part of the body of general international law that binds all nations. In 1998, the Austrian government enacted a federal law requiring the restitution of artworks from Austrian federal museums and collections that had been the subject to a transaction nullified by its 1946 law.

The U.S. policy for restitution of property taken from victims of the Holocaust was clarified in 1947 when the United States promulgated Military Government Law Number 59 (MGL No. 59). This law creates a presumption that sales of personal property by Jewish residents of Germany after 1933 were forced sales, and, thus, constructively property confiscated by the Nazis. This presumption can be rebutted only if the possessor of such property can demonstrate the payment of a fair purchase price for the property and that the possessor acquired the property from a transferor who had the free right of disposal of the purchase price. Because a Jewish person rarely would have had a "free right of disposal of the purchase price" in Nazi Germany, MGL No. 59 creates a presumption that the Nazi regime confiscated artifacts "purchased" or taken from Jewish persons between 1933 and 1945. In 1949, Jack Tate, the Acting Legal Advisor for the U.S. State Department, restated the U.S. policy of undoing forced transfers and restitution of identifiable property to persons wrongfully deprived of that property within the period from January 30, 1933 to May 8, 1945.

In 1999, the Parliamentary Assembly of the Council of Europe unanimously adopted a resolution that recognized that while there were moves early after the end of World War II to find and return Jewish looted property, much still remains in private and public hands. The resolution stated that new attempts were being made to complete the process and "to advance the recovery of looted Jewish cultural property before the last of those persons from which it was taken has died."[139] The Assembly invited the parliaments of all member states to give immediate consideration to ways in which they could facilitate the return of looted Jewish cultural property. It specifically stated that attention should be given "to the removal of all impediments to identification, such as laws, regulations or policies which prevent access to relevant information in government or public archives, and to records of sales and purchases, customs and other import and export records."[140] It provided specifically that entities "in receipt of government funds which find themselves holding Jewish cultural property should return it."[141] The AAM published Guidelines Concerning the Unlawful Appropriation of Objects during the Nazi Era. These guidelines state the AAM position that museums should take all reasonable steps to resolve the Nazi-era provenance status of objects before acquiring them for their collections whether by purchase, gift, bequest, or exchange. Research on objects being considered for acquisition and for incoming loans should include a request that sellers, donors, estate executors, or lenders provide as much provenance information as is available with particular regard to the Nazi era. In the Vilnius Forum Declaration, issued at the conference of European nation states, which was held in Vilnius, Lithuania in October 2000, governments were asked "to undertake every reasonable effort to achieve the restitution of cultural assets looted during the Holocaust era to the original owners or their heirs."[142] It asked governments, museums, the art trade, and other relevant agencies to provide all information necessary to such restitution.

Role of Museums as Tax Exempt Charitable Organizations

Museums qualify for tax exempt status in the United States as charitable organizations pursuant to § 501(c)(3) of the Internal Revenue Code. This status provides a twofold governmental benefit. A museum will not be taxed on its receipts, and donors to the museum will obtain a tax deduction for contributions, both cash and property donations. For property donations, § 170(e) of the Code permits contributors to deduct the property's fair market value if the donated property qualifies as a capital asset under § 1221 of the Internal Revenue Code and the donor has held the property for more than one year. A painting that was not created by the donor or the donor's heirs is a capital asset to the donor. Thus, a taxpayer who is not the artist can deduct on the taxpayer's income tax return the fair market value of a painting the taxpayer has held more than one year if the taxpayer donates the painting to a museum. This Code provision attaches a significant tax benefit to the donor of a valuable painting to a museum, particularly if the donor paid a bargain price for the painting. Further, § 2055 of the Code relieves a decedent's estate from estate tax with respect to testamentary donations of cultural property to museums.

A collector of valuable cultural treasures often finds advantage in tax laws in order to receive a monetary benefit from acquiring works with questionable provenances. This is because a questionable provenance will reduce substantially the amount for which the collector can sell a cultural treasure. However, a purchaser of a valuable artwork can reap a financial benefit by the reduction in income taxes the purchaser will procure by donating the work to a museum. The purchaser undoubtedly would have bought the cultural treasure at a bargain price because of its title problems. By deducting on the purchaser-donor's income tax return the fair market value of the artwork, with no reduction in value because of title questions, the donor can save in income taxes 35 percent of that value. In past years, when the highest income tax rate was 70 percent and later 50 percent, the donor saved in income taxes either 70 percent or 50 percent of that value. If a collector continues in possession of a valuable cultural treasure that has a questionable provenance, the collector may seriously consider bequeathing the property to a museum. For example, if a valuable painting remains in the estate upon the collector's death, the painting will subject the decedent's estate to an estate tax of 45 percent of the painting's value with no reduction in its value because of title problems.[143] Later the collector's heirs could be subjected to a successful suit by the original owner for return of the painting to the rightful owner at a date when the limitations period to file a claim of refund for the estate taxes on the painting had expired. Because of these tax benefits and tax concerns, many possessors of valuable artworks with questionable provenance donate them to museums.

Section 501(c)(3) of the Internal Revenue Code requires a museum as a charitable organization to meet an operational test to maintain its charitable tax-exempt status. The operational test requires a charitable organization to be "operated exclusively" for its charitable purposes. None of the earnings of the organization can inure in whole or in part to the benefit of private individuals or entities. The policy underpinnings of the noninurement rule derive from the tenet that charities should promote the public good rather than provide private benefits.

The Supreme Court pointed out, in *Bob Jones University v. United States,*[144] that Congress sought to provide tax benefits to charitable organizations to encourage the development of private institutions that serve a useful public purpose. The Court referred to the first charitable exemption statute Congress enacted, in 1894, which set out the congressional intent that "charities were to be given preferential treatment because they provide a benefit to society."[145] The Supreme Court recognized in *Bob Jones University* that the corollary to the public benefit principle is the requirement that "the purpose of a charitable trust may not be illegal or violate established public policy."[146] The Court commented that when Congress "grants exemptions or allows deductions, all taxpayers are affected. . . . " According to the Court, "the very fact of the exemption or deduction for the donor means that other taxpayers can be said to be indirect and vicarious 'donors.'"[147] The Supreme Court stated in *Bob Jones University*:[148]

> Charitable exemptions are justified on the basis that the exempt entity confers a public benefit—a benefit which the society or the community may not itself choose or be able to provide, or which supplements and advances the work of public institutions already supported by tax revenues. History buttresses logic to make clear that, to warrant exemption under § 501(c)(3), an institution must fall within a category specified in that section and *must demonstrably serve and be in harmony with the public interest*. The institution's purpose *must not be so at odds with the common community conscience* as to undermine any public benefit that might otherwise be conferred. (Emphasis added.)

The Supreme Court recognized in *Bob Jones University*[149] that "public benefit and public policy questions are sensitive matters with serious implications for the institutions affected . . . " but it decided that racial discrimination in education "violates deeply and widely accepted views of elementary justice" and agreed with the Internal Revenue Service that tax exempt status should be revoked for Bob Jones University because of its racially discriminatory policies.

Some posit that a museum's acquisition and retention of stolen and/or illegally exported artifacts contribute to the illegal international trade in cultural property and that this complicity violates "elementary justice." The governmental interest at stake with respect to a private school maintaining a racial discriminatory policy was, according to the Supreme Court in *Bob Jones University*, "compelling enough" to warrant revoking the school's tax exempt status. Some might contend that there is an important governmental interest at stake that is "compelling enough" to warrant revocation of tax exempt status of those museums that continue to retain in their collections stolen and/or illegally exported cultural property, if they also refuse to mediate ownership and return/restitution issues relating to that property. Some members of the public argue that encouraging the illicit international market in stolen and illegally exported artifacts, whether by purchasing such objects or by accepting them as donations, points to a purpose at odds with the "common community conscience" to which the Supreme Court referred in *Bob Jones University*, and that such a posture undermines the public benefit a museum should confer.

Ethical Principles Relating to Stolen and/or Illegally Exported Cultural Property

Because museums serve the public interest, museum directors should maintain transparency with respect to museum activities and collections. Records applicable to their collections should be open for public scrutiny. If there are title questions or provenance gaps for some objects in the collection, the museum director should be amenable to mediating ownership issues. Further, those involved in the mediation process should consider ethical principles, as well as laws, in their approach to return/restitution issues. Ethical precepts provide a better and higher standard for evaluation of the rights of the parties than do the differing and inadequate legal principles that exist in the many countries involved.

The international code of professional ethics for ICOM, published by ICOM in 1989, and amended in 2006, dictates certain ethical obligations for members of the museum profession. It admonishes museums to initiate dialogues for the return of cultural property to the country or people of origin.[150] It states that, when a country or people of origin seeks the restitution of an object that can be demonstrated to have been exported or otherwise transferred in violation of the principles of international and national conventions and that can be shown to be part of that country's or people's cultural or natural heritage, the museum concerned, if legally free to do so, should take prompt and responsible steps to cooperate in the object's return.[151] The Code cautions museums to respect fully all laws and conventions that regulate the import, export, and transfer of cultural property.[152] The Code suggests that museum policies acknowledge international conventions as standards in interpreting the ICOM Code of Ethics.[153] These ethical and moral responsibilities, which call for international cooperation to end the illicit traffic in cultural property, should instill in all ICOM members a willingness to mediate ownership and return/restitution issues relating to objects in their collections.

Mediation Can Lead to Shared Cultural Heritage Partnerships

Bernice Murphy, the current chair of the ICOM Ethics Committee, opined that many museums "have moved beyond a fixation of their exclusivity of ownership" and have begun to act "according to tenets of shared custodianship and stewardship of cultural heritage."[154] She reported that museums have "sought to build new kinds of partnerships in research and heritage care" and that such partnerships often "open up possibilities for research, acquisition or exchange."[155] She pointed out that some museums in Europe have repatriated cultural property from their collections voluntarily while others have "embarked on long-term loans," in what she termed as "a faster course of action than discussion of permanent repatriation."[156] She referred to the fact that museums today are becoming "both mediators and (re)mediators" as signaling "a new phase of greater ethical maturity on the part of the museums of the world and a more active engagement with the societies they serve."[157] Patrick Boylan, who, as noted earlier, was the first chair of the ICOM Legal Affairs Committee, characterized mediation as a means to "build new bridges between potential partners adrift and create a new relationship between former adversaries."[158] Boylan endorsed the new ICOM mediation process as a means wherein ICOM can promote mediation in the resolution of disputes over the ownership of cultural property because, as Boylan concluded, "there can be win-win solutions devised out of court at minimal cost, with the anonymity of the participants preserved in the process."[159] He commented that the ICOM Code of Ethics and ICOM's support of UNESCO conventions imply "a high level of involvement in promoting the restitution of illicitly acquired cultural property to countries of origin and international cultural exchanges."[160]

Mediation Can Protect Heritage

As the international museum community seeks to "build new kinds of partnerships in research and heritage care" that will "open up possibilities for research, acquisition, or exchange," mediation of international cultural property ownership issues provides a feasible and attractive means to settle ownership questions and to provide a corresponding avenue for increased protection of cultural property. Alternative dispute resolution is the most effective means of resolving conflicts without one party becoming subject to another party's national court system, which may be unfamiliar, slow, and expensive. The alternative dispute resolution mechanism established by ICOM can provide a more effective system for museums to resolve ownership questions relating to collections with gaps in provenance. Patrick Boylan considers the objective of mediation to be the establishment or reestablishment of relationships and concludes that "much is at stake:

the public's access to art in the present, respect and consideration for the individual and/or community whose past is embedded in the work of art, and the museum's ability to perform its service to society of protecting heritage for future generations."[161] When fully and effectively utilized by museums worldwide, the ICOM mediation process will provide the most fair and equitable manner of addressing return/restitution issues. Indeed, the mediation process may be vital to the long-term preservation of the cultural heritage of humanity. It also is the "right thing to do."

Notes

1. *See* "Promoting the Use of Mediation in Resolution of Disputes over the Ownership of Objects in Museum Collections: Statement by the President of ICOM Alissandra Cummins," at http://icom.museum/statement_mediation_eng.html. Alissandra Cummins, current President of ICOM, is the Director of the Barbados Museums and Historical Society.
2. *Id.*
3. *Id.*
4. Conversation with John McAvity, current chair of the ICOM Legal Affairs Committee and Executive Director of the Canadian Museum Association, September 17, 2008.
5. Patrick Boylan, "What Does Mediation Mean for ICOM?" ICOM News, No. 3/2006, 4. Patrick Boylan is Emeritus Professor of Heritage Policy and Management at City University, London.
6. *Id.* Boylan opined that when "a court of justice or judge is involved or an arbitrator is selected to resolve a dispute, the process is expensive and the outcome of the conflict determines a winner or loser." He referred to the fact that some cases "make front page news, much to the chagrin of the parties involved." *Id.*
7. Statement from John McAvity, September 17, 2008.
8. Statement by the President of ICOM, Alissandra Cummins, cited in note 1.
9. *Id.*
10. Document: LegComm 2007–Guidance Notes on ICOM Mediation Process, ICOM News, No1/2006. The document can be obtained from the Chairperson of the ICOM Legal Affairs Committee at Maison de l'UNESCIO, 1 rue Miollis, Paris 75032 Cedex 15, France or by e-mail: legalaffairs@icom.museum
11. *Id.*, p. 1.
12. *Id.*, p. 1.
13. *Id.*

14. The four conventions are: 1954 Hague Convention for the Protection of Cultural Property in the Event of Armed Conflict, 249 U.N.T.S. 240 (1954); discussed in notes 51-54 and accompanying text; the 1970 UNESCO Convention on the Means of Prohibiting and Preventing the Illicit Import, Export, and Transfer of Ownership of Cultural Property, 823 U.N.T.S. 231 (1970), discussed in notes 56-58 and accompanying text; 1972 UNESCO Convention for the Protection of the World Cultural and Natural Heritage, 1037 U.N.T.S. 151 (1977); discussed in notes 67-75 and accompanying text; 1995 UNIDROIT Convention on Stolen or Illegally Exported Cultural Property, available at http://exchanges.state.gov/culprop/unidroit.html and discussed in notes 76-93 and accompanying text; and 2001 UNESCO Convention on the Protection of the Underwater Cultural http://portal.unesco.org/cultureHeritage, available at http://portal.unesco.org/culture and discussed in notes 98-100.
15. See, e.g., *Autocephalous Greek-Orthodox Church of Cyprus v. Goldberg*, 917 F.2d 278 (7th Cir. 1992), in which the court applied Indiana law to determine the right of possession of four Byzantine mosaics created in the early sixth century, as between the Church of Cyprus, the Republic of Cyprus, and the purchaser of the mosaics. *Id.* at 280. The court determined that because the mosaics were stolen from the rightful owner (the Church of Cyprus), the purchaser of the mosaics never obtained title to, or right to possession of, the mosaics. *Id.* at 290-1; 294.
16. Nemo dat quoid non habet. (He who hath not cannot give.)
17. *See Menzel v. List*, 246 N.E.2d 642, 820 (N.Y. 1969), in which the New York court stated that the "principle has been basic in the law that a thief conveys no title as against the true owner." [*See also Menzel v. List*, 267 N.Y.S.2d 804, 819 (1966).]
18. U.C.C. Article 2.403.
19. *Menzel v. List*, 267 N.Y.S. at 820.
20. *See O'Keeffe v. Snyder*, 416A.2d 862, 875 (N.J. 1980), in which the Supreme Court of New Jersey decided that it should protect an innocent purchaser from an owner who "sleeps on his rights." The court stated that a possessor has the right to retain property except as against the true owner. As the court concluded, the only imperfection on a bona fide purchaser's claim is the original owner's right to repossess the property. According to the New Jersey Supreme Court, once that imperfection is removed, the possessor should have good title for all purposes. *Id.* at 862.
21. *See Kunstsammlungen Zu Weimar v. Elicofon*, 678 F.2d 1150 (2nd Cir. 1982) in which a Federal appellate court refused to impose a due diligence requirement upon the rightful owner. The court ordered the return to the original owner of two priceless Albrecht Durer portraits, which were created around 1499 and were stolen in 1945 from a castle in Germany. *Id.* at 1152. The possessor, an

American citizen, purchased the paintings in good faith 20 years earlier. *Id.* at 1153. The purchaser was concerned that a bona fide purchaser had to wait for a demand from the true owner before the statute of limitations would begin to run. *Id.* at 1163. *See also Solomon R. Guggenhein Found. v. Lubell*, 569 N.E.2d 426, 430 (N.Y. 1991), wherein the highest court in New York ruled that New York does not impose a due diligence requirement upon original owners of property.

22. *See* decision of the courts in *Autocephalous Greek-Orthodox Church of Cyprus v. Goldberg*, cited in note 15, 917 F.2d at 288, wherein the court held that the plaintiff's cause of action did not accrue until the plaintiffs, using due diligence, knew or were on reasonable notice of the identity of the possessor of the mosaics. The court concluded that the plaintiffs exercised due diligence in their search to locate and to recover the mosaics. *Id.* at 293-4. *See also Solomon R.Guggenheim Found. v. Lubell*, cited in note 21.
23. In *O'Keeffe v. Snyder*, 416 A.2d at 869.
24. See, e.g., *O'Keeffe v. Snyder*, 416 A.2d at 872.
25. *See Guggenheim Found. v. Lubell.* In New York, case law has long protected the rights of owners whose property has been stolen, allowing recovery even if it is the possession of a good faith purchaser. As the court ruled in *Guggenheim Foundation v. Lubell*, 569 N.E.2d at 430, the statute of limitations does not begin to run against a true owner's claim until the true owner makes demand of a good faith purchaser for return of the property and the possessor refuses to return it.
26. California has adopted a three-year statutory limitation period that begins to run at "the discovery of the whereabouts of the article by the aggrieved party. . . ." Cal. Civ. Proc. Code § 338.
27. In *O'Keeffe v. Snyder*, 416 A.2d. at 872, the Supreme Court of New Jersey commented that the statute of limitations on a suit to recover stolen paintings would begin to run when the true owner "discovers, or by exercise of reasonable diligence and intelligence should have discovered, facts which form the basis of a cause of action." The court stated that apart from the discovery rule, the statute of limitations in replevin actions ordinarily runs against the owner of lost or stolen property from the time of the wrongful taking. However, as the court commented, this was ordinarily true "absent fraud or concealment." *Id.* According to the court, where a chattel is fraudulently concealed, the general rule is that the statute is tolled. *Id.* at 873. The New Jersey statute of limitations, which was at issue in O'Keeffe, provided that a suit for recovery of goods must be commenced within six years after the cause of action accrues. N.J. Stat. Ann. §2A:14-1. According to the court in O'Keeffe, this discovery rule avoids the harsh result of a mechanical application of the limitations statute. *Id.* at 869.
28. In *O'Keeffe v. Snyder*, 416 A.2d at 857, the court thought that an innocent purchaser should be protected from an owner who "sleeps on his rights" and, thus,

placed "due diligence" requirements on the original owner. However, as noted previously, in more recent court decisions, courts have shifted the "due diligence" requirement to the purchaser of valuable cultural property. See, e.g., *Autocephalous Greek-Orthodox Church of Cyprus v. Goldberg*, 917 F.2d at 294 and *Guggenheim Foundation v. Lubell*.

29. *See Hoelzer v. City of Stamford, Conn.*, 933 F.2d 1131 (2d Cir. 1991) and *Solomon R. Guggenheim Found. v. Lubell*, 469 N.E.2d at 430. In *Guggenheim*, the New York Appellate Division recognized that, under New York law, the statute of limitations does not begin to run as against a true owner until demand for a return on the property was made and refused. The court ruled that absent a demand for the property, there is no cause of action against a bona fide purchaser and, absent a cause of action, the statute of limitation does not begin to run. *Id.*
30. *See Guggenheim*, 569 N.E.2d at 431. The court did state, however, that an owner's failure to exercise reasonable diligence to locate a stolen artwork would be considered in the context of the defense of laches.

The New York court in *Guggenheim* referred to the discovery rule in other states in which the statute of limitations in suits to recover stolen works of art begins to run from the time the true owner discovers or should have discovered the whereabouts of the stolen art. at 430. It explained that New York rejected the discovery rule because New York courts decided the rule did not provide a reasonable opportunity for individuals or foreign governments to receive notice of a possessor's acquisition of artwork and sufficient time to take action to recover a work. The court was concerned that New York would become a "haven for cultural property stolen abroad" because such works would be immune from recovery under limited time periods. The court concluded it was inappropriate to shift the burden to the wronged owner.

In *Republic of Turkey v. Metropolitan Museum of Art*, 767 F. Supp. 44, 45 (S.D.N.Y. 1990), the Republic of Turkey sought recovery of artifacts in possession of the Metropolitan Museum of Art. The Republic of Turkey contended that the artifacts were excavated from burial grounds in the Ushak region of Turkey and exported to the United States in contravention of Turkish law; it also claimed that all artifacts found in Turkey belong to the Republic of Turkey. The New York court held that "unreasonable delay" requirements apply only to the equitable defense of laches. at 46. It ruled that the statute of limitations had not run on Turkey's cause of action against the Metropolitan. at 47.

The equitable laches doctrine applies to delay that causes a defendant harm or prejudice. It permits a court to cut off a right of action when a plaintiff has delayed unreasonably and inexcusably in instituting litigation and thereby has prejudiced the defendant significantly. As the Supreme Court stated in *Holmberg v. Armbrecht*, 327 U.S. 392, 396 (1946):

> Equity eschews mechanical rules; it depends on flexibility. Equity has acted on the principle that laches is not, like limitation, a mere matter of time; but principally a question of the inequity of permitting the claim to be enforced—an inequity founded upon some change in the condition or relations of the property or the parties.

The Supreme Court further stated in *Costello v. United States*, 365 U.S. 265, 282 (1961), that laches requires "proof of (1) lack of diligence by the party against whom the defense is asserted, and (2) prejudice to the party asserting the defense."

31. 421 N.E.2d 500, 502 (1981).
32. *Id.*
33. *Id.*
34. *Id.*
35. Cited in note 15.
36. *Id.*, 917 F.2d at 294. The organizations a potential purchaser should contact include: International Foundation for Art Research (IFAR), which monitors trafficking in stolen art; Art Loss Register, which was created in 1991 by IFAR, and by several insurance companies and art world investors in London and which maintains one of the largest private international data bases of stolen and missing art; International Criminal Police Organization (INTERPOL), which is a group of police agencies that computerize information on stolen artifacts and which has a DVD, updated every two months, containing stolen art information; International Council of Museums and Sites, which coordinates and develops measures and security systems for museums throughout the world; Europa Nostra, which is a European organization interested in the conservation of the architectural heritage of Europe; Christie's; Sotheby's; FBI, which maintains a central archive of stolen art in the United States; Harvard University's Dumbarton Oaks Institute for Byzantine Studies, which is the leading center in the United States for the study of Byzantine Art; and Art Dealers' Association of America.
37. See, e.g., Italian Civil Code, Article 1153; Spanish Civil Code, Article 464; Sweden Personal Property (Bona Fide) Acquisitions Act (1986:796).
38. See, e.g., Italian Civil Code, Article 1153.
39. *See Republic of Austria v. Altmann*, 541 U.S. 677, 688, 702 (2004), wherein the U.S. Supreme Court affirmed a decision of the Ninth Circuit Court of Appeals that U.S. courts had jurisdiction to hear a claim of a victim of the Holocaust as against the Republic of Austria. Maria Altmann brought a claim against the Republic of Austria for the recovery of six Gustav Klimt paintings the Nazis took from her now deceased Jewish uncle, Ferdinand Bloch. *See* 317 F.3d 954, 958 (9th Cir. 2002), 327 F.3d 1246 (9th Cir. 2003). The Republic of Austria contended it was immune from the jurisdiction of U.S. courts under a federal statute, the Foreign Sovereign Immunities Act (FSIA), which was enacted in 1976. *Id.*

317 F.2d at 958.The Ninth Circuit Court of Appeals affirmed the decision of the district court that a foreign state is not immune from the jurisdiction of U.S. courts when the issue is whether rights in property were taken in violation of international law. *Id.* at 968. The Ninth Circuit decided that Austria could not expect immunity in light of its complicity in, and perpetuation of, the discriminatory expropriation of the Klimt paintings. It noted that the seizures violated both Austria's and Germany's obligations under the 1907 Hague Convention on the Laws and Customs of War on Land and that Austria's Second Republic officially repudiated all Nazi transactions in 1946. Although the U.S. Supreme Court did not endorse the reasoning of the Court of Appeals, it affirmed the Ninth Circuit's judgment because it determined that the FSIA clearly applies to conduct that occurred prior to the Act's enactment in 1976. 541 U.S. at 702.

See also Malewicz et. al. v. City of Amsterdam, 517 F.Supp.2d 322 (D.D.C. 2007), wherein the heirs of Kazimir Malevich filed a complaint in the U.S. District Court for the District of Columbia against the City of Amsterdam for its alleged wrongful possession of fourteen artworks of Malevich. The district court denied the City of Amsterdam's motion to dismiss. at 340. The Malevich heirs alleged the City of Amsterdam should not be immune from suit pursuant to the Foreign Sovereign Immunities Act, 28 U.S.C. §§ 1603(a) and 1605(a)(3). at 327. The Malevich heirs alleged that Malevich entrusted his works to several friends in Germany, including Hugo Haring. All the works he had brought to Berlin were shipped to a Hannover museum where they later were concealed in the museum's basement when the Nazis ascended to power and began their attacks against "degenerate art." at 325. The post-World War II director of the Stedelijk in Amsterdam met with Haring who later agreed to a loan of the Malevich works to the Stedelijk. The Stedelijk Museum was established and is operated by the City of Amsterdam. at 326. The Malevich works came to the Stedelijk on loan in 1957. In 2001, Amsterdam responded to the heirs' claims for the paintings that its acquisition of the Malevich Collection was valid and that, at any rate, it became the owner of the Malevich Collection in 1993 though acquisitive prescription under Article 3:105 of the Dutch Civil Code. It issued its decision in 2001 that it would not continue to negotiate with the heirs to try to achieve a settlement. In 2008, the City of Amsterdam and the Malevich heirs reached an amicable settlement wherein the City of Amsterdam agreed to transfer to the Malevich heirs five of the fourteen Malevich paintings in its collection. The heirs agreed that it would no longer contest title to the nine other paintings, which would remain with the City. The U.S. action was withdrawn permanently. The nine paintings in the Malevich Collection continue to be housed at the Stedelijk. Over the years, their value has increased significantly.

40. Discussion in *United States v. McClain*, 545 F.2d 988, 996 (5th Cir. 1977). *See* further discussion in Marilyn Phelan, "Legal and Ethical Considerations in Museum Acquisitions," MUSEUM PHILOSOPHY FOR THE TWENTY-FIRST CENTURY, Hugh H. Genoways, Editor, AltaMira Press, 2006, pp. 38-9.
41. *Id.* In *Peru v. Johnson*, 720 F. Supp. 810, 814 (C.D. Cal. 1989), the court noted that restrictions on the export of certain artifacts are addressed to protection of such artifacts and that such restrictions do not imply ownership. The court commented that possession of such artifacts is allowed to remain in private ownership and that such objects may be transferred. The court characterized an export restriction as an exercise of the police power of the state. It stated that such restrictions do not create ownership in the state. [*See also Jeanneret v. Vichey*, 693 F.2d 259 (2nd Cir. 1982).]

    The general rule that export restrictions do not prevent a possessor in another country from acquiring good title to such artifacts can be qualified by statutes or treaties. For example, in the United States, the Pre-Columbian Art Act, 19 U.S.C. 2091-2095, provides that any pre-Columbian monumental or architectural sculpture or mural imported into the United States in violation of the Act is to be seized and is subject to forfeiture under the U.S. customs laws. The Convention on Cultural Implementation Act, 19 U.S. C. 2601 et seq., discussed at notes 59-66 and accompanying text, provides that import restrictions will be placed on designated archaeological or ethnological material exported from a nation which properly requests such restrictions. If such objects are imported into the United States, they are subject to seizure and forfeiture.
42. For example, the trade in antiquities became illegal in Italy in 1939 with the enactment of the Law for the Protection of Works of Artistic and Historic Interest (law n.1089/39). Under this law, all archaeological objects belong to the state unless they were in private ownership prior to 1902. Further, only the state (or a private citizen by special permit) can conduct excavations.

    As noted in *United States v. Antique Platter of Gold*, 184 F.3d 131 (2nd Cir. 1999), cert. den., 120 S. Ct. 978 (2000), the Egyptian government has declared ownership of all its archaeological artifacts pursuant to its Antiquities Protection Law, Article 6, which was adopted in 1983.

    The 1932 Act with Respect to Antiquities in Greece provides that all antiquities belong to the State. Individuals cannot acquire ownership of antiquities.
    In 1926 the Republic of Turkey declared in force and effect a 1906 Decree that all antiquities found in or on lands in Turkey were owned by the Republic. Also, in 1926, the Republic adopted a Turkish Civil Code which remains in effect today. Article 697 of the Turkish Civil Code declares that antiquities found on Turkish land are the property of the Republic.

43. 18 U.S.C. §§ 2314-15. The National Stolen Properties Act makes it a felony knowingly to sell or receive stolen goods in interstate or foreign commerce.
44. 593 F.2d 658 (5th Cir. 1979).
45. *Id.* at 671. In *Peru v. Johnson*, 720 F. Supp. at 812, the court decided that Peru had not sufficiently stated a claim of ownership to pre-Columbian artifacts it claimed were excavated from historical monuments in Peru. The court ruled against Peru because evidence did not indicate for certain in what country the artifacts were found and from which they were exported. In addition, it determined that the extent of Peru's claim of ownership as part of its domestic law was uncertain. at 815.

    In *Republic of Turkey v. OKS Partners*, 797 F. Supp 64, 66 (D.Mass 1992), the Republic of Turkey brought suit against the possessor of ancient Greek and Lycian silver coins, which the Republic of Turkey maintained were unearthed in Turkey. The Republic of Turkey maintained that the sale of such coins could be in violation of the National Stolen Properties Act. The Republic of Turkey declared that under Turkish law all artifacts within Turkey's borders are Turkish property even before they are discovered. The court ruled that the statute of limitations did not bar Turkey's claim. at 69. The court stated that the discovery rule applied and that facts giving rise to a cause of action were "inherently unknowable" to the Republic of Turkey for purpose of tolling the statute of limitations under either the discovery rule or the doctrine of fraudulent concealment. at 69-70.
46. 333 F.3d 393 (2nd Cir. 2003).
47. *See* notes 121-136 and accompanying text.
48. *See* Anthee Carassava,"Greek Court Dismissed Case Against Ex-Curator," NEW YORK TIMES, November 28, 2007, available at http://www.nytimes.com/2007/11/28/arts/design/28true.html. *See also* Elizabetta Polvoledo, "Getty Pact Appears to Ease Rome Trial," September 27, 2007, available at http://www.nytimes.com/2007/01/18/arts/design/18gett.html
49. *Id.*
50. *Id.*
51. *See* discussion in John Henry Merryman, "Two Ways of Thinking about Cultural Property," 80 Amer. J. Int'l L 831 (1986). Merryman discusses the work of Francis Lieber, a German emigre professor at Columbia College in New York, who argued for protection of cultural property during combat. As Merryman pointed out, the Lieber Code was the first attempt to provide a set of principles governing the conduct of belligerents in enemy territory.

    Further discussion in Hays Parks, "Protection of Cultural Property from the Effects of War," Chapter 3, THE LAW OF CULTURAL PROPERTY AND THE NATURAL HERITAGE, Marilyn Phelan, Gary Edson, and Kimberly Mayfield, editors, Kalos Kapp Press, 1998.

52. Pursuant to the 1954 Hague Convention, cited in note 14, Article 16, cultural property bears a distinctive emblem (a blue shield) during military conflict to facilitate its recognition. The emblem repeated three times is used as a means of identification of immovable cultural property under special protection, the transport of cultural property, and improvised refuges. *Id.*, Article 17. Transport exclusively engaged in the transfer of cultural property, whether within a territory or to another territory, at the request of a contracting party, may take place under special protection. Articles 12 and 13, Parties to the Convention must refrain from any act of hostility directed against transport.
53. 1954 Hague Convention, cited in note 14, Article 4(3).
54. Preamble, 1954 Hague Convention.
55. Cited in note 14.
56. *See* discussion in *Autocephalous Greek-Orthodox Church v. Goldberg*, note 15.
57. 1970 UNESCO Convention, note 14.
58. Tariff Schedule, Pub. L. No. 97-446, 1982 U.S.C.C.A.N. (96 Stat. 4098, 4100, 4101, 4106). Art objects had been sold in increasing quantities from churches, museums, and collections. at 4099-100. The governments of the victimized nations became disturbed at the outflow of their artifacts to foreign lands and organized the convention to combat the increasing illegal international trade in national art treasures, which in some countries had led to wholesale pillaging. at 4100. To this end, the parties to the convention undertook to protect their own cultural heritage and to establish an export certificate for cultural property designated by each country as being of importance. The parties further agreed to take what measures they could, consistent with existing national legislation, to prevent museums and similar institutions within their territory from acquiring cultural property originating in another country that had been illegally exported. at 4101.
59. 19 U.S.C. §2601 et seq.
60. *See* 19 U.S.C. §2611. The Convention on Cultural Property Implementation Act is not applicable to any designated archaeological or ethnological material or any article of cultural property imported into the United States if such material or article has been held in the United States for a period of not less than three consecutive years by a recognized museum and was purchased by the museum for value, in good faith, and without notice that such material or articles were imported in violation of the act, but only if

    (1) the acquisition of the material or article has been reported in a publication of the museum, any regularly published newspaper or periodical with a circulation of at least fifty thousand, or a periodical or exhibition catalog which is concerned with the type of article or material sought to be exempted from the act,

    (2) the material or article has been exhibited to the public for a period or periods aggregating at least one year during the three-year period or

(3) the article or material has been cataloged and the catalog material made available upon request to the public for at least two years during the three-year period. at §2611(2)(A).

The act also does not apply to such material or articles that have been in the United States for less than ten consecutive years but that have been exhibited for not less than five years during that period in a recognized museum in the United States open to the public. at §2611(2)(B). It does not apply to material and articles that have been in the United States less than ten consecutive years but in an instance wherein the country concerned has received or should have received during that period fair notice of location of the material or articles within the United States. at §2611(2)(C). The act is not applicable to material and articles that have been in the United States for at least twenty consecutive years if the claimant establishes that it purchased the material or article for value without knowledge or reason to believe it was imported in violation of law. at §2611(2)(D).

61. *See* 4 U.S.C.C.A.N. 4100 (1982). Congress first acknowledged a need to protect cultural property of other nations when it adopted the Pre-Columbian Art Act in 1972, cited in note 41. As noted previously in note 41, this Act prohibits the importation into the United States of any pre-Columbian monumental or architectural sculpture or mural unless the government of the country of origin issued a certificate that exportation of the artifact from that country did not violate any of its laws. The Act defines a pre-Columbian monumental or architectural sculpture or mural as any stone carving or wall art, or any fragment or part thereof, which is the product of a pre-Columbian Indian culture or Mexico, Central America, South America, or the Caribbean Islands. 19 U.S.C. §2095(3). It is an immobile monument or architectural structure or part of such monument or structure and is subject to export control by the country of origin.

A pre-Columbian monumental or architectural sculpture or mural will be permitted entry into the United States if the importer files with the district director of customs, at the time of making entry, a certificate issued by the government of the country of origin certifying that the exportation was not in violation of the laws of that country. 19 C.F.R. §12.107. If the importer does not have a certificate from the government of the country of origin at the time of making entry, the director of customs will store the sculpture or mural and permit the importer ninety days to produce such a certificate. 19 C.F.R. §12.109. If the importer fails to do so, the sculpture or mural is forfeited to the United States. If the country of origin presents a request in writing, the director of customs will return the sculpture or mural to that country. 19 C.F.R. §12.109. Any pre-Columbian monumental or architectural sculpture or mural imported into the United States in violation of the act is to be seized and is subject to forfeiture under the custom laws. I9 U.S.C. § 2093.

62. 4 U.S.C.C.A.N 4100.
63. 19 U.S.C. 2602.
64. *Id.* at §2606. No article of cultural property documented as appertaining to the inventory of a museum, or a religious or secular public monument in any nation, that has been stolen from that nation or from an institution, can be imported into the United States. 19 U.S.C. §2607. Any designated archaeological or ethnological material or article of cultural property that is imported into the United States is subject to seizure and forfeiture.
65. *Id.* at §2601.
66. *Id.*
67. 1972 UNESCO Convention, cited in note 14.
68. Article 5 requires parties to the convention to "foster the establishment or development of national or regional centres for training in the protection, conservation and presentation of the cultural and natural heritage and to encourage scientific research in this field." Article 6 notes that parties to the convention recognize that the cultural and natural heritage of outstanding universal value" constitutes a world heritage for whose protection it is the duty of the international community as a whole to cooperate." Parties to the convention agree to give their help to the identification, protection, conservation, and preservation of such heritage. Article 7 affirms that "international protection of the world cultural and natural heritage" means the "international cooperation and assistance designed to support" individual nations "in their efforts to conserve and identify that heritage."
69. 1972 UNESCO Convention, cited in note 14, Preamble.
70. *Id.*
71. *Id.*, Article 8.
72. *Id.*, Article 11(2).
73. *Id.*, Article 11(4).
74. *Id.* Article 15. The World Heritage Committee may provide international assistance to national or regional centers for the training of staff and specialists at all levels in the field of identification, protection, conservation, presentation, and rehabilitation of the cultural and natural heritage. Part of the cost of necessary work is borne by the international community, but the State benefiting from international assistance bears a substantial share of the cost unless that country's resources will not permit its contribution. Articles 22-26.
75. *See* Pub. L. No. 96-515, 1980 U.S.C.C.A.N. (94 Stat.) 6406. The legislation was part of the 1980 amendments to the National Historic Preservation Act. 16 U.S.C. §470a-1.
76. 1995 UNIDROIT Convention, cited at note 14, Appendix.
77. *Id.*, Article 3(1). The Convention does not require that a theft be proven.
78. *Id.*, Article 3(2).

79. *Id.*, Article 5. A cultural object that was exported temporarily for purposes such as exhibition, research or restoration, under a permit but that is not returned in accordance with the permit is deemed to have been illegally exported.

    The court of the country addressed must order the return of an illegally exported cultural object if the requesting nation establishes that removal of the object from its territory significantly impaired the physical preservation of the object or of its context, the integrity of a complex object, the preservation of information of a scientific or historical character, the traditional or ritual use of the object by a tribal or indigenous community, or establishes that the object is of significant cultural importance for the requesting nation.
80. *Id.*, Article 3.
81. *Id.*, Article 3(3).
82. *Id.*, Article 3(4).
83. *Id.*, Article 3(5). The Kingdom of the Netherlands has declared that it will consider a claim subject to a time limitation of 75 years.

    The Convention provides that a claim for restitution of a cultural object displaced from a monument, archaeological site or public collection is also subject to that time limitation.
84. *Id.*, Article 3(7). Claims for restitution of a sacred or communally important cultural object belonging to and used by a tribal or indigenous community as part of a community's traditional or ritual use, are also subject to the time limitations applicable to public collections. Article 3(8).
85. *Id.*, Article 4(1). Article 4(2) provides that reasonable efforts must be made to have the person who transferred the cultural object to the possessor, or any prior transferor, pay the compensation where to do so would be consistent with the law of the nation in which the claim was brought.
86. *Id.*, Article 4(4).
87. *Id.*, Article 6(2).
88. *Id.*, Article 10(1).
89. *Id.*, Article 10(2).
90. *Id.*, Article 10(2).
91. *Id.*, Article 8(1).
92. *Id.*, Article 10(3).
93. The countries are: Afghanistan, Argentina, Azerbaijan, Bolivia, Brazil, Burkina Faso, Cambodia, China, Cote d'Ivoire, Croatia, Cyprus, Ecuador, El Salvador, Finland, France, Gabon, Georgia, Guatemala, Guinea, Hungary, Iran, Italy, Lithuania, Netherlands, New Zealand, Nigeria, Norway, Pakistan, Paraguay, Peru, Portugal, Romania, Russian Federation, Senegal, Slovakia, Slovenia, Spain, Switzerland, and Zambia.

94. See, e.g., *Menzel v. List*, note 17; *O'Keeffe v. Snyder*, note 20; *Autocephalous Greek-Orthodox Church v. Goldberg*, note 15; *Republic of Turkey v. Metropolitan Museum of Art*, note 30; *Solomon R. Guggenheim Found. v. Lubell*, note 21; *Republic of Turkey v. OKS Partners*, note 45; and *Naftzger v. American Numismatic Society*, 42 Cal. App. 4th 421, 49 Cal. Rptr. 2d 784 (1996).
95. 25 U.S.C. §§3001-13. After Native Americans claimed ownership in, and demanded repatriation of, their tribal artifacts, Congress enacted NAGPRA in 1991. Through passage of this act, Congress provided the legislation Native Americans had long judged necessary to procure their ancestor's remains and religious and funerary objects.
96. NAGPRA, cited at note 95, §3003(a).
97. *Id.* at §3005(a)(1). The act provides that a museum will not be liable for claims from an aggrieved party for breach of fiduciary duty or good faith if the museum repatriates in good faith, that is, follows the process set forth in the law. *Id.* at §3005(f).
98. 2001 UNESCO, Convention, cited in note 14, Resolution, p. 1.
99. *Id.*, Article 20.
100. *Id.*, Article 19(4).
101. The leadership of the AAM articulated this view in an *amicus curiae* brief it filed in *United States v. An Antique Platter of Gold*, cited in note 42.
102. Cited in note 42.
103. 184 F.3d at 133. The country of origin of the phiale was listed on Customs Form 3461 as "CH,' the code for Switzerland.
104. *Id.* at 134.
105. *Id.*
106. *Id.* at 133.
107. *Id.* Brief of Amici Curiae American Association of Museums, et al. in Support of Appeal of Claimant Michael H. Steinhardt, pp. v-vi.
108. *Id.* at i-ii.
109. *Id.* at ii.
110. *Id.*
111. *Id.*
112. *Id.* at iii.
113. *Id.*
114. *Id.* at iv.
115. *Id.* at v. The AAM argued in its brief that the United States had used its "extraordinary forfeiture powers in order to circumvent the demanding burden of proof, both as to legal and factual issues, that it would have faced in a NSPA prosecution or that Italy would have faced in a civil replevin case to recover the Phiale in its own right." at v-vi.

116. *Id.* at viii.
117. *Id.* at xiv.
118. *Id.* at xxxiii.
119. *Id.* at lvii.
120. 184 F.3d at 140.
121. Cited in note 46.
122. 333 F.3d at 395.
123. Cited at note 43.
124. 333 F.3d at 395-6.
125. *Id.* Schultz met Jonathan Tokeley Parry (Parry), a British national, through a mutual friend in 1992. Parry showed Schultz a photograph of an ancient sculpture of the head of Pharaoh Amenhotep III, and told Schultz that he had obtained the sculpture in Egypt earlier that year from a man who represented himself to be a building contractor. 333 F.3d at 396. Parry had used an Egyptian middle-man named Ali Farag (Farag) to facilitate the transaction. Parry had smuggled the sculpture out of Egypt by coating it with plastic so that it would look like a cheap souvenir. He removed the plastic coating once the sculpture was in England. Schultz offered Parry a substantial fee to serve as the agent for the sale of the Amenhotep sculpture. Parry and Schultz then set out to create a false provenance for the sculpture so that they could sell it. Parry later sold the sculpture to Schultz for $800,000, and Schultz sold it to a private collection in 1992 for $1.2 million. Parry and Schultz became partners in an effort to bring more Egyptian antiquities into the United States for resale, smuggling them out of Egypt disguised as cheap souvenirs, assigning a false provenance to them, and restoring them with 1920s techniques. Parry was arrested in Great Britain in 1994 and Farag was arrested in Egypt. 333 F.3d at 397-8. Each was charged with dealing in stolen antiquities. at 398. Although Parry was arrested, he, with Schultz, continued to obtain Egyptian antiquities. After a jury found Schultz guilty, he was sentenced to a term of 33 months' imprisonment. He appealed his conviction. Upon appeal, organizations filed *amicus curiae* briefs in his defense: the National Association of Dealers in Ancient, Oriental & Primitive Art, Inc., the International Association of Professional Numismatists, the Art Dealers Association of America, the Antique Tribal Art Dealers Association, the Profession Numismatists Guild, the American Society of Appraisers, and an ad hoc group called Citizens for a Balanced Policy with Regard to the Importation of Cultural Property. These groups contended in their briefs that permitting Schultz's conviction to stand would threaten the ability of legitimate American collectors and sellers of antiquities to do business. *See* Brief of Amici Curiae Citizens for a Balanced Policy with Regard to the Importation of Cultural Property in Support of the Appeal of Defendant-Appellant, Frederick Schultz.

126. 333 F.3d at 396-8.
127. *Id.* at 396.
128. *Id.* at 396-7.
129. *Id.* at 398.
130. *Id.*
131. Amici brief, cited in note 125, Addendum.
132. *Id.* at 1.
133. *Id.* at 7. The group stated that the "risks of importing art objects have become so substantial that established dealers" were "abandoning the field." They contended that Congress did intend this result in 1983 when it implemented in part the 1970 UNESCO Convention on the Means of Prohibiting and Preventing the Illicit Import, Export and Transfer of Ownership of Cultural Property, cited in note 14 and notes 56-58 and accompanying text. The group argued in their brief that the "very core" of the Cultural Property Implementation Act of 1983, which ratified in part the 1970 UNESCO Convention, was the "principle that the United States will act to bar the importation of specified cultural properties, except in narrowly defined emergencies, only as part of a concerted international response to a specific problem of serious pillage." Amici brief at p. 3.
134. *Id.* at 7.
135. 333. F.3d at 416. The Second Circuit concluded that NSPA applies to property that is stolen from a foreign government where that government asserts actual ownership of the property pursuant to a valid patrimony law.
136. *Id.* at 411.
137. 8 Dep't St.Bull 21.
138. Austrian Nullification and Restitution Law, BGB1 No.106/1946.
139. Council of Europe Resolution 1205 (November 1999), 5.
140. *Id.*, 11.
141. *Id.*, 12.
142. Vilnius Forum Declaration, 1.
143. *See* I.R.C. §2001(c). Prior to 2003, the highest estate tax rate was 55 percent so that, prior to 2003, a valuable painting would be taxed at 55 percent of its value with no reduction in value because of title questions.
144. 461 U.S. 574, 588 (1974).
145. *Id.* at 589.
146. *Id.* at 591.
147. *Id.*
148. *Id.* at 591-2.
149. *Id.* at 592.
150. ICOM Code of Ethics, 6.2.
151. *Id.* at 6.3.

152. *Id.* at 6.4.
153. *Id.* at 7.2.
154. Bernice Murphy, "Museums (Re)mediating History," ICOM News, No. 3/2006. Bernice Murphy, Chairperson of the ICOM Ethics Committee, is a former Vice President of ICOM and former Chief Curator and Director of the Museum of Contemporary Art in Sydney, Australia. She was the first Curator of Contemporary Art at the Art Gallery of New South Wales.
155. *Id.*
156. *Id.*
157. *Id.*
158. *Id.* The new "partnerships" that can be forged as a result of mediation can provide for a sharing of each nation's cultural treasures as a feasible and vital alternative to the tacit approval given in the past to powerful nations looting and pilfering the artifacts of smaller and often underdeveloped countries. The sharing of cultural property through loans, or traveling exhibits, is a means of increasing knowledge and goodwill among the countries involved. International loans of cultural treasures were hindered in the past by the cost of insuring such exhibitions. To solve the problem of funding to acquire international exhibitions on loan, the U.S. Congress enacted the Arts and Artifacts Indemnity Act (20 U.S.C. §§971 et. seq.) to provide indemnification by the federal government for museum exhibitions of works of art and other objects or artifacts that are of educational, cultural, or scientific value and that are certified by the Secretary of State as being in the national interest. Note 154, at 972. The act is administered by the Federal Council on the Arts and Humanities. The Arts and Artifacts Indemnity Act has provided the means to accomplish the objective of permitting United States citizens to share in cultural treasures of the world and has fostered international cooperation and goodwill through this sharing of cultural property.
159. Patrick Boylan, cited in note 5.
160. *Id.*
161. *Id.*

ARTICLE

Risk as a Relevant Factor in Determining the Fair Market Value of Donated Antiquities

• • •

Jillianne M. Arguello

Finalist 2008 LCCHP/Andrews Kurth LLP Law School Writing Competition

Background

"Broken Chain" of Title Versus "Unbroken Chain" of Title

In recent years, a focus of the debate about the illicit trade in antiquities has been on institutions and individuals found to possess items that were, at some point in time, acquired or imported in violation of law or are fakes. Very little, if any, attention has been paid to the incentives for individuals to acquire and donate antiquities that are later found to be controversial. Controversial antiquities can be repatriated by the donee directly to their country of discovery, forfeited to the United States (to be repatriated to their country of discovery), ordered by a court to be repatriated to their country of discovery, or be deemed worthless.

In a report released on June 4, 2008, the Association of Art Museum Directors (AAMD) recognized the year 1970 as the relevant threshold date for applying a more rigorous standard to the acquisition of archaeological material and ancient art.[1] A month later, the American Association of Museums (AAM) approved standards regarding the new acquisitions of archaeological material and ancient art.[2] The updated AAM standards recommend that museums require documentation that an object left its probable country of modern discovery by November 17, 1970.[3] For objects exported from their country of modern discovery after November 17, 1970, the AAM guidelines recommend that museums require documentation to verify that the object has been or will be legally exported from its country of modern discovery and legally imported into the United States.[4] These new industry standards are significant because, by emphasizing the importance of obtaining a chain of title or ownership history to evidence that an antiquity was legally exported from its country of probable modern discovery after 1970, they uphold a commitment to responsible acquisition practices.[5] The AAMD Report and AAM guidelines also provide a specific framework for addressing how objects without a complete ownership history dating back to 1970 should be considered for acquisition purposes.[6] Both the AAMD report and AAM standards serve as examples of how the art market has reacted to the recent developments involving the acquisition or donation to charitable institutions of antiquities having a broken chain of title. Going forward, the acquisition of such objects likely will be scrutinized in order to adhere to the AAMD and AAM industry standards.

Apart from the obvious importance of the recent AAMD and AAM developments and the policies they embody regarding general acquisitions of antiquities, their timing is interesting, as they were produced shortly after a cooperative federal agency investigation uncovered the alleged systematic abuse of the current IRS donation scheme in the donations of antiquities to four southern California museums.

In January 2008, much of the attention that hitherto had been focused on the repatriation of antiquities from high-profile museums such as the Metropolitan Museum of Art and the J. Paul Getty Museum was diverted toward an alleged tax fraud scheme involving donations of overvalued ancient art to four southern California museums.[7] This scheme, uncovered by the Internal Revenue Service, Department of the Interior, and Immigration and Customs Enforcement Agency, involved inflated appraisals and the manipulation of the value assigned to donated antiquities in order to avoid triggering an IRS rule on the provision of documented fair market value in exchange for a tax deduction.[8]

One particular part of the multifaceted tax fraud scheme uncovered in California has isolated and made public the reality of donor-related tax fraud, specifically how the appraisals of antiquities have the high potential for enabling such fraud. The alleged involvement of the late Roxanna Brown, former director of the Southeast Asian Ceramics Museum at Bangkok University, and the related warrant affidavit for Ms. Brown's AOL Internet account, issued as part of the January investigations in California, provide specific guidance and relevant information related to the operation of the tax fraud scheme.[9] According to the warrant affidavit, Brown's name had been used for purposes of creating fraudulent appraisals for Thai antiquities that donors hoped to contribute to local California museums in order to get a tax write-off for their value.[10]

The warrant affidavit details how the allegedly fraudulent appraisals, bearing Ms. Brown's name, were used in a transaction initiated by an undercover federal agent, whereby Ms. Brown's name was included in an appraisal of an object whose value had been inflated by a party to the ongoing federal investigation.[11] Specifically, the inflation involved an object whose fair market value (or the price paid for it by a potential donor, in this instance) was $1,500, but for appraisal purposes, and more importantly, tax purposes, it was assigned an appraised value of $4,900.[12] The inflated $4,900 amount, not its fair market value of $1,500, was deemed the appraised value of the object, and the appraisal document further falsely stated that it had been prepared by Brown and that the object had been "personally inspected" by Brown.[13]

Also included in the warrant affidavit for Ms. Brown's AOL email account was copy of an email exchange between Brown and one of the parties to the federal investigation. In this email exchange, Brown was instructed to sign forms to be used for current and future appraisals; presumably, these forms would be used in the same fashion that they were used in the aforementioned transaction involving the undercover federal agent.[14] Further, Brown was assured by the email sender that if she was nervous about taking such action, "the Republicans are in office and the IRS doesn't have enough personnel to review small time appraisals, and the appraisals are very well written and will never be challenged even if they do."[15] Brown subsequently agreed that she would "be delighted" to do as she was asked.[16]

Inflated appraisal values have scarcely factored into the scholarly debate about the illicit trade in antiquities, yet altogether, deductions for art- and antiquity-related donations reportedly cost the federal government nearly one billion dollars in tax expenditures each year.[17] The determination of the fair market value of an antiquity, which becomes the dollar amount deducted by a taxpayer from his or her gross income (subject to some limitation under I.R.C. §170), is a key component of the current IRS valuation mechanism.[18] The January 2008 investigations in southern California widely publicized possible manipulation of the tax code for the purpose of obtaining tax benefits for antiquities donated to not-for-profit museums or other cultural institutions.[19]

In light of the allegedly fraudulent donor-related activity uncovered in California, and the significant amount of government revenue expended on tax write-offs related to the Internal Revenue Code's current donation mechanism, it is necessary to address how a fair market value is, and should be, assigned to donated antiquities.

The difference between an antiquity with documented ownership history and an antiquity without ownership history is significant for the purposes of assigning value. A distinction of greater significance, however, relates to the point in time from which the ownership history for an antiquity should extend in order for it to support a claim of title. To make a proper value distinction between objects with broken and unbroken chain of title, the IRS needs to establish a threshold date upon which it can base a value distinction for antiquities with an unbroken chain of title and antiquities with a broken chain of title.

Following the initiative of several prominent cultural institutions such as the Indianapolis Museum of Art, the J. Paul Getty Museum, and most recently the Association of Art Museum Directors and American Association of Museums, the IRS could establish 1970 as its threshold year for requiring documentation.[20] Setting 1970 as a threshold would mean that the IRS could require documentation for any donated object reaching back from the present to 1970; an object with such documentation would be classified as having an unbroken chain of title, and an object without such documentation would be classified as having a broken chain of title. Regarding objects that might have left their country prior to 1970 and do not have documentation, or objects that have been in the U.S. without documentation prior to 1970, the IRS should consider the objects to possess a broken chain of title, as they carry the enumerated risks that should be included in an assessment of fair market value.

Given its significance for the preservation of world cultural heritage, and the fact that several institutions have begun to incorporate this year into their acquisition policies and guidelines, 1970 could serve as an optimal threshold by which the IRS could base a determination of when a chain of title becomes "broken."[21]

The thesis of this paper is that by not making a value distinction between antiquities with an unbroken and a broken chain of title, the current valuation standards of the IRS fail to account for the relevant factor of risk to the United States Government that donated antiquities with a broken chain of title will ultimately fail to serve the donee's charitable purpose, resulting in an undeserved tax deduction for certain individuals.[22] As the IRS must take into account "relevant facts" when it considers the fair market value of an antiquity, and since there is a risk that a donated antiquity with a broken chain of title could fail to serve a donee's charitable purpose, the failure of the IRS to consider this risk constitutes a failure to consider a relevant fact.[23] Thus, the IRS is not properly performing its delegated task when it reviews the value assigned to an antiquity and does not account for the relevant factor of risk in the valuation of antiquities with a broken chain of title.

This paper proposes that the IRS account for the heightened risk to the United States Government that donated antiquities with a broken chain of title ultimately will fail to serve the donee's charitable purpose by assigning separate and distinct values to donated objects based on whether their chain of title is broken or unbroken. In doing so, the IRS could take an affirmative and effective step towards reducing the United States Government's current expenditures on both fraudulent donation schemes and donations that ultimately fail to deserve a tax benefit under I.R.C. §170.

Donating Antiquities with a Broken Chain of Title Increases Risk of Failing to Serve Donee's Charitable Purpose

The Object Could Be Stolen

In a 2003 case that generated much press and raised the eyebrows of many in the art world, *United States v. Schultz*,[24] the conviction of a well-known antiquities dealer, and former president of the National Association of Dealers in Ancient, Oriental, and Primitive Art, Frederick Schultz, was upheld by the United States Court of Appeals for the Second Circuit. The facts of this case provide a clear example of one of the heightened risks presented to the U.S. government by donated antiquities with a broken chain of title—the antiquities could be stolen.

Schultz was convicted of conspiracy to receive stolen property that had been transported in interstate and foreign commerce, in violation of the National Stolen Property Act.[25] Initially, Schultz moved to dismiss his indictment. He claimed that the items he was charged with conspiring to receive (among them the sculpted head of Pharaoh Amenhotep III, smuggled out of Egypt disguised as a cheap souvenir, and sold to a private collector for $1.2 million), which had left Egypt in the 1990s, were not stolen within the meaning of the National Stolen Property Act.[26] The court instead held that the Egyptian government, pursuant to a patrimony law declaring that all antiquities found in Egypt after 1983 were the property of the Egyptian government, owned the antiquities in question. Thus, Mr. Schultz's argument that the Egyptian law in question was not a patrimony law failed, and his conviction for violation of the National Stolen Property Act was upheld. As a result, the antiquities in question were returned to Egypt.

The *Schultz* case provides an example of a heightened risk associated with antiquities with a broken chain of title, namely that as a result of a conviction under the National Stolen Property Act for receiving an antiquity known to be taken in violation of a nation's patrimony laws, an antiquity will be repatriated to its country of discovery.

The Object Could Be Contraband

The Second Circuit's decision in the 1999 case *United States v. Antique Platter of Gold*,[27] provides a second example of a heightened risk associated with an antiquity having a broken chain of title: the antiquity could be contraband, and thus subject to seizure by the United States and repatriation to its country of discovery.

In *Steinhardt*,[28] Michael Steinhardt purchased a Sicilian phiale (bowl) with a largely unknown provenance from a Swiss dealer with whom he had previously engaged in 20 or 30 transactions.[29] The dealer, acting for Steinhardt, finalized the purchase of the phiale for just over $1 million and charged a 15% commission on the transaction, meaning that Steinhardt altogether paid close to $1.2 million for the object.[30]

On February 16, 1995, the Italian government sent a request to the United States seeking assistance in investigating the circumstances surrounding the phiale's export, and asked the U.S. government to confiscate the phiale and return it to Italy.[31] The phiale was seized, and an *in rem* forfeiture action was subsequently filed by the United States, which asserted that the forfeiture was proper under 18 U.S.C. §545 because the phiale was stolen property under the National Stolen Property Act, based on the existence of Italian patrimony law.[32] On appeal, the Second Circuit affirmed the lower court's decision on the grounds that the false designation of the phiale's country of origin satisfied the materiality requirement of 18 U.S.C. 542.[33]

Although the phiale had not been donated prior to its forfeiture, the breadth of Steinhardt's charitable contributions of antiquities to institutions such as The Metropolitan Museum of Art (which has a gallery dedicated in his name) suggests the phiale might have eventually joined the Greek antiquities donated by Steinhardt to the Met, and served as a significant tax deduction for him. As to the museum donee, had Steinhardt maintained possession of the phiale long enough to donate it, not only would the institution be forced to endure the bad press of having to forfeit an item from its collection due to a violation of law, but it could lose credibility in the eyes of the public.

Losing credibility with its patrons and the public at large could have a detrimental effect on museums and cultural institutions, especially because the main purpose of these institutions is to provide an educational and aesthetic benefit to the public, and not serve as a conduit for restituting stolen property.

The Object Could Be Fake

Any discussion in the art world regarding the forgery of antiquities intended for sale in the art market as originals frequently leads to the kouros on display at the J. Paul Getty Museum. According to the museum, neither art historians nor scientists have been able to completely resolve the issue of the kouros' authenticity.[34] Chief among the elements that raise questions are the mixture of earlier and later stylistic traits and the use of marble from the island of Thasos at a date when its use is unexpected.[35] An additional barrier to authentication with certainty is that the kouros has no clear provenance. Nevertheless, the kouros is unique; if it is also authentic, it is one of the most important works of ancient art to enter the United States since World War II.[36]

The kouros was brought to the Getty by a former curator, the late Jiri Frel.[37] Frel brought the work to Malibu to be examined and presented papers to the museum's trustees that he claimed vouched for the sculpture's authenticity and provenance.[38] After it was discovered that Frel had participated in a tax scheme to inflate the value of archaeological material donated to the Getty, and further that he had recommended that the museum purchase other expensive objects which turned out to be fakes, the authenticity of the kouros was called into question.[39] Specifically, there was much speculation regarding the kouros' provenance papers.[40] As Frel was known to have fabricated provenances for other purchases, the Getty was concerned that he had done so for the kouros.[41] To this day, the museum has not been able to establish with certainty the origin of the kouros, and whether it is an authentic antiquity or a forgery.

The lack of information about the kouros' authenticity and chain of title provides another example of the heightened risk associated with an object that has a broken chain of title, namely, that the antiquity could be a forgery.

Donee Might Voluntarily Repatriate Object to Avoid Costs of Risky Title Litigation

On January 4, 2008, the University of Virginia announced that it would return two ancient Sicilian sculptures to Italy.[42] The acroliths—statues usually made with wooden trunks and stone heads and extremities—were once owned by New York businessman Maurice Tempelsman, and had been on display after their donation to the University of Virginia Art Museum, in Charlottesville, in 2002.[43] The donor and university originally had agreed that Tempelsman would loan the museum the acroliths for five years and then transfer all his interest in them to the university.[44] This transfer, often used for charitable contributions of art, is known as a "partial contribution."[45]

While Tempelsman's agreement with the university was permissible under the current law, nevertheless, upon the presentation of evidence by Italy that the acroliths had been looted, the museum quickly repatriated them to Italy. That a museum will acquire an antiquity and then repatriate it upon the presentation of evidence (even if disputed) about its ownership history or the way in which it was discovered is a significant risk to any museum that acquires antiquities with a broken chain of title. In fact, a museum might prefer this scenario of quick repatriation instead of bearing the cost of litigating ownership or title for an antiquity. In this case, if Mr. Tempelsman structured his donation as a vehicle by which to obtain an income tax deduction, not only would the museum lose a piece of its collection through the transfer, but the federal government would lose tax revenue as a result of Mr. Tempelsman's deduction. Considering that the acroliths, in 1980, reportedly were sold to Mr. Tempelsman for $1 million, at minimum, Tempelsman most likely would have used that amount as a deduction from his gross income.[46]

Discussion

Currently Mandated IRS Valuation Mechanism for Antiquities

According to Internal Revenue Code §170, an individual can make a donation or gift to, or for the use of, a qualified organization and claim a deduction for his or her charitable contribution.[47] While the Internal Revenue Code provides the statutory framework for the charitable donation deduction, the IRS determines the process by which a value is assigned to a donated object, and informs the public of this process through publications such as IRS Publication 561 and the Internal Revenue Manual.[48] These sources provide insight into the complex administrative scheme surrounding the charitable donation deduction in § 170.

IRS Publication 561

The purpose of Publication 561 is to help donors and appraisers determine the value of donated property.[49] Publication 561 outlines the specific kind of information needed to support the charitable donation deduction that is claimed on an individual tax return.[50]

According to the publication, an individual's deduction for charitable contributions is generally limited to 50% of the individual's adjusted gross income, but in some cases 20% and 30% limits are applied.[51] With regard to paintings, antiquities, and other objects of art, the IRS stipulates that the value of such items "should be supported by a written appraisal from a qualified and reputable source, unless the deduction is $5,000 or less."[52] Thus, if an antiquity listed on a tax return is valued at $5,000 or less, the taxpayer is not currently required to have *any* documentation to verify its fair market value or ownership history. This $5,000 amount was significant in the allegedly fraudulent tax scheme uncovered through the southern California museum searches in January 2008, as the values assigned to many of the items involved in the scheme remained at a value under $5,000 in order to avoid the necessity of IRS scrutiny of a written appraisal.[53]

Generally, for donations with a claimed value exceeding $5,000, the burden is on the individual taxpayer to provide documentation of the appraised fair market value for an object they wish to donate. "Fair market value," according to the publication, is "the price that property would sell for on the open market; it is the price that would be agreed on between a willing buyer and a willing seller, with neither being required to act, and both having a reasonable knowledge of the relevant facts."[54] An object's fair market value becomes the amount that the taxpayer will be eligible to deduct from his or her taxes in a given year.[55] Publication 561 further notes that while there is no single formula that always applies when determining the value of property, all facts and circumstances connected with the property must be considered.[56]

As written, the current language of Publication 561 supports the conclusion that even if a taxpayer is audited, he or she will not be required to provide documentation to support the fair market value or ownership history of an object if the object is valued at $5,000 or less on a tax return.

Next, for "art, antiquities, or other objects of art" that are valued at $20,000 or more, the IRS requires that a complete copy of a signed appraisal of the item be attached to the individual's tax return.[57] The $20,000 threshold triggers the potential involvement of the Art Advisory Panel, a federal advisory committee to the IRS comprised of individuals representing various segments of the art world that assists Art Appraisal Services.[58] Art Appraisal Services is an office within the IRS that is primarily responsible for reviewing fair market value claims on works of art and cultural property in cases selected for audit; it functions as a subsidiary group within Appraisal Services under the IRS Chief, Appeals.[59] In addition, according to the Internal Revenue Manual, when a tax return has been selected for audit and it includes art or cultural property valued at $20,000 or more, the IRS local office must refer the case to Art Appraisal Services.[60] Thus, if a tax return lists an antiquity valued at $20,000, the Art Advisory Panel *may* review the fair market value of that antiquity *if* that tax return is selected for audit. Donating an object valued at over $20,000 does not automatically result in a review by Art Appraisal Services.

Finally, for "art, antiquities, or objects of art are valued at $50,000 or more, the IRS, through the Art Appraisal Services, may provide a Statement of Value for the object." The Statement of Value, in turn, represents the value agreed upon by the Art Advisory Panel. Similar to the preceding value thresholds, this dollar amount simply corresponds with a *potential* issuance of a Statement of Value; the presence or absence of a Statement of Value does not preclude a tax benefit from being conferred in a donee taxpayer. Further, Art Appraisal Services and the Art Advisory Panel are not obliged to review a donation with an appraised fair market value; it is only a possibility that a tax return listing a donated object worth $50,000 or more will be audited or reviewed by Art Appraisal Services.

Internal Revenue Manual's Procedural Guidance for Valuation of Antiquities

The Internal Revenue Manual, which contains the policies, procedures, instructions, guidelines, and delegations of authority that direct the operation and administration of the Internal Revenue Service, is an important tool for understanding how the IRS examines the appraisal value of antiquities in its review and audit process.[61] The Internal Revenue Manual lists the responsibilities of the Office of Art Appraisal Services, including the management of the Commissioner's Art Advisory Panel.[62] In addition, the Internal Revenue

Manual sets forth specific items that should be included in an appraisal submitted for a valuation.[63] One of the items listed is the history, or "provenance," of an item.[64]

Immediately following the Internal Revenue Manual's list of information that may be used to make an art-related valuation is an addendum in the form of a note. The note stipulates that

> While the items listed in subparagraphs (2)-(11) represent the ideal informational background required for valuation determinations by Art Appraisal Services, *it is understood that each item of information will not be readily available in every case.* However, it is emphasized that the validity of the FMV findings and recommendations of the Art Advisory Panel are greatly enhanced and facilitated by complete and accurate information. Scant information hinders or in some cases precludes meaningful consideration.[65]

The above section concludes by stating that for objects valued at less than $20,000, the Office of Art Appraisal Services is available to provide telephone assistance to examiners in determining the fair market value of many objects of art that have return values of less than the $20,000 threshold.[66]

If Not Currently Required to Account for an Object's Ownership History, the IRS Does Not Distinguish Fair Market Value Between an Object with a Broken Chain of Title and an Object with an Unbroken Chain of Title

The Internal Revenue Manual recommends, but does not require, that a taxpayer's income tax return include an object's ownership history, or provenance.[67] While the Internal Revenue Manual notes that not all of the information that it requires might be available to a taxpayer, it is silent with regard to whether an incomplete provenance precludes a tax deduction from being taken by an individual taxpayer for the fair market value of a donated antiquity.[68] Thus, an appraisal of the fair market value for an antiquity that disregards a chain of title does not preclude the IRS from allowing a tax deduction, nor is the fair market lowered to account for the missing information.

While the IRS makes clear in Publication 561 that documentation is required for objects with a claimed value of $20,000 or more, the Internal Revenue Manual contradicts this statement by acknowledging that the required material might not be available to a taxpayer in some cases. This contradiction is problematic because it creates a potential loophole whereby a donor can obtain a deduction for the fair market value of an antiquity without providing documentation establishing chain of title. Thus, the IRS forecloses the possibility that an object's chain of title will be considered in a determination of its fair market value, and an object with a broken chain of title and one with an unbroken chain of title currently receive the same fair market value from the IRS.

By failing to require the consideration of an object's provenance or ownership history, and making a value distinction between antiquities with broken and unbroken provenance, the IRS is ignoring the higher risk that donated antiquities with a broken chain of title ultimately will fail to serve the donee's charitable purpose. Furthermore, that an antiquity with either an inflated or fraudulent fair market value could still slip through the IRS tax return auditing process unnoticed supports the conclusion that failure of the IRS to consider the presence or absence of a donated object's documented provenance or chain of title stifles its ability to accurately determine fair market value. If provenance is not referenced, then the IRS is not considering a relevant factor in the donated antiquity's fair market value.

If the IRS Does Not Make a Value Distinction Between an Antiquity with a Broken Chain of Title and One with an Unbroken Chain, then It is Not Accounting for Higher Risk to the U.S. Government Associated with Donations that Have a Broken Chain of Title

Documentation of an antiquity's chain of title is not a prerequisite to obtaining a charitable donation deduction for the fair market value of an antiquity. The case examples presented above demonstrate, however, that there *is* a nexus between whether or not an antiquity has a chain of title and the heightened risk that ultimately a donated antiquity will not deserve a tax benefit. In order to make a fair market value determination that accounts for the risk attached to the donation of objects with a broken chain of title, information about the ownership history of an item is necessary. Thus, the IRS should be required to consider the presence or absence of a donated antiquity's chain of title before it allows a donor to take a deduction.

A mandatory consideration of an antiquity's chain of title in the valuation process would address the problems of undervaluation and overvaluation, and its effect would be to reduce the expenditure of tax revenue on antiquities that carry a higher risk of repatriation, and tax revenue loss, among other potential risks. Donations of antiquities would still be permitted, regardless of whether their chain of title was broken or unbroken, but their fair market value and, consequently, the allowable deduction for their donation, would be less if they had a broken chain of title.

By Failing to Account for the Risk Involved with Antiquities that Have a Broken Chain of Title, the IRS Constructively Fails to Determine the Fair Market Value of These Donations

When the IRS decides to determine the fair market value of a donated antiquity, it must take into account relevant factors that have the potential to affect the antiquity's value. Establishing whether or not an antiquity has an unbroken chain of title is one of those relevant factors because doing so allows the IRS to evaluate the risk that the purpose of a donation will not be effectuated and that, consequently, the government's tax expenditure will not have been worthwhile. Thus, when the IRS does not account for this risk by assigning separate values to antiquities having a broken chain of title and antiquities having an unbroken chain of title, arguably, it is improperly ascertaining fair market value.

By assigning separate and distinct values to donated antiquities based on whether they have a broken or unbroken chain of title, the IRS could give purchasers who acquire antiquities with the thought of eventually donating them and receiving a tax deduction good reason to protect their investment-backed expectations. As a result, the marketplace for antiquities will respond to an IRS policy of considering chain of title to be a relevant factor in determining fair market value by preferring antiquities having an unbroken chain of title. As for the federal government, assigning separate values to antiquities based on their chain of title documentation will reduce the government expenditure of tax revenue related to charitable donation deductions involving higher-risk antiquities.

Recommendations

Learning from the Past and Preventing Future Antiquities-Related Tax Fraud

Tax fraud schemes such as the one allegedly uncovered during the southern California museum searches have persisted despite IRS and Congressional attempts to thwart them. From 1973 to 1985, the Getty Museum accepted at least $14 million in donated Greek and Roman antiquities from a network of wealthy "collectors."[69] Most of the antiquities brought to the Getty during this time were handled by Jiri Frel, who was later found to have inflated their values through forged appraisals.[70] Many of the donors who participated in the Getty scheme never saw or owned the objects they gave, but they agreed to lend their names to the transactions in return for significant tax write-offs.[71]

A second example of tax fraud took place in 1982, when two undercover IRS agents, posing as wealthy donors, donated overvalued antiquities to the Los Angeles County Museum of Art (LACMA) and the University of California, Santa Barbara. Senior officials at LACMA accepted the donations and signed backdated donation forms for the agents.[72] A third example, in 1983, was the discovery by the IRS that gems donated to the Smithsonian Institution had been appraised at five times their fair market value.[73]

Historically, the federal government has sought to balance the incentives to donate art for the public's benefit with the risk of donor tax fraud, and in doing so, has borne a cost of nearly $1 billion in tax expenditures. Today, in response to the southern California museum searches and the alleged discovery of yet another tax fraud scheme, as well as the ever increasing risk that donated antiquities having a broken chain of title ultimately will fail to serve the donee's charitable purpose, the IRS charitable donation structure needs to be examined.

To Properly Account for the Risks Involved When Antiquities with a Broken Chain of Title Are Donated to a Charitable Institution and a Tax Benefit Is Conferred, the IRS Should Assign Separate and Distinct Values to Objects Based on Whether the Antiquity Has a Continuous and Unbroken Chain of Title Going Back To 1970

If the IRS were to agree that provenance is a relevant factor in determining the fair market value of a donated antiquity, and make a value distinction based on whether an antiquity has a broken or unbroken chain of title, it would be taking an important first step in addressing the waste and fraud related to charitable donations of antiquities.

Translating the risk that a donated antiquity lacking a chain of title will not effectuate the purpose of the charitable donation into a formula for valuation presents a task that is done every day by actuaries, insurance agents, and economists: doubtless, this task could be performed by agents of the IRS. However, in order to do so, the IRS first must fix the baseline for establishing the rebuttable presumption that an uninterrupted chain of title is deemed unbroken.

A Continuous and Unbroken Chain of Title Going Back to 1970, As Advocated by the American Association of Museums, Should be the Baseline for Chain of Title Determinations by the IRS

According to their recently promulgated guidelines, both the American Association of Museums (AAM) and the Association of Art Museum Directors (AAMD) regard the year 1970 as an important benchmark date for the acquisition policies related to antiquities. Indeed, by virtue of the UNESCO convention, 1970 is significant for recognizing and addressing the illicit trafficking of cultural heritage, and would be an appropriate year to incorporate into an IRS policy. Thus, if a taxpayer were to present to the IRS evidence establishing that the title to a donated antiquity is traceable directly and without interruption back to 1970, then, absent evidence to the contrary, the antiquity would be presumed to have an unbroken chain of title. Otherwise, the antiquity would be deemed to have a broken chain of title, and a value would be assigned accordingly.

The IRS Should Require That Every Donated Antiquity for Which a Tax Benefit Is Claimed Be Accompanied by an Appraisal of Its Fair Market Value, and That the Appraiser State Whether the Appraisal Is Based On an Unbroken or a Broken Chain of Title

A second way for the IRS to address the issues of waste and fraud involving tax expenditures for donated antiquities is by requiring that every donated antiquity for which a tax benefit is claimed be accompanied by an appraisal of its fair market value. Additionally, it could require the appraiser to state whether the appraisal is based on an unbroken chain of title or a broken chain of title. The recent alleged tax fraud scheme involving the southern California museums revealed that the $5,000 threshold for requiring documentation to support a claim for a tax deduction was intentionally avoided by those allegedly involved. Requiring that every donated antiquity be accompanied by an appraisal, or at least lowering the threshold from $5,000 to, say, $1,500, would be an effective deterrent to fraud. In addition, the IRS could eradicate the $20,000 and $50,000 distinction for treating donations of antiquities—presently, the prescribed actions are discretionary—and expand the size of the Art Appraisal Services. Doing so could allow a larger number of audits to be done each year by this group, in order to verify that the Fair Market Values assigned to the antiquities accurately reflect the risks to the federal government associated with the donation of antiquities lacking a chain of title.

Adjusting the dollar amount at which the IRS scrutinizes the fair market value of donated antiquities would not be the first downward adjustment involving value in order to protect antiquities and defer offensive conduct directed towards them.[74] The 1988 Congressional amendments to the Archaeological Resources Protection Act lowered the threshold for a felony violation from $5,000 to $500 based, in part, on the archaeological value or commercial value of the archaeological resource involved in the offensive conduct.[75]

Conclusion

Each year many millions of tax dollars are spent by the federal government to compensate antiquities donors for the contributions that they make to cultural institutions. In order to (1) preserve the individual and public benefit of the Internal Revenue Code's charitable contributions structure, and (2) simultaneously address the risk that donated antiquities with a broken chain of title will not have their charitable purpose effectuated, the IRS should determine the fair market value of donated antiquities using the relevant factor of whether or not an antiquity has an uninterrupted chain of title reaching back to 1970.

Notes

1. Association of Art Museum Directors' New Report on Acquisition of Archaeological Materials and Ancient Art, issued by Association of Art Museum Directors, June 4, 2008, available at http://aamd.org/newsroom/documents/2008ReportAndRelease.pdf. [hereinafter AAMD Report]
2. American Association of Museums' Standards Regarding Archaeological Material and Ancient Art, Approved July 2008, available at http://www.aamus.org/aboutmuseums/standards/stbp.cfm [hereinafter AAM Guidelines]
3. *Id.*
4. *Id.*
5. *See* AAMD Report at 3.
6. *See* AAMD Report at 1.
7. Edward Wyatt, *Four Museums Are Raided in Looted Antiquities Case*, NEW YORK TIMES, Jan. 25, 2008, at A14, available at 2008 WLNR 1461215.
8. *Id.*
9. *See* Roxanna Brown (rxbrown@aol.com) AOL Internet Account Warrant Aff. 13, July 16, 2008. (Central District of California, Docket No. 08-1665M) (On file

with author); *see also* Bob Pool, *Asian Art Expert Dies in Custody*, LOS ANGELES TIMES, May 15, 2008, at 8, available at 2008 WLNR 9140090.

10. *See* Brown Aff. 13.
11. *See* Brown Aff. 13-14.
12. *See* Brown Aff. 14.
13. *See* Brown Aff. 14.
14. *See* Brown Aff. 52.
15. *See* Brown Aff. 52.
16. *See* Brown Aff. 51.
17. Jason Felch & Doug Smith, *Inflated art appraisals cost U.S. government untold millions*, LOS ANGELES TIMES, March 2, 2008, available at 2008 WLNR 4124504 [hereinafter Inflated art appraisals].
18. *See* I.R.S. Publication 561, "Determining the Value of Donated Property" 2 (Rev. Apr. 2007) available at http://www.irs.gov/publications/p561/index.html
19. *See* Inflated art appraisals, *supra* note 17.
20. Randy Kennedy, *Museums Set Stricter Guidelines for Acquiring Antiquities*, NEW YORK TIMES, June 6, 2008, at E2 (describing the new acquisition policy set out by the Association of Art Museum Directors).
21. In 1970, the United Nations Educational Scientific and Cultural Organization (UNESCO) held the Convention on the Means of Prohibiting and Preventing the Illicit Import, Export, and Transfer of Ownership of Cultural Property, which is the most recognized international convention to date regarding the protection of cultural heritage.
22. For purposes of clarity, "chain of title" is a legal term of art used frequently in the context of property law, and is defined in the 8th Edition of Black's Law Dictionary as "ownership history." In this paper, and consistent with the June 4, 2008 AAMD report, antiquities with an unbroken chain of title are those that *have* an uninterrupted ownership history, which would tend to show that they were legally exported from their country of origin or modern discovery after 1970, or already were in the United States prior to 1970.
23. *See* I.R.S. Publication 561 *supra* note 18, at 2.
24. *United States v. Schultz*, 333 F.3d 393 (2003).
25. Id; *see* also National Stolen Property Act, 18 U.S.C. § 371(West 2008).
26. *Schultz* at 395; *see* National Stolen Property Act, 18 U.S.C. § 2315 (West 2008) (providing for a cause of action against those who import stolen property into the U.S., and defining a "stolen" object as an object that is taken in violation of a patrimony law).
27. *United States v. Antique Platter of Gold*, 184 F.3d 131 (1999).
28. Steinhardt refers to Michael H. Steinhardt, the Claimant-Appellant in the *in rem* action of *United States v. an Antique Platter of Gold.*

29. *Antique Platter of Gold*, 184 F.3d at 133.
30. *Id.*
31. *Id.* at 134.
32. *Id.*; *see also* 18 U.S.C. § 545 (West 2008) (stating that whoever "knowingly and willfully, with intent to defraud the United States, smuggles, or clandestinely introduces or attempts to smuggle or clandestinely introduce into the United States any merchandise which should have been invoiced, or makes out or passes, or attempts to pass, through the customhouse any false, forged, or fraudulent invoice, or other document or paper will face imprisonment of 20 years or less or a fine, and that Merchandise introduced into the United States in violation of this section, or the value thereof, to be recovered from any person described in the first or second paragraph of this section, shall be forfeited to the United States."
33. 18 U.S.C. § 542 (West 2008) states that "Whoever enters or introduces . . . into the commerce of the United States any imported merchandise by means of any fraudulent or false invoice, declaration, affidavit, letter, paper, or by means of any false statement as to any matter material thereto without reasonable cause to believe the truth of such statement [shall be guilty of a crime]."
34. J. Paul Getty Museum Website, http://www.getty.edu/art/gettyguide/artObjectDetails?artobj=12908
35. *See Id.*
36. Michael Kimmelman, *Absolutely Real, Absolutely Fake?* New York Times, Aug. 4, 1991, at 21, available at 1991 WLNR 3068483.
37. *Id.*
38. *Id.*
39. *Id.*
40. *Id.*
41. *Id.*
42. *UVA To Return Looted Statues to Italy*, Associated Press, Jan. 4. 2008, available at 2008 WLNR 298001.
43. Elizabeth Povoledo, *Two Marble Sculptures to Return to Sicily*, New York Times, Sept. 1, 2007, at B7, available at 2007 WLNR 17115474.
44. *Id.*
45. *See* 26 I.R.C. § 2522 (c)(2)(A) (West 2008) (allowing for a deduction where a donor transfers a partial interest in property, and a remainder trust is established to which a donee is entitled at the end of an agreed upon period of time); *see also* IRS Publication 526 *supra* note 8 at 9 (explaining that a charitable contribution of a partial interest in property can be deducted if the partial interest is transferred to certain qualified organizations.
46. Elizabeth Povoledo, *Tempelsman Sculptures Return to Italy*, New York Times, Feb. 26, 2008, at E2, available at 2008 WLNR 3723076.

47. *See* 26 I.R.C. § 170 (a)(West 2008); *see also* IRS Publication 526 "Charitable Contributions" at 1 (2006).
48. *See* IRM 4.48.2 (CCH)(Jan. 1, 2006) (providing an overview of valuation assistance for cases involving works of art).
49. *See* IRS Publication 561, *supra* note 18, at 1.
50. *Id.*
51. *Id.* at 4.
52. *Id.*
53. Felch & Smith, *Inflated art appraisals*, *supra* note 17.
54. IRS Publication 561, *supra* note 18 at 2.
55. *Id.*
56. *Id.*
57. *See* Publication 561, *supra* note 18 at 4.
58. The Art Advisory Panel is a Federal Advisory Committee that must adhere to the statutory duties set forth by the Federal Advisory Committee Act, 5 U.S.C.A. App. 2 §1-16 (West 2008); All meetings of the Art Advisory Panel are closed to the public. A summary of their activity is available via the IRS website, www.irs.gov
59. *See* IRM 4.48.2.1 (1) (CCH) (Jan. 1, 2006) (summarizing the responsibilities of Art Appraisal Services); *see also* IRS Publication 561, *supra* note 18, at 2 (defining fair market value as the price that property would sell for on an open market: it is the price that would be agreed on between a willing buyer and a willing seller, with neither being required to act, and both having reasonable knowledge of the relevant facts).
60. IRM 4.48.2.1(2) (CCH) Jan. 1, 2006.
61. *See* Tax Almanac, www.taxalmanac.org (providing a summary of the purpose of the Internal Revenue Manual).
62. *See* IRM 4.48.2.1 (1) (CCH) (Jan. 1, 2006); *see supra* note 59.
63. *See Id.*
64. For purposes of this paper, the term "chain of title" is synonymous with "provenance"; "provenance" is a term used frequently in the art world to refer to the history of an object's ownership.
65. *See* IRM 4.48.2.3.1 (CCH) (Jan. 1, 2006).
66. *See Id.*
67. *See* IRM 4.48.2.3.1(11) (CCH) (Jan. 1, 2006).
68. *Id.*
69. *Inflated art appraisals*, *supra* note 17.
70. *Id.*
71. *Id.*
72. *Id.*
73. *Id.*

74. *See also* Sherry Hutt, Caroline M. Blanco & Ole Varmer, *Heritage Resources Law, Protecting the Archaeological and Cultural Environment,* 188-189 (National Trust for Historic Preservation 1999).
75. Pub. L. 100-588, § 1(c), Nov. 3, 1988, 102 Stat. 2983; *see* Hutt, Blanco, & Varmer, *supra* note 75, at 188-189.

In Defense of Site-Specific Art

The Visual Artists Rights Act's Pragmatism Gone Awry in the First Circuit

• • •

Jessica Kennedy

Finalist 2008 LCCHP/Andrews Kurth LLP Law School Writing Competition

Introduction

The concept of site-specific art, the creation of an inextricable fusion between an art object and an unique location, is not limited to modern and contemporary art. We need only look to the proliferation of church-specific art of the Middle Ages and the Renaissance, or even to prehistoric cave paintings, to find artists creating art in a discrete environment. However, artists of the 1970s used site specificity to drastically reject museums and galleries in a new and distinct manner.[1] While the impetus of each historical period and artist may be dramatically different, the use of site specificity has an extensive lineage.

The cultural and historical significance of site-specific art is irrefutable and vital to our nation's cultural heritage. Unfortunately, the First Circuit placed that heritage into jeopardy when it ruled in *Phillips v. Pembroke Real Estate* that the Visual Artists Rights Act of 1990 "does not apply to site-specific work at all."[2] By excluding site-specific art from the Visual Artists Rights Act (VARA), the First Circuit eliminated an important source of protection for an entire class of artwork.

In this paper, I explore how the First Circuit's ruling in *Phillips* undermines VARA, and argue that it reached this result by misreading VARA's plain language and legislative history. I argue that the First Circuit's purported reliance on the plain language of VARA was contradictory to Congressional intent, and that the elimination of site-specific art from VARA is an untenable result not contemplated by Congress. By focusing on VARA's public presentation exception and the concepts of placement and destruction as applied to site-specific art, I propose to demonstrate that the First Circuit's reasoning was not in accord with VARA's purpose and basic pragmatism.

I begin with an in-depth explanation of site-specific art and briefly chronicle its rich history. Next, I explain the statutory framework of VARA. In addition, I use VARA's legislative history to parse out the Congressional purpose and intent behind VARA. I conclude this section with a brief review of pre-*Phillips* litigation to examine the preceding case law on VARA and its limited application by the courts. I then critically assess the *Phillips* ruling by tracking the progression of the case from the state level to the First Circuit. Then, in opposition to the First Circuit, I argue that VARA encompasses site-specific art. This section concludes with a review of *Kelley v. Chicago Park District* to suggest that the acquiescence with the First Circuit's ruling provides dangerous precedent.[3] In conclusion, I provide alternatives to the First Circuit's interpretation of VARA as applied to site-specific art and set out the practical effects of these alternatives.

Site-Specific Art

Definition

At its most basic, site-specific art is "a sculpture commissioned and/or designed for a particular spot."[4] Sculpture often takes on an expanded role when it is site-specific.[5] At their essence these artworks "establish an inextricable, indivisible relationship between the work and its site."[6] Therefore, when a permanent site-specific work is removed, especially if it is relocated, the artwork is completely destroyed. Removal is not mere decontextualization.

As early as 1969 artists were declaring the integral relationship between an artwork and its site in an attempt to move away from the white space of museums and galleries.[7] A site-specific artwork is "made to suit the place in which it was installed," and cannot "be moved without being destroyed."[8] Bound by the conceptual notion of location, site-specific art is not necessarily permanent.

An integral element of site-specific art, or any art form, is artistic intent. Artistic intention determines when artistic creation becomes a work of art. More often than not, the birth of a work of art is determined by its context, the place it is destined for after creation. Context is critical to all artwork, whether it is a photograph, a painting hung on a wall, a sculpture placed on a pedestal, or a site-specific work installed in a singular location. However, site-specific art differs in that it is destined for only one location. As Richard Serra steadfastly declared, "To remove the work is to destroy the work."[9] Therefore, two elements become critical when defining an artwork—artistic intention and context.

The underpinning of moral rights is to give artists the right of integrity (prevention of intentional destruction, mutilation, or modification) and the right of attribution (claim of authorship and prevention prejudicing honor or reputation). These rights are inextricably bound with artistic intent. One commentator has defined site specificity as "contextual integrity."[10] Yet, site specificity demands more than contextual integrity because the site is inextricable from the art object. Context can merely suggest where an artwork is seen or created, not necessarily an elemental aspect of the artwork. To maintain the integrity of a permanent site-specific artwork, removal must be prevented even if it merely results in relocation.[11] For site-specific art there is only one context: the context where the artist installed the work. The crux of any artwork is artistic intent, and moral rights serve as a protective measure, at least to a limited degree, for an artist's intent.

A Brief Historical Overview

Artists such as Robert Smithson, Michael Heizer, Nancy Holt, and Walter DeMaria defined site specificity in the late 1960s and early 1970s through earthworks. Earthworks are the most dramatic examples of site-specific artworks. Artists create earthworks by taking their materials directly from the ground and the landscape in which they create.

Robert Smithson's monumental "Spiral Jetty" (1969–1970), in the Great Salt Lake, is emblematic of site specificity and the nascent earthworks movement of the 1970s. *Spiral Jetty* is a massive earthen and rock jetty that juts out into Utah's Great Salt Lake. After securing a twenty-year lease on the land, Smithson took earth from the surrounding site to create his massive spiral.[12] The artwork is contingent on the site. Smithson knew that the fluctuations of the lake would continually change the appearance of the spiral whether it is fully above ground, partially submerged, or completely salt encrusted.[13] The site is integral to the physical form of the jetty.

Site specificity burst into maturity in the 1980s. Maya Lin's *Vietnam Veterans Memorial* (1981–1983) is probably the most recognizable American site-specific artwork from the 1980s. Lin's poignant tribute to Vietnam veterans is nestled into the landscape of Constitution Gardens in Washington, D.C. The 1980s also signaled a clash between the art world and the American legal system.[14] In fact, Lin's memorial was not without its own controversy, although not legal, when protestors felt the wall was an inappropriate memorial for Vietnam veterans.

A more recent example of temporary site-specific art is Christo and Jeanne-Claude's *The Gates* (1979–2005, installed 2005). Their installation of vibrant orange cloth gates remained in New York City's Central Park for sixteen days in February 2005.[15] *The Gates* was an excellent example of temporary site specificity and indicative of the broad range of site-specific art. The artists worked for almost thirty years to have *The Gates* project approved by New York City. Once installed, it received a stellar reception.

Perhaps the most legendary site-specific work is Richard Serra's *Tilted Arc*. Removed because of public disapproval, Serra's *Tilted Arc* was a 120-foot-long by 12-foot-high Cor-Ten steel sculpture in the Federal Plaza at Foley Square in lower Manhattan. Commissioned for the General Services Administration (GSA), the artwork was installed in 1981, and completely removed by March 16, 1989.[16] Approximately one hundred and eighty people testified regarding the removal of *Tilted Arc*. One hundred and twenty of those people advocated that the artwork remain in place. In a plea for the GSA to retain *Tilted Arc* Serra stated:

> *Tilted Arc* was conceived from the start as a site-specific sculpture and was not meant to be "site-adjusted" or "relocated." Site-specific works deal with the environmental components of given places. The scale, size, and location of site-specific works are determined by the topography of the site, whether it be urban or landscape or architectural enclosure. The works become part of the site and restructure both conceptually and perceptually the organization of the site.[17]

Hoping to rescue his artwork from brutal destruction, Serra sued to prevent the removal of *Tilted Arc* by claiming violations of his moral rights and First Amendment rights, and injury under constitutional tort. Serra later dropped his moral rights claim after his attorneys convinced him it would be a fruitless claim.[18] The district court ultimately rejected all of his arguments, with the Second Circuit Court of Appeals affirming the decision.[19]

Serra's case signaled a crisis point for public, site-specific art.[20] *Tilted Arc* proved that a world-renowned artist could have his artwork destroyed due to minor public dissatisfaction despite prior public approval through the commissioning process. Disheartened, Serra stated "this Government . . . is eating its culture. . . . People now recognize that lip service to the Berne is hypocritical."[21]

Arguably Congress paid more than lip service to the Berne Convention when it enacted VARA. On the other hand, the *Phillips* ruling makes Serra's statement more powerful and more acutely pertinent than it was twenty years ago.

The Visual Artists Rights Act

Based on the Berne Convention, the United States codified moral rights protection with the enactment of VARA. Moral rights are an artist's right to artistic attribution and integrity. The protection of artistic attribution and integrity is "of the utmost importance to professional artists who build their future on the integrity and authenticity of art in public and private collections and to the public for preserving its cultural heritage."[22]

Prior to the passage of VARA the U.S. relied on the utilitarian benefits of copyright and rejected the natural rights theory of moral rights.[23] In addition, because moral rights are inherently antithetical to pecuniary property interests, the United States was hesitant to give moral rights effect. Nevertheless, the codification of VARA permits an artist to control the attribution and integrity of her artwork. In turn the Act created an exception to the personal property rights of the owner of the artwork. Congress endowed artists with an enormously important set of rights that not only protect the artist's reputation, but also preserve our nation's cultural heritage.[24]

U.S. Adherence to the Berne Convention was Slow and Cautious

The U.S. reluctance to adopt moral rights protection was grounded in a fear of interfering with property rights. As we will see in the *Phillips* opinion, a landowner's property rights is at the heart of the issue when VARA is being applied to site-specific art. Essentially, the U.S.'s hesitation and refusal to grant moral rights to artists signaled the diminished value that the American legal system placed on visual artists and art.[25] Moral rights were sometimes recognized in state and federal court, but there was a categorical refusal to codify these rights until VARA.[26] However, Congress was quick to act once the U.S. joined the Berne Convention in 1989 and codified VARA within one year.

In 1989 the U.S. joined the Berne Convention for the Protection of Literary and Artistic Works. More than one hundred years after the formation of the convention the U.S. modeled VARA after Article 6bis of the Berne, which protects an artist's right of integrity and attribution.[27] The U.S. joined the Berne Convention out of a "desire to achieve greater international protection for other forms of intellectual property, particularly computer software, rather than by a desire to expand artists' rights in the United States."[28] Accession to the Convention was fueled by a need to protect and fight international copyright piracy, not to grant artists moral rights.[29]

Moral rights, as viewed by French law, are rights of personality, which "are deriv[ed] from the nature of artistic creation and from the 'mystical presence of the author's personality in his work.'"[30] The recognition of moral rights was perhaps the largest stumbling block to the U.S. joining the Berne Convention. Moreover, legislators believed that moral rights were adequately protected through "existing federal copyright laws, state moral rights statutes and a patchwork of other federal and state statutes, and common law causes of action."[31] The perceived existence of protection, coupled with a reluctance to recognize natural rights, led the U.S. to focus primarily on the protection of economic copyright benefits.[32] Eventually artists received the much-needed protection of moral rights with the implementation of VARA. The adoption of VARA increased the bargaining power of artists by attempting to remedy the historical inferior bargaining power of artists.[33]

VARA Grants an Artist the Right of Attribution and the Right of Integrity and the Right to Prevent the Destruction of an Artwork of Recognized Stature

Subject to fair use, and independent of the exclusive right of copyright, VARA recognizes an author's right of attribution and right of integrity in a work of visual art.[34] The right of attribution mandates that an author:

> shall have the right (A) to claim authorship of that work, and (B) to prevent the use of his or her name as the author of any work of visual art which he or she did not create; (2) shall have the right to prevent the use of his or her name as the author of the work of visual art in the event of a distortion, mutilation, or other modification of the work which would be prejudicial to his or her honor or reputation.[35]

With one exception,[36] the right of integrity protects an artist's honor and reputation, and prevents works of visual art that have recognized stature from being destroyed. Subject to 17 U.S.C. § 113(d), an author:

> shall have the right (A) to prevent any intentional distortion, mutilation, or other modification of that work which would be prejudicial to his or her honor or reputation, and any intentional distortion, mutilation, or modification of that work is a

> violation of that right, and (B) to prevent any destruction of a work of recognized stature, and any intentional or grossly negligent destruction of that work is a violation of that right.[37]

For a work of visual art to be of recognized stature, the stature must be "meritorious" and the recognition must come from "art experts, other members of the artistic community, or some cross-section of society."[38] The recognized stature standard has been widely criticized for its inability to encompass artists that may not be appreciated at the time the destruction occurs.[39]

VARA is limited to an author of a work of visual art,[40] and is not available to works made-for-hire.[41] Importantly, VARA applies whether or not the artist still has possession of the artwork. The statute also applies if the artist has relinquished copyright in the work.[42] An artist may waive her rights under VARA, per § 106A (e), but an artist's rights under VARA are not transferable.[43] VARA's protection lasts for the lifetime of the author, [44] in contrast to copyright protection, which lasts for the life of the author plus seventy years.[45]

Two important limitations on VARA's right of integrity are modifications to an artwork that either are caused by normal degradation or are undertaken for purposes of public presentation:

> (1) The modification of a work of visual art which is a result of the passage of time or the inherent nature of the materials is not a distortion, mutilation, or other modification described in subsection (a)(3)(A). (2) The modification of a work of visual art which is the result of conservation, or of the public presentation, including lighting and placement, of the work is not a destruction, distortion, mutilation, or other modification described in subsection (a)(3) unless the modification is caused by gross negligence.[46]

This provision is at the core of the *Phillips* case. Site-specific art's protection under VARA turns on whether or not the concept falls under the public presentation exception. If it does not, then the artwork is protected. Remedies available for a violation of VARA include injunctive relief, actual damages, profits made by the infringer (statutory damages), and attorney's fees.[47] These remedies parallel the remedies for copyright infringement, although VARA explicitly excludes criminal sanctions from its remedial scheme.[48] There is no distinction between the remedies that are available for a violation of the right of attribution and those available for a violation of the right of integrity. In theory, an artist may recover monetary damages for both a violation of her reputation and honor and a violation of her right of integrity.[49]

VARA's Legislative History Indicates That Congress Was Aware of Site-Specific Art and Discussed the Issue

Congress enacted VARA to grant artists the moral rights of attribution and integrity, which they saw as a "pragmatic response to a real problem."[50] The statute created a flexible standard that includes a broad range of works of visual art with a few specific exceptions. Congress gave the courts an express directive to defer to "common sense and generally accepted standards of the artistic community" when defining a work of visual art.[51] Moreover, this flexible approach was to encompass the wide "variety of media artists work with."[52] Likewise, the recognition of an artwork as a work of visual art "should not depend on the medium or materials used."[53]

Ultimately, the versatility behind VARA recognizes an artist's personal and professional identity, her dignity, and her moral rights:

> An artist's professional and personal identity is embodied in each work created by that artist. Each work is a part of his or her reputation. Each work is a form of personal expression (oftentimes painstakingly and earnestly recorded). It is a rebuke to the dignity of the visual artist that our copyright law allows distortion, modification and even outright permanent destruction of such efforts.[54]

Artistic intent is at the heart of each artist's personal identity and expression. VARA places the right of attribution and right of integrity in the hands of the artist; therefore artistic intent is implicated when applying the statute.

During the House Hearing before the Subcommittee on Courts, Intellectual Property and the Administration of Justice, sculptor Weltzin Blix described his battle with the State of Oregon when the State attempted to remove his sculpture, "Oregon Capital Fountain," in order to build a parking garage below his sculpture without his consultation.[55] Blix came to an understanding with the State, which ultimately preserved his work, but only after a hard-fought battle to retain control over the artwork's integrity. In response to the experience, he stated that "any distortion of such works is automatically a distortion of the artists' reputation and cheats the public of an accurate account of the culture of our time. . . . The Visual Artists Rights Act militates against this and protects our historical legacy."[56] Interestingly, the primary artist who provided testimony before Congress creates site-specific artwork.[57] Blix's testimony is just one instance that proves that Congress was aware of the issues that site-specific art posed and that they considered the movement of works when enacting the statute.

In addition, a clear debate runs through the testimony given at the subcommittee hearing that questions the public presentation exception and its practical implications.[58] Beginning the debate, Attorney John Koegel testified that the public presentation exception "talk[s] about a change to the object not how it's hung or where it is hung. Also we're not talking about the whole problem of site-specific works either[;] . . . 'distortion,' 'mutilation'. . . are directed at significant changes in the piece itself."[59] Koegel's understanding of distortion and mutilation is nothing less than ambiguous, but it is a particularized instance of a discussion regarding site-specific art.

The debate continued, with Blix testifying again. Blix's exchange with Rep. Robert Kastenmeier, the chairman of the subcommittee, resulted in a critical recognition that certain changes in presentation might constitute destruction therefore not encompassed under the public presentation exception:

Mr. Kastenmeier: In other words, there was discussion earlier that presentation of a work would not constitute distortion in and of itself, but you are saying it is possible—

Mr. Blix: Very possible.

Mr. Kastenmeier [continuing]: Presentation of a work could be, in your view, should be distortion. Is that correct?

Mr. Blix: It could be . . .

Mr. Kastenmeier: I want to raise this because, you know, I think I can see where different people would come to different conclusions about what constitutes a presentation or distortion and it may be somewhat different, whether you are referring to a [*sic*] oil painting or a sculpture; that is to say; I would understand why a sculptor would be concerned about changing the environment in which a sculpture appeared.[60]

This statement from Rep. Kastenmeier is an explicit recognition of site-specific art. More importantly, his statement recognized that a change in a sculpture's environment might affect an artist's integrity. Further, Arnold Lehman declared that the public presentation exception is directed at museums and galleries and not particular forms of art:

> I believe the museum community, working very closely with the artist community, generally is exceptionally sensitive to these issues. . . . There are may [*sic*] instances in which we are concerned about the potential for what we would not like to see as a kind of frivolous confrontation over the exhibition of works of art of living artists.[61]

Lehman continued to discuss the responsibility that museums and public entities have when commissioning large sculpture works: "There is no question that in decades—in future decades, we all may find ourselves with difficult situations. But that is no reason to allow for the destruction of a work of art."[62] Kastenmeier concluded the debate with an account of yet another site-specific artist, Kenneth Snelson, and detailed how his work was destroyed without his consent.[63] In response to Snelson's predicament, Kastenmeier stated that the bill "will make . . . people aware of their responsibilities and rights with respect to sculpture and other art."[64]

Kastenmeier proposed that artists and commissioning entities should "determin[e] at the outset" an artwork's future with VARA guiding that discussion.[65] Clearly, the legislative record indicates that Congress was acutely aware of the potential problems that might arise with site-specific art and the public presentation exception. Critically, this history indicates that Congress believed VARA created rights in site-specific artists that were to inform and to be recognized during the commissioning process.

The House discussion occurred a mere three years after the destruction of *Tilted Arc*. There was far more than conceptual destruction when the GSA removed Serra's artwork from Foley Square. There was literal destruction when the work was cut into several pieces and removed to a government parking lot.[66] There is an account in the legislative history that is analogous to Serra's situation. In response to Picasso's *Trois Femmes* being cut into hundreds of pieces and sold by two Australian entrepreneurs, Congress stated emphatically "this is clearly not a presentation question."[67] It is difficult not to draw a comparison to *Tilted Arc* with the Picasso example. While Serra's work wasn't sold off as originals, *Tilted Arc* was nonetheless destroyed when it was cut into pieces.

The assertion made by several commentators and the First Circuit in *Phillips*—that Congress must have been aware of the *Tilted Arc* battle but, nonetheless, was not considerate of site-specific art—is misguided.[68] Further, the suggestion that Congress meant to exclude site-specific art based on the plain language of VARA, the absence of an express provision providing for site-specific art, and VARA's legislative history is untenable.

A Survey of Pre-*Phillips* Litigation Indicates that the Courts Apply VARA Sparingly

Carter v. Helmsley-Spear, Inc.

The case of *Carter v. Helmsley-Spear, Inc.* examined an attempt by an artists' collective to preserve the sculptural work they installed in a building lobby in Queens, New York.[69] The artists, under contract, incrementally created the sculpture over a three-year period. While the defense challenged the categorization of the sculpture as a work of visual art, and argued for its exclusion from VARA, the court ultimately held that the artwork under consideration was a work of visual art, but also held that it was a work for hire and, therefore, exempt from VARA. Nonetheless, the case established the framework necessary for evaluating whether or not a particular work is a work of visual art falling within the scope of VARA.

After detailing the history of VARA and the concept of moral rights, the *Carter* court recognized three rights in VARA—"the right of attribution, the right of integrity and, in the case of works of visual art of 'recognized stature,' the right to prevent destruction."[70] A critical issue for the Court was whether the right of integrity is meant to serve the "public interest in preserving a nation's culture" or the "author's personality."[71] If the former is intended, then destruction is prohibited in order to preserve the integrity of national culture. On the other hand, preserving the artist's personality does not preclude destruction, because destruction does not truly misrepresent the artist like a mutilation or deformation of the work of art.[72]

Carter also provided a roadmap for determining whether a work of art is of recognized stature. The district court proposed a two-prong test: (1) the work must have stature, "i.e. is viewed as meritorious" and (2) the stature must be "'recognized' by art experts, other members of the artistic community, or by some cross-section of society."[73] The Court's test grants judges wide discretion in determining which witnesses are qualified to make this showing.[74]

Martin v. City of Indianapolis

Similar to the *Phillips* case, *Martin v. City of Indianapolis* considered the destruction by the city of Indianapolis of a stainless steel sculpture which had been installed on recently purchased city land.[75] The city began, but subsequently ceased, communication with artist Jan Martin about removing his sculpture from the land, eventually destroying the artwork without his consent. The majority in *Martin* found no liability under VARA because the city had not willfully destroyed the sculpture. Instead, the Court held that the city's destruction of the sculpture constituted a breach of contract.

Cautioning that "purchasers or donees of art had best beware,"[76] the dissent suggested that, "[t]o avoid being the perpetual curator of a piece of visual art that has lost (or perhaps never had) its luster," persons acquiring artwork should obtain a waiver and, thereby, avoid liability.[77] Otherwise, according to the dissent, an artwork of questionable value involved in a VARA violation could end up costing an owner dearly.[78]

Board of Managers of Soho International Arts Condominium v. New York

Board of Managers of Soho International Arts Condominium v. New York (Soho) was the first case to touch on site-specific artwork in terms of VARA.[79] In dicta, the *Soho* court held that VARA makes no distinction between site-specific and freestanding artworks.[80] By further stating that "[t]he point of VARA is not to preserve a work of visual art where it is, but rather to preserve [a] work as it is,"[81] the district court laid the groundwork for the exclusion of site-specific work from VARA.

Soho is distinguishable from *Phillips*, as the work in *Soho* was attached to a building, and VARA clearly provides a course of action for artworks attached to buildings with the building exception.[82] Thus, the Court did not need to address differences between site-specific art and freestanding artwork. Nonetheless, the *Soho* court's dicta were picked up by the First Circuit in *Phillips*.[83]

Concerns Regarding VARA's Applicability to Site-Specific Art Prior to *Phillips*

Various commentators have expressed their concern that site-specific art might face trouble under VARA because of the nature of site-specific art and VARA's public presentation exception. The legacy of *Tilted Arc* undoubtedly exacerbated such concern. One commentator suggested that artists could only hope that courts would understand the principle of site-specific art when applying VARA to site-specific cases.[84] Further, it was argued the court would have to comprehend the fact that "any change in the whole creation, the sculpture as well as the setting, affects both the expression of the work as well as the artist's honor and reputation."[85] However, mere comprehension of site specificity by the court was not enough to protect site-specific art. In fact, comprehension became its death knell.

The First Circuit's Exclusion of Site-Specific Art from the Scope of VARA in *Phillips v. Pembroke*

In 2000, David Phillips completed a series of sculptures based on a marine theme for Eastport Park, in Boston. The works consisted of both realistic marine creatures, such as frogs and shrimp, and abstract pieces that were continuous throughout the park.[86] Phillips also "selected and directed the placement of mosaic paving stones, granite feature strips, and rough stone walls at the base of the sculpture *Chords*."[87] An axis united all the sculptural elements of the park with spiral and circular forms. Within one year of Phillips' completion of the artwork, the park's managing authority, Pembroke Real Estate, decided to modify the park because of problems with the stone work and a general dissatisfaction with the design.[88] Phillips considered all of his artworks in the park to be site-specific and rejected Pembroke's proposal to remove and relocate his work.

Another redesign was proposed in 2003, which retained all but one of his artworks, but relocated a considerable number of them. Phillips initiated litigation to preserve his work in situ. He went so far as to claim that the entire park was one site-specific artwork that could not be changed without his consent. In response, Pembroke removed all of Phillips' artworks to a private campus in Rhode Island.[89]

Supreme Judicial Court of Massachusetts: MAPA Does Not Protect Artwork from Removal if the "Crafted Components" Can be Removed without Physical Damage

Phillips first brought his case in state court, claiming that his artwork was protected under the Massachusetts Art Preservation Act (MAPA).[90] Ultimately, he appealed his case to the Massachusetts Supreme Judicial Court. Even though that court's opinion does not directly implicate VARA, it is worth studying because, subsequently, the United States Court of Appeals for the First Circuit adopted much of the Supreme Judicial Court's language and reasoning when it analyzed the same facts under VARA.

The Massachusetts Supreme Judicial Court found that MAPA encompasses site-specific art but does not protect site-specific art from "conceptual destruction" or decontextualization.[91] The statute merely protects the destruction of crafted components of an artwork, not the placement of site-specific art.[92] Thus, the court held, "if the crafted components of the site-specific art can be extracted from their surroundings without physical damage to them, the statute is not violated by their removal."[93] The Court justified its decision by declaring that a site is not an artist's material, and site specificity is not a technique that is protected.[94] Instead, they are inspiration for an artist, in contrast to the tangible materials an artist manipulates. Crucially, the Court failed to consider that when an artist creates a site-specific work, the artist physically alters the site by manipulating the location. As the site and the work created there become inextricably bound, the site transcends mere inspiration.

Declaring that MAPA's protection is against "physical rather than conceptual harm," the Court found, with respect to Phillips' artwork, that "the harm presented is decontextualization."[95] While harmful to the artist, that harm "is not the same harm as the actual physical alteration or physical destruction of the artworks crafted by the artist."[96] The Massachusetts court also expressed a real concern for the "radical consequences for owners of land" if site-specific art were to be protected under MAPA.[97]

U.S. District Court for the District of Massachusetts: VARA's Public Presentation Exception Allows for the Removal of Phillips' Site-Specific Artwork

After his loss in state court, Phillips pursued his case in federal court, claiming that Pembroke acted in violation of VARA. In its opinion, the United States District Court for the District of Massachusetts addressed VARA's public presentation exception.[98] The Court held that VARA, as a whole, protected site-specific art,[99] but that site-specific artworks fell under the Act's public presentation exception in § 106A(c)(2). Therefore, Pembroke was not "obligated to display the works in the Park, as VARA provides no protection for a change in placement or presentation."[100] True, Pembroke was not allowed to "alter, modify or destroy the 'works of visual art,'"[101] but they were not obligated to display the works, either, which meant they could move them. Unfortunately, the Court failed to address the issue of whether the removal from the site constituted destruction for purposes of VARA.

According to the district court's analysis, Phillips' "sculptures along the northwest to southeast [sic] axis of the Park, including 'Chords' and the medallion sculpture, as well as the Stone Elements" constituted the site-specific works of visual art that could not be altered, modified, or destroyed by Pembroke.[102] The realistic marine bronzes were freestanding works that were not part of this singular "integrated" work of visual art, and were subject to the public presentation exception.[103]

Phillips' contention that the entire park was a single work of art protected in its entirety by VARA was dismissed by the Court.[104] As Phillips did not create all of the artworks in the park, and only assisted in the design of the park, the park, as a whole, could not be Phillips' work of art.[105] Moreover, the park's constituting one site-specific sculpture was refuted by Phillips' own expert as being unsupported by the traditional definition of sculpture.[106]

The federal district court recognized that site-specific art was protected under VARA, but also declared that the public presentation exception allowed for the removal of site-specific artwork as long as the removal did not alter, modify, or destroy the work. Later, the United States Court of Appeals for the First Circuit would affirm the district court's decision, but on other grounds.

The First Circuit Holds that the Plain Language of VARA Excludes Site-Specific Artwork

On appeal from the district court, the United States Court of Appeals for the First Circuit agreed that Pembroke could remove Phillips' work from the park because, the Court held, VARA did not protect site-specific art.[107] The Court found that the plain language of the statute denied protection to site-specific art.[108] According to the First Circuit's reasoning, VARA could not both protect site-specific artwork and then allow for "its destruction by removal from its site pursuant to the statute's public presentation exception," as the district court had ruled.[109]

Looking at VARA's public presentation exception, the court declared that "the word placement inescapably means location"[110] and not, as Phillips argued, "non-permanent changes in public presentation."[111] Finding no ambiguity in the meaning of "placement," rejecting the idea that the public presentation exception could mean one thing when applied to freestanding artwork and another when applied to site-specific art,[112] and reasoning that site-specific art cannot be moved without the movement constituting destruction, the Court concluded that Congress meant to exclude site-specific art from VARA's protection.

The court agreed with Phillips that "the possibility of change without destruction is implicit in the public presentation exception,"[113] yet held that "VARA does not protect site-specific art and then permit its destruction by removal from its site pursuant to the statute's public presentation exception."[114] In doing so, the Court constructively created a new exception to VARA whereby, if the public presentation exception cannot apply to a work of art, then that work of art is completely excluded from VARA's scope. The First Circuit's acceptance of the concept of site-specific art, thus, was used as the basis for excluding site-specific artwork from the statute.

The First Circuit's Exclusion of Site-Specific Art from VARA's Protection is Erroneous Because It Contradicts VARA's Legislative History

The legislative history of VARA clearly shows that the public presentation exception was not intended to apply to categories of artwork. Rather, it was included in the statute so that galleries and museums could "continue to have normal discretion to light, frame, and place works of art."[115] The presentation exception is, therefore, applicable to the typical reframing, moving, or lighting of freestanding, movable works of visual art. Moreover, Congress explicitly stated "conduct that goes beyond presentation of a work to physical modification of it is actionable."[116] Nowhere does VARA or its legislative history state that if a work of visual art cannot be accommodated under the public presentation exception, then the entire category of artwork to which it belongs is excluded. Moreover, the First Circuit's assertion that site-specific art is never mentioned by name in VARA's legislative history is erroneous.[117] On the contrary, the legislative history explicitly mentions site-specific art once and implicitly references it numerous times in discussing the public presentation exception and the idea of destruction.

The practical implication of the First Circuit's ruling is that Phillips' artwork could be moved to Pembroke's proposed private site in Rhode Island or reinstalled somewhere other than its intended location and Phillips is left with no recourse under federal law for violation of either his right of attribution or his right of artistic integrity. Categorical exclusion from VARA means that, in the First Circuit, any site-specific artwork can be removed from its site, reassembled, and completely reconfigured into something new, and yet still retain the artist's name. This result clearly is contrary to Congress's "pragmatic response to a real problem . . . [to] enable visual artists to protect the integrity of their works and the fact of their authorship."[118]

The First Circuit Did Not Adequately Address VARA's Statutory Framework

The First Circuit concluded that, as VARA could not necessarily protect a piece of site-specific art in every situation,[119] consequently, site-specific art was entirely excluded from VARA. In doing so, the Court did not address the issue of whether or not site-specific art is a work of visual art suited to VARA's other protections. In construing a statute, "a court should not read one part of a statute so as to deprive another part of meaning."[120] In eliminating all of VARA's rights for site-specific art, the First Circuit subsumed both the right of attribution and the right of integrity under the public presentation exception when, in fact, the public presentation exception expressly applies only to the right of integrity.[121] Site-specific art having been left devoid of VARA protection altogether, today, in the First Circuit, someone could cut up a site-specific work, or mutilate it in some other way, and display it as a work of art by the artist without the artist having a cause of action for violating an artist's right of attribution under § 106 (a)(2).

Congress indicated that the works of visual art protected under VARA are "narrowly defined,"[122] and include paintings, drawings, prints, or sculptures, existing in single copies in an edition of 200 or less.[123] The narrow definition was aimed at excluding motion pictures and audiovisual works from the scope of the Act[124] while, at the same time, acknowledging a wide and flexible acceptance of what constitutes a painting, drawing, print, or sculpture: "Whether a work falls within the definition should not depend on the medium or materials used. . . . sculpture includes, but is not limited to, castings, carvings, modelings, and construction."[125] The inclusion of this last category of sculpture, "construction," argues for bringing site-specific sculpture within VARA's ambit.

Art, as Congress clearly contemplated when enacting VARA, is a broad and diverse set of objects that should be defined by "common sense and generally accepted standards of the artistic community."[126] Yet, the First Circuit did not determine, as an initial matter, whether site-specific artworks fit the definition of a work of visual art, and it is that determination that should, as a matter of law, be dispositive for VARA protection. Instead, the Court, claiming not to "denigrate the value or importance of site-specific art, which unmistakenly enriches our culture and the beauty of our public spaces," nonetheless excluded it from VARA.[127]

The Heart of the Matter: If Protected by VARA, Site-Specific Art Would Encumber Real Property Rights

Beyond its purported reliance on the plain language of the statute, the First Circuit explicitly considered the effect of protecting site-specific artwork on real property rights: "Once a piece of art is considered site-specific, and protected by VARA, such objects could not be altered by the property owner absent consent of the artist. Such a conclusion could dramatically affect real property interests and laws."[128] As offered by Pembroke and accepted by the Court, one such dramatic effect might be that changes or development to the landscape around the park would give Phillips a cause of action under VARA if site-specific art was protected by the statute.[129]

Of course, the issue in *Phillips* was not changes to the landscape but, rather, actual physical removal of site-specific artwork. Even so, site-specific art is just one of any number of discrete, independent interventions into a landscape that alters a viewer's conception of that site, and nothing in VARA precludes changes to the viewshed. In fact, Congress directly addressed the encumbrance of real property in the building exception at § 113(d), which contains no provision concerning separate land rights in the artist.[130]

Ultimately, the First Circuit relied on the United States Supreme Court's holding in *United States v. Texas*,[131] that a statute's abrogation of real property must be stated directly, in finding that VARA could not conceivably entail this purpose.[132] Curiously, the First Circuit overlooked another portion of the Supreme Court's opinion in *Texas*, in which the Court stated that "Congress need not affirmatively proscribe the common-law doctrine at issue, but . . . courts may take it as a given that Congress has legislated with an expectation that the [common law] principle will apply except when a statutory purpose to the contrary is evident."[133] Land rights aside, Congress's intention in enacting VARA was to grant an artist moral rights, and those moral rights abrogate some of the property rights of an owner of the artist's artwork. As these moral rights extend to all artworks that are statutorily encompassed by VARA, and as VARA's legislative history shows that Congress intended that VARA extend to site-specific artwork by inserting "construction" as a category of sculpture, site-specific artwork should be protected by VARA.

In *Phillips*, the First Circuit did not differentiate between site-specific works that are intended to be permanent and those works that are intended to be ephemeral. Protecting an artist's moral rights in an artwork thus requires a court to examine the artist's intent regarding the placement of the work.

Kelley v. Chicago Park District Creates Another Precedent Unfavorable to Site-Specific Art

The recent decision in *Kelley v. Chicago Park District* follows the First Circuit's holding in *Phillips*. Artist Chapman Kelley brought suit against the Chicago Park District to recover damages under VARA for harm to his reputation and integrity for the willful destruction of his artwork, *Wildflower Works I* in Grant Park, Chicago (Wildflower Works).[134] Wildflower Works was composed of two large circular forms that covered one and a half acres in Grant Park.[135] First installed in 1983, the installation remained unaltered until 2004, when the Park District abruptly removed the flowers inside the forms and fenced off the space without Kelley's consent or notification.

The District Court stated that Kelley's VARA claim depended, *inter alia*, on whether his work is considered site-specific.[136] The is not bound by the First Circuit's holding in *Phillips*, but it indicated that "due weight is accorded," and that if Wildflower Works is site-specific, then it is not protected under VARA.[137] In its initial statement the Court indicated that it was leaning toward a finding of site-specificity: "the flowers were growing out of the ground" in Grant Park and "could not exist without the ground in which they were planted."[138]

Kelley had the burden of proving that his work is not site-specific, an element of proof not required by Congress from parties pursuing VARA claims.[139] On the other hand, Kelley's work was site-specific, and he refused to argue anything less.[140] Under VARA, Kelley only should bear the burden of proving that his artwork is a work of visual art,[141] yet if courts follow the First Circuit, then any work of art that is incapable of being subjected to the public presentation exception is necessarily excluded from VARA. In fact, the District Court found that Wildflower Works was a work of visual art.[142] Deeming the work either a painting or a sculpture, the court declared that it was "loath to take too literalist an approach to determining whether a given object qualifies as a sculpture or a painting. There is a tension between the law and the evolution of ideas in modern or avant garde art."[143] Despite the court's deference to the art world it found that Wildflower Works was a site-specific artwork, and therefore unprotected based on the "persuasive reasoning set forth by the First Circuit in *Phillips*."[144]

Alternatives to the First Circuit's Application of VARA

VARA Protects Site-Specific Art

In light of VARA's legislative history, a colorable claim exists for the law's protection of site-specific art. As the legislative history of the Act clearly shows, the public presentation exception was meant to affirmatively apply to certain artworks situated in certain classes of sites—mainly to museums and galleries—under certain circumstances, and not as an exclusion for all site-specific artworks. Nowhere does VARA or its legislative history say that an artwork exempt from the public presentation exception is denied all of VARA's protection. On the contrary, the legislative history states that a modification of an artwork that exceeds the parameters of the public presentation exception could constitute a destruction of the artwork.[145] Consequently, if the removal of a site-specific work would exceed the public presentation by constituting a destruction of the work, VARA would prohibit the removal. Analogizing the landscape in which a site-specific sculpture is situated to a canvas, and the sculpture itself as the paint on that canvas, just as scratching the paint off the canvas violates VARA, so, too, should removing a permanent site-specific work from its site.

When the law protects an expansive, albeit defined class of things, such as art, it must look at the specific facts of each individual case in determining legal outcomes. VARA protects works of visual art, and its legislative history indicates that the artistic community should have a say in what should be considered a work of visual art for purposes of applying the Act. The field of art has an extensive legion of practitioners, historians, and critics who have devoted their lives to the creation and interpretation of artwork, and the artists who create and are better suited than judges to make judgments regarding whether certain site-specific art should be considered a work of visual art.[146]

Artists and Art Patrons Should Contract Explicitly When Commissioning Site-Specific Artworks

Regardless of whether or not VARA protects site-specific art, the artist and art patron have the ability to create a contract governing the installation of a site-specific artwork that includes a waiver of the artist's VARA rights. True, Congress found the use of waivers undesirable, but the ability to contract around a transaction is part and parcel to the commercial traditions in the United States.[147] Essential to the waiver of VARA rights, though, is a mutual ability of the artist and the art patron to bargain.

Artists might best be advised to contract explicitly about their intention with regard to the placement of their artwork, as not all site-specific works are intended to be kept in perpetuity. The College Art Association (CAA), which has set out recommended guidelines for public art, suggests that artists and public art patrons should contract in terms of permanence and temporariness when commissioning public artworks, and that the artist's intent should inform the contract process.[148] Congress perceived an inherent inequality in bargaining power between the artist and the art patron, and hoped that VARA would work to remedy the historical imbalance.[149] Consequently, VARA provides an explicit framework for waiving VARA rights,[150] so that the informed artist may act knowingly.[151] Nevertheless, an express provision on the treatment of site-specific art, rather than a complete waiver of the artist's rights, is offered as the best practice with respect to site-specific transactions.

Responding to a Finding that VARA Does Not Protect Site-Specific Art

If the courts find that site-specific art does not fall within the scope of VARA, then artists might seek redress of the matter from Congress, as suggested by the First Circuit in *Phillips*,[152] by advocating for the explicit inclusion of this category of art in VARA. Meanwhile, artists and art patrons will need to contract fairly and with specificity.

Conclusion

As VARA approaches its twentieth anniversary, it is readily apparent that the statute has been used ineffectively to protect artists' moral rights. The *Phillips* case and now the *Kelley* case show that courts are excluding certain artworks from federal protection. The time is ripe for the American legal system and the American public to prove Richard Serra wrong. We must no longer be a society that allows its government to eat its culture. Instead, our legal system needs to build upon VARA's foundation and fully recognize and preserve the vitally important achievements of America's artists

Notes

1. E.g. Douglas Crimp, *On the Museum's Ruins* (MIT Press, 1993).
2. *Phillips v. Pembroke Real Estate*, 459 F.3d 128, 143 (1st Cir. 2006).
3. *Kelley v. Chicago Park District*, 2008 WL 4449886 (N.D. Ill. Sep. 29, 2008).
4. Marilyn Stokstad, *Art History*, glossary 12 (2d rev. ed., Pearson Prentice Hall 2005).
5. Rosalind Krauss, *Sculpture in the Expanded Field*, 8 October 30 (Spring 1979).
6. Miwon Kwon, *One Place After Another: Site-Specific Art and Locational Identity,* 12 (MIT Press 2002).
7. Kwon, *supra* n.6, at 12.
8. *Id.*
9. *Id.*
10. Carrie Jones, *Site-Specific Art Parks on Moral Ground: Distilling Old Whine in New Battles over the Visual Artists Rights Act,* 9 Comp. L. Rev. & Tech. 355, 382 (Winter 2005).

11. Eric M. Brooks, *"Tilted" Justice: Site-Specific Art and Moral Rights After U.S. Adherence to the Berne Convention*, 77 Cal. L. Rev. 1431, 1433(1989).
12. Robert Smithson, *The Collected Writings of Robert Smithson*, 146 (Jack Flam ed., Univ. Cal. Press 1996).
13. Unfortunately, Smithson's work is now threatened by oil drilling in the Great Salt Lake, as are numerous other environmental resources. However, Smithson believed in the entropic nature of his artwork and he may not have been opposed to the oil drilling or slow destruction of his work. See Smithson, *supra* n. 12, at 10. Ultimately this proves that artistic intention is crucial to the understanding and application of VARA. Smithson died tragically in a plane crash in 1973; therefore VARA is not applicable to Spiral Jetty, but there is a strong movement to protect the work from the drilling. Spiral Jetty lives beyond Smithson and has become one of our nation's greatest artworks. *See* generally Dia Art Foundation, www.spiraljetty.org (accessed Apr. 29, 2008).
14. *See National Endowment for the Arts v. Finley*, 524 U.S. 569 (1998).
15. *See* Christo and Jeanne-Claude, www.christojeanneclaude.net (accessed Apr. 29, 2008).
16. Brooks, *supra* n. 11, at 1432-33.
17. Kwon, *supra* n. 6, at 12.
18. Brooks, *supra* n. 11, at 1432.
19. *Serra v. Gen. Services Admin.*, 847 F.2d 1045 (2d Cir. 1988).
20. Kwon, *supra* n. 6, at 13.
21. Brooks, *supra* n. 11, at 1433.
22. H.R. Rep. 101-514 pt. 1 (June 1, 1990) (reprinted 1990 U.S.C.C.A.N 6915, 6916) (testimony of Oregon sculptor and professor Weltzin Blix) [hereinafter H. Rep.].
23. Rebecca Stuart, *A Work of Heart: A Proposal for a Revision of the Visual Artists Rights Act of 1990 to Bring the United States Closer to International Standards,* 47 Santa Clara L. Rev. 645, 659 (2007) (detailing the U.S.'s reliance on the utilitarian view of copyright instead of natural rights as employed by many civil law countries).
24. Brooks, *supra* n. 11, at 1434.
25. Stuart, *supra* n. 23, at 646.
26. *Carter v. Helmsley-Spear, Inc*, 71. F.3d 77, 82 (2nd Cir. 1995).
27. "(1) Independently of the author's economic rights, and even after the transfer of the said rights, the author shall have the right to claim authorship of the work and to object to any distortion, mutilation or other modification of, or other derogatory action in relation to, the said work, which would be prejudicial to his honor or reputation." Berne Convention for the Protection of Literary and Artistic Works (Paris Text 1971), http://www.law.cornell.edu/treaties/berne/6bis.html (accessed Mar. 27, 2008).

28. Patty Gerstenblith, *Art, Cultural Heritage, and the Law: Cases and Materials,* 169 (Carolina Academic Press 2004).
29. Stuart, *supra* n. 23, at 648.
30. Brooks, *supra* n. 11, at 1436.
31. Gerstenblith, *supra* n. 28, at 169.
32. Stuart, *supra* n. 23, at 652.
33. Brooks, *supra* n. 11, at 1474. The waiver provision of VARA is the ultimate expression of this bargaining power.
34. Visual Artists Rights Act of 1990, 17 U.S.C. § 106A (Lexis current through 2008).
35. 17 U.S.C. § 106A(a).
36. The right of integrity is limited by the commonly referred to building exception found in 17 U.S.C. § 113(d).
37. 17 U.S.C. § 106A(a)(3).
38. *Carter v. Helmsley-Spear, Inc.*, 861 F.Supp. 303, 325 (S.D.N.Y. 1994), *aff'd in part, vacated in part, and reversed in part*, 71. F.3d 77 (2nd Circ. 1995) [hereinafter *Carter I*].
39. Stuart, *supra* n. 23, at 658.
40. A work of visual art is defined as: "(1) a painting, drawing, print, or sculpture, existing in a single copy in a limited edition of 200 copies or fewer that are signed and consecutively numbered by the author, or, in the case of a sculpture, in multiple cast, carved, or fabricated sculptures of 200 or fewer that are consecutively numbered by the author and bear the signature or other identifying mark of the author; or (2) a still photographic image produced for exhibition purposes only, existing in a single copy that is signed by the author, or in a limited edition of 200 copies or fewer that are signed and consecutively numbered by the author." 17 U.S.C. §101 (Westlaw current through 2008). Excluded from this category is "(A)(i) any poster, map, globe, chart, technical drawing, diagram, model, applied art, motion picture or other audiovisual work, book, magazine, newspaper, periodical, data base, electronic information service, electronic publication, or similar publication; (ii) any merchandising item or advertising, promotional, descriptive, covering, or packaging material or container; (iii) any portion or part of any item described in clause (i) or (ii); (B) any work made for hire; or (C) any work not subject to copyright protection under this title." 17 U.S.C. §101.
41. 17 U.S.C. § 106A(c)(3).
42. "Scope and exercise of rights. Only the author of a work of visual art has the rights conferred by subsection (a) in that work, whether or not the author is the copyright owner. The authors of a joint work of visual art are co-owners of the rights conferred by subsection (a) in that work." 17 U.S.C. § 106A (b).
43. 17 U.S.C. § 106A(e).
44. 17 U.S.C. § 106A(d)(1).

45. 17 U.S.C. § 302(a) (Westlaw current through 2008).
46. 17 U.S.C. § 106A(c).
47. 17 U.S.C. § 504 (Westlaw current through 2008).
48. 17 U.S.C. § 506(f) (Westlaw current through 2008).
49. 74 Am. Jur. 3d Proof of Infringement of the Visual Artists Rights Act of 1990 § 13 (2008).
50. H. Rep., *supra* n. 22, at 6915.
51. *Id.* at 6921.
52. *Id.*
53. *Id.*
54. *Id.* at 6925.
55. H.R. Subcomm. on Cts., Intell. Prop., & the Admin. of Just. of the Jud. Comm., The Visual Artists Rights Act of 1989—Hearings of H.R. 2690, 101st Cong. 1 at 119-120 (Oct. 18, 1989) [hereinafter subcomm. hearing].
56. H. Rep., *supra* n. 22, at 6916.
57. See W. B. Blix Sculptor, http://www.wbblix.com/ (accessed Apr. 28, 2008).
58. Subcomm. Hearing, *supra* n. 55.
59. *Id.*
60. *Id.* at 132-133.
61. *Id.* at 133.
62. *Id.* at 134.
63. *Id.*
64. *Id.*
65. *Id.*
66. Rachel E. Nordby, *Off of the Pedestal and into the Fire: How Phillips Chips Away at the Rights of Site-Specific Artists,* 35 Fla. St. U. L. Rev. 167, 177-178 (Fall 2007) (the remnants of Tilted Arc rested in a parking garage for ten years, but then were moved to a government storage facility in Maryland, where they remain today).
67. H. Rep., *supra* n. 22, at 6927.
68. Nordby, *supra* n. 66, at 178.
69. Carter, 71 F.3d 77.
70. *Id.* at 83.
71. *Id.* at 81-82.
72. *Id.*
73. *Carter I,* 861 F.Supp. at 325 ("In making this showing, plaintiffs generally, but not inevitably, will need to call expert witnesses to testify before the trier of fact").
74. *Id.*
75. *Martin v. City of Indianapolis*, 192 F.3d 608 (7th Cir. 1999).
76. *Martin*, 192 F.3d at 616.
77. *Id.*

78. *Id.*
79. *Board of Managers of Soho International Arts Condominium v. New York*, 2003 WL 21767653 at 3 (S.D.N.Y. 2003).
80. *Id.* at 3.
81. *Id.* at 10.
82. 17 U.S.C. § 113(d).
83. *Phillips,* 459 F.3d at 138.
84. Rebecca J. Martel, *The Should-it-Stay Spotlight: Protection of Site-Specific Art Under VARA*, 13 DePaul-LCA J. Art & Ent. L. 101, 119 (Spring 2003).
85. *Id.*
86. *Phillips v. Pembroke Real Estate*, 819 N.E.2d 579, 581 (Mass. 2004).
87. Phillips, 288 F.Supp.2d at 94.
88. *Id.* (Pembroke employed another designer to redesign the park and add more walkways and plants for shade).
89. *Id.* at 99.
90. Mass. Gen. Laws ch. 231, § 85S (1984).
91. *Phillips*, 819 N.E.2d at 580-581.
92. *Id.* at 580.
93. *Id.* at 581.
94. *Id.* at 585.
95. *Id.* at 586.
96. *Id.*
97. *Id.* at 584-585.
98. *Philips*, 288 F.Supp. 2d at 100.
99. *Id.*
100. *Id.*
101. *Id.*
102. *Id.* at 98 (directional description should read northeast to southwest as pointed out by the First Circuit).
103. *Id.*
104. *Id.* at 99.
105. *Id.* (noting sculptures by other artists were part of the park, and a renowned landscape architect was actually hired to design the park).
106. *Id.* (Phillips' expert admitted that "a park does not fit within the traditional definition of sculpture").
107. *Phillips*, 459 F.3d at 143.
108. *Id.*
109. *Id.*
110. *Id.* at 141.
111. *Id.*

112. *Id.* at 143.
113. *Id.* at 141.
114. *Id.* at 143.
115. H. Rep., *supra* n. 22, at 6927.
116. *Id.*
117. *Phillips*, 459 F.3d at 143 (noting in footnote 12 that the legislative history never mentions site-specific art explicitly).
118. H. Rep. *supra* n. 22, at 6915.
119. Nordby, *supra* n. 66, at 190.
120. *Carter*, 71 F.3d at 85 (citing *U.S. Nat'l Bank of Or. v. Independent Ins. Agents of America, Inc.*, 508 U.S. 439, 113 S. Ct. 2173, 2182 (1993).
121. 17 U.S.C. § 106 (a)(3).
122. H. Rep., *supra* n. 22, at 6921.
123. 17 U.S.C. § 101.
124. H. Rep., *supra* n. 22, at 6919.
125. *Id.* at 6921.
126. *Id.*
127. *Phillips*, 459 F.3d at 143.
128. *Id.* at 142.
129. *Id.*
130. 17 U.S.C. § 113(d).
131. *U.S. v. Tex.*, 507 U.S. 529 (1993).
132. *Phillips*, 459 F.3d at 142.
133. *U.S. v. Tex.*, 507 U.S. at 534 (internal quotations omitted).
134. *Kelley v. Chicago Park District*, No. 04 C 07715 (N.D. Ill. Sep. 14, 2007).
135. See ChapmanKelley.com, http://chapmankelley.com (accessed Apr. 28, 2008).
136. *Kelley*, No. 04 C 07715 at 10.
137. *Id.* at 11.
138. *Id.*
139. H. Rep., *supra* n. 22, at 6923. The burden of proof that a particular artwork is a work of visual art as defined by VARA, and not one of the enumerated exceptions, is placed on the plaintiff. However, the fact remains clear that nowhere in the list of enumerated exceptions is site-specific art mentioned or otherwise indicated.
140. *Kelley*, 2008 WL 4449886, at 7.
141. H. Rep., *supra* n. 22, at 6923.
142. H. Rep., *supra* n. 22, at 6927.
143. *Kelley*, 2008 WL 4449886, at 7.
144. *Id.*
145. *Id.*, at 6-7.

146. *See Bleistein v. Donaldson Lithographing Co.*, 188 U.S. 239, 251 (1903).
147. *Brooks, supra* n. 11, at 1433. ("waivable paternity and integrity rights is imperative to set the interests of the artist, the purchaser, and the public into proper balance, consistent with the American commercial tradition").
148. Sub-Committee on Public Art of the Artists' Committee of the College Art Association of America, Guidelines: Public Artworks, The College Art Association, http://www.collegeart.org/guidelines/publicwork.html (accessed Apr. 28, 2008). "Removal or Relocation. Provisions for removal or relocation are not recommended. Commissions for both permanent and temporary works are to be preferred instead. In the event that a removal or relocation provision is included in a contract, however, the provision should clearly define the procedure to be followed in deciding whether to remove or relocate, as well as the procedure for the selection of a future site."
149. H. Rep., *supra* n. 22, at 6928.
150. 17 U.S.C. § 106A(e).
151. H. Rep., *supra* n. 22, at 6928.
152. *Phillips*, 459 F.3d at 143.

Preserving Sacred Places

Religious Free Exercise and Historic Preservation in the Context of Third Church of Christ, Scientist, Washington, D.C.

Bryan Stockton

2nd Place Winner 2008 LCCHP/Andrews Kurth LLP Law School Writing Competition

Introduction

Churches are more than mere bricks and mortar. For congregants, they are sacred places of worship, contemplation, and fellowship. For the community-at-large, churches define neighborhood skylines and often provide valuable social services. For preservationists, churches represent some of the most ambitious (and controversial) architectural and design efforts of past generations. As surrounding shops and residences have deteriorated or been destroyed for redevelopment, churches often remain, as symbols of times past.

Historic preservation of churches, synagogues, and other religious buildings can create unique tensions between congregations, which want to be able to alter or demolish their buildings to meet changing needs, and preservationists, who want to preserve their architectural integrity. Historic preservation imposes substantial financial constraints on congregations.[1] Landmarking may make maintenance more expensive and hinder the transferability of the property.[2] Religious groups, citing the free exercise clause of the First Amendment,[3] the Religious Freedom Restoration Act (RFRA), and the Religious Land Use and Institutionalized Persons Act of 2000 (RLUIPA)[4] claim that historic preservation laws do not apply to churches. Preservationists argue that religious groups should not receive special exemptions from neutral laws of general applicability.

This paper will analyze the tension between the historic preservation of sacred places and the free exercise of religion as seen through the recent controversy surrounding the landmarking of Third Church of Christ, Scientist, in Washington, D.C. In August 2008, Third Church filed a complaint in U.S. District Court alleging that the District of Columbia's June 2008 denial of a demolition permit violated the church's free exercise rights, RFRA, and RLUIPA.[5] This paper will examine how Third Church's suit would likely fail in federal court.

After describing the factual background, the paper will evaluate questions of standing and ripeness. The mere fact of landmarking does not necessarily create a cause of action, so any successful suit would have to be brought after administrative remedies are exhausted. The paper will then analyze the potential challenge under pre-RLUIPA free exercise jurisprudence and conclude that despite cases to the contrary in Kansas and Washington State, the denial of a demolition permit is not a violation of free exercise under the Supreme Court's analysis in *Employment Division v. Smith*.[6] The paper will then address the inherent contradictions within RLUIPA when religious entities try to invoke strict scrutiny to challenge historic preservation laws. While claiming to codify existing free exercise jurisprudence and not confer immunity from land use regulations to religious entities, RLUIPA contradictorily seems to expand free exercise protections by triggering strict scrutiny review upon a showing of an "individualized assessment" by a government body in land use decisions.

Although a court likely would not find the District's denial of a demolition permit to violate the free exercise clause, a court's determination of a RLUIPA violation is a much closer question and would depend on how it interprets "substantial burden." Circuit courts are split, but the more compelling precedent suggests that the District's insistence on preserving the landmarked church would not violate RLUIPA. The mere denial of a demolition permit to Third Church—absent a showing by the church of economic hardship triggering a taking—would not violate the expanded protections afforded religious groups through RLUIPA because the denial does not make religious exercise "effectively impracticable" and increased costs on religious beliefs are not alone a substantial burden.

Controversy Surrounding the Landmarking of Third Church of Christ, Scientist

Third Church of Christ, Scientist in Washington, D.C. does not look like a traditional church. Situated two blocks north of the White House, the church is an octagonal structure, with high concrete, windowless walls, that stands in an unadorned plaza on 16th St. NW. Araldo Cossutta, a principal architect in the renowned firm of I.M. Pei, designed the structure, which was finished in 1971.[7] The church is considered an example of Brutalist architecture—a mid-twentieth century movement that emphasized the use of rough, poured-in-place concrete as the building medium.[8]

In late 2007, the District of Columbia Preservation League and the Committee of 100 of the Federal City, which had originally nominated the church for landmark status in 1991, renominated the church for landmark status after learning of Third Church's intent to demolish the church.[9] On November 20, 2007, Third Church filed an application to raze the church building, but the church postponed proceedings on the permit application until mid-2008.[10] In December 2007, the District of Columbia Historic Preservation Review Board (HPRB), based on the testimony of multiple architects, architectural historians, and other knowledgeable experts regarding the building's architectural significance,[11] granted landmark status to the entire church complex: the octagonal church itself, the rectangular office building that housed the offices of the *Christian Science Monitor,* and the triangular courtyard between the church and office building.[12] The congregation opposed the landmark designation at the December meeting. They claimed the structure, which holds 400 people, was too large for the congregation of forty to sixty weekly worshippers. The congregants expressed concern about the costs of maintaining the aging structure. They also stated that the building's fortress-like design impeded their worship and ability to attract new members.[13] HPRB's authority to grant landmark status, though, is not dependent on the property owner's agreement.[14]

The landmarking has frustrated the plans of the congregation. The Mother Church of Christian Science had conveyed the property to a commercial real estate developer, ICG, who promised to construct a smaller sanctuary on the site, but the HPRB denied Third Church's application for its raze permit in July 2008. In October 2008, Third Church, represented by the Becket Fund for Religious Liberty, a public interest law firm that provides legal services to religious organizations, filed a complaint in U.S. district court alleging that HRPB's designation of Third Church violated RLUIPA, RFRA, and the First Amendment.[15] The church sought to rescind HPRB's landmark designation and permanently enjoin HPRB from applying its laws in a way that substantially burdens the church's religious exercise.[16]

Background on Free Exercise Law

Supreme Court Free Exercise Jurisprudence

The Supreme Court's free exercise jurisprudence has changed significantly over the past forty years and has been a source of much controversy. In *Sherbert v. Verner*, the Warren Court held that burdens upon religious exercise were subject to strict scrutiny—that is, for the government action or law to survive judicial review the government had to assert both a compelling interest and that its action or law was narrowly tailored to achieve this objective.[17] Commentators saw this standard to be extremely favorable to religious groups. The *Sherbert* compelling interest test was the prevailing free exercise standard until the Court's 1990 decision in *Employment Division v. Smith*, which held that neutral, generally applicable laws were subject to rational basis review, not strict scrutiny.[18] The *Sherbert* compelling interest test still applied to government action that was not neutral toward religion or not generally applicable.

There were, however, two exceptions to the *Smith* rule imposing rational basis review. First, where the claim is "hybrid"—in that it combines free exercise with another constitutional right (like freedom of speech)—strict scrutiny is appropriate.[19] Second, "where the State has in place a system of individual exemptions, it may not refuse to extend that system to cases of 'religious hardship' without compelling reason."[20] The individualized exemption exception can be summarized as follows: as long as a law does not contain any exemptions, it is considered generally applicable and religious groups cannot claim a right to exemption; however, if a law has secular exemptions, then religious groups can challenge the law.[21] In the words of the Tenth Circuit, "the general applicability test gives religious groups something akin to a disparate treatment claim."[22] By requiring the government to merely show a rational basis for its actions in most cases, the Court immediately made it more difficult for individuals and religious entities to bring successful free exercise challenges.

Religious Freedom Restoration Act

Unsurprisingly, the *Smith* decision was not popular with certain constituencies. Several years later Congress approved and President Clinton signed into law the Religious Freedom Restoration Act of 1993 (RFRA), which attempted to overturn *Smith* and "restore" the compelling interest test for federal and state actions that "substantially burdened" the free exercise of religion, even if such burdens derived from neutral rules of general applicability.[23] Four years later, in *City of Boerne v. Flores*,[24] the Supreme Court held RFRA to be unconstitutional, although subsequent courts have suggested that RFRA would still apply to federal governmental action.[25]

The Court in *City of Boerne* dismissed a church's RFRA challenge to a Texas town's denial of a demolition permit for a historic sanctuary building.[26] Although Congress may enforce constitutional rights pursuant to Section Five of the Fourteenth Amendment, the Court in *City of Boerne* held that Congress had not simply enforced First Amendment rights but had exceeded its constitutional authority by defining the boundaries of those rights.[27] The Court stressed that RFRA was out of proportion to its supposed remedial or preventative object, considering that Congress had presented no evidence in the legislative record of any widespread pattern of religious discrimination by states or the federal government.[28]

Religious Land Use and Institutionalized Persons Act

Not dissuaded, Congress passed new legislation, the Religious Land Use and Institutionalized Persons Act of 2000 (RLUIPA), which President Clinton signed into law in September 2000. RLUIPA reinstated the same general rule of RFRA: state action that substantially burdens religious exercise can be justified only as the "least restrictive means" of furthering a "compelling governmental interest."[29] However, RLUIPA, unlike RFRA, did not apply to all government action but only to state or federal government action involving land use or institutionalized persons. Within the context of land use regulation, RLUIPA applies where the "burden is imposed in the implementation of a land use regulation or system of land use regulations, under which a government makes . . . individualized assessments of the proposed uses for the property involved."[30]

The purpose in passing RLUIPA's land use provisions was to eliminate covert discrimination against religious groups by zoning boards.[31] Despite its sweeping language, the statute was not intended to immunize religious institutions from local land use laws.[32]

To date, the Supreme Court has upheld the constitutionality of RLUIPA, but only in regard to its application to institutionalized persons.[33] While lower courts have generally agreed that RLUIPA is constitutional in regard to land use regulations,[34] no court has yet addressed RLUIPA's constitutionality as applied to historic preservation laws. Still, the legislative record of RLUIPA does not contain any examples of religious discrimination in the application of historic preservation ordinances.[35]

Considering that the Supreme Court struck down RFRA in *City of Boerne* because Congress had not provided any evidence of religious discrimination to justify its use of its enforcement powers, RLUIPA as applied to the historic preservation context could very well be found unconstitutional. Nevertheless, for this paper, the constitutionality of RLUIPA is assumed.

Thus, under the current constitutional and statutory framework, an individual or religious entity can bring a challenge to a burdensome government action both under the First Amendment and under RLUIPA.

Considerations of Standing and Ripeness

Standing

The first issue that must be addressed is whether the church has standing to bring a free exercise or RLUIPA claim when it no longer owns the land. The standing analysis is hindered by the uncertainty surrounding the terms of the church's lease with the developer. While the church controls the church building, ICG owns the underlying land. In all other cases where a religious organization has challenged historic preservation regulations, it has owned the entire property being regulated.[36] In contrast, while the Christian Science Mother Church, based in Boston, originally owned the land on which Third Church currently sits and leased the land to the congregation, a developer currently owns the land and continues to lease it back to Third Church.

Standing for a Free Exercise Claim

To have standing for a free exercise challenge, plaintiffs must prove that particular religious freedoms are or will be infringed.[37] Third Church can assert that the burdens imposed by the historic preservation regulations limit the space in which the congregation worships and impose financial costs that detract from religious and social initiatives. Moreover, the fact that no court has yet dismissed a challenge to a historic preservation law on standing grounds strongly suggests that even though Third Church does not own the underlying land, it satisfies the standing requirements for a free exercise claim.[38]

Standing for a RLUIPA claim

The general rules of standing under Article III of the Constitution also govern standing for purposes of RLUIPA; so the standing analysis is identical for potential constitutional and statutory challenges.[39] But RLUIPA's protections apply only to two areas: institutionalized persons and land use regulations. As a consequence, Third Church's claim has to be related to a land use regulation in order for it to bring a suit.

Nevertheless, courts have recognized that plaintiffs who have a definite but non-possessory interest in the land—such as those who will receive the land as part of a contract or other agreement—do have standing to challenge zoning decisions.[40] In *DiLaura v. Ann Arbor Township*, a religious organization entered into an agreement with a land development company to receive a residential home for free, if the home could be used for religious purposes. The court held that the contingency interest did not render the religious organization's interest unenforceable because a definite agreement existed.[41]

The *DiLaura* court cited RLUIPA, which defined a "land use regulation" that could be challenged under RLUIPA as any "zoning or landmarking law, or the application of such a law, that limits or restricts a claimant's use or development of land, including a structure affixed to land, if the claimant has an ownership, leasehold, easement, servitude, or other property interest in the regulated land or a contract or option to acquire such an interest."[42] Therefore, the religious group in *DiLaura* successfully met the standing requirement because it had an option to acquire a property interest in the property at issue.

Without more information about the structure of the contractual agreement between the developer and Third Church, it is difficult to completely analyze the standing question. Nevertheless, if the developer and Third Church have a similar arrangement that grants Third Church some type of property interest, even if nothing more than a lease, Third Church can likely satisfy the standing requirement, particularly because courts sometimes liberalize standing requirements with respect to the raising of First Amendment issues.[43]

Ripeness

Assuming that Third Church would have standing to bring a suit under both the First Amendment and RLUIPA, the next issue becomes at what point the challenge becomes ripe for judicial review. The mere act of landmarking a historic church building does not present a justiciable controversy under the First Amendment.[44]

In *Metropolitan Baptist v. Department of Consumer & Regulatory Affairs*, the D.C. Court of Appeals upheld the dismissal of the church's free exercise challenge to the inclusion of five church-owned rowhouses in the Greater 14th

Street Historic District.[45] The court stated that historic designation did not impede the current use of the buildings and that because the church had not yet applied for a permit to alter or demolish the rowhouses, its claim was based solely on harm that might occur in the future.[46] The court stressed that one of the purposes of the ripeness doctrine was to protect "'agencies from judicial interference until an administrative decision has been formalized and its effects felt in a concrete way by the challenging parties,'" and that allowing the church's challenge to go forward in the absence of a final administrative decision would needlessly entangle the courts in administrative policies.[47]

The *Metropolitan Baptist* court specifically declined to follow the precedent of the Washington State courts, which have found landmark designations, as applied, to be violations of free exercise under the federal and state constitutions.[48] The Court of Appeals distinguished the Washington case partly on the grounds that the Washington State Constitution provided broader protection for religious freedom than the federal Constitution.[49]

Third Church's claim will not be ripe until an administrative decision is formalized. In other words, for the claim to be ripe, first the HPRB must deny the demolition permit and the Mayor's Agent, through the normal appeals process, must affirm the HPRB's decision. At the time of this writing, the Mayor's Agent had not affirmed or overruled the HPRB's denial of the demolition permit.

Analysis of a Potential Challenge by Third Church under the Free Exercise Clause

Historic Preservation Laws Are Neutral and Generally Applicable

The threshold question in a free exercise challenge under the First Amendment is whether the government action allegedly burdening the exercise of religion is neutral and generally applicable. If it is not, then strict scrutiny will apply. On the other hand, if the historic preservation regulation is neutral and generally applicable, and the regulations do not implicate hybrid rights or do not have individualized exemptions, then rational basis will apply.

Historic preservation laws are neutral and of general applicability, as they do not aim to infringe upon or restrict practices because of their religious motivation, and do not in a selective manner impose burdens only on conduct motivated by religious belief.[50] Thus, these laws permissibly may burden free exercise. The Supreme Court's decision in *Church of the Lukumi*

Babalu Aye v. City of Hialeah strongly suggests that historic preservation laws may be viewed as generally applicable, even if a demolition permit may be denied through an individualized hearing process. The Tenth Circuit Court of Appeals, in applying *Lukumi* to a zoning ordinance, explained that in order for a plaintiff to successfully invoke strict scrutiny, the individual must present evidence "suggesting that the ordinance was passed due to religious animus"; evidence showing that "the city specifically targeted religious groups . . . in its enforcement of the ordinance"; or evidence that the municipality, through its ordinances, "ha[d] 'devalue[d] religious reasons . . . by judging them to be of lesser import than nonreligious reasons.'"[51]

The animosity toward religious practice addressed in *Lukumi* is not relevant here, because local historic preservation boards only decide to landmark buildings that meet specific threshold criteria, which are predetermined, explicit, and not religiously motivated.[52] The HPRB voted to landmark Third Church because of the church's architecture, not out of any religious motivation.[53] While the decision to landmark a particular building does involve discretion and subjective tastes about aesthetics, in *Penn Central Transportation Co. v. City of New York* the majority of the Supreme Court explicitly stated that subjective elements considered in the landmarking process do not make the final decision arbitrary.[54] Instead, historic preservation laws, like zoning laws, are generally applicable because they treat similar property in a similar manner within a generally applicable scheme.[55] In *St. Bartholomew's Church v. City of New York*, the United States Court of Appeals for the Second Circuit explicitly held that landmarks laws are "facially neutral regulations of general applicability within the meaning of Supreme Court decisions."[56] In addition, the Supreme Court, in *City of Boerne v. Flores*, assumed, in dicta, that the preservation ordinance at issue was a law of general application.[57] Therefore, historic preservation laws are likely to be found both neutral and generally applicable.

Regulation of Religious Property Does Not Implicate Freedom of Speech

Assuming historic preservation laws are neutral and generally applicable, plaintiffs may still attempt to invoke strict scrutiny under *Smith* by asserting a hybrid claim: that the historic preservation law infringes both free exercise and free speech.[58] Professor Angela Carmella has argued that, because architecture is closely intertwined with expression, religious architecture constitutes religious speech and is consequently protected by not only the Free Exercise Clause but also the Free Speech Clause.[59] "The semiotic nature of the house of worship," she writes, "renders its 'religious' and 'aesthetic' aspects indistinguishable."[60] Therefore, when the government attempts to control ecclesiastical design for purely aesthetic reasons,[61] it "severely compromises the religious community's freedom to adapt its worship structure to its liturgical, theological, doctrinal, and missional goals" as well as the congregation's ability to protect its "expression and vitality."[62]

The Washington State courts, in *First Covenant Church v. City of Seattle* and *First United Methodist Church v. Hearing Examiner for Seattle Landmarks Preservation Board*, have embraced the idea that ecclesiastical architecture is an expression of religious ideas, and that landmarking churches implicates both free speech and free exercise.[63] In striking down Seattle's landmark designation of First Covenant Church, the court held that "regulation of the church's exterior impermissibly infringes on the religious organization's right to free exercise and free speech."[64]

In another case, *Society of Jesus v. Boston Landmarks Commission*, the Supreme Court of Massachusetts struck down the interior designation of a Jesuit church. Citing its state constitution, the Court held that the "configuration of the church interior is so freighted with religious meaning that it must be considered part and parcel of the Jesuits' religious worship."[65]

Unlike *Society of Jesus*, the landmark designation for Third Church applies only to the exterior of the building. Meanwhile, Washington State remains, to date, the only state to have made landmark designation subject to a hybrid claim.

The issue of a hybrid claim was not before the D.C. Court of Appeals in *Metropolitan Baptist*. Nonetheless, the court's distinguishing that case from *First United Methodist* and *First Covenant* likely means that the D.C. Court of Appeals would reject a hybrid claim argument by Third Church, although a decision by the federal district court is less certain.[66] Moreover, the Washington State cases conflict with the Supreme Court's dicta in *Berman v. Parker*, which suggests that even municipal regulations solely based on aesthetics, and without any historic element, would be constitutionally permissible and not subject to First Amendment challenges.[67]

The United States Court of Appeals for the Ninth Circuit rejected the idea that land use regulations always implicate the Free Speech Clause. In *San Jose Christian College v. City of Morgan Hill*, the Ninth Circuit held that zoning ordinances restricting religious entities from fully developing their properties do not implicate the Free Speech Clause unless the ordinances contain content-based discrimination or unless the city enacted or enforced the ordinances as a "pretext for suppressing expression."[68] In *San Jose Christian*, the city denied a religious group's petition to rezone a parcel to educational use. The religious college, the owner of the property, claimed that the building on the property was itself "speech."[69] Ignoring the idea that the property itself constituted symbolic speech, the court, in upholding the rezoning denial, instead looked to the effect and purpose behind the ordinance.[70] The court held that because the ordinance did not prohibit all religious uses within the city and was not a "pretext for suppressing expression,"[71] it was not a content-based restriction on religious speech.[72] The court distinguished cases where land use laws were subject to free speech protections because those cases involved adult movie theaters that the city was attempting to zone out of existence.[73] Because Morgan Hill was not motivated by a disdain of the college's religious orientation, or by the message that would have been communicated by the property, "no viable impingement of speech claim has been asserted."[74]

Like Morgan Hill's ordinance, the District of Columbia's landmarking of religious buildings does not prohibit all religious uses within the city and is not a pretext for suppressing expression. The landmark designation does not prevent religious uses within the landmarked building; it merely prevents a change in the status quo. While the preservation restrictions undoubtedly impose costs on religious exercise, courts generally have not considered the effects of freezing current uses sufficient to rise to the level of an economic taking or a substantial burden on free exercise.[75] Therefore, absent a showing of discriminatory treatment, the District of Columbia courts likely would dismiss Third Church's hybrid claim.

Denial of a Demolition Permit Is Not an Individualized Exemption under *Smith*

In a First Amendment challenge, the issue of whether the historic preservation laws contain individualized exemptions—and thus fall under *Sherbert*'s compelling interest test—is a much closer case. Courts have disagreed on whether preservation ordinances contain a system of individualized exemptions.[76] Nevertheless, the individualized exemption exception to the rational basis test articulated by the Supreme Court in *Smith* and applied in *Lukumi* should not be read to provide religious entities "special treatment," so long as the administrator has some criteria to narrow decision-making and there is no evidence of religious discrimination.

Five Circuits Refuse to Apply Strict Scrutiny Notwithstanding Individualized Exemptions

The Second, Sixth, Eighth, Tenth, and Eleventh Circuits have held that neither land use nor historic preservation regulations trigger strict scrutiny, notwithstanding the fact that they may have individualized procedures for obtaining special use permits or variances.[77] In *Grace United Methodist Church v. City of Cheyenne*, the Tenth Circuit declined to apply strict scrutiny to the town's denial of a license authorizing a religious day care center.[78] The court rejected a per se test that would subject any land use regulation to strict scrutiny, and adopted a fact-specific inquiry to determine the existence of discriminatory animus or an application of the rule in "a discriminatory fashion that disadvantages religious groups or organizations."[79]

The Tenth Circuit distinguished the land use exemptions at issue in *Grace United* from *Axson-Flynn v. Johnson*. In *Axson-Flynn*, the court found that a system of individualized exemptions might exist where a Mormon student in an actor's training program had been required, while reciting a script, to utter certain words offensive to her religious beliefs, but a Jewish student had received permission to miss certain class exercises for religious reasons without suffering adverse consequences.[80] In addition to the absence of any criteria for the university to exempt students from the academic program, the court also stressed the possibility of religious animus.[81] The court in *Grace United* thus reasoned that although special use permits or variances generally require individualized assessments about the property, the ordinances are motivated by secular purposes and equally impact all land owners within the city that seek a variance or special use permit.[82]

In *St. Bartholomew's*, the Second Circuit assumed, without deciding, that the demolition provision in the New York City landmarks law did not constitute an individualized exemption. Although the exemption exception was announced by the Supreme Court in *Smith* before the Second Circuit decided *St. Bartholomew's*, the Second Circuit ultimately decided it was worth only a brief mention. Acknowledging that the landmarks law "accords great discretion" to the city's Landmarks Commission, the court went on to state that "absent proof of the discriminatory exercise of discretion" such discretion was constitutionally irrelevant.[83] The court compared historic preservation to zoning, in which "the exercise of discretion is [hardly] constrained by scientific principles or unaffected by selfish or political interests," yet still "passes constitutional muster."[84]

Interestingly, on very day the Supreme Court denied certiorari in *St. Bartholomew's*, it vacated and remanded the Washington State Supreme Court's decision in *First Covenant* for further consideration in light of *Smith*, thereby implying that Seattle's historic preservation law did not warrant strict scrutiny.[85] While the denial of certiorari is not binding precedent, the Supreme Court has effectively endorsed the Second Circuit's opinion in *St. Bartholomew's* by denying certiorari in that case and by vacating and remanding *First Covenant*.

A Few Courts Have Found Individualized Exemptions and Have Applied Strict Scrutiny

Several courts have differed with the refusal of the five circuits to apply strict scrutiny. In *Keeler v. Mayor & City Council of Cumberland*, the United States District Court of Maryland held that the city's preservation ordinance had implemented a system of individualized exemptions that triggered strict scrutiny.[86] The court analyzed the circumstances under which the preservation board could allow an alteration or demolition of a protected property: when the retention of the landmark (1) would prevent a "major improvement program which will be of substantial benefit to the City," (2) "would cause undue financial hardship," or (3) "would not be to the best interest of a majority of persons in the community."[87] The court concluded that the city's ordinance embodied a legislative judgment that the city's interest in historic preservation should, in some individual circumstances, give way to other interests, such as furthering major development and exempting property owners from financial hardship.

The Cumberland ordinance regarding demolition of historic landmarks is similar to the District of Columbia's. Section 6-1104 of the District of Columbia Code states, "No permit shall be issued unless the Mayor finds that issuance of the permit is necessary in the public interest, or that failure to issue a permit will result in unreasonable economic hardship to the owner."[88] The statute details the information required for a finding of economic hardship,[89] but the finding of "in the public interest" is a subjective determination.

Admittedly, courts in Maryland as well as Kansas might apply strict scrutiny in analyzing the matter of the Third Church. Nonetheless, the Supreme Court's decision to deny certiorari in *St. Bartholomew's* and, during the same term, to vacate *First Covenant* strongly suggests that the Supreme Court would consider historic preservation laws to be neutral, generally applicable laws not subject to strict scrutiny.

The Required Maintenance of a Landmarked Church Is Not Necessarily a Substantial Burden on the Free Exercise of Religion

The strict scrutiny inquiry asks whether the government has placed a substantial burden on the observation of a central religious belief or practice and, if so, whether a compelling governmental interest justifies the burden.[90] It is a "basic precept" of First Amendment jurisprudence that not every governmental act that burdens religion violates the free exercise clause: "The First Amendment is only offended if there is a substantial burden on religious exercise."[91] Consequently, even if a court in the District of Columbia were to apply the individualized exemption of *Smith*, thereby triggering strict scrutiny, Third Church still must show a substantial burden on its religious exercise for its free exercise claim to prevail. Because courts repeatedly have held that indirect financial or aesthetic burdens on religious groups are not substantial, the denial of a demolition permit likely would not rise to the level of a substantial burden on religion.

Substantial burdens arise when the government coerces a person to engage in an action that violates a fundamental tenet of his or her genuinely held religious beliefs.[92] Substantial burdens also occur when the government forces an individual to choose between following a basic tenet of his or her faith and forfeiting a government benefit.[93] However, states do not substantially burden religious exercise when laws indirectly make the practice of religion more expensive.[94] In *Brownfield v. Brown*, the Supreme Court upheld Pennsylvania's Sunday closing law, even though it imposed a serious financial burden on an Orthodox Jew, whose faith prevented him from also working on Saturday.[95] Although the state law increased financial hardship and made practicing one's religion more difficult, the Court held that the law did not interfere with or impede a religious observation.[96]

A refusal by a landmarking body to allow religious groups to alter or demolish historic structures has repeatedly been held not to substantially burden free exercise.[97] In *St. Bartholomew's*, the Second Circuit rejected an Episcopal church's claim that the city's refusal to allow it to tear down a historic auxiliary building was a violation of free exercise.[98] Just as the developer has planned to replace Third Church with an office building, St. Bartholomew's Church sought permission to replace its community building with a forty-seven-story office tower.[99] Citing its weak financial condition, the unsuitability of the building for its activities, and the cost of structural and mechanical repairs of its historic property, St. Bartholomew's—like Third Church—claimed the new office tower would provide better space for its activities and generate needed revenues.[100]

While the preservation law "drastically restricted" the church's opportunity to raise funds and to expand its activities, the Second Circuit held that the denial of the demolition permit did not prevent the church from following its beliefs and was thus not a violation of the free exercise clause.[101]

Key to the court's holding in *St. Bartholomew's* was the church's inability to prove it could no longer continue its religious practice in its historic structure. Thus, if the D.C. jurisdiction follows *St. Bartholomew's*, Third Church could only escape the persuasive authority of *St. Bartholomew's* by a showing that the current structure effectively prevents its religious practice. The fact that religious practice might be better served in a new facility is irrelevant. While Third Church can argue that the present structure is foreboding and unwelcoming, they will likely be unable to prove that the facility is unsuitable for religious exercise, especially because the church originally approved the architect's plans.

In contrast to the Second Circuit, courts in Washington State, Kansas, and Maryland have held that historic preservation laws impose unconstitutional burdens on religion. For example, in *First Covenant Church of Seattle v. City of Seattle*, the Washington State Supreme Court held that Seattle's historic preservation ordinances, as applied, burdened religious exercise "administratively," by requiring a religious entity to seek the approval before alteration or demolition, and "financially," by reducing the value of the landmarked property by fifty percent.[102] The court acknowledged that not all financial burdens upon religion violate free exercise but found that the fifty-percent reduction in value of the church property at issue was a "gross" financial burden.[103]

In *Keeler v. Mayor & City Council of Cumberland*, the United States District Court for the District of Maryland held that a city's refusal to allow demolition of a monastery and chapel in a historic district violated the free exercise of religion under the U.S. and Maryland constitutions.[104] The Catholic Archdiocese of Baltimore wanted to demolish a historic structure and replace it with a newer building in order to improve accessibility, parking, and meeting space.[105] The *Keeler* court found that the city's historic preservation law contained a series of individualized exceptions and applied strict scrutiny.[106] The court accepted as true the archdiocese's claims that the denial of the demolition permit burdened its free exercise rights, but it applied strict scrutiny without first determining whether those free exercise rights were substantially burdened.

In *Mount St. Scholastica, Inc. v. City of Atchison*, the United States District Court for the District of Kansas, applying strict scrutiny, held that a city's denial of a demolition permit for a historic monastic property violated free exercise.[107] The city did not dispute that it had burdened religious practice, so the Court, as in *Keeler*, accepted as true the plaintiff's alleged burden on religious exercise and, just as in *Keeler*, applied a strict scrutiny analysis without initially analyzing whether the alleged burden was substantial.[108]

First Covenant, Keeler, and *Mount St. Scholastica* do not necessarily conflict with the holding of *St. Bartholomew's*. First, the courts in *Keeler* and *Mount St. Scholastica* did not analyze, as a threshold matter, whether a substantial burden had occurred. Second, although *First Covenant* held a fifty-percent reduction in value to be a substantial burden, the Washington State Supreme Court, acknowledging its dislike of the *Smith* test,[109] grounded its decision in the Washington State Constitution, which the Court characterized as "significantly different and stronger than the federal Constitution."[110] While the First Amendment limits government action that prohibits free exercise, the Washington Constitution "absolutely" protects freedom of worship and prohibits any conduct that merely "disturbs" religious conduct.[111] Therefore, in light of the unique provisions of the Washington Constitution, the analysis of *First Covenant* would be inapplicable in the District of Columbia.

The application of strict scrutiny in *Keeler* and *Mount St. Scholastica* absent a finding of a substantial burden conflicts with Supreme Court dicta in *Smith*. Fearing the "anarchy" that would result from a liberal application of strict scrutiny to neutral laws, the majority in *Smith* cautioned:

> "[W]e cannot afford the luxury of deeming presumptively invalid, as applied to the religious objector, every regulation of conduct that does not protect an interest of the highest order. The rule respondents favor would open the prospect of constitutionally required religious exemptions from civic obligations of almost every conceivable kind. . . ."[112]

Even Justice O'Connor, who dissented in *Smith* and wanted to preserve the *Sherbert* compelling interest test, recognized that courts must first consider the scope of the alleged burden: the proper approach is "to determine whether the burden on the specific plaintiffs before us is constitutionally significant and whether the particular criminal interest asserted by the State before us is compelling."[113] Therefore, by applying strict scrutiny before determining whether a substantial burden on religious exercise has occurred, the courts in *Keeler* and *Mount St. Scholastica* depart from the proper compelling interest test they purport to follow.

Analysis of a Potential Suit under RLUIPA

Protections to Religious Exercise under RLUIPA

As discussed above, RLUIPA prohibits the federal and state governments from imposing substantial burdens on religious exercise unless the government shows its action is the least restrictive means of achieving a compelling state interest.[114] RLUIPA does not define what constitutes a "substantial burden" of religious exercise, but it expands the scope of "religious exercise" to include not only "any exercise of religion, whether or not compelled by, or central to, a system of religious belief" but also "the use, building, or conversion of real property" for religious purposes.[115]

The substantial burden analysis under RLUIPA is supposed to be identical to that under the First Amendment, and yet different outcomes have resulted in a few jurisdictions.[116] Sen. Orrin Hatch (R-UT), one of the sponsors of RLUIPA, explained to the Senate, "it is not the intent of this Act to create a new standard for the definition of 'substantial burden' on religious exercise. Instead, that term as used in the Act should be interpreted by reference to Supreme Court jurisprudence."[117]

Not all courts have agreed with Sen. Hatch's interpretation. The United States District Court for the Eastern District of Pennsylvania commented: "Viewed in the light that the RLUIPA effectively changed the type of burdens that require judicial intervention, it appears that there are two types of burdens on the exercise of religion: those defined by free exercise case law both prior to and during the effectiveness of the RFRA, and those that have been recognized since the passage of the RLUIPA."[118] Thus, according to the Eastern District of Pennsylvania court, a government action can be a violation of RLUIPA but not a violation of the free exercise clause.[119] This problem arises because the language of the statute conflicts with its legislative history.[120] RLUIPA was intended to remedy intentional discrimination against religion in zoning decisions, yet if interpreted broadly the statute can give religious organizations a per se exemption from historic preservation regulations, even in the absence of discrimination.[121]

As already discussed, RLUIPA applies only in specific contexts, the most relevant of which is where a substantial burden results from a regulation that allows the government to make "individualized assessments of the proposed uses for the property involved."[122] There are two sequential steps in the analysis: first, whether the regulation makes individualized assessments and next, whether a substantial burden exists. If the regulation does not make individualized assessments, then even if the regulation substantially burdens free exercise, RLUIPA does not apply. Additionally, if the regulation does make individualized assessments, RLUIPA will not be relevant unless there is a substantial burden.

Individualized Assessments and Strict Scrutiny

The "individualized assessments" language in RLUIPA purposefully mirrors and codifies the "individualized exemption" language in *Smith*. The general consensus of courts is that RLUIPA encompasses zoning and historic preservation laws that allow for individualized exemptions.[123] In one example, *Episcopal Student Foundation v. City of Ann Arbor*, a federal district court found that a denial of a demolition permit for a contributing building in a historic district constituted an individualized assessment.[124] In a second example, *Corp. of Presiding Bishop v. City of West Linn*, the Oregon Court of Appeals stated that even though zoning or preservation ordinances "are neutral laws of general applicability, their application to particular facts nevertheless can constitute an individualized assessment—particularly where . . . the application does to involve a mere numerical or mechanistic assessment."[125]

Even though the HPRB applies criteria in deciding whether or not to deny a demolition permit, those criteria are nevertheless subjective and require individualized assessments. For example, § 6-1104 of the D.C. Code prohibits any demolition permit for a landmark from being issued unless the Mayor finds the permit "is necessary in the public interest" or that a failure to issue the permit "will result in unreasonable economic hardship to the owner."[126] The term "necessary in the public interest" is defined as being consistent with the purposes of the act or necessary to create a project "of special merit."[127] A project can be considered of special merit if it contains "exemplary architecture," "specific features of land planning," or "social or other benefits."[128] Each of these determinations requires an individual, fact-specific assessment. In addition, while the Code standardizes the economic hardship review by listing specific financial information an owner must submit,[129] the determination of whether the hardship is unreasonable is nevertheless individualized. Thus, even absent any evidence of discrimination, RLUIPA is triggered because the denial of a demolition permit requires an individualized assessment.

Historic Preservation of a Religious Property Does Not Create a Substantial Burden Unless Religious Exercise Is Effectively Impracticable

It is important to note that strict scrutiny is not automatically invoked once an individualized assessment is found. Every zoning and historic preservation system has exemptions and requires individualized assessments, and to impose strict scrutiny without any other showing would effectively create immunity from any individualized assessment, be it a variance or a permit. Such an interpretation of RLUIPA conflicts with the legislative intent of Congress when passing the Act. In describing the effects of RLUIPA, the Senate sponsors of the Act stated, "This Act does not provide religious institutions with immunity from land use regulation, nor does it relieve religious institutions from applying for variances, special permits or exceptions, hardship approval, or other relief provisions in land use regulations, where available without discrimination or unfair delay."[130] That Congress intended religious groups to apply for variances and special permits shows that Congress intended many of these variances and permits to be upheld under RLUIPA barring the showing of a substantial burden on religious exercise.

Once it is determined that RLUIPA applies because an individualized assessment is made, the crucial question becomes whether a substantial burden exists. Once a substantial burden is found, local preservation ordinances will rarely survive strict scrutiny review, in part because historic preservation has never been held to constitute a compelling state interest.[131] While RLUIPA does not define substantial burden, the legislative history states that courts should "reference...Supreme Court jurisprudence" to establish what constitutes a substantial burden.[132] Indeed, recent Supreme Court decisions show that the substantial burden test is a difficult standard to meet[133] and is rarely satisfied without a showing of coercion,[134] animus toward religion,[135] or the threat of criminal sanctions for religiously motivated activities.[136]

Five Circuits Narrowly Interpret "Substantial Burden"

The Second, Third, Fifth, Ninth, and Eleventh Circuits have narrowly interpreted the term "substantial burden," holding that inconveniences or financial difficulties do not rise to the level of substantial burdens. The Second Circuit, suggesting in dicta that a town's denial of a special use permit for a religious day care center would not be a substantial burden, cautioned that if RLUIPA is construed too broadly, "a serious question arises whether it goes beyond the proper function of protecting the free exercise of religion into the constitutionally impermissible zone of entwining government with religion in a manner that prefers religion over irreligion and confers special benefits on it."[137] In other words, courts should narrowly interpret what constitutes a substantial burden on religion to avoid a potential Establishment Clause violation.

The Seventh Circuit, in one of the first cases addressing the question of what constituted a substantial burden under RLUIPA, recognized that although RLUIPA expanded the definition of religious exercise to include mere use of property for religious purposes, not every infringement on use would be substantial. In upholding Chicago's requirement of a special use permit for any church that sought to operate in a business or commercial zone, the court reasoned that applying the substantial burden provision to any government action or regulation that constrained the use of property for religious purposes "would render meaningless the word 'substantial,' because the slightest obstacle to religious exercise incidental to the regulation of land use—however minor the burden it were to impose—could then constitute a burden sufficient to trigger" RLUIPA's strict scrutiny.[138] Thus, the Seventh Circuit defined a substantial burden for RLUIPA purposes as a government action that "necessarily bears direct, primary, and fundamental responsibility for rendering religious exercise—including the use of real property for the purpose thereof within the regulated jurisdiction generally—effectively impracticable."[139] The court justified its holding by claiming that a broader interpretation would impermissibly create religious exemptions from land use and that "no such free pass for religious land uses masquerades among the legitimate protections RLUIPA affords."[140]

Other circuits have followed this approach. For example, the Third Circuit held that a city's denial of a variance to build a church in a commercial district did not constitute a substantial burden because the denial was not a "significantly great restriction" making religious exercise "effectively impracticable."[141] The Fifth Circuit, in the context of an institutionalized persons claim, held a "substantial burden" arises if government action "truly pressures the adherent to significantly modify his religious behavior and significantly violate his religious beliefs."[142] Echoing the element of coercion necessary for a substantial burden, the Ninth Circuit held that a "substantial burden" must be "oppressive" and "render religious exercise effectively impracticable."[143] Finally, the Eleventh Circuit, defining a "substantial burden" as one that "directly coerces the religious adherent to conform his or her behavior accordingly," held that a city requirement limiting churches and synagogues to the central business district did not impose a significant burden to a synagogue whose members did not live nearby and had to walk farther to attend services.[144]

Historic Preservation Laws, Unless They Make the Practice of Religion Effectively Impracticable, Are Not a Substantial Burden on Religious Exercise

Historic preservation laws, while they add financial expense and inconvenience, do not necessarily rise to the level of a substantial burden. In *Episcopal Student Foundation v. City of Ann Arbor*, the United States District Court for the Eastern District of Michigan applied a narrow interpretation of substantial burden in the context of historic preservation. The City of Ann Arbor denied a demolition permit to an Episcopal organization near the University of Michigan that sought to demolish its two-story building in a historic district. The group alleged its ministry had outgrown the historic structure and it wanted to erect a "large and multi-faceted church."[145] The organization wanted to cater to students, but alternative sites near the university campus were impossible to obtain. The court found no substantial burden because the preservation ordinance's financial burden and inconvenience did not "prevent the group from pursuing its religious beliefs, coerce its members into abandoning or violating those beliefs, or dissuade members from practicing their faith."[146] It explicitly rejected the idea that the financial burdens on the religious organization constituted a substantial burden.[147] The court recommended a variety of alternatives, which included renting worship space in another facility or constructing an addition on the site.[148]

The holding of *Episcopal Student* strongly supports the constitutionality of not exempting religious groups from historic preservation regulations. In fact, the holding of *Episcopal Student* is in some regard even more compelling than *St. Bartholomew's* because the building at issue in *Episcopal Student*—like Third Church—is used for worship, not merely social services or offices, as was the case in *St. Bartholomew's*. Thus, even though the building was more closely tied to a central religious exercise, the burden in not being able to demolish the structure was insufficient to violate RLUIPA.

Circuits Retreat from Narrow Interpretation of Substantial Burden upon a Colorable Showing of Religious Discrimination

Several recent decisions have retreated from the narrow interpretation of substantial burden. The United States Court of Appeals for the Seventh Circuit, in the year after its decision in *Civil Liberties*, significantly broadened the scope of a substantial burden. Distinguishing, and not overruling, *Civil Liberties*, the Seventh Circuit in *Saints Constantine & Helen Greek Orthodox Church v.*

City of New Berlin held that "delay, uncertainty, and expense" resulting from the denial of a request to rezone for religious use constituted an impermissible substantial burden.[149] The burden need "not be insuperable" to be substantial.[150] However, in addition to the denial, the city had committed a series of legal errors, and the court found that the mayor was "playing a delaying game," all of which created the inference of less than good faith on the part of the city.[151]

In *Guru Nanak Sikh Society of Yuba City v. County of Sutter*, the United States Court of Appeals for the Ninth Circuit, applying the reasoning of *San Jose Christian*, held that Sutter County's repeated denials of a conditional use permit to build a Sikh temple constituted a substantial burden.[152] The court suggested the possibility of subtle discrimination from the county's inconsistent application of zoning law and its explanation for the denial, despite the group's good faith efforts to satisfy every mitigation condition.[153]

A Broad Interpretation of Substantial Burden Is Not Applicable to Third Church Because No Evidence of Religious Discrimination Exists

New Berlin and *Guru Nanak* raise issues of administrative incompetence or, at worst, discrimination and, thus, are distinguishable from *Episcopal Student* and the issue in Third Church. In the matter of Third Church, the HPRB has signaled its willingness to work with the Church to reach a compromise resolution.[154] Moreover, the administrative record shows that the church was landmarked because it was an example of Brutalist architecture, not because the HPRB wanted to restrict the religious practice of Christian Scientists. *New Berlin* and *Guru Nanak*, on the other hand, deal with the siting and creation of new houses of worship. By repeatedly denying the conditional use permit to the Sikhs, the County of Sutter was severely restricting their ability to locate. The burden involved in not being able to establish a house of worship is far greater than the burden in not being able to alter an established church building. While the denials of siting approval do not directly coerce a religious adherent to alter his beliefs, it does make religious exercise, to adopt the term from the Seventh Circuit in *Civil Liberties*, "effectively impracticable."

Preservation Regulations Impose Financial Costs on the Level of a Substantial Burden on Free Exercise

In contrast, preventing the demolition of Third Church of Christ, Scientist, would not necessarily make religious exercise "effectively impracticable" because religious exercise would continue as it had since the building was completed in 1971. The matter of Third Church, thus, is different from cases in which courts have been willing to find a substantial burden when a church is denied a permit to construct a building for religious worship.[155] While congregants claim that the church is unwelcoming and that it costs $8,000 to erect scaffolding to change the light bulbs,[156] government actions that make the practice of religion more inconvenient or expensive—without making religious use impractical—have not been found to constitute a substantial burden upon religion.[157] This is not to say that a financial burden on religious exercise could never rise to the level of a significant burden. Applying the test adopted by the Seventh Circuit and other courts, Third Church would have to show that its finances are in such poor shape that the maintenance costs made religious exercise "effectively impractical."[158] Considering that the congregation has declined from several hundred to approximately fifty or sixty weekly worshippers,[159] this is not unrealistic.

To date, no court has decided what level of financial burden would amount to a substantial burden for either RLUIPA or First Amendment purposes,[160] but based upon *St. Bartholomew's* and *Episcopal Student*, the court's inquiry would be detailed and searching. Following *St. Bartholomew's*, Third Church would have to provide "financial projections or cash flow analyses" to prove that financing of repairs and maintenance would be infeasible and would "prohibit" religious exercise, not merely make it more difficult.[161] In addition, the Second Circuit has implied that a court would not run afoul of the Constitution by requiring a church to mount a good faith fundraising drive.[162] While *St. Bartholomew's* is a pre-RLUIPA case, using the *St. Bartholomew's* analysis as a guide is appropriate because the legislative history of RLUIPA suggests that the meaning of substantial burden should be in line with legal precedent.[163]

The District of Columbia Court of Appeals in *900 G Street Associates v. Department of Consumer and Regulatory Affairs* held that an owner had to undertake good faith efforts to rent or sell a building before the court would make a finding of economic hardship.[164] That case involved a takings claim, and not a free exercise claim, but it nevertheless reinforces the contention that a plaintiff carries a significant burden in alleging economic hardship. The opinion in *900 G Street* thus implies that Third Church may have to undertake good faith efforts to rent out parts of the building (perhaps for conferences) before the court would be willing to find the financial burdens substantial.

Substantial Burden Determination Resembles Fifth Amendment Takings Analysis

Third Church's showing that religious exercise was "effectively impractical" would be similar to the Church's showing a Fifth Amendment takings claim. This is not to say that Third Church must bring a successful takings claim first, but merely that the level of the burden is very similar for each claim.[165]

In *Society for Ethical Culture v. Spatt*, the Court of Appeals of New York rejected the claim that the landmark designation of a historic mansion used by a charitable organization constituted an unconstitutional taking.[166] The court stated that the landmark designation of a nonprofit organization would be constitutionally permissible so long as "it does not physically or financially prevent, or seriously interfere with the carrying out of the charitable purpose."[167] The *Society for Ethical Culture* had claimed its historic building was ill suited for its needs. In response, the court said the society had not proved its activities within the building were "wrongfully disrupted" by the landmark designation and that the society was not entitled to put the property to its most beneficial use.[168]

The Court, in *Ethical Culture*, distinguished an older case, *Lutheran Church in America v. City of New York*, which had found that landmark designation of a church-owned property constituted a "naked taking."[169] In *Lutheran Church*, the landmark structure had become so "hopelessly inadequate to the church needs" that had the regulations been applied, the charitable activity would have had no alternative but to cease.[170] By contrast, the Society for Ethical Culture—like Third Church—had not shown that the building was so "hopelessly inadequate" that the regulations would have had "no alternative" but to cause the charitable activity to cease.[171] Third Church could argue that the historic preservation regulations "seriously interfere" with their religious activity, but following *Ethical Culture*, only if the religious activity would cease could the landmark designation be deemed to work a taking.[172]

The Second Circuit has stated in *St. Bartholomew's* that a preservation law does not cause a taking—even though the regulation interfered with the church's mission—if the religious entity could continue its existing activities in its current facilities.[173] In adapting the Supreme Court's *Penn Central* test to property used for religious or charitable purposes, the court stated that "so long as the Church can continue to use its property in the way that it has been using it, there is no unconstitutional taking."[174] In essence, then, the trigger for a takings claim in both *Ethical Culture* and *St. Bartholomew's*—the inability to continue use—is the same as for a free exercise claim: that religious exercise is "effectively impracticable."

Role for Accommodation

Considering that the Third Church matter would be a case of first impression were it to come before a court in the District of Columbia, the District might consider an accommodation of Third Church. True, accommodation creates a problem, in that each and every landmark is supposed to be protected to the same extent; however, a combination of political realities and the shifting of burdens imposed by RLUIPA make accommodation an option for the D.C. government to consider. In addition, accommodation reduces litigation costs and removes the controversy from the uncertainty of the courts.

The statutory language of RLUIPA provides that the government can alleviate substantial burdens by proposing accommodations to religious entities.[175] Moreover, the legislative history of RLUIPA states that a claimant has the burden of showing that any proposed accommodation by the government to relieve the burden on religion is either "unreasonable or ineffective" before the claimant can prevail under the statute.[176] As a consequence, assuming a substantial burden exists, the HPRB can propose a compromise—perhaps an alteration to the entrance to make it more welcoming—that addresses its preservation concerns as well as Third Church's concerns, and then, in response, Third Church would bear the burden of showing the accommodation to be "unreasonable or ineffective."

Accommodation might be preferable for political reasons. Even if a potential Third Church challenge to the Mayor's Agent's denial of a demolition permit were rejected by the courts, the controversy could jeopardize the District's overall ability to protect churches, as well as public support for including religious buildings within the overall historic preservation regime.[177] Indeed, the initial landmarking decision caused vocal outrage from some segments in the community, and resulted in District of Columbia Councilmember Jack Evans introducing a bill (which he withdrew a few days later) that would exempt houses of worship from historic preservation laws upon a statement of opposition from the religious entity.[178] Evans' proposal presents its own constitutional challenges—it might present an unconstitutional establishment of religion to allow religious entities to opt out of historic preservation laws[179]—but a similar law was enacted and upheld as constitutional in California.[180] Consequently, while the preservation laws stand a good chance of surviving a free exercise and RLUIPA challenge by Third Church, the realities of preserving the integrity of preservation laws as applied to religious structures might steer the District of Columbia's efforts toward accommodation.

Conclusion

Historic preservation of religious properties raises constitutional and policy questions. The parameters of historic preservation in the context of religious properties are complex because religious entities have a constitutional protection of free exercise that ordinary landowners do not enjoy. The discrepancies in case law underscore the difficulty courts are having in applying free exercise jurisprudence to this activity.

Despite conflicting opinions, the Supreme Court's denial of certiorari in *St. Bartholomew's* and its vacation of *First Covenant* during the same court term strongly suggest that the Court would not consider the preservation of a religious property to be a violation of the free exercise clause. Also, the decision in *Episcopal Student*, which is factually similar to the situation involving Third Church, suggests that the denial of a demolition permit would not be a substantial burden on religious exercise under RLUIPA. In light of the District of Columbia Court of Appeals' preservation-friendly opinions in *Metropolitan Baptist* and *Embassy Real Estate Holdings, LLC v. District of Columbia*,[181] and if *St. Bartholomew's* and *Episcopal Student* are followed by the courts, Third Church will have to show that the preservation regulations made its religious exercise "effectively impracticable" in order to prevail in a lawsuit.

The tension between historic preservation of churches and religious exercise will become more pronounced as congregations with historic churches suffer from shrinking congregations.[182] Faced with increased maintenance costs and decreased attendance and tithing, Third Church's might be only the first of many challenges based on religious freedom.

Notes

1. See Melanie E. Homer, *Landmarking Religious Institutions: The Burden of Rehabilitation and the Loss of Religious Freedom*, 28 Urb. Lawyer 327 (1996).
2. See Stephen M. Watson, *First Amendment Challenges to Historic Preservation Statutes*, 11 Fordham Urb. L. J. 115, 121 (1982); see also Evelyn B. Newell, *Model Free Exercise Challenges for Religious Landmarks*, 34 Case W. Res. L. R. 144, 154-57 (1983) (describing in detail four hypothetical burdens on religious exercise).
3. U.S. CONST. amend. I.
4. 42 U.S.C. §§ 2000bb-2000bb-4 (2000) (RFRA); 42 U.S.C. §§ 2000cc-2000cc-5 (2000) (RLUIPA).

5. See Complaint, *Third Church of Christ v. D.C. HPRB*, 1:08-cv-01371 (D.D.C. Aug. 7, 2008), *available at* http://www.dcpreservation.org/Third_Church/Third-Church-v-DCHPRB-cmp.pdf
6. 494 U.S. 872 (1990).
7. Paul Schwartzman, *Church Gets Landmark Status over Congregation's Objections,* WASH. POST., Dec. 7, 2007, at B03.
8. *Id.*
9. See Application for Historic Landmark, Nov. 19, 1991, *available at* http://www.dcpreservation.org/Third_Church/Landmark_Nomination.pdf; D.C. Preservation League, http://www.dcpreservation.org/thirdchurch.html (last accessed Dec. 21, 2008).
10. Application for Raze Permit, Nov. 20, 2007, *available at* http://www.dcpreservation.org/Third_Church/Raze_Permit.pdf; D.C. Preservation League, http://www.dcpreservation.org/thirdchurch.html (last accessed Dec. 21, 2008).
11. D.C. Historic Preservation Office, Staff Report for Third Church of Christ, Scientist (Nov. 1, 2007) (on file with author). The Historic Preservation Office's staff report noted that the church "was one of the best examples of Brutalism in the Washington area and one of the most important Modernist churches." *Id.* at 2. In addition, the design won the Washington Board of Trade's Award for Excellence in Architecture and a craftsmanship award for the concrete work from the Washington Building Congress. *Id.* at 4. Thus, the church complex satisfied the Historic Preservation Review Board's designation criterion F, for "notable works of craftsmen, artists, sculptors, architects, landscape architects, urban planners, engineers, builders, or developers whose works have influenced the evolution of their fields of endeavor, or are significant to the development of the District of Columbia or the nation." *Id.* at 10. Richard Longstreth, a George Washington University architectural history professor, testified before the board that the Third Church complex is "in a league of its own" as a "distinctive and original work." Mark Fisher, State vs. Church: March of the Preservation Police, WASH. POST., Dec. 7, 2007, http://blog.washingtonpost.com/rawfisher/2007/12/state_vs_church_march_of_the_p.html
12. Designation by the D.C. Historic Preserv. Review Bd. in Historic Landmark Designation Case No. 91-05.
13. Schwartzman, supra note 7. Darrow Kirkpatrick, a congregant who opposed the designation, testified: "We know of no way to adapt the building to meet our needs. . . . It's not a welcoming building." *Id.*
14. See D.C. Mun. Regs. tit. 10, § 201–202 (2004) (describing criteria for landmarking).
15. Complaint at 16-17.
16. Complaint at 18.

17. 374 U.S. 398 (1963).
18. 494 U.S. 872, 876-77 (1990).
19. *Id.* at 882.
20. *Id.* at 884.
21. See *Grace United Methodist Church v. City of Cheyenne*, 451 F.3d 643, 650 (10th Cir. 2006).
22. *Id.*
23. See 42 U.S.C. §2000bb-1 (2000).
24. 521 U.S. 507 (1997).
25. *See Sutton v. Providence St. Joseph Med. Ctr.*, 192 F.3d 826, 832 (9th Cir. 1999) (collecting cases).
26. *City of Boerne*, 521 U.S. at 507.
27. *Id.* at 508-09.
28. *Id.* at 509.
29. See 42 U.S.C. §§ 2000cc(a)(1), 2000cc-1(a) (2000). The full text of § 2000cc is in Appendix A.
30. § 2000cc(a)(2).
31. See Daniel Lennington, *Thou Shalt Not Zone: the Overbroad Applications and Troubling Implications of RLUIPA's Land Use Provisions,* 29 Seattle U. L. Rev. 805, 816 (2006).
32. A joint statement issued by the sponsors of the legislation, Senators Hatch and Kennedy, explains, "This Act does not provide religious institutions with immunity from land use regulation, nor does it relieve religious institutions from applying for variances, special permits or exceptions, hardship approval, or other relief provision in land use regulations, where available without discrimination or unfair delay." 146 Cong. Rec. S7774-01, S7776 (daily ed. July 27, 2000).
33. See *Cutter v. Wilkinson*, 544 U.S. 709 (2005).
34. See, e.g., *United States v. Maui County*, 298 F. Supp. 2d 1010 (D. Haw. 2003) (upholding constitutionality of RLUIPA against establishment clause, enforcement clause, commerce clause, and Tenth Amendment challenges); *Guru Nanak Sikh Society of Yuba City v. County of Sutter*, 456 F.3d 978 (9th Cir. 2006) (upholding RLUIPA as valid exercise of Congress's enforcement powers).
35. See Julia Miller, Regulating Historic Religious Properties Under RLUIPA, SL014 ALI-ABA 719, 731 (2005).
36. See, e.g., *Soc'y of Jesus v. Boston Landmarks Comm'n*, 409 Mass. 38 (1990).
37. *Sch. Dist. of Abington Tp. v. Schempp*, 374 U.S. 203, 225 (1963).
38. However, the lack of a concrete property interest would implicate standing if Third Church sought to also bring a Fifth Amendment takings challenge. This paper will not address a separate Fifth Amendment takings challenge, but does

analyze how a "substantial burden" on religion resembles the burden of proving an unconstitutional taking.

39. 42 U.S.C. 2000cc-2(a) (2000).
40. *Dilaura v. Ann Arbor Charter Tp.*, 30 Fed. Appx. 501, 506 (6th Cir. 2002).
41. *Id.*
42. 42 U.S.C. § 2000cc-5(5).
43. See *Flast v. Cohen*, 392 U.S. 83 (1968) (granting taxpayer-plaintiff standing to challenge funding scheme that allegedly violated the Establishment Clause of the First Amendment).
44. *Metro. Baptist Church v. D.C. Dep't of Consumer & Reg. Affairs*, 918 A.2d 119 (D.C. 1998); *see also Church of St. Paul & St. Andrew v. Barwick*, 496 N.E.2d 183 (2d Cir. 1986), *cert. denied*, 479 US. 985 (1986) (rejecting church's free exercise challenge to landmark designation where church had not yet applied for a permit). But *see* First *United Methodist Church v. Hearing Examiner for the Seattle Landmarks Preservation Board*, 916 P.2d 374 (Wash. 1996) (holding that landmark designation violated church's free exercise under federal and state constitutions because the designation restricted the church's ability to sell its property to further its religious mission); *Munns v. Martin*, 930 P.2d 318 (Wash. 1997) (holding that landmark designation of religious school is a violation of the state constitution). The United States District Court for the District of Connecticut held that in regard to a ripeness inquiry, it was not necessary to distinguish a RLUIPA claim from a First Amendment free exercise claim. *Murphy v. New Milford Zoning Comm'n*, 402 F.3d 342, 350 (2d Cir. 2005).
45. 918 A.2d at 130.
46. *Id.*
47. *Id.* (quoting *Abbot Lab. v. Gardner*, 387 U.S. 136, 148 (1967)).
48. *Id.* at 131-32 (distinguishing *First United Methodist*, 916 P.2d 374 (1996)).
49. *Id.* at 132. In a footnote, the court also distinguished *First United Methodist* on the grounds that the church in that case was suffering from deterioration, unlike the rowhouses of *Metropolitan Baptist*, and that repairs would only be affordable absent government regulations. This footnote suggests that if a court finds that Third Church is deteriorating and maintenance costs would be prohibitively expensive, the church may have a stronger case of distinguishing *Metropolitan Baptist*. Nevertheless, it is unlikely that even this would overcome the court's reluctance to intervene before a final administrative determination.
50. *Church of the Lukumi Babalu Aye v. City of Hialeah*, 508 U.S. 520, 533 (1993); see also *San Jose Christian Coll.*, 360 F.3d 1024, 1031 (9th Cir. 2004) (finding that city's denial of Christian college's petition for rezoning was not targeted on basis of religion and thus not a violation of free exercise).

51. *Grace United*, 451 F.3d 643, 650 (10th Cir. 2005) (citing *Lukumi*, 508 U.S. at 537).
52. For the seven criteria that HPRB uses in determining whether to approve landmark status, see 10 DCMR § 200.1 (2002). For example, subsection (e) provides: "No permit shall be issued unless the Mayor finds that issuance of the permit is necessary in the public interest, or that failure to issue a permit will result in unreasonable economic hardship to the owner." § 200.1(e).
53. In contrast, the Supreme Court struck down a municipal ordinance that criminalized animal sacrifice within city limits because the Court found that the city council, in passing the ordinance, was motivated by animus toward Santerians and excluded many other activities that killed animals (medical research, butchers) from the ban. See *Lukumi*, 508 U.S. at 530.
54. 438 U.S. 104, 132 (1978). "[C]ontrary to appellants' suggestions, landmark laws are not like discriminatory, or 'reverse spot,' zoning: that is, a land-use decision which arbitrarily singles out a particular parcel for different, less favorable treatment than the neighboring ones. . . . In contrast to discriminatory zoning, which is the antithesis of land-use control as part of some comprehensive plan, the New York City law embodies a comprehensive plan to preserve structures of historic or aesthetic interest wherever they might be found in the city. . . . Equally without merit is the related argument that the decision to designate a structure as a landmark "is inevitably arbitrary or at least subjective, because it is basically a matter of taste." *Id.*
55. *Id.*
56. *St. Bartholomew's Church v. City of New York*, 914 F.2d 348, 353 (2nd Cir. 1990).
57. *City of Boerne*, 521 U.S. 507, 513-14 (1997).
58. The hybrid rights claim is not without controversy. As the Tenth Circuit in *Grace United* stated, "The hybrid rights doctrine . . . has been characterized as mere dicta not binding on lower courts, *Knight v. Conn. Dep't of Pub. Health*, 275 F.3d 156, 167 (2d Cir.2001); criticized as illogical, *Kissinger v. Bd. of Trs. of Ohio State Univ.*, 5 F.3d 177, 180 (6th Cir.1993); and dismissed as untenable." *Grace United*, 451 F.3d 643, 656 (D. Wyo. 2006). For simplicity, this paper assumes the validity of the hybrid rights exception in *Smith*.
59. See Angela Carmella, *Landmark Preservation of Church Property*, 34 Cath. Law. 41, 60 (1991); Russell S. Bonds, *First Covenant Church v. City of Seattle: The Washington Supreme Court Fortifies the Free Exercise Rights of Religious Landmarks Against Historic Preservation Restrictions, Comment*, 27 GA. L. Rev. 589, 614 (1992).
60. Angela Carmella, *Houses of Worship and Religious Liberty: Constitutional Limits to Landmark Preservation and Architectural Review*, 36 Vill. L. Rev 401, 405 (1991).
61. Prof. Carmella does not dispute that health and safety regulations would trump this freedom of ecclesiastical architectural expression. *Id.*

62. *Id.*
63. *First Covenant Church v. City of Seattle*, 840 P.2d 174, 182 (1992) ("The relationship between theological doctrine and architectural design is well recognized."); *First United Methodist Church v. Seattle Landmarks Preservation Bd.*, 916 P.2d 374 (1996) ("[T]he Landmarks Preservation Ordinance posed a potential threat to both the free exercise of religion and free speech. . . .").
64. *First Covenant*, 840 P.2d at 182.
65. 564 N.E.2d 571, 573 (1990).
66. *See Metro. Baptist Church v. D.C. Dep't of Consumer & Reg. Affairs*, 718 A.2d 119, 132 (D.C. 1998).
67. 348 U.S. 26, 33 (1954).
68. 360 F.3d 1024, 1033 (9th Cir. 2004).
69. *Id.* at 1032.
70. *Id.*
71. *Id.* (quoting *City of Renton v. Playtime Theatres, Inc.*, 475 U.S. 41, 47 (1986)).
72. *Id.* at 1032.
73. *Id.* at 1032 (discussing *Renton v. Playtime Theaters*).
74. *Id.* at 1032.
75. *See St. Bartholomew's Church v. City of New York*, 914 F.2d 348 (2d Cir. 1990), *cert. denied*, 499 U.S. 905 (1991) (holding that no First Amendment violation occurs absent a showing of discriminatory motive, coercion in religious practice, or an inability to carry out its religious mission in its existing facilities).
76. Compare *St. Bartholomew's* (holding landmark law to be generally applicable) with *Mt. St. Scholastica v. City of Atchison*, 482 F. Supp. 1281 (D. Kan. 2007) (holding historic preservation to be a system of individualized exemptions).
77. *See Grace United Methodist Church v. City of Cheyenne*, 451 F.3d 643, 651 (10th Cir. 2006); *First Assembly of God v. Collier County*, 20 F.3d 419, 423 (11th Cir. 1994); *Cornerstone Bible Church v. City of Hastings*, 948 F.2d 464, 472 (8th Cir.1991); *Mt. Elliott Cemetery Ass'n v. City of Troy*, 171 F.3d 398, 405 (6th Cir.1999); *St. Bartholomew's Church v. City of New York*, 914 F.2d 348, 354 (2d Cir.1990); *Civil Liberties for Urban Believers v. City of Chicago*, 157 F. Supp. 2d 903, 914-15 (N.D. Ill. 2001), *aff'd*, 342 F.3d 752 (7th Cir. 2003).
78. *Grace United*, 451 F.3d at 651.
79. *Id.* at 651.
80. *Id.*
81. *Axson-Flynn v. Johnson*, 356 F.3d 1277, 1298-99 (10th Cir. 2004).
82. *Grace United*, 451 F.3d at 651 ("[S]everal federal courts have held that land use regulations . . . are neutral and generally applicable notwithstanding that they may have individualized procedures for obtaining special use permits or variances. . . . According to these courts . . . [zoning laws] are generally applicable if

they are motivated by secular purposes and impact equally all land owners in the city seeking variances."); *Collier County*, 20 F.3d at 423-24; *City of Troy*, 171 F.3d at 405; *Civil Liberties*, 157 F.Supp.2d at 914-15.

83. *St. Bartholomew's Church v. City of New York*, 914 F.2d 348, 354-55 (2nd Cir. 1990).
84. *Id.* at 355.
85. Homer, *supra* note 1, at 341. While the denial of certiorari in *St. Bartholomew's* and the vacation and remand "appeared to make First Covenant an easy victory for preservationists," the Washington court surprisingly refused to change its opinion in light of *Smith* and grounded its second decision in the state constitution to insulate it from further review. *Id.* at 342.
86. *Keeler v. Mayor of Cumberland*, 940 F. Supp. 879, 886 (D. Md. 1996).
87. *Id.* at 886.
88. D.C. Code § 6-1104(e) (2000).
89. See § 6-1104(g). The full text of this section is in Appendix B.
90. *Hernandez v. Comm'r of Internal Revenue*, 490 U.S. 680, 699 (1989).
91. *Congregation Kol Ami v. Abington Tp.*, 2004 WL 1837037 at 5 (E.D. Pa., Aug. 12, 2004).
92. *See Wisconsin v. Yoder*, 406 U.S. 205 (1972) (holding that state law requiring Amish parents to send their children to high school a substantial burden on free exercise).
93. *Sherbert v. Verner*, 374 U.S. 398, 404 (1963) (finding free exercise violation when Seventh Day Adventist was forced to choose between working on Saturday—which her faith prohibited—and receiving generally available unemployment benefits).
94. *See Braunfeld v. Brown*, 366 U.S. 599 (1961); *see also Lakewood Cong. of Jehovah's Witnesses, Inc. v. City of Lakewood*, 699 F.2d 303 (6th Cir.1983) (finding no substantial burden when city zoning ordinance required new religious groups to purchase land in the expensive commercial section of the city for religious structures).
95. *Braunfield*, 366 U.S. at 605.
96. *Id.*
97. *See St. Bartholomew's Church v. City of New York*, 914 F.2d 348 (2nd Cir. 1990); *First Church of Christ, Scientist v. Historic Dist. Com'n of Ridgefield*, 738 A.2d 224 (Conn. Super. Ct. 1998), *aff'd*, 737 A.2d 989 (Conn. App. Ct. 1999), *cert. denied*, 742 A.2d 358 (1999) (holding that denial of alteration of historic church was not a substantial burden); *Diocese of Toledo v. Toledo City-Lucas County Planning Comm'n*, No. CI97-3710 (Lucas County Ct. C.P. 1999), *rev'd on other grounds*, No. L-98-1150 (Ohio Ct. App., Mar. 12, 1999), 1999 WL 128563 (Ohio App. 6

Dist.) (holding that denial of permission to tear down house for church parking lot was not an undue burden on the church's free exercise).

98. *St. Bartholomew's*, 914 F.2d at 355.
99. *Id.* at 352.
100. *Id.* at 353-54.
101. *Id.* at 355.
102. *First Covenant Church v. City of Seattle*, 840 P.2d 174, 183 (1992).
103. *Id.*
104. *Keeler v. Mayor of Cumberland*, 940 F. Supp. 879, 887 (D. Md. 1996).
105. *Id.* at 883.
106. *Id.*
107. 482 F. Supp. 2d 1281, 1295 (D. Kan. 2007).
108. *Id.* at 1292.
109. The Washington State Supreme Court criticized the United States Supreme Court's analysis in *Smith* as "depart[ing] from a long history of established law and adopt[ing] a test that places free exercise in a subordinate, instead of preferred, position." *First Covenant,* 840 P.2d at187.
110. *Id.* at 186.
111. *Id.* at 186.
112. *Employment Div. v. Smith*, 494 U.S. 872, 888-89 (1990).
113. *Id.* at 899. (O'Connor, J., dissenting) (emphasis added).
114. 42 U.S.C. § 2000cc(a)(1) (2000).
115. § 2000cc-5(7)(A)-(B).
116. *See Congregation of Kol Ami v. Abington Township*, 2004 WL 1837037 (E.D. Pa., Aug. 12, 2004) (finding that denial of variance not a free exercise violation but a violation under RLUIPA).
117. 146 Cong. Rec. S7776 (daily ed. July 27, 2000) (statement of Sen. Hatch). Hatch continued: "Nothing in this Act, including the requirement in Section 5(g) that its terms be broadly construed, is intended to change that principle. The term "substantial burden" as used in this Act is not intended to be given any broader interpretation than the Supreme Court's articulation of the concept of substantial burden or religious exercise." *Id.*
118. *Kol Ami*, 2004 WL 1837037 at 8-9. However, it should be noted that *Kol Ami* is an unreported opinion and therefore lacks precedential weight.
119. *See id.*; see also *DiLaura v. Ann Arbor Charter Twp.*, No. 00-1846, 2002 U.S. App. LEXIS 3135, at *20 (6th Cir., Feb. 25, 2002) (holding that denial of variance seeking to use a donated house for a religious retreat was a substantial burden under RLUIPA but not a violation of the Free Exercise Clause).
120. *See Lennington*, *supra* note 26, at 834.
121. *See id.* at 835.

122. 42 U.S.C. § 2000cc(a)(2)(C) (2000).
123. *See Freedom Baptist Church v. Twp. of Middleton*, 204 F. Supp. 2d 857, 868-69 (E.D. Pa. 2002) (holding that zoning ordinances impose individual assessments involving case-by-case evaluation of the propriety of proposed activity against the ordinance); *Shepherd Montessori Center Milan v. Ann Arbor Charter Tp.*, 675 N.W.2d 271 (Mich. App. Ct. 2003) (finding that denial of variance constituted "individualized assessment" under RLUIPA).
124. 341 F. Supp. 2d 691, 698 (E.D. Mich. 2004).
125. *Corp. of Presiding Bishop v. City of West Linn*, 86 P.3d 1140, 1148 (Or. App. Ct. 2004) (finding that denial of variance to construct church was individualized assessment, although not a substantial burden on religious exercise).
126. D.C. Code § 6-1104(e) (2000).
127. D. C. Code § 6-1102(10).
128. D.C. Code § 6-1102(11).
129. D.C. Code § 6-1104(g).
130. 146 Cong. Rec. 7776 (daily ed. July 27, 2000) (statement of Sen. Kennedy).
131. See *Mt. St. Scholastica v. City of Atchison*, 482 F. Supp. 2d 1281, 1294 (D. Kan. 2007) (citing *Keeler v. Mayor of Cumberland*, 940 F. Supp. 879, 886 (D. Md. 1996)).
132. 146 Cong. Rec. S7776 (daily ed. July 27, 2000).
133. *See Braunfeld v. Brown*, 366 U.S. 599, 605 (1961) (finding no substantial burden when Sunday closing law merely made practice of religion more expensive); *Bowen v. Roy*, 476 U.S. 693 (1986) (finding no substantial burden even though government's use of Social Security number would allegedly negatively affect plaintiff's soul); *Lyng v. Northwest Indian Cemetery Protective Ass'n*, 485 U.S. 439 (1988) (finding no substantial burden when government built road through forest held sacred by Native Americans because action interfered with, but did not coerce, individual beliefs).
134. *See Sherbert v. Verner*, 374 U.S. 398 (1963) (finding substantial burden when individual forced to choose "between following the precepts of her religion and forfeiting benefits, on the one hand, and abandoning one of the precepts of her religion . . . on the other").
135. *See Church of the Lukumi Babalu Aye v. City of Hialeah*, 508 U.S. 520, 533 (1993).
136. *Id.*
137. *Westchester Day Sch. v. Vill. of Mamaroneck*, 386 F.3d 183, 189 (2d Cir. 2004).
138. *Civil Liberties for Urban Believers v. City of Chicago*, 342 F.3d 752, 761 (7th Cir. 2003).
139. *Id.* at 760-61. However, the Seventh Circuit's inclusion of a requirement that the challenged governmental action be the "direct" cause of an effective impracticability of using the real property for religious purposes appears to be inconsistent with the test under the Free Exercise Clause stated by the Supreme Court in *Sherbert*. *See Sherbert v. Verner*, 374 U.S. 399, 404 (1963) (explaining that, if the

purpose or effect of a law is to impede religious practice, the law is constitutionally invalid even though it has such effect only indirectly). Thus, perhaps the more complete standard is one that either indirectly or directly makes religious exercise impracticable. The issue is of little importance because the Supreme Court has shifted away from examining the directness or indirectness of the burden to the substantiality of the burden. Compare *Braunfeld v. Brown*, 366 U.S. 599 (1961) and *Sherbert*, 374 U.S. at 404 with *Employment Div. v. Smith*, 494 U.S. 872, 899 (O'Connor, J.,[dissenting]).

140. *Civil Liberties*, 342 F.3d at 761.
141. *Lighthouse Inst. for Evangelism Inc. v. City of Long Branch*, 100 F. Appx. 70, 77 (3d Cir. 2004) (not precedential).
142. *Adkins v. Kaspar*, 393 F.3d 559 (5th Cir. 2004).
143. *San Jose Christian Coll. v. City of Morgan Hill*, 360 F.3d 1024, 1035 (9th Cir. 2004).
144. *Midrash Sephardi v. Town of Surfside*, 366 F.3d 1214, 1227 (11th Cir. 2004).
145. *Episcopal Student Found. v. City of Ann Arbor*, 341 F. Supp. 2d 691, 694 (E.D. Mich. 2004).
146. *Id.* at 704.
147. *Id.* at 706 ("Finally, although Canterbury House may incur additional financial burdens, such as rental expenses to accommodate its entire congregation on occasion, or if it seek additional growth, such financial burdens are not 'substantial' under RLUIPA.").
148. *Id.*
149. 396 F.3d 895, 901 (7th Cir. 2005); *Lennington, supra* note 26, at 821.
150. *New Berlin*, 396 F.3d at 901.
151. *Id.* at 899.
152. *Guru Nanak Sikh Society of Yuba City v. County of Sutter*, 456 F.3d 978, 992 (9th Cir. 2006).
153. *Id.* at 990-91.
154. Transcript of Dec. 6, 2007 HPRB hearing (on file with the Office of Historic Preservation).
155. *See Cottonwood Christian Ctr. v. Cypress Redev. Agency*, 218 F. Supp. 2d 1203, 1226 (C.D. Cal. 2002) ("Preventing a church from building a worship site fundamentally inhibits its ability to practice its religion. . . . If Cottonwood could not build a church, it could not exist."); *Elsinore Christian Ctr. v. City of Lake Elsinore*, 291 F. Supp. 2d 1083, 1090 (C.D. Cal. 2003) ("Denial of the [conditional use permit] bars the Church's use altogether, thereby imposing the ultimate burden on the use of that land.").
156. Charles Paul Freund, *A Brutalist Bargain,* The American Spectator, Dec. 18, 2007, available at http://www.spectator.org/dsp_article.asp?art_id=12460.
157. *See Braunfeld v. Brown*, 366 U.S. 599 (1961).

158. *See Civil Liberties for Urban Believers v. City of Chicago*, 342 F.3d 752, 760-61 (7th Cir. 2003).
159. *See* Schwartzman, *supra* note 6.
160. The court in *First Covenant* held that a substantial burden arose because the church's property was reduced in value by 50%, but this was largely based on the Washington State constitution. *First Covenant Church v. City of Seattle*, 840 P.2d 174, 182 (Wash. 1992).
161. *See St. Bartholomew's Church v. City of New York*, 914 F.2d 348, 355 (2nd Cir. 1990) (quoting *Lyng v. Northwest Cemetery Protective Ass'n*, 485 U.S. 439 (1988)) ("The crucial word in the constitutional text is 'prohibit.'").
162. *See id.* at 359.
163. *See* 146 Cong. Rec. S7776 (daily ed. July 27, 2000) (statement of Sen. Hatch).
164. 430 A.2d 1387, 1391 (D.C. 1981).
165. This paper does not fully explore a potential taking claim; this paragraph is included to illustrate how the showing of impracticability under RLUIPA is similar to a takings claim under the Fifth Amendment.
166. *Society for Ethical Culture v. Spatt*, 415 N.E.2d 922, 926 (N.Y. 1980).
167. *Id.*
168. *Id.*
169. *Id.*
170. *Id.*
171. *Id.*
172. *See also Sailors' Snug Harbor v. Platt*, 29 A.D.2d 376 (N.Y. App. Div. 1968) (upholding landmark designation of historic building owned by charitable organization because the designation neither "physically or financially prevents" nor "seriously interferes" with the organization's charitable purpose.).
173. *See St. Bartholomew's*, 914 F.2d at 357.
174. *Id.*
175. 42 U.S.C. § 2000cc-3(e) (2000).
176. 146 Cong. Rec. S7776 (daily ed. July 27, 2000). *See* Julia H. Miller, Regulating Historic Religious Properties Under RLUIPA, SM056 ALI-ABA 817, 829 (2007).
177. Local media figures and property rights advocates have severely criticized the HPRB's decision to landmark Third Church. *See* Fisher, *supra* note 7.
178. Bill on file with author.
179. To avoid an Establishment Clause violation under the Supreme Court's test in *Lemon v. Kurtzman*, a government action or law must "have a secular legislative purpose;" its "principal or primary effect" must "neither advance[] nor inhibit[] religion," and it must not foster "'excessive government entanglement with religion.'" 403 U.S. 601, 612-13 (1971) (quoting *Walz v. Tax Comm'n*, 397 U.S.

664, 674 (1970). Exempting only religious properties arguably has neither a secular purpose nor a secular effect.

180. *See East Bay Asian Local Dev. Corp. v. California*, 13 P.3d 1122 (Cal. 2000). The California law exempts all noncommercial properties from historic preservation laws if the organization objects to application of the regulations and makes a declaration in a public forum that it would suffer substantial hardship if the regulations were applied. See Felipe M. Nunez & Eric Seidman, *California's Statutory Exemption For Religious Properties From Preservation Ordinances: A Constitutional and Policy Analysis,* 12 J.L. & Religion 271-322 (1995).
181. *Embassy Real Estate Holdings, LLC v. District of Columbia*, No. 06-AA-1083 (D.C. Mar. 20, 2008).
182. For example, the diocese of Pittsburgh closed over 40 churches from 1988 to 1994. Megan McCloskey, *Historic Church Closes Its Doors Forever*, PITTSBURGH TRIB. REV., Dec. 7, 2004. In Boston, the Roman Catholic archdiocese recently closed 83 churches, many of them historic. Marilyn M. Fenollosa, *The Boston Archdiocese Parish Closing Process*, *in* QUEL AVENIR POUR QUELLES EGLISES? [WHAT FUTURE FOR WHICH CHURCHES?] 139 (2007).

Appendix A

42 U.S.C. §§ 2000cc (2000)
Protection of land use as religious exercise

(a) Substantial burdens

(1) General rule

government shall impose or implement a land use regulation in a manner that imposes a substantial burden on the religious exercise of a person, including a religious assembly or institution, unless the government demonstrates that imposition of the burden on that person, assembly, or institution—

(A) is in furtherance of a compelling governmental interest; and

(B) is the least restrictive means of furthering that compelling governmental interest.

(2) Scope of application

This subsection applies in any case in which—

(A) the substantial burden is imposed in a program or activity that receives Federal financial assistance, even if the burden results from a rule of general applicability;

(B) the substantial burden affects, or removal of that substantial burden would affect, commerce with foreign nations, among the several States, or with Indian tribes, even if the burden results from a rule of general applicability; or

(C) the substantial burden is imposed in the implementation of a land use regulation or system of land use regulations, under which a government makes, or has in place formal or informal procedures or practices that permit the government to make, individualized assessments of the proposed uses for the property involved.

(b) Discrimination and exclusion

(1) Equal terms

No government shall impose or implement a land use regulation in a manner that treats a religious assembly or institution on less than equal terms with a nonreligious assembly or institution.

(2) Nondiscrimination

No government shall impose or implement a land use regulation that discriminates against any assembly or institution on the basis of religion or religious denomination.

(3) Exclusions and limits

No government shall impose or implement a land use regulation that—

(A) totally excludes religious assemblies from a jurisdiction; or

(B) unreasonably limits religious assemblies, institutions, or structures within a jurisdiction.

Appendix B

D.C. Code § 6-1104(e) (2000)

(1) In any instance where there is a claim of unreasonable economic hardship, the owner shall submit, by affidavit, to the Mayor at least 20 days prior to the public hearing, at least the following information:

(A) For all property:

(i) The amount paid for the property, the date of purchase and the party from whom purchased, including a description of the relationship, if any, between the owner and the person from whom the property was purchased;

(ii) The assessed value of the land and improvements thereon according to the two most recent assessments;

(iii) Real estate taxes for the previous two years;

(iv) Annual debt service, if any, for the previous two years;

(v) All appraisals obtained within the previous two years by the owner or applicant in connection with his purchase, financing or ownership of the property;

(vi) Any listing of the property for sale or rent, price asked, and offers received, if any; and

(vii) Any consideration by the owner as to profitable adaptive uses for the property; and

(B) For income-producing property:

(i) Annual gross income from the property for the previous two years;

(ii) Itemized operating and maintenance expenses for the previous two years;

(iii) Annual cash flow, if any, for the previous two years

Review of Books, Articles, and Other Resources

• • •

Compiled by Gary Nurkin

The editors invite information on new items as they are published, past items of ongoing value to readers, as well as information on new websites and in film.

Selected Bibliography of Recent Books and Articles

Books

Catherine Bell and Val Napoleon (eds.), *First Nations Cultural Heritage and Law* (UBC Press, 2008).

Catherine Bell and Robert K. Paterson, *Protection of First Nations Cultural Heritage: Laws, Policy, and Reform* (UBC Press, 2008).

Barbara Bundy, *Archaeological Looting and Vandalism in the Pacific Northwest: A Quantitative Analysis of Causes and Prevention* (VDM Verlag 2008).

Heather Burke, Claire Smith, Dorothy Lippert, Joe Watkins, Larry Zimmerman (eds.), *Kennewick Man: Perspective on the Ancient One* (Left Coast Press, 2008).

Nina Burleigh, *Unholy Business: A True Tale of Greed and Forgery in the Holy Land* (Collins 2008).

James Cuno (ed.), *Whose Culture?: The Promise of Museums and the Debate over Antiquities* (Princeton University Press 2009).

James Cuno, *Who Owns Antiquity?: Museums and the Battle over Ancient Heritage* (Princeton University Press 2008).

Wendy J. Eliason, *Indigenous Peoples, Archaeologists, and Cultural Property Law in the United States: A Bibliography* (Scarecrow Press 2008).

Geoff Emberling, Katharyn Hanson (eds.), *Catastrophe! The Looting and Destruction of Iraq's Past* (Oriental Institute Museum Publication 28, 2008).

Mille Gabriel and Jens Dahl (eds), *Utimut —Past Heritage—Future Partnerships: Discussions on Repatriation in the 21st Century, IWGIA Document No. 21* (Transaction Publishers, 2008).

Patty Gerstenblith, *Art, Cultural Heritage and the Law* (Second Edition) (Carolina University Press, 2008).

Jeanette Greenfield, *The Return of Cultural Treasures* (Third Edition) (Cambridge University Press, 2007).

Christopher Hitchens, *The Parthenon Marbles: The Case for Restitution: New and fully updated edition* (Verso, 2008).

Sherry Hutt and David Tarler (eds.) *Yearbook of Cultural Property Law* (Left Coast Press, 2008).

J. Myrick Howard, *Buying Time for Heritage: How to Save an Endangered Property* (University of North Carolina Press, 2007).

Thomas W. Killion, *Opening Archaeology: Repatriation's Impact on Contemporary Research and Practice* (School for Advanced Research Press, Santa Fe, 2008).

Thomas F. King, *Our Unprotected Heritage: Whitewashing the Destruction of Our Culture and National Heritage* (Left Coast Press, 2009).

Argyro Loukaki, *Living Ruins, Value Conflicts (Heritage, Culture and Identity)* (Ashgate Publishing Limited, 2008).

Margaret M. Miles, *Art as Plunder* (Cambridge University Press, 2008).

Milikin Institute, *Financial Innovations for Developing Archaeological Discovery and Conservation: Financial Innovations Lab Report* (Miliken Institute, 2008).

Robin F. Rhodes (ed.), *The Acquisition and Exhibition of Classical Antiquities* (University of Notre Dame Press, 2008).

Peter Stone and Joanne Farchakh Bajjaly (eds.), *The Destruction of the Cultural Heritage of Iraq* (Boydell & Brewer Ltd., 2008).

Ana Filipa Vrdoljak, *International Law, Museums, and the Return of Cultural Objects* (Cambridge 2008).

Sharon Waxman, *Loot: The Battle Over Stolen Treasures of the Ancient World* (MacMillan, 2008).

Jonathan Webb and Julian Radcliffe, *Stolen: The Gallery of Missing Masterpeices* (Herbert Press Ltd., 2008).

Elizabeth Weiss, *Reburying the Past: The Effects of Repatriation and Reburial on Scientific Inquiry* (Nova Science Publications, 2008).

Articles

Andrew Adler, *An Unintended and Absurd Expansion: The Application of the Archaeological Resource Protection Act to Foreign Lands*, 38 N. M. L. Rev. 133 (2008).

Kimberly Alderman, *The Ethical Trade in Cultural Property: Ethics and Law in the Antiquity Auction Industry*, 14 ILSA Journal of International and Comparative Law 549 (2008).

Raechel Anglin, *The World Heritage List: Bridging the Cultural Property Nationalism-Internationalism Divide*, 20 Yale J.L. & Human. 241 (2008).

Alexander Bauer, *Essay: New Ways About Thinking About Cultural Property: A Critical Appraisal of the Antiquities Trade Debates*, 31 Fordham Int'l. L. J. 690 (2008).

David J. Bederman and Brian D. Spielman, *Refusing Salvage*, 6 Loy. Mar. L.J. 31 (2008).

Carrie Betts, *Enforcement of Foreign Cultural Patrimony Laws in U.S. Courts: Lessons for Museums From the Getty Trial and Cultural Partnership Agreements of 2006*, 4 S.C. J. Int'l L. & Bus. 73 (2007).

Colonel Matthew Bogdanos, *Essay: Thieves of Baghdad: Combating Global Trafficking in Iraqi Antiquities*, 31 Fordham Int'l. L. J. 725 (2008).

Cinnamon Carlarne, *Putting the "and" Back in the Culture-Nature Debate: Integrated Cultural and Natural Heritage Protection*, 25 UCLA J. Envtl. L & Pol'y 153 (2007).

Kristen A. Carpenter, *Real Property & Peoplehood*, 27 Stan. Envtl. L. J. 313 (2008).

Kristen A. Carpenter, Sonia Katyal, and Angela Riley, *In Defense of Property*, found at: http://papers.ssrn.com/sol3/papers.cfm?abstract_id=1220665

Madeline Chimento, *Lost Artifacts of the Incas: Cultural Property and the Repatriation Movement*, 54 Loy. L. Rev. 209 (2008).

David Curfman, *Note: Thar Be Treasure Here; Right To Ancient Shipwrecks In International Waters: A New Policy Regime*, 86 Wash. U. L. Rev. 181 (2008).

Piers Davies and Paul Myburgh *The Protected Objects Act in New Zealand: Too Little, Too Late*, 15 International Journal of Cultural Property 321 (2008).

Alexis Derrossett, *The Final Solution: Making Title Insurance Mandatory for Art Sold in Auction Houses and Displayed in Museums That Is Likely to Be Holocaust-Looted Art*, 9 T. M. Cooley J. Prac. & Clinical L. 223 (2007).

Stacey Falkoff, *Note & Comment: Mutually Beneficial Repatriation Agreements: Returning Cultural Patrimony, Perpetuating the Illicit Antiquities Market*, 16 J. L. & Pol'y 265 (2007).

Derek Fincham, *How Adopting the Lex Originis Rule Can Impede the flow of Illicit Cultural Property*, to be published Columbia Journal of Law and Arts found at: http://papers.ssrn.com/sol3/papers.cfm?abstract_id=1287365

Derek Fincham, *A Coordinated Legal and Policy Approach to Undiscovered Antiquities: Adapting the Cultural Heritage Policy of England and Wales to Other Nations of Origin*, 15 International Journal of Cultural Property 347 (2008).

Gillian Flynn, *The Recovery of Stolen Cultural Property in the State of Maryland*, 38 U. Balt. L. F. 103 (2008).

Patty Gerstenblith and Lucille Rousssin, *Art and International Cultural Property*, 42 Int'l. Law. 729 (2008).

Saby Ghoshray, *Essay: Repatriation of the Kohinoor Diamond: Expanding the Legal Paradigm for Cultural Heritage*, 31 Fordham Int'l. L. J. 741 (2008).

Linsey Gleason, *"Possession" and the Abandoned Shipwreck Act: Promoting the Discovery of Historic Shipwrecks and Preventing the Unconstitutional Destruction of Federal Admiralty Jurisdiction*, 2007 Mich. St. L. Rev. 1017 (2007).

Stefan Gruber, *Protecting China's Cultural Heritage Sites in Times of Rapid Change: Current Developments, Practice and Law*, 10 Asia Pacific Journal of Environmental Law 253 (2007).

Dick Jackson, *Cultural Property Protection In Stability Operations*, Army Law. 47 (Oct. 2008).

Lawrence M. Kaye, *Cultural Heritage: Dispute Resolution and Avoidance: Article: Avoidance and Resolution of Cultural Heritage Disputes: Recovery of Art Looted During the Holocaust*, 14 Willamette J. Int'l. L. & Dispute Res. 243 (2006).

Jenifer Anglim Kreder, *The Holocaust, Museum Ethics and Legalism*, 18 S. Cal. Rev. L. & Soc. Just.___ (2008), found at: http://papers.ssrn.com/sol3/papers.cfm?abstract_id=1119449

Jennifer Anglim Kreder, Monica Dugot, Thomas R. Kline, Lucille A. Roussin, *Legal and Ethical Issues in Art Restitution*, International Lawyer, International Law News 2008 found at: http://papers.ssrn.com/sol3/papers.cfm?abstract_id=1098348#PaperDownload

Arthur Leavens, *Beyond Blame—Mens Rea and Regulatory Crime*, 46 U. Louisville L. Rev. 1 (2007).

Simon MacKenzie and Penny Green, *Performance Regulation: A Case Study in How Powerful People Avoid Criminal Labels*, 48 Brit. J. Criminology 138 (2008).

Sarah K. Mann, *What's a Survivor To Do? An Inquiry into Various Options and Outcomes for Individuals Seeking Recovery of Nazi-Looted Art*, 5 Loy. Int'l L. Rev. 191 (2008).

James A.R. Nafziger, *Cultural Heritage: Dispute Resolution and Avoidance: Article: The Protection and Repatriation of Indigenous Cultural Heritage in the United States*, 14 Willamette J. Int'l. L. & Dispute Res. 175 (2006).

Mary Ellen O'Connell, *Beyond Wealth: Stories of Art, War and Greed*, 59 Ala. L. Rev. 1075 (2008).

Patrick O'Keefe, *Cultural Heritage: Dispute Resolution and Avoidance: Article: Using Unidroit to Avoid Cultural Heritage Disputes: Limitation Periods*, 14 Willamette J. Int'l. L. & Dispute Res. 227 (2006).

Melineh S. Ounanian, *Of All the Things I Lost, I Miss My Marbles The Most: An Alternate Approach to the Epic Problem of the Elgin Marbles*, 9 Cardozo J. Conflict Resol. 109 (2007).

Jordan Paradise and Lori Andrews, *Article Tales from the Crypt: Scientific, Ethical and Legal Considerations for Biohistorical Analysis of Deceased Historical Figures*, 46 Temp. J. Sci. Tech. & Env. L. 223 (2007).

Robert K. Paterson, *Cultural Heritage: Dispute Resolution and Avoidance: Article: Resolving Material Cultural Disputes: Human Rights, Property Rights and Crimes Against Humanity*, 14 Willamette J. Int'l. L. & Dispute Res. 155 (2006).

Janene Marie Podesta, *Saving Culture, But Passing The Buck: How The 1970 UNESCO Convention Undermines Its Goals By Unduly Targeting Market Nations*, 16 Cardozo J. In'l & Comp. L. 457 (2008).

Lauren Fiedler Redman, *Article: The Foreign Sovereign Immunities Act: Using a "Shield" Statute as a "Sword" for Obtaining Federal Jurisdiction in Art and Antiquities Cases*, 31 Fordham Int'l. L. J. 781 (2008).

Lauren F. Redman, *A Wakeup Call for a Uniform Statute of Limitations in Art Restitution Cases*, 13 UCLA Ent. L. Rev. 203 (2008).

Michael J. Reppas II, *Empty "International" Museums' Trophy Cases of Their Looted Treasures and Return Stolen Property to the Countries of Origin and the Rightful Heirs of Those Wrongly Dispossessed*, 36 Denv J. Int'l L. & Pol'y 93 (2007).

Samantha M. Ruscavage-Barz, *The Efficacy of State Law in Protecting Native American Sacred Places: A Case Study of the Paseo Del Norte Extension*, 47 Nat. Resources J. 969 (2007).

Omar Carmona Sanchez, *Rights of Treasure Hunters Under Puerto Rico Law: Application of Article 285 of the Civil Code Through The Jones Act, The Puerto Rico Underwater Protection Act and The Abandoned Shipwreck Act of 1987*, 47 Rev. Der. P.R. 347 (2008).

Susan Scafadi, *Symposium On Cultural Property & The Law, Introduction, New Dimensions on Cultural Property*, 31 Fordham Int'l. L. J. 684 (2008).

Geoffrey R. Scott, *Article: Spoliation, Cultural Property, and Japan*, 29 U. Pa. J. Int'l. L. 803 (2008).

Shira T. Shapiro, *Case Note: How Republic of Austria v. Altmann and United States v. Portrait of Wally Replay the Past and Forecast the Future of Nazi Looted-Art Restitution Litigation*, 34 Wm. Mitchell L. Rev. 1147 (2008).

Matthew K. Steen, III, *Collateral Damage: The Destruction of Cultural Property in Armed Conflict*, found at: http://works.bepress.com/matthew_steen/1/ (2008)

Deborah L. Threedy, *Claiming the Shields: Law, Anthropology and the Role of Storytelling in a NAGPRA Repatriation Case*, 28 J. Land Resources & Envtl L. 301 (2008).

Jennifer Tsai, *Curse of the Black Swan: How the Law of Salvage Perpetuates Indeterminate Ownership of Shipwrecks*, 42 Int'l. Law Rev. 211 (2008).

Valentina Sara Vadi, *Cultural Heritage and International Investment Law*, 15 International Journal of Cultural Property, 1 (2008).

Ana Filipa Vrdoljak, *Unraveling the Cradle of Civilization 'Layer by Layer': Iraq, Its Peoples and Cultural Heritage*, found at: http://papers.ssrn.com/sol3/papers.cfm?abstract_id=1267256.

Ana Filipa Vrdoljak, *Reparations for Cultural Loss*, found at: http://papers.ssrn.com/sol3/papers.cfm?abstract_id=1142791

Jennifer C. White, *Conserving the United States' Reefs: National Monument Designation to Afford Greater Protection for Coral Reefs in Four National Marine Sanctuaries*, 32 Wm. & Mary Envt'l. L. & Pol'y Rev. 901 (2008)

Elizabeth Willis, *The Law, Politics and "Historic Wounds": The Dja Dja Warungs Basrk Etchings Case in Australia*, 15 International Journal of Cultural Property 49 (2008).

Katrina Miriam Wyman, *Is There a Moral Justification for Addressing Historical Injustices?*, 61 Vand. L. Rev. 127 (2007).

Peter K. Yu, *Cultural Relics, Intellectual Property and Intangible Heritage*, 81 Temple Law Rev. (2008) found at: http://papers.ssrn.com/sol3/papers.cfm?abstract_id=1272727

Other Resources

Additional Readings

Kimberly DeGraaf, *Should the U.S. Restrict Imports of Chinese Archaeological Materials? An Analysis under the Convention on Cultural Property Implementation Act*, 2 Art & Museum Law Journal 31 (2007).

Monica S. Dugot, Thomas Kline, Jenifer Anglim Kreder and Lucille A. Roussin, *Legal and Ethical Problems in Art Restitution,* found at: http://papers.ssrn.com/sol3/papers.cfm?abstract_id=1098348#PaperDownload

Francesco Francioni, *Beyond Treaties: The Emergence of a New Customary Law for the Protection of Cultural Heritage (Au-Delà Des Traits: L'Émergence D'Un Nouveau Droit Coutumier Pour La Protection Du Patrimoine Culturel)*, EUI Law Working Paper No. 2008/05 found at: http://papers.ssrn.com/sol3/papers.cfm?abstract_id=1093630

Stefan Gruber, *Environmental Law and the Threat of Global Climate Change to Cultural Heritage Sites*, found at: http://papers.ssrn.com/sol3/papers.cfm?abstract_id=1285741

Brian Hole, *Playthings for the Foe: Repatriation of Human Remains in New Zealand*, 6 Public Archaeology 5 (2007).

Douglas J. Krupka and Dogulas S. Noonan, *Determinants of Cultural Heritage and Cultural Landmark Designation: Why We Preserve What We Preserve*, IZA Discussion paper 3777, found at: http://papers.ssrn.com/sol3/results.cfm?RequestTimeout=50000000

Simon Mackenzie, *Dealing in Cultural Objects: A New Criminal Law for the UK*, 71 Amicus Curiae, 8 (2007).

Sally McCausland, *Protecting Aborigianl Cultural Heritage in Australia: Looking for Solutions in the Canadian Experience (L.L.M. Thesis University of British Columbia)*, found at: http://papers.ssrn.com/sol3/papers.cfm?abstract_id=1285392

John Henry Merryman, *Thinking About the Sesvo Treasure*, found at: http://papers.ssrn.com/sol3/papers.cfm?abstract_id=1105584#PaperDownload

Christopher Pala, *Paradise Almost Lost: Hawaii's Bishop Museum Grapples with NAGPRA*, Museum (March/April 2008).

Charles Palmer, *Holocaust Art*, 86-Sep Mich. B. J. 20 (2007).

Laura Elizabeth Young, *A Framework For Resolution of Claims For Cultural Property*, (M.A. Thesis University of Oregon) found at: https://scholarsbank.uoregon.edu/dspace/bitstream/1794/6575/1/Laura_Young_Dec07.pdf

New Web Sites

elginism found at: http://www.elginism.com/2008/01/

U.S. Committee for the Blue Shield found at: http://uscbs.org/news/

Blogs

Kimberly Alderman's Cultural Property Law Blog found at: http://culturalproperty-law.wordpress.com

Artifact Replica Blog found at: http://artifact-replicas.com/

Paul Barford's Portable Antiquity Collecting and Heritage Issues found at: http://paul-barford.blogspot.com/

Heather Hopes Truly Educated found at: http://trulyeducated.blogspot.com/

Tom Flynn's blog found at: http://tom-flynn.blogspot.com/search?q=

Thomas F. King's blog found at: http://crmplus.blogspot.com/search?q=

numismatics and archaeology found at:http://coinarchaeology.blogspot.com/search?q=

Lawrence Rothfield's The Punching Bag found at: http://larryrothfield.blogspot.com/.

Ed Shible, A Gift for Polydektes, found at: http://digitalhn.blogspot.com/search?updated-min=2008-01-01T00%3A00%3A00-05%3A00&updated-max=2009-01-01T00%3A00%3A00-05%3A00&max-results=50

Peter Tompa's cultural property observer found at: http://culturalpropertyobserver.blogspot.com/search?q=

UNESCO in theSpotlight: Education and Culture found at http://unescoeducation.blogspot.com/search?q=

DVDs

Rape of Europa (2007).

Recognizing Career Achievements in Cultural Resource Protection

• • •

In the past the *Yearbook* has noted the achievements of those who though not lawyers have greatly advanced the status of cultural property law. This year we recognize two such individuals whose noteworthy careers have been the inspiration for lawyers around the world.

Professor Colin Renfrew

Upon Receiving the SAFE Beacon Award

On January 10, 2009, the international cultural heritage community gathered in Philadelphia to honor the life and contributions of Professor Colin Renfrew. Accolades poured in from his colleagues at the McDonald Institute for Archaeological Research, where he was the director for years, and from the LCCHP, the Penn Cultural Heritage Center, DePaul University, Rutgers, the Cotsen Institute of Archaeology at UCLA, Brown University's Joukowsky Institute, the Archaeological Institute of America, Heritage Watch, the Alaska Peace Center, and others. The program read not just like a Who's Who, but a Who Cares about Saving Antiquities for Everyone, SAFE, the host of the event.

The SAFE Beacon Award, founded in 2006, recognizes outstanding achievement in raising public awareness about our endangered cultural heritage and the devastating consequences of the illicit antiquities trade, which fuels the looting of ancient sites and destroys our ultimate nonrenewable resource: the intact evidence of our undiscovered past. The following comments were compiled for SAFE and are reprinted in part, with permission.

Few can speak with Prof. Colin Renfrew's authority on the grave impact looting has had on humanity's understanding of its past. Early in his storied career he focused on the study of Cycladic figurines, virtually all of which have been looted with few clues remaining to their provenance. Despite this imposing challenge, his work on the Cycladic Islands added immeasurably to not just our knowledge of the figurines but of the Late Neolithic and Early Bronze Age people who created them. Now, after decades of ground-breaking research that has ranged from rewriting Aegean prehistory to pioneering cognitive archaeology, he is one of the world's most eloquent champions of ethical museum acquisition policies and has publicly and forcefully campaigned against the link between museums and the illicit antiquities trade.

Colin Renfrew was born in 1937 in Stockton-on-Tees, in North East England, and was educated at St. Albans School. After serving a stint in the Royal Air Force from 1956 to 1958, he received his B.A. in Archaeology and Anthropology at St. John's College, Cambridge in 1962. As a research student there and at the British School of Archaeology at Athens, he wrote "Neolithic and Bronze Age cultures of the Cyclades and their external relations" and in 1965 received his Ph.D. from the University of Cambridge. He was elected a Research Fellow at St. John's College and took up a post as lecturer at the Department of Prehistory and Archaeology of the University of Sheffield.

In 1972 Renfrew joined the University of Southampton as Professor of Archaeology and Head of the Department. In 1981, he became Disney Professor of Archaeology at the University of Cambridge, a post he held until he retired in 2004. That year he also became Head of the Department of Archaeology and Fellow of St. John's College. In 1986 he became a Fellow of Jesus College, Cambridge, where he served as Master from 1986 to 1997. In 1990 he was appointed the first director of the McDonald Institute for Archaeological Research and the next year was made a life peer, choosing the title "Lord Renfrew of Kaimsthorn." In 1996, with Dr. Neil Brodie, he helped create the Illicit Antiquities Research Centre at the University of Cambridge. He is the author of numerous popular and scholarly books, including *Loot, Legitimacy and Ownership: The Ethical Crisis in Archaeology* (2000).

Among his many awards are the Lucy Wharton Drexel Medal of the University of Pennsylvania Museum (2003) and the European Latsis Prize of the

European Science Foundation, Strasbourg (2003). He has been awarded honorary degrees by the University of Sheffield, the University of Athens, the University of Southampton, the University of Liverpool, the University of Edinburgh, the University of St. Andrews, the University of Kent at Canterbury, and the University of London. He has served as a trustee of the British Museum (1991–2001), as Council member of the British Academy (1997–2000) and as Vice President of the Prehistoric Society (1979–1983), the Council of British Archaeology (1979–1982), and the Royal Archaeological Institute (1982–1984). He currently serves as a trustee of the Antiquity Trust.

Selected Bibliography

Renfrew, Colin. 2000. *Loot, Legitimacy and Ownership: The Ethical Crisis in Archaeology.* London: Duckworth.

Brodie, Neil, Jennifer Doole and Colin Renfrew, eds. 2001. *Trade in Illicit Antiquities: The Destruction of the World's Archaeological Heritage.* Cambridge: McDonald Institute for Archaeological Research.

Renfrew, Colin. 2003. *Figuring It Out: The Parallel Visions of Artists and Archaeologists.* London: Thames and Hudson.

Renfrew, Colin. 2008. *Prehistory: the Making of the Human Mind.* London: Orion, and New York: Random House.

Robert Wittman

Upon Retiring from the FBI Art Crime Team

In the Yearbook 2007, a tribute was offered to Robert Goldman, one-half of the "Two Bobs" international art crime team, and now the second half has retired. In 2008, after 20 years with the FBI, Robert Wittman left the FBI Art Crime Team to enter private investigative practice. Before Bob Wittman, the FBI treated art theft as any other theft. Bob not only changed how art crimes were investigated and prioritized by the FBI, he went further, to train agents within the FBI and other agencies and actively assist prosecutors in the preparation of successful cases. The results were stunning. The FBI now has an entire team of agents devoted to art theft. The agents, who receive special art training, have recovered more than 850 stolen items of cultural and artistic significance.

Art and the antiquities trade were not new concepts to Bob. His family included antiques dealers and he came to the FBI with an interest in art. His first successful case as an agent involved the recovery of a bronze mask that had been taken from the Rodin Museum, and a crystal ball that once belonged to the Empress Dowager in China that had been taken from the University of Pennsylvania Museum of Archaeology and Anthropology.

The FBI was not quick to embrace art crime as a special area of investigation, but then came the looting of the Baghdad Museum in 2003. The incident captured worldwide attention and Bob was one of the agents who were tapped to prepare for the investigation. Although no FBI team actually went to Iraq, the concept of an Art Crime Team was born and Bob was a key part of that team.

Then, in 2006, a Goya, en route from the Toledo Museum of Art to the Guggenheim in New York, was stolen. Bob and the team were ready to respond and recovered the painting. As it turned out, the culprit was a petty thief looking for tools and did not know what he had until he opened the shipping crate. Upon discovering his prize the thief called the FBI, looking for a reward. He was arrested and is serving a prison term.

Bob has thrilled and inspired law students and lawyers in lectures, as well as the general public in presentations for the Smithsonian Associates programs. He has given up what little free time he may have had for his family to travel and give training to other agency law enforcement.

Those who applaud FBI efforts to investigate and solve crimes involving art theft (such as the FBI and its European counterparts) can only hope that the legacy of Bob will continue. Museums seeking to protect and recover assets now have the reconstituted team of the Two Bobs, back in action in the private sector.

Table of Cases

Yearbook 2009 Contributors and Editorial Board

• • •

Jillianne M. Arguello is a 2004 graduate of Tufts University in Medford, Massachusetts, and expects to graduate from American University's Washington College of Law in May of 2009. For most of her law school career, Ms. Arguello has been involved with the State Burial Law Project, a joint effort by American University and the National NAGPRA program at the National Park Service to compile a database with all of the state-specific laws related to the treatment of burial sites and objects that fall outside the jurisdiction of the federal NAGPRA statute. During the summers of 2007 and 2008, Ms. Arguello served as a law clerk with the National NAGPRA Program in Washington, D.C. At the start of her second year of law school, Ms. Arguello developed an interest in tax law, and in early 2008 she presented her research for the article contained herein at a panel held at American University's Washington College of Law entitled "Tax Law and Cultural Property." Upon graduation from law school, Ms. Arguello hopes to professionally pursue her interest in both tax law and its effect on cultural property.

Caroline M. Blanco, Editorial Board and Board member of LCCHP, is coauthor of HERITAGE RESOURCES LAW (1999) and CULTURAL PROPERTY LAW (2004). She is the Assistant General Counsel for the Environment at the National Science Foundation, where she provides advice on the environmental and cultural resources laws implicated by the Foundation's mission in promoting cutting edge science. Prior to assuming her current position, she served as a trial attorney in the Natural Resources Section of the Environment and National Resources Division of the United States Department of Justice where, from 1991 until 2007, she specialized in heritage resources law and, in particular, historic shipwreck litigation. Ms. Blanco, twice a recipient of the Attorney General's Award for Distinguished Service, frequently lectures in the field of heritage resources law at law schools and government training seminars throughout the country. In recognition of her work in cultural resource preservation and outstanding contributions to the legal protection of submerged cultural resources during her tenure at the Department of Justice, she was recently presented with *A Legacy of Excellence in Submerged Resource Preservation* award by the Submerged Resources Center of the National Park Service. In addition, Ms. Blanco serves on the faculty of American University's Washington College of Law as a Professorial Lecturer on cultural property law. Prior to her government service, Ms. Blanco was a litigation associate at the law firm of McCutchen Doyle Brown & Enersen, San Jose, California.

L. Eden Burgess is an associate in the Washington, D.C. office of Andrews Kurth LLP, where she focuses on general litigation matters including art recovery and cultural property cases and has written and spoken on these subjects. She received her JD from George Washington University Law School, with honors.

Kelly Yasaitis Fanizzo, the *Yearbook* editorial board member for the State and Local Practice Area, is a historic preservation specialist with the Advisory Council on Historic Preservation (ACHP). She currently works with a number of federal property management agencies in their Section 106 compliance. She holds a J.D., magna cum laude, from American University, Washington College of Law, and a Graduate Certificate in Museum Studies from George Washington University, Columbian College of Arts and Sciences.

Elise Foster is an attorney with the U.S. Department of Agriculture, Office of the General Counsel, in Ogden, Utah. Since 1997 she has been active in the development of ARPA civil penalty prosecutions. Elise has handled many ARPA civil penalty cases, collecting thousands of dollars which have been used for restoration and repair of archaeological resources on National Forest System lands. She has provided training on the subject of ARPA civil penalty prosecution to a wide range of federal attorneys and government land managers. She is also the author of USING ARPA CIVIL PENALTIES TO PROTECT ARCHEOLOGICAL RESOURCES ON PUBLIC AND INDIAN LANDS, a guide to civil ARPA prosecution, published cooperatively by the Forest Service and the National Park Service in 2007.

Patty Gerstenblith, Editorial Board, International Practice Area, President of Board LCCHP, is a professor of law at DePaul University College of Law, where she is Director of DePaul's program in art and cultural heritage law. She served as Editor-in-Chief of the INTERNATIONAL JOURNAL OF CULTURAL PROPERTY from1995 to 2002, as a public representative on the President's Cultural Property Advisory Committee in the U.S. Department of State from 2000 to 2003, and as Co-Chair of the American Bar Association's International Cultural Property Committee from 2002 to 2006. Her most recent books include ART, CULTURAL HERITAGE, AND THE LAW and IRAQ BEYOND THE HEADLINES: HISTORY, ARCHAEOLOGY, AND WAR (coauthored with Benjamin R. Foster and Karen Polinger Foster). She received her J.D. from Northwestern University and a Ph.D. from Harvard University in Fine Art and Anthropology.

Sherry Hutt, Senior Editor, Board member LCCHP, is the program manager for the National NAGPRA Program, in the Department of the Interior. Formerly a Superior Court Judge in Arizona, an assistant United States Attorney assigned to ARPA cases, and a trustee of the Heard Museum, she is the coauthor of CULTURAL PROPERTY LAW (2004), HERITAGE RESOURCES LAW (1999), ARCHEOLOGICAL RESOURCE PROTECTION (1992), and co-editor of PRESENTING ARCHAEOLOGY IN COURT (2006). In addition to the J.D., she holds a Ph.D. in forestry.

Jessica Kennedy is a 2009 J.D. candidate at Lewis & Clark Law School, in Portland, Oregon. She also holds an M.A. in Modern Art History, Theory and Criticism from The School of the Art Institute of Chicago and a B.A. in Art History from the University of Florida.

Thomas R. Kline, Editorial Board, Art Market Practice Area, Board member LCCHP, is a partner in the Washington, D.C. office of Andrews Kurth LLP, has represented governments, museums, churches, foundations, and families, including Holocaust survivors and heirs, in recovering stolen art appearing in the United States. He has also represented a major American museum in responding to a Holocaust claim. Mr. Kline co-teaches a seminar, Stolen and Illegally Imported Art and Cultural Property, in the George Washington University Museum Studies Program. Mr. Kline writes and speaks on the subject of restitution of stolen art, and appeared before the Presidential Advisory Commission on Holocaust Assets in the United States. He is a member, Editorial Board, KUNST UND RECHT (Art and Law), www.kur-journal.de.

Jennifer Anglim Kreder teaches Cultural Property Law and other courses at Salmon P. Chase College of Law at Northern Kentucky University. Prior to entering academia, Professor Kreder was a Litigation Associate with Milbank, Tweed, Hadley & McCloy, LLP in New York, concentrating on Holocaust era intergovernmental negotiation and litigation issues and art disputes. She has published extensively, including in legal academic journals at Harvard, Vanderbilt, Virginia, Georgetown, University of Southern California, Brooklyn, University of Melbourne, and University of Heidelberg. She has given presentations about legal issues affecting the international art market in many domestic and foreign venues, serves as Co-Vice Chair of the Art & Cultural Heritage Committee of the ABA Section of International Law, and engages in pro bono legal work. Professor Kreder is a graduate of the Georgetown University Law Center.

Laina Lopez is an attorney with Berliner, Corcoran & Rowe, LLP in Washington, D.C. Mrs. Lopez concentrates on complex civil litigation. For example, Mrs. Lopez represents Iran in *Rubin v. Iran* and Iran's Bank Melli in *Weinstein v. Iran*, both of which are attachment proceedings in which victims of terrorism are attempting to attach certain assets in satisfaction of default judgments against Iran. Prior to joining BCR, Mrs. Lopez worked at Cohen, Milstein, Hausfeld & Toll, PLLC, litigating a variety of federal antitrust, ERISA, and human rights class action cases. She also assisted claimants before the September 11th Victim Compensation Fund, including some of the most severely injured survivors of the Pentagon attack. For two years, Mrs. Lopez served as law clerk to the Honorable Gregory A. Presnell, U.S. District Court for the Middle District of Florida.

Gary Nurkin was an Assistant District Attorney in Nassau County, New York, where he handled environmental crimes, among others, and was a trial attorney in the Appeals Bureau and then Chief of the Environmental and Frauds Bureau. Gary joined the EPA in 1989 as a Regional Enforcement Counsel, became Assistant Regional Counsel, and, for two years, was a Special Assistant United States Attorney handling environmental cases. A graduate of Chicago-Kent College of Law, Gary has also been an adjunct faculty member at Seton Hall University School of Law and Pace University School of Law, where he taught cultural property law. His undergraduate and graduate degrees are in anthropology.

Nathaniel R. Orpen works in the areas of estate planning, personal injury, real estate, business transactions, and business organization at Galena Law Firm, P.A., in White Bear Lake, Minnesota. He is a graduate of William Mitchell College of Law in St. Paul, Minnesota, and is a member of the Minnesota bar. Nathaniel received his B.A., cum laude, at Gustavus Adolphus College in St. Peter, Minnesota, where he majored in history and political science.

Marilyn Phelan, J.D. (with honors), University of Texas School of Law, and Ph.D, Texas Tech University, is the Paul Whitfield Horn Professor of Law at Texas Tech University. Receipt of a Horn Professor chair is one of the highest honors Texas Tech University can bestow on its professors. Phelan also has served as Professor of Museum Science. She is a certified public accountant and is certified by the Texas Board of Legal Specialization as Specialist in Tax Law. Phelan founded the Tax Clinic at Texas Tech University School of Law and has served as its Director. Marilyn Phelan is the author or coauthor of twelve books and over forty-five articles or book chapters on laws relating to taxation, nonprofit organizations, and museums. Her book on laws relating to museums is listed by the Smithsonian as one of a dozen books every museum should own. She also is the coauthor of a casebook on art and museum law, published by Carolina Academic Press. Phelan is a member of the American Law Institute and a Texas Commissioner to the Uniform Law Commission. Phelan was reappointed for another three-year term on the Legal Affairs Committee of the International Council of Museums (ICOM). As a member of this committee, she prepared the mediation procedure for ICOM to recommend when individuals or countries make claims to stolen or illegally exported objects in museums' collections. She currently serves as Vice-Chair of the Cultural Property Committee of the Section of International Law and Practice of the American Bar Association.

Lucille A. Roussin, Editorial Board, Museum Practice Area, Board Member LCCHP, is an advisor to SAFE, Saving Antiquities for Everyone. She is the founder and director of the Holocaust Restitution Claims Practicum at the Benjamin N. Cardozo School of Law in New York City, where she teaches a seminar, Remedies for Wartime Confiscation. She also teaches a course on "Art, the Law and Professional Ethics" at the School of Graduate Studies at the Fashion Institute of Technology. She is an associate with the firm of McCallion & Associates and earned her law degree in 1996 from the Benjamin N. Cardozo School of Law, where she was a Belkin Scholar. She was Deputy Research Director of the Art and Cultural Property Team of the Presidential Commission on Holocaust Assets and was an associate in the Art and International Law Practice Group at Herrick, Feinstein LLP in New York City. In 2001, she negotiated the first restitution of a rare Jewish ritual object to a private family in the United States.

Rob Roy Smith is of counsel with the Indian Law Group of the law firm Ater Wynne, LLP in Seattle, Washington. He received a JD, cum laude, with a certificate in natural resources and environmental law from Northwestern School of Law of Lewis and Clark College. He has extensive experience advising Indian tribal clients and those doing business in Indian Country on all aspects of federal Indian law, including economic development, cultural resource protection, taxation, tribal sovereignty, and Indian gaming.

Bryan Stockton is a third year law student at Georgetown University Law Center focusing on land use and environmental law. He received his undergraduate degree from Georgetown University's School of Foreign Service. Because of his avid interest in architecture and history, he has explored nearly every historic district in Washington, D.C.

David Tarler, Assistant Editor and Editor Enforcement Practice Area, Board member LCCHP, is a Near Eastern archaeologist and an attorney. From 1978 to 1990 he was a senior staff member of the City of David excavation project, in Jerusalem, Israel. After completing his legal studies, in 1993, he served as a consultant to the Archeology Program and the Native American Graves Protection and Repatriation Act Program of the National Park Service, in Washington, DC. In 2006 he became the enforcement and training coordinator for the National NAGPRA Program and in 2008 he added Designated Federal Official to the NAGPRA Review Committee to his duties. During 2001–2002, he provided assistance to staff at the United States Sentencing Commission working on Federal Sentencing Guideline 2B1.5, which applies to crimes involving cultural heritage resources. He was a contributing editor for Hutt, Blanco, & Varmer, HERITAGE RESOURCES LAW (1999) and PRESENTING ARCHAEOLOGY IN COURT (2006).

James Van Ness, Editorial Board, Board member LCCHP, is the acting Deputy General Counsel (Environment & Installations), Department of Defense. In this capacity, he is responsible for advising senior DoD officials on legal matters related to natural and cultural resources management, environmental planning, and consultation with indigenous peoples. Mr. Van Ness earned an LL.M. from the University of Washington; a J.D. from the University of Iowa; and a B.S. from Iowa State University. He is a member of the adjunct faculty at The George Washington University School of Law.

Index